FLIGHT TO FREEDOM

Barrington Brathwaite, *Zabeth* (2004)

FLIGHT TO FREEDOM

AFRICAN RUNAWAYS AND

MAROONS

IN THE AMERICAS

Alvin O. Thompson

University of the West Indies Press
Jamaica • Barbados • Trinidad and Tobago

University of the West Indies Press
1A Aqueduct Flats   Mona
Kingston 7   Jamaica
www.uwipress.com

10 09 08 07 06   5 4 3 2 1

CATALOGUING IN PUBLICATION DATA

Thompson, Alvin O.
Flight to freedom: African runaways and Maroons
in the Americas / Alvin O. Thompson.
p. cm.
Includes bibliographical references.

ISBN: 976-640-180-2

1. Maroons – Caribbean Area – History. 2. Fugitive slaves –
Caribbean Area. 3. Caribbean Area – History. I. Title.

F1884.T58 2006   972.92

The original manuscript of this book won the literary award in the
category of Political Thought, Prizes of Caribbean Thought 2003–2004.

Cover illustration: Richard Ansdell, *The Hunted Slaves* (1861).
Reproduced by permission of National Museums Liverpool, United Kingdom.

Book and cover design by Robert Harris.
Set in ACaslon 10.5/14 x 24
Printed in the United States of America.

To my wife, Hilda,

with all my love

Contents

Illustrations

Acknowledgements

My research for this study was conducted largely in the Main Library, University of the West Indies, Cave Hill, and the Benson Latin American Collection, University of Texas at Austin. I wish to thank the staff of these institutions, whose courtesy and willingness to assist me in locating information made my task much easier than it might have been. I also wish to thank Dr Pedro Welch of the University of the West Indies, Cave Hill, for reading the manuscript of this work and making valuable suggestions for improving it.

Figures 1 and 4 have been used with the kind permission of Professor Jerome Handler, who, along with Michael L. Tuite Jr., has mounted the Web site "The Atlantic Slave Trade and Slave Life in the Americas: A Visual Record" at http://hitchcock.itc.virginia.edu/Slavery/index.html. Figure 7 has been used with permission of Ian Randle Publishers; figure 8, with permission of the University of North Carolina Press; figure 9, with permission of the Florida Museum of Natural History; figure 17, with permission of Cambridge University Press; and figure 26, with permission of the Bristol Museum/Bristol City Council. I wish also to thank Mr Barrington Brathwaite of Guyana for his artistic impression of Zabeth.

Introduction

Slavery is the most perverse and alienating form of domination of one man by another, the absolute negation of freedom and the corruption of all political order that aspires to protect human dignity.

— Charles Esteban Deive, *Los Cimarrones del Maniel Neiba*

Slavery is a denial of all freedom and, as such, is a denial of humanity, of the very essence of the human condition, for it is an attempt at objectification, at making the person a thing, a chattel.

— Orlando Patterson, "Slavery and Slave Revolts"

This book examines the struggles of enslaved Africans in the Americas to achieve freedom through flight, in the face of overwhelming military odds on the part of their oppressors. The study of *marronage* (*marronnage, maroonage, maronage*), especially in the past few decades, has opened up a new frontier of knowledge in slavery studies in the Americas. It presents a more contextualized discourse on slave resistance than studies that focus on resistance within the geographical framework of the plantation or the White urban centres.

The face of oppression has been, and in many places still is, all too visible in the region. It began with the European assault on the Amerindians and continued with the Africans and Asians. African slavery in the Americas has left indelible marks on the geographical, political, economic, social and cultural landscapes of the hemisphere. An important part of that indelibility is *marronage*, which involved both flight from slavery and the establishment of free communities.

Maroon societies have fascinated writers from almost every discipline – history, sociology, politics, linguistics, anthropology, folklore, music, medicine, journalism and fiction. The authenticity of "Maroon studies" was given a boost in 1992, in the quincentennial year of Columbus's arrival in the Americas, when the Smithsonian Institution in Washington, DC, sponsored two important events: an assembly of people, including the descendants of several Maroon communities, at a Festival of American Folklife, and an exhibition under the theme Creativity and Resistance: Maroon Cultures in the Americas.

There are many reasons for the growing fascination with Maroon history, but one of the most important is the struggle of African peoples in the Americas to achieve human dignity in the face of great adversity. An outstanding feature of Maroon communities is that many of them survived for several decades – and some for over a century – without capitulating to the military expeditions sent against them. Among the most durable were Palmares (literally "palm groves"; also known as *Angola Janga* or Little Angola) in Brazil; Saramaka and Ndjuka in Suriname; San Basilio in Colombia; Esmeraldas in Ecuador; Le Maniel (present-day San José de Ocoa) on the Haitian–Dominican Republic border; and the Leewards and Windwards in Jamaica.[1] The struggle for freedom was a hard one; most enslaved persons sought it in one form or another, but relatively few attained it until the authoritarian state decreed general abolition. It was this circumstance that caused Fuentes (1979, 11) to write about the "phantasm of freedom" that many runaways sought. Once attained, that freedom was constantly in jeopardy from the former slaveholders; thus Jesús (Chucho) García (1996, 63) writes about "the danger of freedom" that was integral to the dialectics of *marronage*. While most Maroon communities knew only an ephemeral existence, the longevity of *marronage* itself constituted a significant aspect of the Blacks' struggles for freedom. García (1989, 62) extols *marronage* as a saga of the redemptive love of freedom and a quest to recapture the beauty of the human form, which had been reduced to a work machine through slavery that created a disjunction between the enslaved person's inner self (soul, spirit) and outer self (body).

The Maroon heritage exists almost everywhere in the Americas – especially in the large plantation societies – in extant contemporary literature, artefacts, place names, icons, and myths and legends. Richard Price (1979, 105) states that the Maroon heritage is deeply intertwined in the history of the French Antilles, that out-of-the-way rural settlements that relate to the Maroon past are not uncommon, and that in Haiti present-day historians glorify the Maroons' role in the revolution that overthrew slavery and colonialism. François Duvalier, president of Haiti at the time, unveiled a statue to *Le Nègre Marron* (The Black Maroon) on the Square of the Heroes of Independence. The monument has become the symbol of freedom in a country once the locale of some of the most draconian slave laws and practices, and a hotbed of Maroon activities. In 1986 the Casa de Africa was founded in Cuba to collect and display artefacts of African history and culture and to carry out archaeological and cultural studies of Black communities. In July 1997 UNESCO (the United Nations Educational, Scientific and Cultural Organisation) sponsored the construction of a giant-sized monument to the runaway miners of El Cobre in that country. In the same year Rokeby Museum, a ninety-acre site in the US state of Vermont, was declared a National Historical Landmark because of the site's significant role in the Underground Railroad's activities. On 14 March 2002 the Black Carib chief Joseph Chatoyer (Chatawe) was declared the first National Hero of St Vincent and the Grenadines and the day proclaimed a national holiday. In the Dominican Republic a radio station bears the name Radio Enriquillo, while in Venezuela the José Leonardo Chirinos International Airport was named in honour of this iconic figure in the country's history of resistance to enslavement.

In the 1890s Enrique Herrera Morena, mayor of Córdoba, built a new hospital and named it after Gaspar Yanga (Ñaga, Ñanga), the most celebrated Maroon leader in Mexico's history. In 1933 the town of San Lorenzo de los Negros, where Yanga's Cofre de Perote group settled some years after signing a treaty with the government, was officially renamed Yanga, and in the mid-1970s a group known as the Yang Bara Club initiated an annual festival on San Lorenzo Day in the Yanga Township, celebrating the birth of the "First Free Town of the Americas".[2] Annual carnivals or other festivals commemorating the Maroon heritage – most of recent origin – are held in the Dominican Republic, Haiti, Mexico, Brazil, Venezuela and other countries. The theme of life and death informs many of these folk festivals, where participants relive in music, dance, song and drama the Maroons' struggle for freedom and their deadly encounters with their oppressors.

Especially since 20 November 1978, when the Brazilian government declared an annual National Black Consciousness Day, Zumbi, the last leader of Palmares, who refused to sign a treaty with the colonial state, has been regarded in popular discourse as the main nationalist figure in that country's history of resistance to racism and colonialism. The 1995 tercentenary of his death was organized around his "immortality". On that occasion the world's largest carnival focused on the theme of Zumbi; country-wide commemorations and celebrations included a pilgrimage to Palmares, where the Brazilian president addressed the gathering. Details of the celebrations were carried in the international press (Anderson 1996, 545–47; chapter 10).

In Jamaica, the almost legendary female Maroon leader, Grandy (Granny) Nanny, referred to today by Jamaicans as Nanny of the Maroons, has been declared a National Heroine (Harris 1994, 46). Kamau Brathwaite (1994, 122) and Mavis Campbell (1990, 51) compare her to several female warriors in Africa, particularly Nzinga, the equally legendary figure who symbolized Angolan resistance to Portuguese rule in the first half of the seventeenth century. Not least among Grandy Nanny's legendary feats was her magical display at the signing ceremony in 1739 that brought an end to warfare between the Windward Maroons and the British. According to Harris's (1994, 48) version:

> At the end of the signing ceremony the Wonder Lady for the last time displayed her unusual capability of rendering harmless the bullets fired at her: she asked the British commandant to give the order for a volley to be fired at her. When the request was at last hesitantly granted, she rose from the stooping position she had taken up and handed him all the bullets fired at her, as a memento of the occasion.

Figure 1. The Black Maroon of Haiti

The Cockpit Country and Blue Mountains of Jamaica, the Bahoruco (Baoruco) region on the border between Haiti and the Dominican Republic, the Bayamón Mountains in Puerto Rico, the Cottica and Marowijne River areas of Suriname and many places in Santiago de Cuba hold strong memories of Maroon dwellings and deeds, and the descendants of Maroons still live as distinctive groups in some of these places. Among the place names resonant of the Maroon heritage that have survived are Lake Enriquillo in the Dominican Republic; Runaway Creek in Belize; Piton des Nègres, Piton des Ténèbres, Crête à Congo, Pic des Platons and Cavernes de Cavaillon in Haiti; Morne Nègre Marron (Morne Laurent) in Dominica; Nanny Falls, Nanny Town, Accompong Town, Guy's Town and Molly Town in Jamaica; Todos Tenemos Stream, Guardamujeres Stream, Guardamujeres Mountain, Ajengiblar Stream, Calunga Stream and Calunga Mountain in Cuba; and Dismal Swamp in the United States. Even the relatively small island of Antigua retains a vestige of Maroon heritage in Runaway Bay, and the tiny islands of Bermuda (with an estimated total size of only twenty-one square miles) have Jeffrey's Cave in memory of a runaway who hid there for some weeks. Towards the end of the last century Suriname's nationalist government named the military barracks in Paramaribo, the nation's capital, *Membre Boekoe* (Boucou, Buku) (Remember Boekoe), in tribute to the brave struggle waged by the Aluku (Boni) Maroons at their capital of that name against the mercenary and regular soldiers that were sent against them (Thoden van Velzen 1995, 112; Hoogbergen 1993, 181).

In other places, small towns, villages and other communities clearly reflect both Maroon and wider African heritage, such as the numerous *pueblos de morenos* of the Costa Chica in Mexico; the settlements of Matta Escura, Armacao, Piraja, Estrada da Liberdade, Itapoa and Cabula in Salvador, Brazil; the *Playeros* ("beach people") of the rivers and coastal areas of Darien in Panama; and the inhabitants of the Pearl Islands on that country's Pacific coast. Even in Costa Rica, with a small Maroon community and heritage, the runaways are remembered as *Zambos* or *Zambos-Moskitos*, whose ancestors established settlements in areas remote from Spanish control and tormented the colonists until the government made peace with them in the eighteenth century. James Lockhart and Stuart B. Schwartz (1983, 220) tell us that in Brazil today more than 150 rural and urban names are derived from *mocambo* (the Kimbundu word for "mountain peak") and *quilombo* ("capital" or "town"). Some settlements had rather curious names, such as Carrion Crow Hill in

Jamaica, Urubu (Vulture) in Brazil, and Todos Tenemos (We All Have) and Guardamujeres (Protect Women) in Cuba.

Archaeological work and field expeditions by scholars in Cuba, Haiti, the Dominican Republic, the United States, Suriname, Jamaica and elsewhere are adding to our knowledge of the exact sites of many of the settlements and the material and social culture of their inhabitants. In the case of Jamaica, such work, aided by historical maps, other contemporary records and oral traditions, has allowed Kofi Agorsah and others to locate more precisely Gun Hill, Watch Hill, Lookout Point (Parade), Kindah, Bathing Place, Petty River Bottom, Gun Barrel, Killdead, Ambush, Peace Cave and several other Maroon sites. They have also uncovered British stone fortifications dating back to the brief period of British military occupation of Nanny Town in 1734–35 (Agorsah 1994, 170–74, 182). Gabino La Rosa Corzo (2003, 231–43 passim), employing similar techniques, has located many settlements in Cuba, including Todos Tenemos and Calunga in El Frijol Mountains. Such finds help to bring to life the events described, sometimes not with great precision, in historical records. They are helping gradually to separate myths from reality and to refine our understanding of the Maroon experience.

The faces behind *marronage* were numerous. The iconography of great leaders includes François Makandal (Macandal), Jérôme Poteau, Polydor, Romaine la Prophetesse, Padre Jean and Boukman Dutty in Haiti; Françisque Fabulé, Grand-Papa and Nocachy in Guadeloupe; Pompée in French Guiana; Juan de Serras, Cudjoe (Kojo), Grandy Nanny, Three-Fingered Jack and Leonard Parkinson in Jamaica; Enriquillo, Diego Guzman, Juan Vaquero, Diego de Ocampo and Lemba in the Dominican Republic; Gaspar Yanga and Macute (Makute) in Mexico; Marcos Xiorro in Puerto Rico; Boni, Jolicoeur and Baron in Suriname; Joseph Chatoyer in St Vincent; Domingo Bioho, Domingo Padilla (Domingo Criollo) and Jerónimo in Colombia; Andresote (Andrés López del Rosario), José Leonardo Chirinos, Francisco Pirela, Miguel Jerónimo (Gerónimo, Guacamayo) and Guillermo Rivas (Ribas) in Venezuela; Zumbi in Brazil; and Alonso de Illescas in Ecuador.

This study looks at how the runaways achieved initial freedom and sought to maintain it, and at the massive loss of life involved in doing so. They went through many trials and tribulations, but at the end of the slavery period quite a few of their settlements survived, and some demonstrated a remarkable degree of political, economic, social and cultural health. The study also looks at the various threats to their freedom, from both inside and outside the Maroon settlements (variously called *palenques, rancherias, ladeiras, mambises, quilombos, mocambos, magotes, cumbes, manieles* and so on). It shows how they utilized the natural landscape and modified it to guard their freedom, and examines the dangers posed by complacency, authoritarianism and militarism.

As Thomas Flory (1979, 117) put it, Maroon communities emerged where those who fled from slavery finally stopped running. This study follows the Maroons where they went. In the words of Kevin Mulroy (1993, 1), "As history unfolded, true liberty would acquire connotations of crossing international boundaries, fighting wars, living in exile, and establishing communities on hostile frontiers." Mulroy (1993, 2) goes on to summarize the commonalities among Maroon communities in the Americas:

> Similarities included the building of settlements in inaccessible, inhospitable areas for concealment and defense; the development of extraordinary skills in guerrilla warfare; impressive economic adaptation to new environments; substantial interaction with Native Americans; existence in a state of continuous warfare, which strongly influenced many aspects of their political and social organization; the emergence of leaders skilled in understanding whites; and an inability, because of various needs, to disengage themselves fully from the enemy which proved to be "the Achilles heel of maroon societies throughout the Americas".

One of the features emphasized in this study is the striking similarity of the problems that Maroons faced and the solutions that they forged. Though most of them enjoyed little or no contact with other communities across geographical and linguistic boundaries, the similarity of these solutions suggests an inner logic to their actions that transcended spatial and linguistic barriers. Of course, Africans (who constituted the vast majority of enslaved persons and Maroons) came with a cornucopia of thoughts, ideologies and skills. These were modified under the circumstances of New World slavery and the new physical and social environments into which they were thrust. Their remarkable resilience and adaptability in the face of the incubus that threatened to destroy them are a tribute no less to their ancestral heritage than to their own ingenuity and willpower.

I hope that what emerges from this study is a strong sense of the need of the people in the Americas to guard against threats to the freedoms that our ancestors won by their sweat and blood. One school of thought holds that no historical, scholarly or political work should be consciously didactic. However, it is a truism that unless we learn from the past we are likely to repeat our mistakes.

The originality of this study is based on two primary factors: its reassessment of several of the views and interpretations that have informed discourse on *marronage*, and its pan-American scope. The bibliography is evidence that a large and growing number of works exist on various aspects of the subject. Some of these are quite good, but few of them focus on the Americas as a whole or provide the panoramic view of the subject that is critical to understanding the role of *marronage* in the region's struggle for freedom and dignity.

In many instances, our only source is a faint voice from the past in the midst of deep troughs of silence, but archaeological work is helping to fill the gap. Much of what has survived in contemporary written records is enmeshed in myths, legends and biased contemporary views. Despite the obvious difficulties that the modern researcher and writer face in unravelling this skein of largely negative contemporary thought concerning Maroons, I have attempted, through careful use of some of the best contemporary and modern works on the subject and reference to the African continent from which the enslaved persons came, to challenge and modify the perspective. For instance, I have tried to provide new insights into the despotism of Maroon leaders, the large-scale abduction of women from the plantations, and Maroon enslavement of others in their communities. I have also attempted to offer more detailed and careful analyses of Maroon economy and ethnicity.

Nonetheless, this study is not a comprehensive one on Maroon societies in the Americas, nor does it provide a detailed chronological framework of *marronage* in different territories. Rather, it is an interpretive work based on selected issues relating to the struggle for freedom. Because of space constraints, I have focused largely on the main Maroon states and colonies in the Americas. Other colonies, such as Barbados, Belize, Dominica, Chile and Ecuador, are given only very brief mention, and a few are not mentioned at all. For the same reason I have not dealt, except in passing, with the social and cultural dynamics of Maroon life, though I have examined those aspects of religion that reinforced the political and governmental apparatus, and had a direct and powerful impact upon both the defensive and aggressive aspects of Maroon polities.

Naturally, there were important variations between states, within a given state, and over various time periods. Unfortunately, it is impossible in such a relatively short study to address those variations all the time, especially when they did not make a qualitative difference to Maroon life. However, every attempt has been made to cite cases or examples from several countries to illustrate the salient points and to provide greater scope for comparative analysis. Of necessity, I have been highly selective in regard to the bibliography and have no doubt omitted several works that would have enriched this study. I trust, though, that the works cited will guide those who want to deal with particular communities or topics in greater depth.

Resistance to enslavement and brutalities constituted an attempt by enslaved persons both to reduce the power of the enslavers and to acquire some power for themselves. William Freehling (2002, 5) observes that "The job of an underclass, when it seeks to overturn a crushing dominion, is to find the spaces where successful resistance can be mounted." Maroons certainly sought and often found such spaces. *Marronage* was the most extreme form of such resistance, since it involved opting out of the system of oppression altogether and establishing a new kind of society in which the former enslaved persons took (or sought to take) control of their own lives and destinies. Jean Fouchard (1972, 170) insists that *marronage* was not a saga about "fugitives interested in timid escapades without a tomorrow, but with true 'rebels', dedicated and aggressive, hostile to slavery". Harriet Beecher Stowe's 1852 novel *Uncle Tom's Cabin* (which sold over three hundred thousand copies in its first year of publication) emphasizes the contribution of fugitive agency to changing the pathetic circumstances under which enslaved persons lived.

Contemporary and occasionally modern writers have criticized the Maroons for their seemingly indiscriminate attacks on people who were not enslavers. We must remember, however, that it was not simply the slaveholders who were responsible for the system of slavery, but almost the entire White community. The system could not have existed without broad sanction, tacit or open, by that community. In the words of Orlando Patterson (1991, 10), "A slave relationship . . . requires at least the tacit support of those not directly involved with it, and calls into being a slave culture, however rudimentary." The validity of this observation is evident in the United States Fugitive Slave Act of 1850, which placed the burden on every free person in the country to apprehend and return runaways (Quarles 1969, 107; Fogel 1989,

341–42; Freehling 2002, 8–9). Also, Maroons on the whole were waging a counter-offensive against slavery. The real aggressors were the enslavers who had held them in bondage, sought to return them to bondage and continued to keep their families and friends in lifelong bondage.

I used the term "former enslaved persons" earlier because, functionally, Maroons were no longer enslaved persons. Patterson (1979, 278) states that arguably Maroons were not "slaves". Jean Fouchard (1972, 339) insists that they were *de facto* free persons, but different from other free persons because they had freed themselves against the express wishes of their overlords. Jesús (Chucho) García (1989, 53, 61) speaks about *marronage* as the Africans' "reconquest of their freedom", and "the reconquest of the human condition of the African and his descendants". Brito Figueroa (1985, 206–7) views it as an attempt by enslaved persons to "take back the freedom that the Spanish had so tyrannically usurped".[3] Occasionally, the colonial authorities spoke about pre-treaty Maroons as free people – for instance, in an official document of the Royal Audiencia in Caracas (Brito Figueroa 1985, 238).

We should also bear in mind that many people were born in Maroon communities and were never enslaved. This was true especially of the large and long-standing communities such as Palmares in Brazil, the Windwards and Leewards in Jamaica, the Saramakas and Ndjukas (Djukas, Ndyukas, Aukas) in Suriname, and Le Maniel (Spanish: Maniel de Neiba) on the border between Haiti[4] and the Dominican Republic. Nevertheless, the slaveholders commonly referred to the progeny of deserters as "slaves". One example comes from the court records of Maroons captured in Brazil in 1877. Although certain women testified that they had been born in the Curuá *mocambo* and that they had children but had never had masters, the records still referred to them as "slave women" (Conrad 1983, 393). Similarly, although the vast majority of Maroons and other groups of African descent in the Miskito population of Nicaragua lived as free persons, working for themselves as traders, woodcutters, fishermen and peasant farmers, in 1766 the writer Robert Hodgson still listed them as "slaves" (Gordon 1998, 35).

Patrick Carroll (1977, 499) refers to Maroons who had signed treaties with the authoritarian states that recognized their freedom as "former maroons". The use of such a term and the larger argument that I have put forward are in a sense semantic, but the objective is to probe more deeply the psyches of both the plantocracy and the escapees in dealing with the issue of bondage and freedom. Part of the process of rethinking *marronage* is to try to view the

Maroons from their perspective rather than that of the enslavers. Maroons had three main identities. In their own view they were self-liberated persons (who, depending upon their other activities later on, might also regard themselves as freedom fighters); to enslaved persons they were successful rebels (people who had beaten the system); whereas to the enslavers they were simply "runaway slaves" (who might also be bandits or vagabonds). A notary act of Guadeloupe specified that runaways should be considered as "present though absent" (Dubois 2004, 45), and it was not unusual for planters in various colonial jurisdictions to include runaways in the rental or sale of their properties.

Maroons drew a clear distinction between enslavement and *marronage*. The creation story among the Jamaican Windward Maroons contrasts their community's founder, Grandy Nanny, who was willing to fight for her freedom, with her sister Shanti, who was too afraid to do so and remained in slavery (Zips 1999, 110–11). The Ndjuka people (descendants of former Maroons) of present-day Suriname remember three definitive periods in their history: *katibo ten*, the period of enslavement; *lowe ten*, the years of escape into the forests and organization of Maroon settlements; and *a fi*, the post-treaty period. They still celebrate their freedom today and ritualistically remember it in their visits to each other. The host inquires, according to the old sentry challenge, "*Wada, wadaa . . . ooo?*" ("Who is there?"). The visitor replies, "*Friman*" ("Freeman") (Thoden van Velzen 1995, 116–17).

Katia Mattoso (1979, 139) states that "[t]he larger quilombos created whole new social organizations, with their own hierarchies and economic and political authorities", and that the *quilombos* generally became "truly independent centers of production". In the same paragraph, however, she expresses the view that Maroons lived "on the very fringes of society". Of course, from the standpoint of the Maroons it was not a question of living on the fringes of any society but rather of creating a new kind of society, where political, social and other distinctions were not based on ascriptive race and colour criteria. Maroon communities had their own distinctive, rich and variegated life. Still, Mattoso's remark is interesting, coming from a person who claims to have written a study from the perspective of the enslaved persons (1979, 1–3), and whose work indeed has a lot of merit. In this instance, however, she falls into the common trap of viewing mainstream society as that to which the enslavers and other upper-class Whites belonged. Her (perhaps inadvertent) statement reflects the orientation of colonial and imperial history for most of the five centuries that the region's written history has existed, and the pervasive nature of a historiography that focused on the oppressors rather than the oppressed. Thus, Alan Burns (1954, 5) wrote of the British Caribbean that its history "is mainly the story of the white conquerors and settlers, as the much larger Negro population, during the centuries of slavery, had little to do, save indirectly with the shaping of events". Colonialist historians like Burns often confined *marronage* to the trash bins of history, but nationalist historians are discovering treasures among the trash.

José Juan Arrom and Manuel A. García Arévalo (1986, 35) insist, in the context of the Dominican Republic (with obvious application to the Americas as a whole), that *marronage* is "a stirring chapter within the womb of the colonial past". In contrast, García (1989, 61) observes that the historiography of enslaved Africans in Barlovento, Venezuela, has generally presented their resistance as a series of isolated episodes without any theoretical or conceptual framework within the wider history of national emancipation (that is, national independence from Spain).[5] Brito Figueroa (1985, 208) implies that instead of writing them into history, historians have sometimes attempted to write them out of it, by ignoring their struggles altogether or treating them as peripheral to the wider struggle for freedom and human dignity. He explains (1985, 243),

> [o]ne of those approaches accepted as gospel truth, consists in denying that the struggle of the Black slaves in colonial society constituted the materialization of the class contradictions and expression of a common class struggle; another approach [is], to ignore the role of *historical agency* among the popular mass – *historically* represented in the society by slaves, freed Blacks, indigenous peoples, mulattos and pardos.

Edison Carneiro (1946, 24) expresses the view that "[f]or three centuries, Palmares remained enveloped in darkness and silence with only its ghost . . . occupying its place". To him, this silence is the more amazing since the Maroon state remains the "example of unparalleled resistance in Brazil, and the bulwark of . . . liberties".

These viewpoints hold good for much of the history of African resistance to slavery and wider oppression in the Americas. However, a growing number of scholars have attempted to jettison this overburden of prejudice and ignorance concerning enslaved persons, and have sought to place their resistance within the ideological context of freedom from brutalities associated with enslavement and from enslavement as a whole. Others have stressed what they perceive as a continuum between such actions and the wider struggle for national independence in Venezuela, Cuba, Haiti, Brazil and elsewhere, in which enslaved persons and Maroons played major roles.

Marronage was political action on the part of enslaved persons and frequently a challenge to the status quo that the enslavers had established (Landers 1998, 358). Incontestably, Maroon settlements constituted the first independent polities from European colonial rule, even if the authoritarian states did not recognize them as such at the time. They had their own independent political, economic and social structures, and occupied definitive land spaces that they often contested with the colonial powers and won. Though "Maroon treaties" compromised the political sovereignty of some of these polities, others retained a good deal of autonomy, and some Maroon leaders absolutely refused to make any arrangement with the colonial state short of a full declaration of their independence.

It is important to recognize that while the vast majority of enslavers in the Americas were Europeans, some Africans (Blacks), Indians and Creoles (Coloureds or Mestizos) were also enslavers. However, there was a great gulf between the Europeans and the other categories of enslavers in terms of access to political, social and other privileges. They only closed ranks, and even so not completely, in cases of heightened slave unrest and pressing Maroon activities. This study focuses largely on the Whites because they exercised extreme dominance within the slavery system, they were by far the most numerous victims of Maroon depredations, and they organized the main military expeditions against Maroons.

Maroon communities included Indians, Africans, Europeans and Creoles; young, middle-aged and elderly people; enslaved and free people; field workers, domestics, drivers, artisans, messengers and soldiers; adherents to African traditional religions, Christianity and Islam. The enslaved people fled from all jurisdictions, regardless of the economic or social circumstances. They fled from the highly developed plantation societies of Brazil, Jamaica, Suriname, Haiti, the United States and Mexico, and from less developed plantation or trading economies such as Paraguay, Uruguay, Argentina, the Bahamas, St Eustatius and Bermuda. Lauren Derby (2003, 11) argues that the Caribbean plantation system spawned

> a frontier society of runaways, vagrants and half-castes who did not live within colonial society but rather in opposition to it in the refuge of the mountains, the

depopulated coasts and the sea. And it was here that a truly Creole society was founded in the sense of a novel social identity and culture that saw itself as autonomous from the metropole.

Slavery was a pathologically wrong socio-economic system, and it negatively affected all people living in the slaveholding states, including those who were not enslavers and did not use the services of enslaved persons. Slavery was a total institution in more than one sense, but particularly in that it defined the relationships between all classes and groups in the society. Thus, in order to defeat or undermine it, the opposition had to be committed to a total struggle against it. The level of commitment of various groups to such a struggle is one of the many moot points to which this discourse will pay some attention. Still, it is important to note Werner Zips's (1999, 12) views here that Blacks had to fight a "physical and psychic battle . . . against the attempted destruction of their religious, social, cultural, political, judicial, and philosophical values and forms of expression by whites".

The existence of Maroon communities also underlined the draconian nature of New World slavery, and the difficulties of escaping totally from it, short of a general abolition of that nefarious institution. Maroons were fugitives, not from justice but from injustice that relentlessly pursued them up to the very gates of their new habitats. But they retaliated fiercely and often effectively. Both the contemporary and modern literature places considerable attention on the depredations that the Maroons wrought on European plantations and urban communities, sometimes bringing the inhabitants to their knees and forcing them to sue for peace. While the literature also refers fairly often to the numbers of Maroons slain in battle, it does not provide us with any coherent data on that subject or on the numbers slain on both sides of the divide. The data suggest that far more Maroons than their pursuers died in such struggles, because of the massive advantage that the latter possessed in terms of weaponry and the size of their military and paramilitary forces. Nevertheless, as far as we know, while many settlements were razed to the ground, the entire population of no large *palenque* was ever completely wiped out, and the human residue often reconstituted itself within a short time by new recruits.

There was always a nexus – perhaps a better word is *symbiosis* – between the slaveholding and Maroon areas. The latter depended heavily on the former for the majority of their population; sometimes for food, arms and various other kinds of materials; for information on what was taking place within the authoritarian state; and at times for physical protection (usually on initial flight, or during some other contingency, such as when they were wounded or were likely to be apprehended). As Jean Fouchard (1972, 169) notes, there were "clandestine networks in the world of the slaves organizing and facilitating flight".

Without such networks *marronage* would have been even more difficult than it was, and much more restricted in demographic and military terms. Many who did not offer physical and emotional help nevertheless revelled quietly in the escape of one of their family members, "and, above all, each escape of a fellow sufferer produced prayers of success, fed the rumor mill, fired dreams, and raised the level of curiosity about freedom throughout the quarters" (Blassingame 1979, 192–93).

On the other side, enslaved persons on the plantations or in the towns depended upon the Maroons to keep their arms open to receive them and provide them with protection and sustenance; to exchange with them commodities – often seized by Maroons on raids – to which the enslaved persons would not otherwise have access; and to create some free space and at times lighten their burdens, when their overlords decided that concessions were necessary to keep the enslaved persons under their control. Of course, Maroon activities could, and sometimes did, lead to tighter control of enslaved persons, but this was usually in times of heightened Maroon activity within a given area.

Patterson (1979, 279) asserts that "all sustained slave revolts" had to be linked with *marronage* since "the only way in which a slave population can compensate for the inevitably superior military might of their masters is to resort to guerrilla warfare, with all its implications of flight, strategic retreat to secret hideouts, and ambush". Wim Hoogbergen (1993, 181–82) also argues strongly that revolts that did not involve prior contacts with Maroons – at least in Suriname in the eighteenth century, when the coercive apparatus of the state had reached unprecedented heights – stood much less chance of success than those that did so. In fact, he seems to view any other approach as a fatal flaw, especially in large-scale revolt. Numerous examples exist of insurgents transforming themselves into Maroons – for example, in the Jamaica revolt in 1760, the Berbice revolt in 1763, and most notably the Haitian revolution of 1791–1804. But smaller revolts often produced the same result, as, for instance, in 1773 when a failed revolt on the Belize River led to eleven insurgents making their way via the Rio Hondo to the Spanish post of Bacalar in Yucatán (Bolland 2002, 55).

Marronage offered enslaved persons the best hope of recapturing their freedom. What Conrad (1983, 360) observes of Brazil is equally appropriate for a number of other jurisdictions, including Suriname, Jamaica, Venezuela, Cuba, Haiti and the United States: "Thousands of offers to reward the capture and return of runaway slaves which appeared in hundreds of newspapers over seven or eight decades are convincing proof that flight was a common solution to the slave's predicament." The durability of Maroon settlements collectively, and the aggressive stance that some of them adopted towards the enslavers, made them the most widespread expression of the enslaved persons' hatred of the slavery system. As Carlos Esteban Deive (1989, 8) observes, *marronage* constituted the most aggressive response of enslaved persons to the servitude and oppression to which they were subjected for centuries by the slaveholding regimes in the Americas.

The vast majority of enslaved persons neither became Maroons in the true sense of the term nor absconded. Fouchard (1972, 153–54) contends that some enslaved persons had no desire to revolt or were incapable of doing so for a variety of reasons, including timidity, submissiveness, resignation, apathy, moral and physical weakness, the holding of certain privileges within the slavery system, brainwashing by the enslavers, and so on. He is quite harsh on those who, he asserts, were incapable of considering the slightest desire to flee yet were prisoners of a savage and unrelenting system. In his view, their failure to flee was no tribute to the humanity of the enslavers, but rather to their own subjective or objective circumstances that prevented them from doing so.

Fouchard is perhaps too harsh on those who remained in bondage. The fact is that no matter how draconian the system of oppression, in societies with a large population rarely do the vast majority of people show open resistance. Large-scale resistance almost invariably has to be carefully planned if there is to be any chance of success, and slave society rarely allowed for such a circumstance to happen. Notable exceptions are the servile revolts in Berbice in 1763 and Haiti in 1791. However, most scholars would probably accept that the vast majority of enslaved persons carried out resistance at a lower level – which Orlando Patterson (1967) dubs passive resistance, and Monica Schuler (1973) and Raymond Bauer and Alice Bauer (1971) call day-to-day resistance – at some point during their enslavement. Others reacted violently against their oppressors by maiming and sometimes killing them. Still others took their own lives in a supreme act of defiance and bravery, in a society where such action was often seen as a form of warfare.

The Maroon story is one not only of bitter struggles of enslaved peoples to achieve freedom but of equally bitter struggles of enslavers to prevent them from doing so. The authoritarian state became a theatre dramatizing the destruction of human beings at the hands of human beings. What strikes one forcefully throughout this drama is the wanton loss of lives, the brutalities with which the slaughter took place, and the sometimes hapless victims on both sides who were caught midstream between the forces of bondage and freedom. But the nobility of the Maroons' struggle looms large in the forfeiture of their lives for a cause in which they believed (one would have liked to say in which all humanity believes): in the words of Eugene Genovese (1981, xiii), a struggle that constituted "the basic assertion of human dignity and of humanity itself". They fought for the ideal of freedom as a right, not a legal prescription. It was all these factors that made *marronage* (and other forms of armed uprising) such a titanic struggle, in some ways comparable to a Greek tragedy – or a series of "great tragic dramas" and "collective explosions of redemption", in the words of Fuentes (1979, 13) – with all its catharsis and *dénouement*. But *marronage* on the whole did not end in tragedy; it ended in triumph for the former enslaved persons.

PART I

Ideological Bases
of Marronage

In a large-scale slave society, the slave relation, like a cancer in the blood, pervades all, degrades all, and magnifies in all the overwhelming goodness and desirability of freedom.

– Orlando Patterson, *Freedom*, vol. 1, *Freedom in the Making of Western Culture*

CHAPTER I

Totalitarianism and Slavery

DOMINION AND DOMINATION

Orlando Patterson (2000, 32) makes the point that "[a]ll human relationships are structured and defined by the relative power of the interacting persons". This suggests that power relations are at the core of human relations. Power relations, of course, have several components, but are usually divided into political, social, economic and psychological categories. A more refined classification would include juridical, military, cultural and sexual components. Enslaved persons felt the heavy hand of the enslavers in all these ways, in practice if not in theory. Here we must understand "the enslaver" to mean not simply the slave-owning class but the authoritarian state as a whole that wielded political and judicial power – though, almost invariably, the state officials did belong to that class. The vast majority of enslaved persons lived (or existed) under regimes of power that some scholars view as almost absolute. While this point may still be open to debate, what is hardly debatable is that slavery in the Americas represented one of the most extreme forms of power relations.

The enslaver perceived himself as all-powerful as far as his enslaved charges were concerned. He sought to control all the material, spiritual, cultural and symbolic elements associated with humanity. Among the powers that he exercised over his servile charges was branding them with his personal trademark. This was not related to any wrong that the enslaved persons were deemed to have committed, but simply to the enslaver's perceived need to identify his "property" properly by permanently searing his name or initials into their flesh. For instance, an advertisement about a runaway in Brazil indicated that he had identifying marks on his forehead and the palms of his hands that read: "Slave of Doña Fortunata" (Conrad 1983, 365). Another enslaver, on this occasion in the Lower Mississippi Valley, seared equally visible marks into the flesh of one of his servile charges: an inch-high cross on his forehead, the letter "O" on his cheek, and "Orleans" across his back (Schweninger 2002, 17). Even the religious orders and so-called humane overlords practised this kind of cruelty.

Enslaved persons looking at cattle could see clearly that they had been assimilated in the enslavers' minds to lower animals – as James Pope-Hennessy (1967, 47) states, "a kind of two-legged domestic animal" – and part of the stock of the plantations. Some enslaved persons underwent multiple brandings, signifying their transfer to different enslavers. Many new enslavers made the former brands unintelligible by superimposing other brands over them, while also burning their own brands on another part of the enslaved person's body. Enslaved people convicted of crimes, real or imagined, might be branded on their cheeks or some other visible part of their body with special marks. Fouchard (1972, 233) informs us of an enslaver named Caradeux who punished his runaways by searing into their flesh, sometimes in more than one place, the statement, "I am a maroon." Branding was one of the features of slavery that no freed person or Maroon could remove entirely (any more than he could remove lash stripes and other signs of brutality, such as loss of limbs). Some Maroons in Haiti, nevertheless, sought to get rid of their brands by various methods, including the use of fire and certain vegetable extracts (Fouchard 1972, 236).

Other powers that the enslaver exercised, legally or otherwise, over his enslaved charges included feeding, clothing and housing them; chastising, rewarding and selling them; giving them a new name, a new language and a new religion; having sexual relations with them; and, not infrequently, maiming and killing them. The enslaver's divestment of the name, language and religion of the enslaved person was an attempt to destroy that individual's identity and recreate him or her in the image of the enslaver. It may be regarded, in today's terminology, as a form of identity theft. The enslaved person was not only uprooted from his or her traditional roots but from all family and social connections – though, especially in the Spanish and Portuguese colonies, enslaved persons' ethnic origins were sometimes pre-

Figure 2. Branding an enslaved person. From *The History of Slavery and the Slave Trade, Ancient, Ancient and Modern,* by William O. Blake (Columbus, OH: J. and H. Miller, 1857).

served as part of their name (for instance, Francisco Angola, Francisco Jolofo and Pedro Mina).

In several jurisdictions the enslaver's power over the life and death of his servile charges was very real, and lasted until almost the end of slavery. Even where the law reserved the power of death to the authoritarian state, it was common for overlords to take the law into their own hands and execute their charges, and then not be charged themselves, or get off scot-free because of lack of acceptable evidence (since in many jurisdictions slave testimony against White people was inadmissible in court), or sometimes pay a small fine. In Berbice, for instance, the killing of an enslaved person by a White person was not deemed a capital offence until the early nineteenth century (Thompson 2002a, 28). While the French *Code Noir* (1685) prohibited it, in practice it was not rigidly enforced until the last days of slavery. According to Fouchard (1972, 114), protected by the state's failure to execute the law, Saint Martin l'Arada assassinated two hundred of his Blacks, and Caradeux buried several enslaved persons alive.

Fouchard (1972, 116–17) goes on to list several other enslavers who gained notoriety for their cruelty and adds a long list of punishments meted out to enslaved persons in Haiti, some of which, in his view, indicated sadism that surpassed the imagination. After reading his list and other evidence of the

Figure 3. Whipping an enslaved person. From *Voyage pittoresque et historique au Brésil*, by Jean-Baptiste Debret (Paris: Firmin Didot Frères, 1834–39).

indecencies and atrocities against the servile population, one begins to understand why some of them wrought similar vengeance on the White community. We cite here only a few of Fouchard's listed atrocities: throwing people alive into ovens and suspending them over spits like barbecuing meat; burning or mutilating men's genitalia and women's genitalia and breasts; priming their anuses with gunpowder which was then set alight; burying them up to the neck alive and pouring sugar over them, to be consumed by flies or ants; making them eat their own faeces and drink their own urine; sewing their lips together with wire; raping women in front of their husbands and children; and cutting up children in front of their parents.

In Berbice around the mid-eighteenth century, manager Gerlach brutalized a seven-year-old girl for what the governor considered trifling offences: he gave her 250 lashes, had her placed in the stocks without food (except what friends and relatives smuggled to her) and kept her there for three weeks.

When the governor saw her at the end of that period, he found that her frail body had been badly torn in places, and it was only his intervention that secured her release (Thompson 1987, 118).

What do we make of the sexual sins of a manager in Suriname who stripped naked a young Coloured woman about eighteen years old, tied her up with her hands suspended to a tree branch and gave her two hundred lashes because she had refused to allow him to invade her body sexually? Stedman (1988, 264–66), who recorded this incident, declared that she was being "skinned alive", and that when he, Stedman, intervened on the young woman's behalf, the manager was so furious that he decided to give her another two hundred lashes! Stedman wrote that after the first whipping she was dyed in blood from her neck to her ankles. The sexual violation of women, both married and single, was one of the cardinal sins of the enslavers and led to frequent violence between them and their enslaved charges. It was often a reason for desertion, as illustrated by reference to the Venezuelan Maroon Juan Antonio, who declared that he had decamped because his overlord violated his wife (who presumably absconded with him) (Brito Figueroa 1985, 241).

Court records in Cartagena from the late seventeenth century recount the statement of Francisco, seventy years old, about why he had deserted. He related before Governor Don Marín de Cevallos Lacerda (Martín de Ceballos y la Cerda) that since his childhood he had served Pedro Pérez, his overlord, with much love, and that he had married an enslaved Mulatto woman with whom he had sired eleven children, eight of whom had survived. Though Francisco had not given his master any motive for umbrage, the latter decided to sell him, thus separating him from his wife and children. When Francisco could find no one to help him, he fled to the Tabacal farm and from there to a *palenque*. Later, he decided to go with other Maroons to Pedro Pérez's place to rescue his wife and four of his children, who were the only ones that he could find (Navarrete 2003, 47–48).

There was also the case of Juan Alejandro, in Venezuela, who declared that he had fled from his overlord five years before because the latter had kept him shackled in irons, given him only a scrap of meat without bread once daily and no water unless he asked for some, forced him to sleep half-naked on the floor, and, for greater torment, during the day kept him in a cattle pen, tied up with a dog chain, because he had refused to perform the duties of headman (Brito Figueroa 1985, 240–41). But this case pales into insignificance in comparison with that of Cadetty, a young man enslaved in Suriname, whose manager practised extreme psychological torture. In Stedman's (1971, 179) words, he tormented the lad for a year by flogging him every day for one month; tying him down flat on his back, with his feet in the stocks, for another month; for a third month keeping an iron triangle or pot-hook around his neck, which prevented him from running away into the woods and even from sleeping, except in an upright or sitting position; for a fourth month chaining him to a dog's kennel on the landing place, night and day, with orders to bark at every boat or canoe that passed; and so on, varying his punishment monthly until the youth became insensible, no longer walked straight, and almost degenerated into a brute.

Covey, to whom Frederick Douglass was hired out for one year, was the ultimate practitioner of physical and psychological brutality and enjoyed a wide reputation for being a "slave-breaker". Slaveholders often sent their recalcitrant charges to him to be broken in, and sometimes he received their labour free of charge for doing so. He often whipped Douglass mercilessly (1973, 63) and for a while broke his spirit. Here are Douglass's own words (1973, 65–66):

> If at any one time of my life more than another I was made to drink the bitter-est dregs of slavery, that time was during the first six months of my stay with Mr. Covey. We were worked in all weathers. It was never too hot or too cold; it could never rain, blow, hail, or snow, too hard for us to work in the field. Work, work, work, was scarcely more the order of the day than of the night. The longest days were too short for him, and the shortest nights too long for him. I was somewhat unmanageable when I first went there, but a few months of this discipline tamed me. Mr. Covey succeeded in breaking me. I was broken in body, soul, and spirit. My natural elasticity was crushed, my intellect languished, the disposition to read departed, the cheerful spark that lingered about my eye died; the dark night of slavery closed in upon me; and behold a man transformed into a brute.

Perhaps the most disturbing case was that of Juana María. Her experience represented one of the most extreme reactions to enslavement, because Africans were intensely religious and showed great respect not only for their own traditional religions but also for Christianity. She had fled because her overlord, whom she described as very cruel, wished to separate her from her only daughter. On being recaptured, she decided to blaspheme against God and the Virgin Mary in order not to be returned to her overlord. When taken before the Inquisition, she asserted that she preferred to make her grave in hell than to serve her overlord (Navarrete 2003, 48). It was not uncommon for enslaved persons in Spanish jurisdictions to blaspheme in the hope of being taken away from their overlords. The judges of the Inquisition usually sentenced them for blasphemy but did not deal with the root cause of the problem (Navarrete 2003, 48; Villa-Flores 2002, 435–68). The brutalities meted out to enslaved persons caused García (1996, 65) to speak about the cross of slavery, and the contemporary Cuban poet Juan Francisco Manzano (once held in slavery) to observe that in the eyes of the enslavers, African life was cheap (Mullen 1981, 71).

Extreme power, appropriated by one set of human beings over another and exercised in a capricious and often arrogant manner, led to all sorts of abuses in the slavery system. It has been argued that in every human society there are psychopaths who commit atrocities, and slave society in the Americas was no different. There is an element of truth in this, but also a considerable degree of distortion. First, the incidence of such brutality was far greater in slave societies than in ostensibly free ones. Second, because people in a free society – at least in theory – had recourse to the law to redress such wrongdoing, and the law officers were themselves monitors of the system, there was a greater possibility of judicial intervention and the granting of some sort of justice to the victims than was the case in slave society, where the perpetrator stood every chance of walking away scot-free.[1]

R.A.J. van Lier (1971b, viii) observes that the slavery system gave psychopathic people an opportunity to pursue their worst inclinations and even encouraged psychopathic behaviour by creating an extreme situation of dominance and submission. Vidiadhar Naipaul (1974, 184) describes Stedman's account of slave life in Suriname as a terrifying catalogue of atrocities reminiscent of the German concentration camps – with the important difference that visitors to Suriname were allowed to survey the scene and make notes and sketches. Patterson (1991, 321) compares slavery in the Americas to warfare, piracy, plague and death. There can be no doubt that the brutalities of slavery registered high on the scale of (in)human atrocities and suffering.

The slavery system was born in sin and shaped in iniquity. It was social oppression at its worst: the classic form of necrophilia. García (1989, 62) refers to it as the negation of life. Oldendorp (1987, 21) claimed that it "accomplished something similar to what is achieved by death". Patterson declares in the title of his 1982 book that it constituted a form of social death, and in a later publication (1991, 331) he argues that enslaved persons suffered from three common disabilities: powerlessness, social degradation (or dishonour) and natal alienation. Some scholars feel that he has been too sweeping in his assignment of all enslaved persons to these three categories since, they argue, the oppressed continuously asserted their rights as human beings in a number of ways, both individually and collectively. Among these were cultural retentions (especially in religion, language, music, song, dance, family and kinship relations, and arts and crafts), the strong gerontocratic basis of their communities, and – particularly significantly, according to Patterson's critics – resistance and revolt.

MARRONAGE AND VIOLENCE

Maroons have had an ambiguous reputation in popular and scholarly literature, as both heroes and villains. Slaveholders commonly explained the flight of individual Maroons in terms of the bad habits that they displayed, such as being drunkards, sluggards, thieves, murderers and prostitutes. Evaristo Ujueta declared that the runaway female Manuela, of Santa Marta, Colombia, was insubordinate, commonly guilty of very bad conduct, and had other despicable character traits (Romero Jaramillo 1997, 183; see also 186). Jacinta, of the same province, was accused of having been a thief and a prostitute since the age of fifteen. It was further alleged that no one was interested in purchasing her because of her bad character (Romero Jaramillo 1997, 183). The numerous pejorative terms employed concerning Maroons as a group included: wild men, beasts (or beastly), snakes, gangrene, vermin, wretches, perfidious villains, cut-throats, pernicious scum, chronic plague, lurking assassins, desperadoes, lawless freebooters, rebellious rabble, sneaking and treacherous rogues, skulking runaways, monsters and hydra.[2] A South Carolina enslaver even referred to one of his runaways as "a stately *Baboon*" (Wood 1975, 246). Esteban Deive (1989, 15) observes that the classic description of the Maroon was that of a common delinquent given over to rapine and robbery. In 1662 Archbishop Francisco de la Cueva Maldonado dubbed the typical Maroon community in the Dominican Republic a den of barbarous thieves, pagan and without laws. However, in the same letter he showed that they did have communal laws, including the death penalty for grave offences (Arrom and García Arévalo 1986, 82–83). Though the penalties were sometimes very harsh by modern standards, they were no more brutal than those that the slaveholding state inflicted, sometimes for far more trivial offences. Of course, in eighteenth-century Europe people could also be hanged for trivial offences such as stealing a sheep.

It was common for contemporary (and many modern) records to refer to the killing of Whites by insurgent Blacks, including Maroons, as "murder", "slaughter", "massacre" or the like, while similar acts by Whites against Blacks were usually referred to as "killing", "execution" or a less evocative term (Bowser 1974, 188; Campbell 1990, 22, 31; Atwood 1971, 242–43). Stedman (1988, 126), who often showed great sympathy for the Maroon cause, once referred to an instance where the Maroons had killed a number of soldiers sent against them as murder. Dr George Pinckard (1806, 2:240–41), who was at best ambivalent on the subject of Black freedom, wrote in 1806 that the Maroons lived in the worst circumstances of savagery and were nothing but brigands or marauders. He went on to say that they were Blacks of the meanest sort – cruel, bloodthirsty and revengeful – and that their crimes would have merited death in European and all other civilized countries. Many of them had murdered White people, massacred their overlords and staged group insurrections in order to take over the colony. Having failed to do so, they sought refuge from punishment by flying into the deep forests, from which they ventured forth to carry out their depredations. Mendoza, a government official in Mexico, felt that Blacks were a bloodthirsty lot: in 1553 he commented that they all wished to purchase their freedom with the lives of their overlords (Davidson 1979, 91).

The use of such pejorative language emphasizes the fact that although, at times, the Whites spoke of their military actions as waging war against the Maroons,[3] they did not perceive – or, rather, accept – the Maroons' quest for freedom as legitimate action or proper warfare; they considered it banditry or roguery. While unquestionably many small groups, especially operating close to the urban areas, practised and lived mainly by banditry, it is a gross exaggeration to suggest, as Carlos Aguirre (1993, 244) does, that *marronage* and banditry were inextricably linked. Though the large Maroon communities engaged in robbery both to obtain vitally needed supplies and as a form of reprisal against the slaveholders, this was not their main way of obtaining a living (see chapter 8).

Moreover, Maroons were not bloodthirsty killers, as their White antagonists stereotyped them. They were often fighting wars to the death against their enemies, and the rules of engagement were brutal on both sides. Those who signed treaties with the slaveholding states generally settled down to a peaceful life, to such an extent that their erstwhile antagonists frequently referred to them as "pacified" Maroons. With the abolition of slavery in the various New World states, *marronage* became a thing of the past, and the so-called brigands, vagabonds and murderers almost completely disappeared. This is perhaps the most striking testimony to the fact that for the Maroons the struggle was about freedom, and once that had been conceded, at least in the physical sense of the term, the rules of engagement changed dramatically from total warfare to other forms of dialogue. They could now beat their swords into ploughshares and study war no more.

The preceding paragraphs touch on the issue of violence as both a containing and a liberating force. The use of violence is one of the most unfortunate and disturbing aspects of human relationships, but it is a common human experience. In most instances, the violence associated with large-scale insurgency and Maroon activities was arguably a *sine qua non* of the achievement and maintenance of freedom. However, it is important to understand that many enslaved persons did not initiate or practise violence against their overlords, either at the time of flight or during their period as Maroons. Frederick Douglass is one outstanding example of such a non-violent approach to *marronage,* and there are numerous others. Nonetheless, Whites often employed extreme violence to keep enslaved people under their thumb. Shahabuddeen (1983, 129), Fuentes (1979, 9) and Lewis (1983, 5) opine that this violence was a form of organized terror and the primary instrument of the overlords' control over their enslaved charges. The oppressed resorted to counter-violence, either to escape the trammels of slavery or as retribution. But it is always a tricky call in human society to use force to settle grievances or achieve specific objectives. Each case has to be judged on its own merits and in the context of the options available to the oppressed peoples. Of course, much of the violence associated with Maroon communities had to do with the defence of their polities.

Recognizing that there are different kinds of violence – physical, mental and psychological – here we will deal essentially with physical violence. Political scientists and behaviourists often distinguish between kinds of physical violence – for instance, state (institutional) and individual (or group), structured (organized) and spasmodic (unorganized), proactive and reactive, enslaving and liberating. Some people argue that the state is often called upon to use the apparatus of violence in order to obtain or maintain a certain level of peace and security within the body politic. They recognize that there are often troubling occasions when the state employs violence without sufficient caution and control, and sometimes to further the interest of a special class or group within the society at the expense of the society as a whole. Examples of this kind of violence abound in despotic regimes, and were ever-present in the slave societies of the Americas. Still, some persons see the use of state violence as being legitimated by the recognition of the authoritarian state internationally. Some scholars have even argued that state despotism should be countered not by acts of counter-violence but by passive forms of resistance. Not so long ago prayer and passive obedience were the preferred tools of the civil disobedience movements led by the Mahatma Mohandas Gandhi and Dr Martin Luther King. Until 1963, passive resistance was also the strategy of the African National Congress against the apartheid regime in South Africa.

On the other side are those who believe that state violence should be countered and neutralized by counter-violence, either through individual or group effort. In *Summa Theologica,* Thomas Aquinas asserted that

> [a] tyrannical law, since it is not in accordance with reason, is not a law in the strict sense, but rather a perversion of law. . . . It only has the character of a law because it is a dictate of a superior over his subjects and is aimed at their obeying law, which is a good that is not absolute but only relative to a specific regime. (Sigmund 1988, 48)

Yet Aquinas was convinced that, under certain circumstances, violence to remove oppression could be legitimate. The most well-known exponent of counter-violence in recent times is Frantz Fanon, especially in his celebrated work *The Wretched of the Earth* (1967). Barbara Marie Perinbam (1982), discussing the philosophy of this "apostle" of counter-violence, referred to it as the advocacy of "holy violence". For Fanon and others, such violence is liberating in physical and psychological terms for both the oppressed and the oppressor. Paulo Freire (1972, 32) writes: "Whereas the violence of the oppressors prevents the oppressed from being fully human, the response of the latter to this violence is grounded in the desire to pursue the right to be human."

In slave societies, state violence raised major questions of how to cope effectively with it, and various enslaved groups and individuals went through the whole gamut of possible reactions: prayer, go-slow, downing of tools, feigned sickness, destruction of crops, poisoning, desertion and armed revolt. It was the last two options, often combined with others, that became the ultimate tool for the enslaved people in their quest for freedom. Naveda Chávez-Hita (1987, 141) points out, in the context of Córdoba, one of the important plantation areas in Mexico, that by the second half of the eighteenth century the sharp confrontation between enslaver and enslaved had become a natural part of social relations.

Ascriptive Criteria for Freedom

Whiteness came to be regarded as the ultimate badge of freedom and Blackness that of bondage. There was, of course, a penumbra along the continuum from bondage to freedom in which Whites and Blacks, free and enslaved, occupied common space, participated in festivals (for instance, Christmas and the feasts of St John and St Louis), and even shared amorous embraces (though these were usually forced rather than voluntary, in the case of Black women). But a wide chasm still existed between Whites and Blacks.

White people did not have to justify their access to freedom: it was taken as a natural condition of their Whiteness. Black people, in contrast, had to justify their claims to freedom, to show themselves deserving of it (Thompson 1995). Ultimately, in slave society Black freedom was viewed, from the legal standpoint, not as a gift from God but as a result of the largesse of the White community. Blacks had to find favour in the eyes of Whites through various behaviours, including fidelity to their masters, willingness to betray servile revolts, and – in the case of women – willingness to have sexual relations with their overlords. Even so, freedom granted could be revoked any time the White authorities felt that the freed persons constituted a burden on White society, failed to live up to specific social, moral and other obligations that the society imposed on them, or engaged in activities that the authoritarian state considered inimical to its interests (Thompson 1990, 138–39; Franco 1979, 38). In 1731 the Jamaican legislature passed a law imposing loss of freedom on any free Black or free Coloured person who refused to serve in the militia against runaways (Campbell 1990, 61). In 1754 the Viceroy of Mexico proclaimed that any freed Black person caught fraternizing with Maroons would lose his freedom (León 1924, 10). In 1769 Laurent Macé, a free Black of Haiti, convicted of giving shelter to two Maroons, was reduced once again to slavery, as was his wife, another free Black, in accordance with a colonial law of 1705 (Fouchard 1972, 364). A French decree of 1802 reiterated the earlier law that free Blacks caught harbouring runaways would lose their freedom, and the same would happen to their families (Franco 1979, 38; Debien 1979, 117). Viewed from this standpoint, at no time were freed persons really free while living within White slave society.

It is this last point that is crucial to appreciating the importance of Maroon communities. Sharp (1976, 148) observes that the passage from slavery to freedom was never easy, nor was assimilation into free society as natural as Frank Tannenbaum (1992, 100) suggested.[4] Richard Wade (1968, 102) notes that in the southern United States the position of the free Black was ambiguous and precarious: his colour indicated that he should be enslaved but his status entitled him to a measure of freedom. But there was another, more positive side to that ambiguity as far as enslaved persons were concerned. As Jordan (1968, 578) sees it, free Blacks became a visible symbol of the freedom for which enslaved persons strove.

During slavery, state laws and social practice reinforced varying degrees of intolerance against free Blacks and free Coloureds. Free Blacks, in particular, lived continuously in the shadow of slavery, were subject daily to the social stigma and stereotypes associated with slavery and Blackness, had to order their lives according to a battery of discriminatory laws imposed on them, and had only very limited access to the legal machinery to redress perceived wrongs and disabilities. Whites tended to tar all Blacks with the same brush. Many so-called slave laws in the United States and elsewhere incorporated all Blacks within their compass. In 1832 the Baltimore legislature decreed that free Blacks and free Coloureds were to be subject in every respect to the same treatment and penalties as enslaved persons, and could to be convicted of any offence for which enslaved persons could be found guilty (Wade 1968, 102). Among the common restrictions imposed indiscriminately in most slavery jurisdictions on free Blacks (and free Coloureds) were carrying arms, except when recruited into the colonial militia; testifying against White persons; wearing certain kinds of clothing; frequenting certain areas; sitting in certain parts of the church; and engaging in certain kinds of employment (Bowser 1974, 179; Fouchard 1972, 79–86, 345; Wade 1968, 106–7).

In Virginia, Tennessee, Georgia and Mississippi free(d) Blacks were required to register their presence in the state, and they were required to carry passes at all times in all the southern states. In Florida, Georgia and some other states they were also forced by law to have White persons as guardians. (Mexico published a similar decree in 1750 [Palmer 1976, 183].) North Carolina banned free Blacks from moving beyond the county adjacent to that in which they normally resided, and most southern states prohibited their free immigration. Failure to observe these laws could lead to a heavy fine and sometimes to reduction to slavery (Franklin 1980, 160). The list of prohibitions and restrictions is very long. Franklin (ibid.) declares that a large majority of free Blacks lived in daily dread of losing the little freedom they enjoyed. Jordan (1968, 123) adds that White attitudes were based on the assumption that "free Negroes were essentially more Negro than free". The truth of this last observation is borne out by the 1857 legislation in Tennessee that a free(d) Black possessed the right to re-enslave himself. Texas, Louisiana and Maryland passed similar laws in 1858, 1859 and 1860 respectively. The ultimate in absurdity was a law passed in Arkansas in 1859 requiring all free Blacks and free Coloureds who chose to remain in the state for more than a year to select guardians who had to post bond guaranteeing not to allow them to act as free persons (Franklin 1980, 163).

On 17 June 1786 the *Saint-Croix Royal Gazette* published a proclamation in the name of the governor general of the Danish West Indies prohibiting enslaved persons, free Blacks and free Coloureds from wearing certain types of jewellery and clothing. The proclamation read, in part:

> It is expressly forbidden to all and every one of the individuals who compose the people of colour, free or slaves, to wear jewellery of diamonds, gold or silver, except in a manner that is hereafter specified. It is likewise forbidden to wear silk and other clothing enriched with gold or silver, any dyed India cloth, cambric, muslins, gauze, linen and any kind of fine clothing and bombazine. (Fouchard 1972, 79)

The proclamation went on to specify restrictions on these same persons in relation to holding fêtes. Similar ordinances relating to dress were proclaimed in the French Caribbean in 1740 and 1779 (Fouchard 1972, 77–78).

In the Chocó mining region of Colombia, Blacks were often classified as unstable persons with an ingrained tendency towards drunkenness and thievery. Spanish officials reported them as completely untrustworthy and a threat to White society (Sharp 1976, 149). The pejorative term *libre vagabundo* (free vagabond) was used frequently to designate them (Sharp 1976, 150). In 1791 an official report in the Dominican Republic stated that Blacks were irre-deemable: they usually preferred life in the bush that allowed them complete freedom and independence; they ran around almost naked and caused a mul-titude of problems for the more settled populations on the island (Derby 2003, 23). Palmer (1976, 182) asserts that in Mexico they formed a "commu-nity of outcasts" and gave evidence of their alienation from the rest of society by their deviant behaviour. In the southern United States, one White racist referred to them as an incubus on the land (Franklin 1980, 157). Reis (1993, 22) writes that in Bahia, Brazil,

> the term *plebe* ('pleb') was current in the vocabulary of the times, along with pejorative terms such as *canalha* ('scum'), *classe baixa do povo* ('low-class folk'), *populaça* ('riffraff'), and so on. The terms refer basically to the free poor: artisans, street vendors, washerwomen, day laborers, vagabonds, prostitutes, men and women in the majority of cases with some African forebears, as well as a relative minority of poor whites.

Collectively, these examples provide a solid body of evidence proving that free(d) Blacks continued to suffer under the duress of legislation and social practice that linked and sometimes virtually relegated them to the slave cate-gory. Moreover, while they might enjoy a certain measure of freedom, before the last years of slavery they usually had no right to redeem members of their family who were still in bondage. The enslaver's right to enslaved persons as his "property" remained virtually unimpaired, including the right to sell or transfer any one of them to another country. Freedom for most manumitted people therefore existed at only the most elemental level and under very pre-carious circumstances. The problem for many was that, while they would have loved to enhance their freedom, they were constrained by various physi-cal circumstances – the most important, perhaps, being that they had almost nowhere to go to escape from White society.

The options available to most freed persons were remaining on the plan-tations, gravitating to the urban communities, becoming members of the colonial militia, migrating to another country and retreating to the non-plan-tation rural areas. Especially in Brazil and the Spanish territories, joining the colonial militias offered a certain measure of social elevation for free Blacks and free Coloureds (Karasch 1987, 315; Sharp 1976, 152). Almost everywhere in the Americas they served in segregated regiments under White commis-sioned officers. In some jurisdictions, as the extirpation of Maroon settlements became more urgent, free Black and free Coloured regiments became the phalanx of slave-catching expeditions, though the Whites always perceived arming them to be risky business. This view remained strong among ordinary Whites – as distinct from government officials, who often felt almost a Machiavellian necessity to employ them in such occupations – in spite of the fact that the men in these regiments were almost universally said to be intensely loyal, courageous and capable.

Another alternative for free Blacks was to settle in the rural areas, beyond the White plantations and small farms, that were referred to in the literature of the day as "the bush" or "the jungle". The term *bush* in relation to runaway Africans was much more than a botanical expression. In the eyes of the planter class, the forest in all its wild magnificence was reduced to "the bush", which became associated with everything that was dark, sinister, even unholy. As in South Africa, "bushmen" were deemed to be wild men. In the Caribbean the bush was contrasted with the plantation: the one primeval, the other cultivated; the one the work of nature in its uncultured state, the other the creation of civilized men. The Whites therefore perceived those who chose to be denizens of the former as opting out of civilization and regressing into barbarism. For the Whites, the bush became the symbol – perhaps even the embodiment – of darkness, primitive evil and anarchy, in contrast to the plantation, which they perceived as the symbol of light, goodness and order. But they also perceived the bush as a major threat to the plantation, not only because of its tendency to creep up on the latter and engulf it when the land was neglected for long periods, but also because Maroons issued forth periodically from it to harass the plantations. Thus the Whites viewed life in the bush as the call of the wild, the evidence of man at his uncivilized worst, at least in relation to Blacks, and the pursuit of a vagabond life. The Blacks, on the other hand, heard the immense forests calling to them, offering them the opportunity of freedom. *Marronage* was for them the clearest political expression of the fact that they were persons with sensibilities similar to those of the Whites. García's (1989, 85) praise of the dense bushes and mountains of Barlovento in Venezuela as "a silent invitation to freedom" is euphonic.

Some freed persons actually decided to take to the bush, far away from all White settlements. Some of them even joined Maroon groups, as was the case with Manuel José Alves da Costa, a freed Creole who became leader of a *quilombo* in Brazil in the early nineteenth century (Karasch 1987, 312). Access to fertile lands was not the sole, and often not the main, reason for such flight. Sharp (1976, 153, 170), writing about the Chocó area in Colombia, asserted that freed persons did not leave the White communities because of a shortage of arable land, but because they desired freedom from Spanish authority, domination and law. Flory (1979, 123) pithily observes, "Contemporaries realized that there were more things in Brazil for a Black man to flee from than slavery." He also advises researchers not to be too ready to translate the term *negros fugidos* as "runaway slaves", since it equally incorporated free Blacks who had fled to Maroon communities, and others engaged in gold or diamond transactions or other trading activities that the authoritarian state deemed illegal. Elsewhere, he (1979, 130n32) notes that a pejorative description of the *quilombos* in the early nineteenth century categorized them as consisting of "creoles, vagrants, the superstitious, thieves, criminals and the sickly, gathered to engage in dancing, religious fanaticism, sartorial excess, and gluttony".

In the fabricated social order of the enslavers, freed persons would have had to establish settlements housing more than a few struggling, straggling individuals to ensure the integrity and viability of their communities. Lockhart and Schwartz (1983, 402–3) point out that in Brazil the development of the plantation economy led to

> the growth of a free rural population of humble people who were for the most part of mixed racial origin. . . . In São Paulo and the south they were often small, independent subsistence farmers, living a rustic life in tiny villages. In the northeast they were more often *moradores,* a new rural category, juridicially free but usually attached to a plantation or ranch. . . . Impoverished, landless, and politically insecure, the moradores, who were in the main pardos, free Blacks, and caboclos, were socially well below the cane growers, who tended to be whites. Droughts periodically drove many of these people into the coastal cities, where they swelled the ranks of the urban poor. In either city or countryside this group had benefited little from the economic boom of the late colonial period. Increasingly, the merchant-planter elite and its spokesmen perceived this class as a threat to the existing social order.

What was true of Brazil was basically true of most of the highly developed plantation societies, where the majority of free Coloureds and free Blacks were socially at just one remove from enslaved persons. Many of them were targets for revolution, and sometimes they led or became involved in social unrest, as happened in Venezuela in 1795, Brazil in 1798 (Lockhart and

Schwartz 1983, 410–11), and notably in Haiti in 1790–91, on the eve of the servile uprising.[5] It is therefore not difficult to envisage some of them opting out of White-dominated society and joining the ranks of the Maroons, but we shall never know how many of them did so.

A number of them sympathized with the Maroons' cause and sometimes assisted them in harassing their common oppressors. Official government sources in Venezuela in 1732 spoke to the extensive, strong links between communities of free persons and Andresote, the feared Maroon leader (Brito Figueroa 1985, 209). Those who actually made the transition from sympathizers, spies or helpers to Maroons might have been fleeing punishments or debts, joining friends or relatives who had absconded, or seeking revenge. In 1826 the Urubu *quilombo* in Brazil comprised an undisclosed number of persons who had attained freedom before joining it (Reis 1993, 57). A 1768 record from South Carolina declared that the colonial forces had battled against a large number of Mulattoes, Mustees, and free Blacks (Aptheker 1979, 153). In 1811 Charles Deslondes, a free Black, led an uprising in Louisiana that involved some four hundred enslaved persons (Blassingame 1979, 216). Aptheker (1979, 157–58) writes that the activities of many Maroon groups in Onslow, Carteret and Bladen Counties, North Carolina, allied with some free Blacks, reached the dimension of a rebellion in the summer of 1821. Plans were in train for a concerted assault involving these various groups and enslaved persons against the slaveholders. Patrick Carroll (1977, 501) states that free Blacks married to Maroons formed part of the Mandinga-Amapa settlement in Mexico.

At the same time, most free persons eschewed all contacts and activities that would associate them, in peoples' minds even if not objectively, with enslaved persons or Maroons. They were therefore trapped by their own ideological stance as much as by the pervasive nature of the slavery system, which reached well beyond the physical contours of the plantations.

Slave society was riddled with contradictions. One of the most significant was the existence of increasing numbers of poor Whites originating in the earliest days of colonialism in the Americas. The United States, Mexico, Colombia, the Dominican Republic, Haiti, Cuba and Puerto Rico had large numbers of them. Many were sent out to the Americas as convicts and insurgents and were often described in very pejorative terms such as riffraff, trash, garbage, scum, and refuse (Goslinga 1985, 231; Thompson 1987, 74, 84; Handler 1974, 73). Josiah Child commented that

Virginia and Barbados were first peopled by a sort of loose, vagrant people, vicious and destitute of means to live at home (being either unfit for labour, or such as could find none to employ themselves about, or had misbehaved themselves by whoring, thieving, or other debauchery, that none would set them to work) which merchants and masters of ships by their agents . . . gathered up about the streets of London and other places, cloathed [*sic*] and transported to be employed upon plantations. (Knight 1990, 120)

Especially as the slavery system expanded, the authoritarian state came to view poor Whites as a distinct class from Blacks because of their skin colour. Still, the poor Whites continued to have limited access to capital, credit, education, medical care, political office and so forth, and there was usually a great social distance between them and their rich brethren. Bryan Edwards (1966, 2:7–8) observes, in the context of Jamaica, that the recognition in colonial society of their inalienable right to freedom gave them a sense of equality with the rich Whites that emboldened them to approach their employers with outstretched hands. Their employers, however, did not reciprocate such gestures, or did so only grudgingly in instances of major slave or Maroon unrest that required all hands on deck. The poor Whites intensely resented their socio-economic position and suffered badly at the hands of the rich Whites, who tended to view them as economic and social failures, even to claim that their skin suggested that they were not "true Whites". One British visitor commented concerning those in the anglophone Caribbean that "Their hue and complexion are not as might be expected; and their colour resembles more that of the Albino than that of the Englishman when exposed a good deal to the sun in a tropical climate; it is commonly sickly white or light red" (Hoyos 1978, 97). This class contradiction in Haitian society on the eve of the French Revolution prevented the Whites from rallying as a united front against the Coloureds and Blacks (James 1963).

In the wider context of slave society, some Whites unsettled the slaveholders almost as much as the free(d) Blacks. They lived close to the edge of slavery and mixed with Blacks with whom they found a comfortable relationship (Wade 1968, 104). Many of them lived, talked, ate and dressed like Blacks, and vied with them for jobs, especially in the urban areas. Some of them even bore the pejorative appellation of "white nigger" or "red nigger". As indentured servants in the early days of the plantation system, they commonly absconded and revolted with Blacks against planter oppression (Peytraud 1897, 37; Beckles 1989a, 98–114), and sometimes threw in their lot with enslaved persons and Maroons.

THE RIGHT TO FREEDOM

Alvin Thompson (2002a, 268) observes that freedom, which is often taken as elemental today, a basic condition of human society and a precondition of social happiness, became in the slave societies almost an end in itself. In 1777, over two centuries earlier, Oldendorp (1987, 233) wrote, in relation to enslaved persons in the Danish West Indies (now the US Virgin Islands), that "They follow their own irrepressible natural drives and consider any and all means of gaining their freedom to be just. To this end, they run away from their masters and flee into the mountains and forests." Every – or almost every – enslaved person desired freedom, but there were different perceptions regarding how it could best be achieved: by violent or non-violent, legal or extra-legal means – negotiation, accommodation, cooperation, purchase, flight, fight, suicide, and so on. *Marronage* was born out of the desire for freedom through flight. Harriet Jacobs (1999, 570), an enslaved woman who fled to freedom in New York, expressed the view that "liberty is more valuable than life". Luciano José Franco (1979, 42, 48) refers to the Maroons in Cuba as people who led a vigorous protest against the infamies of slavery, and were the guardians of the flag of liberation. Aguirre (1993, 243) insists that *marronage* implied a radical questioning of the right of the oppressor to determine the life and work of the oppressed. David Davidson (1979, 89) asserts that severely adverse circumstances intensified the human desire to be free, which was the common factor behind slave resistance.

Mary Karasch (1987, 304) writes that enslaved persons in Rio de Janeiro, Brazil, were preoccupied with the quest to achieve freedom. John Blassingame (1979, 193) declares that freedom was the constant prayer and passion of enslaved persons, and fathers began family worship with prayers for freedom. He cites Josiah Henson, once an enslaved person in the United States, to the effect that from a very small child he always had the ambition to be free, and this informed all his thoughts and actions (ibid.). He also refers to Austin Steward, who declared that he was sick and tired of being in bondage and was willing to do almost anything to obtain his freedom (ibid.).

Robert Fogel (1989, 197) states that historians have produced solid evidence to verify that there was a deep passion for freedom among enslaved persons. It was reflected in the heart-cry of Douglass,[6] who wrote extensively about the trammels of slavery. In lines known as much for their passion as their pathos he wrote: "O, that I were free . . . O, why was I born a man, of whom to make a brute. I am left in the hottest hell of unending slavery. O, God save me! God deliver me! Let me be free!" (Blassingame 1979, 192). In more subdued language but with no less depth of feeling, an enslaved girl in Berbice, Guyana, when asked whether she wanted to be free, replied "[T]o be sure I do Massa, every body like free[dom]" (Thompson 2002a, 268). But the cry for freedom often extended beyond self to include family and friends who laboured under the duress of slavery. We have on record the plea of William F.A. Gilbert, who managed to escape from slavery in the Danish West Indies and find his way to Boston, Massachusetts, from where he wrote in 1847 to the king of Denmark, in "broken" English that bespoke his broken spirit:

> Sir: I taken my pen in hand a runaway slave, to inform your exelcy of the evil of slavery. Sir slavery is a bad thing and if any man will make a slave of a man after he is born free, i should think it an outrage becose i was born free of my mother wom and after i was born the monster, in the shape of a man, made a slave of me in your dominion now Sir i ask your excelcy in the name of God & his kingdom is it wright for God created man kind equal and free so i have a writ to my freedom I have my freedom now but that is not all Sir, i want to see my sisters & my brothers and i now ask your excelcy if your excelcy will grant me a free pass to go and come when ever i fail dispose to go and come to Ile of St. Croix or Santacruce the west indies Sir i ask in arnist for that pass for the tears is now gushing from mine eyes as if someone had poar water on my head and it running down my cheak. . . . (Hall 1992, 137–38)

http://www.pbs.org/wnet/aaworld/reference/images/frederick_douglas.jpg

Figure 4. Frederick Douglass

Solomon Northup (1853, 260), an enslaved person in the United States, explained that enslaved persons understood the privileges that the Whites enjoyed as free persons, and longed for the same. They could not help noticing the difference between their own circumstances and those of the poorest White persons, and they were well aware that this difference was due entirely to their servile condition. The state laws, he opined, were unjust, allowing the Whites to profit immensely from the industry of their enslaved charges and punishing them severely when they resisted.

In the second half of the eighteenth century, American and European philosophical thought was veering increasingly to the view that freedom was an inalienable right of all human beings. The words of the US Declaration of Independence (1776) proclaimed it clearly (though the men who drafted it, many of them slaveholders themselves, did not consider Blacks under the rubric "all men"):

> We hold these truths to be self-evident: that all men are created equal, that they are endowed by their Creator with certain unalienable Rights, that among these are Life, Liberty and the pursuit of Happiness. . . . But when a long train of abuses and usurpations, pursuing invariably the same object evinces a design to reduce them under absolute Despotism, it is their right, it is their duty, to throw off such Government. (Kelly and Harbison 1970, 89)

Somewhat earlier, in 1748, Baron (Charles) de Montesquieu, in *De l'Esprit des lois* (*The Spirit of Laws*), discussed the inequality on which slavery was based and concluded that the system had no proper natural or legal basis: the state of slavery was naturally bad because all men were born equal and bondage was useful to neither the slaveholder nor the enslaved person. Slavery was also not amenable to the civil law, for no such law could restrain an enslaved person from running away. More revolutionary in its implications, only a few years later, was *Du Contrat Social* (*The Social Contract*), written by the Swiss-born philosopher Jean-Jacques Rousseau in 1762, which began with the assertion that "Man is born free; and everywhere he is in chains". In book 1, chapter 4, he commented that since slavery was not based on mutual consent it was illegitimate, absurd and meaningless. He insisted that a person reduced to slavery as a result of war was under no obligation to his conqueror except to obey him under compulsion. The conqueror had not done him a favour by opting for an equivalent for his life, for instead of killing him unprofitably he had killed him profitably. The right of conquest did not imply a peace treaty, and therefore the state of war continued between them. According to him, the words *slave* and *right* contradicted each other.

Then in 1774 Abbé Raynal published a monumental work on the history of European colonialism in the East Indies and West Indies, in which Diderot, one of the main contributors, was highly critical of slavery and predicted that the Blacks would find a person from their ranks to lead them to freedom:

> Nature speaks louder than philosophy or self-interest. Already two colonies of fugitive negroes have been established, whose treaties and power protect them from assault. Those flashes announce the lightning, and what the negroes need now is a courageous leader to wreak vengeance and slaughter. Where is he, that great man whom Nature owes to her vexed, oppressed and tormented children? Where is he? He will appear, do not doubt it. He will come forth and raise the sacred standard of liberty. This venerable leader will gather around him the companions of his misfortune. More impetuous than torrents, they will everywhere leave indelible traces of their just resentment. All their tyrants – Spanish, Portuguese, English, French, Dutch – will become prey to iron and flame. The fields of America will become drunk with the blood for which they have been waiting for such a long time. And the bones of countless unfortunate victims, heaped up for three centuries, will rattle with joy. The Old world will applaud with the New. Everywhere people will bless the name of the hero who shall have re-established the rights of the human race; everywhere they will raise monuments in his honour. (Raynal 1780, 3:204–5)[7]

The Haitian Revolution (1791–1804) proved a landmark in Black freedom struggles in the Americas. The insurgents did not wait for a promise of freedom from their overlords; they took it by force, and ended both colonial slavery and colonialism itself in the country. Out of the seeming chaos of the conflict, an entire society of Blacks had been freed in principle, though they had to undergo the troubling cosequences of giving meaning to that freedom. Their success was deeply constrained by the continuing internal contradictions of class and colour, and external embargoes that kept them out of the comity of newly independent nations within the hemisphere for several decades.

While the various writings and revolutions encouraged Blacks in several parts of the Americas to revolt, enslaved persons did not depend upon these writings or revolutions to give legitimacy or rationality to their struggles for freedom. The life force came from an innate sense that freedom rather than bondage was the natural condition of human beings. One contemporary source attributes to Miguel Jerónimo, the Venezuelan Maroon leader in the mid-sixteenth century, the declaration that he and his followers had justifiably taken their freedom forcefully from the Spanish because God had created them as free as all other men (Brito Figueroa 1985, 207). Fouchard (1972, 165, 169) explains that even the kindness of some overlords could never remove the enslaved persons' natural desire and thirst for freedom.

What else would have made Alonzo, or Madeline, or Marie-Rose run away with their chains on (Moitt 2001, 134; Stampp 1968, 53)? Why else would London do so with "an iron head-piece on his head" (Wood 1975, 247)? Or Magdeleine with an iron collar on? Or Clémence with both chains and iron collar (the latter instrument described by her overlord as long and sturdy)? Why else would Tripe, captured after two years, who had broken his leg trying to free himself from his chains, later take his own life when his manager tried to force him to use a wooden leg (Debien 1974, 434)? Why else would Congo André, at least eighty years old and suffering from hernia and deformed fingers and toes, abscond, taking his machete with him (Fouchard 1972, 284–87)? Or Pierre, forty-eight years old, who absconded twice in 1790, though suffering from physical disabilities, some of which were due to punishments? He was said to have "two unreadable brand-marks on each side of his chest, a large burn on his lower stomach, a very considerable hernia, and both ears cut off" (Geggus 1986, 125). And what force drove Lafortune to the seeming madness of trying to escape yet another time against all odds? Described as twenty-two years old and only five feet three inches tall, he had recently been chastised but fled shortly after, carrying with him a chain with a fifty-pound weight attached to his leg (Fouchard 1972, 392).

Though we speak of "runaways", the examples above indicate that it was impossible for some of them to run, in the literal sense of the term. Many of them were too old, too infirm, too bruised and battered, too bowed down by pregnancy or suckling infants, or too confined by chains and weights to do so. What possibility did the (unnamed) Connecticut deserter have of literally running away, since his back was so deformed that when he bent over it appeared as though it had been broken (Greene 1944, 136)? But perhaps he did manage to run; after all, an advertisement of a Boston deserter named Caesar (ibid.) declared that he had no legs but that he was said to be strolling about the country! Thousands like these, broken in body but not in spirit, with mutilated stride hobbled their way to freedom. Physical disabilities were not an impenetrable barrier to freedom or to political mobility within

Maroon societies. Cudjoe, a "humpback", was leader of the Leeward Maroons of Jamaica when the group signed a treaty with the British in 1739 (Mullin 1992, 54).[8]

Many runaways individually were "elusive shadows", as Fouchard (1972, 390) calls them, in the sense that we might hardly hear about them; but collectively they were a clearly identifiable people. They responded to the inner call to freedom despite the many risks to life or limb, including not only harsh punishments if they were apprehended but also natural obstacles and insalubrious environments. Many of them succumbed to hunger, fevers and wild-animal attacks, and sometimes they turned back (Santos Gomes 2002, 481). One such example comes from Paraguay, where a young Frenchman named Escoffier sought to lead five deserters to a safe haven, but tragedy struck: a tiger devoured one of them, another was bitten by a viper, and a third fell victim to fever. The survivors fell once again into the hands of the enslavers (Plá 1972, 156). In the United States, topography and climate often weighed heavily against successful flight, though many persons made the effort to escape. According to Mullin (1992, 39–40), it was not uncommon for runaways to be recaptured exhausted, cold, badly clothed or naked, and sometimes frost-bitten. Whether or not deserters weighed their options carefully, they must have felt that the new environment was likely to be friendlier than the one from which they were fleeing. Given the generally accepted view among modern scholars that field labourers on sugar plantations in the Americas lived between seven and ten years after beginning their labour, the deserters' probable assumption that they were likely to live longer as Maroons than as plantation slaves seems highly reasonable.

Friar Jerome de Merolla, an Italian Capuchin missionary on a visit to Bahia in 1682, was told, concerning enslaved persons in the mines of Minas Gerais, that their work was so hard and their food so inadequate that they were considered to have lived long if they survived for seven years (Boxer 1962, 174). In 1734, Martinho de Mendonça, after extensive enquiry into the matter, opined that the mining overlords did not usually expect their servile charges to provide them with more than twelve years' labour (ibid.). Sebastião Ferreira Soares wrote in 1860 that he had been informed that the planter calculated that of every one hundred enslaved persons introduced into plantation culture, only about twenty-five were likely to be alive at the end of three years (Freyre 1963, 131).[9] The situation was not unique to Minas Gerais or to Brazil as a whole. Cornelis Goslinga (1985, 463) estimates that the average lifespan of enslaved persons after introduction into the plantation economy of Berbice was about eight years. Extremely short lifespans were the common reality of enslaved persons in all the plantation and mining areas in the Americas.

Thus, an important reason for becoming Maroons was that they expected to enjoy a longer life of better quality in their own settlements. When those expectations were dashed, it seems in most instances to have resulted from military expeditions and bounty-hunting activities that killed and maimed a lot of them. Though a single example does not prove the point, it is interesting to note the deposition of Louis (1979, 314), a captive from the André settlement in French Guiana in 1748, that none of its inhabitants had died in the previous two years. But even for those Maroons or potential Maroons whose lives were abridged shortly after, or in the very act of, desertion – some of whom realized that they stood only the slimmest chance of reaching a safe haven – their martyrdom testifies to their love of freedom.

Some enslavers (and others) viewed slavery as the only appropriate system of government under which Blacks should live (Thompson 1995). More than once, contemporary Spanish documents referred to Maroons as fugitives from the "dominion of their natural masters" (Brito Figueroa 1985, 209). It was the resurrection of the Aristotelian doctrine of natural slaves. Venezuelan overlords complained bitterly that many of their servile charges were casting off "the yoke of subordination" (ibid., 241), but they clearly did not appreciate the burden of that yoke to the enslaved persons.

It is necessary here to draw a distinction between the *primary* and the *primitive* desire for freedom. While the distinction may not be wholly relevant today, it was very relevant during – and, indeed, for some years after – the slavery period. The primary desire for freedom is inborn in all persons (and indeed all living creatures). However, enslavers and other Europeans saw *marronage* as a *primitive* (not *primary*) desire for freedom that linked the Maroons to animals or, at best, wild men – as depicted, for instance, in Alejo Carpentier's *Los fugitivos* (Fleischmann 1993, 573; chapter 2). The fact that there was a preponderance of African-born, as distinct from Creole, Maroons – a view on which scholars are unanimous – reinforced their perception that they were dealing with wild men or "savages". Roberto de la Guardia (1977, 77) cites Armando Fortune who, writing in 1970, interpreted the quest of the Maroons of Panama for freedom as an attempt to "resume their primitive lifestyle". Luis A. Díez Castillo (1981, 23), another Panamanian author, writes in much the same vein that they lived a savage life in the bush. César de

Rochefort, writing in 1681, was convinced that Maroons lived an unhappy and savage life like vile beasts, in contrast to the more comfortable ones that their well-treated counterparts enjoyed under their overlords (Fouchard 1972, 34). In 1667 Pére Dutertre (1667–71, 2:498) declared that they lived a miserable existence, and several centuries later, in 1952, Pérez de la Riva (1979, 58) said much the same thing.

Perhaps the most bizarre and durable myth about the Maroons emerged in the eighteenth century, concerning a group of refugees from Haiti who had ensconced themselves in the Bahoruco Mountains. In the late nineteenth century, Father Nouel described these strange beings, called *Biembienes* or *Vien-Vien*,[10] in this way:

> These mountains are inhabited today by those men, semi-savage, known by the name *Vien-Vien*; a name that they have acquired because of their usual yell; the only sound that anyone has heard them articulate. Without societal laws, they go about naked, and have retreated to the deepest recesses of those forests. For some time they have given no intimation of their existence, because they have ensconced themselves in those impenetrable bushes, and according to reliable informants, have chosen as their refuge the Gualorenzo summit which is one of the most isolated and desolate parts of that region. . . . The *Vien-Vien* possess extraordinary agility; like the monkeys, negotiating the ravines and the steepest rocks with astonishing speed. . . . Among the *Vien-Vien* is a group called *mondongo* signifying that they are anthropophagi. (Larrazábal Blanco 1998, 165)

Europeans were prone to dub Africans as savages at this time, no matter how cultured they were. For instance, in 1488 Pina, writing about the Wolof prince Bemoym, who had paid a visit to Portugal and displayed intelligence and elegance in his bearing, nevertheless commented that such princely bearing did not appear to emanate from a savage African but from a person educated in Athens (Purchas 1950, 6:390). Almost three centuries later, Africans suffered equally unkind remarks from the pen of the Jamaican planter-historian Edward Long. He not only reiterated the view that they were savages, but went into a long invective about their vices, "with scarce a single virtue" (1774, 2:351–78).

The enslavers viewed *marronage* as freedom from all restraint and all sense of community – in Hobbesian terminology, "the war of all against all". The Spanish word *cimarrón,* from which the English term *Maroon* is derived, is translated in the *Collins Spanish Dictionary* as "wild", "rough", "uncouth", and its historical origin is given (wrongly) as "*negro* – (Hist) runaway slave, fugitive slave". Likewise, *The Shorter Oxford English Dictionary* (third edition) defines *Maroon* as "wild, untamed run-away slave".[11]

Some overlords viewed *marronage* as resulting mainly from shortage of food and surfeit of physical brutalities inflicted by insentient overlords and managers. For instance, López de Cerrato, a Spanish official in the Dominican Republic around the mid-sixteenth century, expressed the view that out of every hundred runaways, ninety-nine had deserted because of such ill treatment (Esteban Deive 1989, 45). In 1820 a government official in Belize declared that the first Blacks who had absconded and had excited others to join them had been treated very mildly, and definitely did not have just cause to complain (Bolland 2002, 55). More sentient overlords could understand why ill-fed and generally badly treated enslaved persons would abscond, but the vast majority could not understand – or behaved as though they could not understand – the writhing of the Black soul for freedom as reason enough for deserting.[12] A few lonely voices here and there among the enslavers articulated why their so-called faithful Blacks deserted them even in their hour of travail. In the 1730s the Jamaican government reflected the sentiment of these few when it observed ruefully that the hope of freedom had undermined the fidelity of the most trustworthy Blacks (Campbell 1990, 80). Governor Trelawny saw unrest in the island among the servile population as the manifestation of a dangerous spirit of liberty (Campbell 1990, 105). A few years earlier, in 1719, Count Pedro de Almeida, captain-general of Minas Gerais in Brazil, was even more candid about the "problem" of servile unrest:

> [S]ince we cannot prevent the . . . Blacks from thinking, and cannot deprive them of their natural desire for freedom; and since we cannot, merely because of this desire, eliminate all of them, they being necessary for our existence here, it must be concluded that this country will always be subjected to this problem. (Conrad 1983, 396)

We should note carefully the reason that, in his view, it was impolitic to "eliminate all of them".

Fouchard (1972, 33) asserts that in Haiti no witness of the period had attributed to the Maroons an ideal of or even a need for freedom. Thus César de Rochefort wrote in 1681 that enslaved persons who had the good fortune to be under a kind overlord preferred their present servitude to their former liberty (Fouchard 1972, 34). Another colonist in the same country was nonplussed that although (in his own view) he was more liberal than any other enslaver in providing his Blacks with food, easy working conditions and many other inducements, they had proved incapable of being grateful and had absconded (Manigat 1977, 496). But let us listen to this piece of talk from a Maryland enslaver in 1755 about his chief confidant among his servile charges:

> That this slave should run away and attempt getting his liberty, is very alarming, as he has always been too kindly used, if any thing, by his master, and one in whom his master has put great confidence, and depended on him to overlook the rest of the slaves, and he had no kind of provocation to go off. (Blassingame 1979, 205)

Gabriel Debien, a modern writer, is convinced that some flights had inexplicable causes; indeed, that some enslaved persons fled without motive, plan or preparation (Fouchard 1972, 165–66). For Debien, flight in such instances was sudden and completely irrational. In fact, he comes close to suggesting that such flight constituted result (or action) without causation! He fails to understand that the motive for flight lay in the very condition of servitude. But he is not alone in this view. In 1783 the colonial legislature of Antigua voiced the concern of the slaveholders that their servile charges were absconding "without any other reason, than the dictates of their own vicious inclinations" (Goveia 1965, 257). Miguel Lazo de la Vega, administrator of San José in Peru during the eighteenth century, spoke about the enslaved persons' vice of always fleeing to the mountains at their fancy without any motive (Kapsoli 1975, 60). In the same vein, another enslaver in that country who considered himself a good overlord was bewildered by the fact that one of his female charges had, without cause, jumped over a high wall that enclosed his dwelling (Bowser 1974, 189).

Enslavers and others living in slaveholding societies generally regarded desertion as proof that the Africans and their Creole descendants were lazy, crafty, evil-minded and insolent, characteristics that many of them viewed as pathological and perhaps genetic (Fouchard 1972, 33; Esteban Deive 1989, 45; Long 1774, 2:351–78). It is said that Southerners in the United States viewed running away as "a disease – a monomania, to which the negro race is peculiarly subject", while a New Orleans physician called it "drapetomania", an hereditary disease afflicting Blacks (Schweninger 2002, 18). João Saldanha da Gama, governor of Bahia in Brazil, exemplified this kind of thinking in a dispatch to the Portuguese Overseas Council in 1807:

Seeing that slaves frequently and repeatedly escaped from masters in whose service they had been engaged for years . . . I became curious (an important trait in this land) about where it was they went. I soon learned that in the outskirts of this capital and in the thickets that surround it, there were innumerable assemblages of these people, who, led by the hand of some industrious charlatans, enticed the credulous, the lazy, the superstitious, those given to thievery, criminals, and the sickly to join them. They lived in absolute liberty, dancing, wearing extravagant dress, phoney amulets, uttering fanatical prayers and blessings. They lay around eating and indulging themselves, violating all privilege, law, order, [and] public demeanor. (Reis 1993, 42)

Even Yvan Debbasch (1961, 40), writing more than a century after the abolition of slavery in the French Caribbean, seemed unable to understand the importance of freedom in *marronage*. According to him, statistically, the desire for freedom played only a minor role in flight when compared with fear of punishment, insufficient food, overwork, sickness and so on. In one case a captured Maroon gave as his reason for desertion overwork and sickness, and Debbasch (1961, 20) seized on this, arguing that he became a Maroon precisely because he was ill. Debien (1979, 133–34) follows the same basic line of argument as Debbasch about the main causes of *marronage*, adding, however, what he considers minor causes, such as the desire to escape after committing theft or assault, drunkenness on long holidays, and transfer from one plantation to another.[13] He says absolutely nothing about the importance of freedom to the enslaved persons. In much the same vein, David Rueda Mendez (1995, 127) and Josefina Plá (1972, 149, 151) emphasize the treatment of enslaved persons rather than the desire for freedom as the principal cause of *marronage* in Tunja (part of Colombia) and Paraguay respectively.

Maltreatment was doubtless an exacerbating circumstance, and was also clearly a reason why some enslaved persons deserted, but it was not the dominant reason for the widespread flight by enslaved persons of all occupational strata and differential access to "privileges" within the system. As Aguirre (1993, 243–44) points out, such an approach leads to the false conclusion that enslaved persons questioned only the excesses of the system and not the system itself. Rather, he asserts, the decision to remain under the enslaver did not necessarily mean an acceptance of the ideology of slavery but was a pragmatic response to a situation that the enslaved found difficult to get rid of in the short term.[14] Lucien Peytraud (1897, 343) is close to the truth when he asserts that liberty is so natural to the human condition that *marronage* began from the time that enslaved persons were introduced into the Americas. Toussaint Louverture is said to have explained his decision to join the Haitian Revolution on the basis that, though born into slavery, he had received the soul of a free man (Fouchard 1972, 159–60).

The British anti-slavery lobby in the late eighteenth and early nineteenth centuries insisted that the mere state of freedom uplifted a person regardless of his material condition (Ragatz 1977, 255). J.P. Gannon gave one of the clearest expressions of the ideology that informed *marronage* when he wrote:

> [W]hy men, whose ideas of freedom are so very confined and so free from romance, should prefer an uncertain mode of subsistence to the certainty of rations in food, clothing, &c. such as they formerly received, I am unable to account, otherwise than by supposing, that they find their condition on the whole to be improved by the change. A desire of being free from control, and the power of disposing of their time and labour in the way that should appear most agreeable to themselves, would, no doubt, be sufficient to induce men in every *Zone* to prefer for a time, a precarious mode of living accompanied by freedom, to more certain means of subsistence if attended with control.[15]

This rationale, however, was lost on most enslavers and some modern writers. Gilberto Freyre (1963, 132), for instance, implicitly challenged the anti-slavery view when he asserted that freedom was not sufficient in itself to make the life of an urban runaway more bearable, at least materially. In his opinion, the runaway became submerged in the urban proletariat with its shanty dwellings, and his diet and living conditions worsened; many former enslaved persons, degraded by such freedom, ended up as street idlers, ruffians, thieves, prostitutes and murderers.

Some writers, such as Fernando Ortiz, declared that flight, or freedom, was the ideal of the enslaved person (Deschamps Chapeaux 1983, 11). However, it is important to understand that deserters did not see freedom as an end in itself but rather as the precondition for ordering their lives according to precepts that improved their self-worth as human beings and gave them an opportunity to live with a certain measure of dignity (García 1996, 63). Among the rights that they sought were freedom from hunger, harassment, and unjust punishments, and also freedom to associate, to raise a family and to worship as they saw fit. Arlette Gautier (1985, 227) must have been thinking of these rights when she wrote about the Maroons' quest for concrete liberties.

Enslaved and freed Blacks were kept in their place through the watchful eye of the enslavers, state authorities and military forces. With little room to manoeuvre, they were subject to the daily trammels of the slavery system. The Maroons' situation was just the opposite. They enjoyed a recognizable, and in some instances a substantial, measure of freedom – though, as we will see, nothing close to complete freedom. Apart from the philosophical question of whether anyone can enjoy *complete* freedom, the Maroons lived with the threat that what freedom they had attained could be lost as a result of the military expeditions sent against them by the slaveholding states. Constant vigilance and preparedness therefore had to be their watchwords. Nevertheless, they enjoyed a much greater measure of freedom than any other African communities in the Americas during the slavery period, and what was even more irksome to the White overlords was that this freedom had been taken by the Blacks rather than given by the Whites. Maroon communities demonstrated that Blacks were capable of forging a life outside the boundaries of the plantation system and the more populous White-dominated societies.

CHAPTER 2

Forms of Marronage

PETIT MARRONAGE AND GRAND MARRONAGE

Colonial authorities generally divided flight from slavery into short-term and long-term desertion (in French, *petit marronage* and *grand marronage* respectively; in Spanish, *cimarronaje pequeño* [or *cimarronaje simple*] and *gran cimarronaje*). The laws usually classified persons who ran off or hid, individually or in small groups, for short periods as engaging in petty desertion. However, among the factors that were in practice considered in determining the seriousness of *marronage* were the length of time that the person stayed away, the distance he or she had travelled from the usual place of abode, the time of the year that the absence took place, and whether the deserter returned voluntarily or was apprehended and brought back. The kind and degree of punishment were determined on the basis of such factors as the person's record of desertion, the Maroon community that the runaway had joined, and the crimes for which he or she was convicted.

La Rosa Corzo (2003, 6–9) submits a third category, in the case of Cuba: armed bands of runaways (*caudrillas de cimarrones*) who moved from place to place without any permanent location, though they tended to seek refuge in hilly or swampy terrain. The groups usually did not number more than about twenty, and were often much smaller. The tripartite division does not conflict with the earlier division into two basic categories, since everywhere *grand marronage* comprised both roving bands and settled groups. Reis (1993, 41) refers to the mobile *quilombos* in Brazil that reappeared in another place when driven out of a particular area. Armed bands were also common in Peru, Mexico, the Dominican Republic and the United States, among other places (Bowser 1974; Esteban Deive 1989; Pereira 1994; Blassingame 1979). An official report to the Spanish Crown concerning what was taking place in Mexico in the late sixteenth century stated that the highways had become so perilous that people could not travel them except accompanied by a large military guard, and still much fear existed. The danger was compounded by coalitions involving Chichimeca raiders, Mulattos, Mestizos, vagabonds and formerly peaceful Indians (Palmer 1976, 123).

The periods during which enslaved persons most commonly absented themselves temporarily were the Christmas holidays (which usually lasted two or three days) and the crop season. Most managers granted passes to their servile charges for the holiday seasons (such as Christmas and Easter) to visit friends and relatives on neighbouring plantations, though these trips were usually limited to a single day. Frequently, however, people stayed away for several days without receiving any sanctions, except perhaps a warning. State laws generally regarded absenteeism without permission for more than a few days as desertion. However, few modern scholars regard such absence, without any evidence of intent to stay away permanently, as *marronage*.

Debien (1979, 110) dismisses the use of the term in speaking of absences of up to a week that, according to him, enslaved persons took because they were lazy and libertines. Esteban Deive (1989, 13–14) asserts that such absences usually related to some temporary disaffection with the working conditions, escape from punishment, or desire to visit a companion, and could hardly be called *marronage*. Fouchard (1972, 382) views it as more like truancy from school than a determination to abscond. He dismisses detailed analysis of this kind of activity with the comment that usually when these persons returned, their overlords would forgive them with a simple reprimand or a few strokes with the rod of correction. Manigat (1977, 484) submits that in its original etymological sense, *marronage* meant "to run wild", and a person who absented himself to visit a girlfriend, for instance, cannot be said rightly to have been "running wild".

Frederick Bowser (1974, 190) makes the rather startling statement that in Peru some instances of flight seem to have been a game or a symbolic gesture. Here he fails to distinguish between "fleeting absence" – that is, absence with intent to return shortly – and "flight", which we take to mean the intention to stay away indefinitely or permanently from the place of bondage. Flight, at least in this sense, was a dangerous game to play, a dalliance with death through the activities of bounty hunters or the caprice or sadism of a given overlord. It was not a game of trivial pursuit (see chapter 5). For instance, in the early nineteenth century, Virginian militiamen could legally seize any Black found away from his supposed place of abode and shoot him on sight, unless they could stop him in some other way (Schweninger 2002, 13). The same was true of Maroon hunters in the Danish West Indies in the eighteenth century (Donoghue 2002, 150). As Werner Zips (1999, 7–8) notes, *petit marronage* sometimes brought about severe punishments. Therefore, Fouchard, Manigat and Bowser take all too lightly the significance of short-term absence in relation to the safety and well-being of the enslaved people.

The case of Michael, an enslaved person in Berbice, Guyana, belonging to the British Crown, is an interesting one of desertion without intent to stay away permanently, though he absconded frequently as a way of expressing his discontent with the operation of the system of bondage. The extant record of his life as a deserter began in July 1821, when Michael was twenty-seven, with his superintendent's observation that his colleagues had probably been providing asylum for him and his companion, Andries, for the previous month. These young men, like other enslaved persons belonging to the Crown, were driven to this situation by the failure of the colonial authorities to take seriously their complaints against the manager of the Crown's plantation Berenstein. They had gone to the manager a little over a month earlier, complaining of heavy task work and unfair and cruel treatment. Michael was particularly peeved that the manager had refused to allow him to visit his mother, and also that he, in common with the other people at Berenstein, was suffering from shortage of rations.

The young men therefore chose to desert, moving from place to place, until in August they were apprehended on plantation Prospect and delivered over to the judicial authorities in town. The fiscal (chief judicial officer) sentenced them to fifty-five lashes each at the public market place and three months on the chain gang, but released them after confinement of a little over a month. The superintendent later dispatched them again to Berenstein, from where Michael absconded in less than a week. However, his freedom was abridged once again, this time within five days. On this occasion the fiscal gave the superintendent permission to work him in chains, either on the plantation or in town, for three months. Gone again at a time not recorded, he was apprehended on plantation Smithson's Place, sent to town and given fifteen lashes before being sent back to work.

Six weeks later he was repeating his familiar act, but this time for only three days before being hospitalized. About two weeks later he was in the public jail, awaiting trial as a deserter, and he subsequently received forty lashes on the fiscal's order. After his release, Michael's urge to desert remained unsatisfied, for some months later, in December 1823, he was picked up on plantation Vryheid, where he had beaten an enslaved person violently, for which he received twenty-four lashes.

We do not know what turned Michael's life around, but it might well have been the abandonment of Berenstein as a production unit. He disliked the plantation intensely. He was relocated to town, where he was listed in January 1825 as a member of the Government House staff, and remained there until he fell once again under the direct charge of the superintendent when the governor decided to reduce his staff (Thompson 2002a, 226–27).

Michael was more fortunate than many others, who lost their lives attempting to escape from tyrannical overlords. Demby, for instance, attempted to escape from a brutal whipping inflicted on the orders of Gore, a Maryland overseer notorious for his gory deeds. He fled into a creek where he was soon discovered and from which he refused to come out. Gore threatened to shoot him if, after three admonitions to come out, he still refused to do so. Demby refused, and Gore shot him: "His mangled body sank out of sight, and blood and brains marked the water where he had stood." Gore's justification for this murder was that if one did not take a firm line with recalcitrant individuals, the Blacks would be free and the Whites enslaved (Douglass 1973, 25).

Price (1979, 105) describes *petit marronage* in the French Caribbean as a constant thorn in the planters' sides. However, according to him, while these Maroons might have done some damage to their overlords' material interests, their absence was essentially a nuisance rather than a threat to the integrity of the slavery system. Esteban Deive treats only *grand marronage* as a phenomenon worthy of serious scholarly inquiry. He asserts (1989, 14) that, as a social phenomenon, *petit marronage* doubtless constituted an outward manifestation of the contradictions within the slave mode of production, but it did not signify any consciousness capable of offering enslaved persons the possibility of liberating themselves as a social class. He argues further that enslavers scarcely showed any concern for this kind of absence, clearly demonstrating that it did not pose any danger to the dominant class.

Esteban Deive (1989, 14–15) regards classic or grand desertion (*cimarronaje clásico* or *gran cimarronaje*) as a much higher level of class struggle: in his view, people engaging in such activity displayed a greater consciousness of their state of servitude and of the real possibility of satisfying their longing for freedom. *Grand marronage* also offered the deserters an opportunity to create for themselves a way of life that was structurally and socially of a much higher order than that to which they had been subjected as enslaved persons. It is for this reason, he argues, that while the enslavers regarded *petit marronage* as a deep-seated vice that had to be arrested, they considered *grand marronage* as sedition and as a crime that they had to combat vigorously and without remorse, using all means at their disposal. Jean-Pierre (2000, 109) posits that the colonists in Haiti perceived *grand marronage* not simply as an act of brigandage but as the germ of revolution. He goes on to say that the Maroon settlement was a real war academy where the enslaved person learned that the options were conquest or death (ibid., 111).

Sometimes the quest for personal freedom led people to make very hard – and sometimes not entirely rational – decisions. This was the case with those runaways, both men and women, who left spouses and children behind. It is perhaps rightly assumed that this practice was less frequent among women than men. Vanony-Frisch (1985, 33–36) identifies seven female runaways who had left children behind, among the forty-two who had absconded from the Lepreux plantation in Guadeloupe between 1768 and 1783. Blassingame (1979, 199–200) tries to recapture the moments of parting, based on the autobiographies of some American deserters:

> Mothers and wives argued passionately against it. . . . Henry Bibb said that when he left his family enslaved it was "one of the most self-denying acts of my whole life, to take leave of an affectionate wife, who stood before me on my departure, with dear little Frances in her arms, and with tears of sorrow in her eyes as she bid me a long farewell. It required all the moral courage that I was master of to suppress my feelings while taking leave of my little family."

No doubt, on many occasions, people who for various reasons could not join the ranks of deserters nevertheless encouraged family members to do so. William Wells Brown (1999, 688 passim), an enslaved man in Missouri from 1816 to 1834, told of his determination not to leave his beloved mother and sister behind, and of their pleading with him to go. He also wrote of his agony on bidding these women farewell when their overlords took them away to sell them to others – a loss that finally broke down his resistance to flight without them.

Slaveholders claimed that collusion among family members took place frequently, and we know that there were instances in which runaways returned periodically to the plantations and elsewhere to visit their kin. Even when they did not return, family members must have presumed that the fact that they were not brought back, dead or alive, meant that they had made it to some safe haven. Of course, newspaper advertisements of deserters – who sometimes were on the authoritarian states' most-wanted lists – also informed their friends and relatives that slave-hunting parties had not apprehended them.

Some deserters promised to return for their loved ones or to keep in contact with them. In 1844 two runaways who used the Railroad to escape to Canada regretted that they had had to leave their wives behind. Rachel Gilpin Robinson, a White Railroad worker, wrote that these men seemed to feel the separation deeply. One of them, she observed, told her that he would not have departed if he did not believe that he could easily contrive the escape of his wife later on. Both men seemed very despondent, apparently grieving at the absence of their loved ones (Williamson 2002, 11). Usually, such promises stood little chance of being fulfilled. Both parties knew this, but they lived in hope. Douglass (1973, 108) is one of the few people known to us who made good on his promise to re-establish the broken links: he sent for his sweetheart and married her in New York. Still, one of the troubling issues of male flight was the decision to leave behind wives and children, who, the deserters knew, might well become the vicarious targets of the enslaver's wrath. Dorothy White (1996, 64) asserts that there is no doubt that runaways regretted leaving their wives and children behind.

INDIVIDUAL AND COLLECTIVE MARRONAGE

While we have discussed *marronage* in terms of the usual classifications of short-term and long-term desertion, it would perhaps be more useful here to focus attention on those people who sought to take permanent leave of their overlords. We will divide the subject into two broad categories: individual *marronage* and collective *marronage*. Like short-term *marronage*, individual *marronage* has historically been treated as a peripheral issue within the wider context of desertion, but perhaps this activity had much more significance than scholars have attributed to it in terms of the ideology of freedom. García (1989, 85) argues that *marronage* in itself was an act of valour, hardship and risk taking, all in the quest to regain one's dignity as a human being.

At the same time we accept, even at the risk of being contradictory, that the freedom enjoyed by Maroons living a solitary life was very limited. Most of them could not establish a permanent presence anywhere but lived largely as wanderers, without family, kin or friends. They must have lived mainly by foraging rather than cultivating the land. Thus it is tempting to view them as trees without roots. It is true that individual *marronage* cost the enslavers money, especially if the deserter was a highly valued worker. It also increased the fear in the White community because it helped to swell the ranks of the permanent deserters who became potential, and sometimes actual, members of Maroon settlements. But in reality, the Maroon dwelling alone did not usually pose a serious threat to the plantocracy, since his chances of long-term survival as a free person would have diminished considerably had he attempted to carry out assaults on the White community. Maroon life was hard physically and psychologically, and became much more so when individuals chose or were forced to live alone for long periods. Because of one Suriname Maroon's troubles with both his overseer and his Maroon leader, he chose to live alone in the forest for two years and endured, according to his own testimony, great mental hardships and anxieties (Stedman 1988, 482).

The biography of the Cuban deserter Esteban Montejo, one of the best-known stories of individual *marronage,* may – curiously enough – both challenge and reinforce such views of the solitary Maroon. In his middle or late teens when he absconded the second time, Montejo believed that he was compelled to do so because he had the spirit of a runaway guarding him, which never left him. He was constantly thinking about deserting; the thought pervaded – at times tormented – his mind and would not leave him alone (Barnet 1996, 37).[1] He declared that this urge was fed by the fact that he had no freedom and had to do everything that his overlord or overseer commanded him to do. He described slavery as a plague that he could not endure indefinitely. His overseer was both strong and cruel, and all the Blacks respected him because he could flay the skin off a person's back with one stroke of his whip (ibid.). Montejo hated this man intensely; simply looking at him filled him with rage. On making his flight to freedom, he wandered listlessly for several days up and down the hilly forest terrain, until he hit on

Figure 5. A solitary Maroon. From *Voyage à Surinam,* by P.J. Benoit (Bruxelles: Société des Beaux-Arts, 1839).

the idea of making his habitat in the entrance to a deep cave. There he spent several months, with snakes (which he thought were venomous but, in fact, were not) and bats as his only bedfellows. The place stank terribly, but he had to endure it. He eventually left the cave and built a simple thatch-roofed shelter to protect him from the elements. He lived off the largesse of the forest, which provided honey, various kinds of nuts, and medicinal and other plants, and for additional food he discreetly raided the plots of the small independent farmers; suckling pigs became his main sustenance.

In all this, Montejo lived alone, and a lonely life it was. He declared that he had trusted no one, since "Runaway with runaway sells runaway" (ibid., 41). In his old age (about 105 years at the time of his testimony) he rationalized that he had liked his solitude, which offered him his best chance of maintaining his freedom, though he lived for the most part on the periphery of White settlements. He declared that he had lived a half-wild existence as a runaway (ibid., 43) but had lacked nothing in the forest except sex, for which he was not prepared to risk his freedom. His life had become rather elemental: he thought only about eating, sleeping, keeping watch and listening to the birds and trees. He apparently had washed himself regularly but did not bother to shave. He recalled that he had become so hairy that his beard hung down in ringlets, a sight that would generate fear (ibid., 47, 50). Because of this, he had apparently aged significantly in appearance, though not in chronological time. When later he left the forest and a barber cut off his dreadlocks, he seemed rejuvenated and "looked like a thoroughbred" (ibid., 50–51). He left the forest in 1880, around age twenty-two, after the declaration abolishing slavery in Cuba. Whenever people asked him what he had done as a runaway, he replied, "Nothing" (ibid., 51).

Whether Montejo's life in the forest was typical for Maroons who chose to live alone is a matter of debate. What his life clearly reveals is his overriding concern with maintaining his freedom, though this entailed at times extreme hardships, especially in the early months. His narrative also indicates that he never disturbed the peace among the small farmers and that most likely they did not sense his presence close to their dwellings. He claimed that he did nothing that would leave a lasting impression on the stage of life or the pages of history. Yet he leaps out of the pages of history through his biography, which has evoked intense interest and has been published in several languages (Spanish, English, Portuguese, Italian, German, Dutch and French).[2] What gives strength to his narrative is not a corpus of heroic deeds but the simple heroism and humanism of his struggle for freedom, and the fact that he beat the odds against long-term survival in an environment in which he was pitted against nature, wild animals, hunting dogs, military expeditions and bounty hunters. Writers view him as a symbol of the personal freedom that most humans hold as inalienable. The same might be said of all Maroons who chose to live singly rather than in communities.

Frederick Douglass, the Coloured American runaway who later became an international figure and a fervent spokesperson for the abolitionist cause, had a somewhat different story to tell. Born in Talbot County, Maryland, he first became aware of his situation as an enslaved person at about twelve, through reading the book *The Columbian Orator* (Douglass 1973, 41). His initial desire for freedom slowly became a passion. He wrote about the perpetual thoughts of his servile status that tormented him and pressed upon him through everyday objects, animate and inanimate (ibid., 43). These thoughts were reinforced by an encounter with two Irishmen who told him that he could be free if he could find his way to New York, which, along with the other northern states, had abolished slavery several decades earlier. From then on he experienced periodic strong urges to flee, followed by a lack of desire to do so.

He was shifted from one overlord to another, and sometimes hired out. A few of them showed some concern with his personal welfare, but the majority were distinguished from each other mainly by the degree of cruelty with which they treated their servile charges. He (ibid., 5) remembered, in particular, a brutal whipping that one of them administered to his Aunt Hester, after having her tied up with her hands in the air and her toes barely touching the stool on which she was placed. He whipped her on her bare back: "No words, no tears, no prayers, from his gory victim, seemed to move his iron heart from its bloody purpose. The louder she screamed, the harder he whipped; and where the blood ran fastest, there he whipped longest. He would whip her to make her scream and whip her to make her hush, and not until overcome by fatigue would he cease to swing the blood-clotted cowskin."[3] Douglass (ibid., 6) put the whipping down to the jealous rage of her overlord at her having been out with a particular young man.

Douglass prepared himself for eventual flight by learning to read and write so he could write his own passes in the name of his employer or overlord – though his avid pursuit of literacy suggests that he loved knowledge for its own sake. Like Montejo, his first bid for freedom was aborted. In fact, it never really got underway, since someone had informed the security forces that he and a few of his companions intended to abscond. They were apprehended but later released to their overlords.

It took Douglass about eight years from his first awakening to the possibilities of freedom to the time that he made good his escape. His second attempt at flight was much more carefully planned and was a solo effort. To run away, he saved up money that he had earned through self-hire and extra hours of work as a caulker. He made his way to New York through the Underground Railroad. After a few days' residence in that state he was approached by an abolitionist who was working with the Railroad, and was given the necessary means of moving to New Bedford, where a large number of runaways were living in relative safety and comfort. While in New York he had sent for his sweetheart, a free woman, who travelled to meet him, and they got married. In New Bedford he was able to find steady employment, but not as a skilled artisan, since there was still strong White prejudice against Blacks and Coloureds taking up skilled labour. After residing there for about three years, he was gradually initiated into the ranks of active abolitionists.

Douglass, like Montejo, was a lone deserter, but his life took an entirely different turn for a number of reasons. In the first place, he was largely an urban employee with a skilled trade. This enabled him to have greater mobility and to pass relatively easily among free persons without betraying his true status. Second, he planned his escapes much more carefully than did Montejo. Third, he had a specific destination in mind and a network of support in the abolitionists who constituted the Railroad, working secretly to aid runaways to freedom. Fourth, he was fleeing not to the solitude of the wilderness but to the jostle of a cosmopolitan city, where – theoretically, at least – he could enjoy many of life's comforts. Fifth, he married and settled into a stable family life in a place where slavery had been abolished, though it had not yet ended within the United States as a whole. Montejo emerged from hiding after slavery was abolished in his country; Douglass enjoyed his freedom openly while the slavery system was still vibrant in other parts of his country. Finally, Douglass gained international fame, through both anti-slavery and other activities and the books that he wrote, which influenced many minds against the institution of slavery.[4] He was an adviser to President Abraham Lincoln. He demonstrated how a single runaway could influence national discourse on the evils of slavery. Montejo's biography was published about three-quarters of a century after the abolition of slavery in Cuba, and he himself had no discernible impact on the course of abolition.

Because the record of Douglass's deeds exists in published form, through his own writings and those of other contemporary and modern writers, we can appreciate more fully his contribution to that cause. But hundreds of other lone deserters may also have been influential in chipping away at the system of slavery by their fierce physical onslaughts against the enslavers in Suriname, Haiti, Cuba, Jamaica, Mexico and elsewhere. Some of them may eventually have become leaders of large Maroon communities.

Many other deserters did not make much of a mark on contemporary society, but their testimonies to the importance of freedom speak loudly to us today. To look at only a few of them: Marquis escaped alone from a plantation in St Domingue but was apprehended soon after. The manager voiced his reluctance to whip him for fear of killing him, because he was very frail. Nevertheless, he requested either a chain or collar to restrain him (Debien 1979, 122). Frail Marquis, on the periphery of death, was still prepared to risk what little life was left in him to achieve freedom.

The case of Jasmin Barbe-Blanche, a Congolese by birth and escapee from a plantation in Haiti, is also worthy of note. An elderly individual, according to his manager, he was the leader of a trio that included old Nanette, his wife. They were apprehended after about three weeks. We do not know whether Jasmin was a habitual deserter. Not long before, he had been transferred from a sugar plantation in the west to a coffee plantation in the south as part of a group whose work performance had declined because of some disaffection with their driver. Their overlord hoped that the change would have a salutary effect on their performance. The immediate cause of their desertion may have been the compulsory move that took them away from their friends and possibly other family members. Strangely, the manager declared that they had absconded without motive (Debien 1979, 121–22).

Jasmin's flirtation with freedom did not end with this first apprehension. Placed under the guard of the driver of his new plantation, he was off sometime before the following daybreak, only to be picked up a few days later, showing signs of intense suffering due to inclement weather and hunger. He had survived on green corn and raw yams. He had constant diarrhoea and swollen feet (Debien 1979, 122). The old man died two days later. It is clear that he and his companions could no longer bear the burdens of slavery, in which, even at an old age, they had no control over their lives. He made what the manager considered an almost suicidal bid for freedom or for home. The manager claimed that Jasmin confessed before he died that he had intended to return to his home on the sugar plantation. As a possible explanation for his flight, that is highly improbable, since he and his companions must have realized that they were likely to be punished or, at the very least, sent back to the coffee plantation from which they had fled.

Enslaved persons of all ages ran away. Two enslaved children in Peru, Angelina Criolla, eleven years old, and Juan Criollo, twelve, ran away, but in both cases it was to the house of one of their parents. The Haitian list includes Rosette and Mars, ten years old; L'Amérique, Jean-Pierre Belaly, Henri and Azar, all between twelve and fourteen; Marie, thirty-eight; Alexis, sixty; Lisette and Frances, seventy; and Congo André, at least eighty. The oldest fugitive in the records consulted was a ninety-year-old unnamed Fulani man in Haiti (Bowser 1974, 193, 195; Fouchard 1972, 284–87; Geggus 1986, 124). Although there was a wide age spread, the main age range of runaways in Haiti was seventeen to thirty-five years, followed by the eight-to-sixteen cohort (Fouchard 1972, 286–87). A study of 134 eighteenth-century newspaper advertisements of runaways in the United States revealed that 76 per cent of them were under thirty-five years of age (Blassingame 1979, 202). Lorenzo Greene's (1944, 131) much smaller sample of New England runaways broadly confirms Blassingame's statement. Aguirre (1993, 248–49) found that, of 121 Maroons reported for Lima between 1840 and 1846, 81 per cent of the men and 93.7 per cent of the women were less than thirty years old; the average age of the men was twenty-two years and of the women twenty-three and a half. Writers do not seem to differ on the age range of the vast majority of fugitives.

This is not surprising, since the data correspond roughly to the age cohort of the people imported from Africa. Moreover, given the trials and tribulations of the flight to freedom and life in the *palenques*, it was only the most hardy and innovative of the enslaved population who were likely to survive. Young people are also usually more ambitious, more enterprising and more visionary of a brave new world than their elders.

Most writers agree that outside of special circumstances, such as internal warfare or large-scale revolt, enslaved persons generally ran off in small groups, and some of them sought to join large, settled entities. Geggus (1986, 126) tells us that 75 per cent of the deserters in Haiti in 1790 fled alone. A statistical analysis of advertisements of runaways in South Carolina indicates that just under half of them ran away in groups of two (Morgan 1986, 72). Debien (1979, 107, 126), Hoogbergen (1993, 165, 177), Borrego Plá (1973, 25) and Jordan (1968, 392) agree that most deserters fled in ones and twos, and formed groups (or, presumably, joined existing ones). This appears to be accurate statistically and logically. The contemporary records of plantation managers and newspapers (the latter especially from the late eighteenth century) are replete with instances of persons absconding in ones and twos and mention few large-scale desertions. The small logwood settlements in Belize were ideally suited for such small-scale desertion (Bolland 2002, 54–55). It was the constant trickle, like water out of a leaking container, that best represents the Maroon flow away from the plantation.

Desertion on a large scale would have required considerable planning, good timing and extreme confidentiality to prevent betrayal or suspicion. Though we cannot probe the minds of individual Maroons, their flight seems to have been largely unplanned. We have, of course, the testimony of Esteban Montejo, whose biography indicates clearly that he had made up his mind long before to abscond. In this sense we can say that he planned his escape. However, when the actual time came it was a rush of blood, a sudden urge that compelled him to throw a projectile at his overseer and propelled him into flight (Barnet 1996, 37).

There were occasions on which deserters found companionship in larger numbers. The following examples, drawn from a few slavery jurisdictions, must suffice to illustrate this point. In 1766 forty-two enslaved persons ran away from Leary's plantations in Essequibo and Demerara (parts of modern Guyana); in 1773 Leary lost seventeen more through desertion. In 1778 fourteen people absconded from the Achtekerke plantation in Essequibo, and in 1783 another twenty ran off (Thompson 1987, 138). In 1769 in Haiti seventeen persons ran off from a plantation in Gonaïves, and twenty from a plantation in Petite-Anse (Fouchard 1972, 406n1).

Jamaica was one of the few territories in which large-scale desertion took place with some frequency, especially in the late seventeenth century. In 1673 as many as two hundred people deserted a plantation there, killed fourteen Whites, seized all the arms and ammunition that they could find, and ran off into the mountains. Later (for example, in 1685, 1686, 1690 and 1696), insurgents from other plantations joined them and formed the feared group known as the Leeward Maroons. In 1685 enslaved persons from several plantations revolted and beat off a force of seventy soldiers sent against them. However, after dividing into several groups and trying every means to elude their pursuers, about thirty-seven of them were killed or captured, while another fifty surrendered. In 1690 as many as four hundred people on Sutton plantation revolted and made a bid for permanent freedom in the mountains. The colonial forces managed to kill ten of them and seventy others surrendered, while the others remained at large, most of them joining the Leeward Maroons (Patterson 1979, 256–58).

William Sharp (1976, 156) suggests that in the case of the Chocó Maroons of Colombia, small-scale desertion, and certainly small bands, stood a much better chance of evading capture than large ones; that, in fact, it was almost impossible to capture them. He attributes this to the terrain in which these Maroons operated: a maze of forests, rivers, streams, swamps and rocky escarpments. Presumably their operations were very covert if and when they ventured into White settlement areas.

Sharp (ibid.) also suggests, perhaps rightly, that small groups of Maroons may have engaged in defensive tactics against military expeditions that led to the destruction of their houses but no physical harm to their persons. Clearly, small groups were more able than large ones to shift the physical location of their settlements when necessary. Strategically and operationally, it would have been much more difficult to wipe out twenty or more small groups than a few large ones, because the former were more amorphous and lacked a central authority or headquarters that the expeditionary forces could target. Still, we cannot make any definitive statement about the survival capacity of small as against large groups, mainly because small groups did not enter the historical record as often as large ones, and some of them entered simply as a footnote in the diaries of military leaders who encountered them. More often than not, while the places of encounter might be mentioned, the groups are not identified by name either collectively or in relation to their leaders. Still, in some countries – for example, Peru – small groups played a significant role in harassing the slaveholders (Bowser 1974, 187–221).

It was the large collectives that the Whites feared most and that received the greatest attention from the colonial state and the plantocracy. Contemporary records speak often of Maroon "camps" or "encampments", suggesting that these were temporary phenomena rather than well-established communities, and that their denizens lived largely by brigandage. Doubtless, some settlements were of this character, but there were others that were more stable, catering to fairly large populations. Though modern scholars believe that the Whites considerably exaggerated the size of the largest communities, many of them were substantial enough to be regarded by contemporary writers as *states* and their operational centres as *towns*. This was grudging, and no doubt unintended, tribute to their survival capacity and the organizational abilities of their leaders. Palmares is writ large in the annals of Maroon history because these features were more prominently displayed in it than elsewhere; it has often been dubbed in both scholarly and popular literature as a *republic* of warriors.

GENDER AND MARRONAGE

The gender imbalance in most Maroon communities has led some writers to conclude that women were not as interested as men in absconding. The common view is that the female adult population in Maroon communities comprised largely women who were abducted, mainly to satisfy the biological and social needs of male Maroons. Debien (1979, 109) strongly implies that this was the case, stating that the most common "crime" was the abduction of

Black women. Gautier (1985, 233) states that to be owned by a White master or by a Black Maroon was really not very different, since in both cases the woman's integrity was violated. While this is undeniably so, we need to be careful not to read into the Maroons' actions the intention to transfer women from a White to a Black enslaver. Maroons wanted them as wives, home-makers and mothers of their children, not simply as labour hands and sexual objects (see chapters 7 and 8).

We need to revisit the question of whether women were abducted by men rather than joining Maroon settlements voluntarily. Schwartz (1979, 218–19) asserts that whenever Maroons in Brazil visited the urban areas, these "para-sitic" individuals not only "spoiled" the enslaved persons of the produce that they had brought to market but also, in "traditional" fashion, they carried off "the most appealing women". He states further that they preferred Black or Coloured women. He does not explain why they did not abduct enough of them to meet their sexual needs but rather "seemed to suffer from a chronic lack of females".

Celsa Albert Batista (1990, 41) and Paul Lokken (2004b, 52) believe that men usually carried off the women – or, rather, the women might have allowed the men to carry them off. William Sharp (1976, 156) states that women in the Chocó region of New Granada, Colombia, seem to have absconded as often as men. Thomas Atwood (1971, 226–27) declares that in Dominica, in the latter part of the eighteenth century, whole families ran off into the mountains. Pére Dutertre (1667–71, 1:153) stated that in 1639 more than sixty enslaved persons absconded from Capesterre with their wives and children. He also wrote that, in the French Caribbean, women often ran off along with their husbands, and others deserted on their own or with their children as young as seven or eight years old (ibid., 2:498, 534, 529).

Nicole Vanony-Frisch (1985, 135) argues that mothers' concern for their children was not a deterrent to women becoming Maroons. Bernard Moitt (2001, 133) states that neither pregnancy nor the children's ages appear to have hindered some women in the French Caribbean from absconding, though childless women were more likely to run away. He provides several examples of pregnant and lactating women who absconded, including Coralie, with chains and an infant no more than eight months old (ibid., 134–35). When apprehended and imprisoned, she asserted that she preferred to die, along with her infant, than return to her overlord. While emphasizing the degree to which some women went to recapture their freedom, Moitt makes it clear that pregnancy and motherhood did constrain other women in respect of *marronage*.

Stedman (1988, 80) gives the impression that fleeing women were a common sight in Suriname in the 1770s. According to him, enslaved persons – men, women and children – often rose up against their overlords, killed the White inhabitants, ravaged the plantations and fled as a group to the woods. Gautier (1985, 237) declares that some women deserted while pregnant, which to her is a clear indication of their refusal to bring up their children under slavery. Among the examples that Fouchard cites is Marie, who took off with her children, aged seventeen, four and two years: "The procession continues with babies of all ages. There were those born on slave ships, whose mothers attempted to snatch them from slavery, spiriting them away into marronage as soon as they arrived in port" (1972, 285).

It is possible that Maroon abduction of Indian rather than African women occurred on a proportionately larger scale in societies where the number of Indian women was large, such as Mexico, Peru and Colombia. We cannot, however, assume that all, or almost all, Indian women found in Black Maroon settlements were abducted. In Mexico, for instance, the colonial authorities complained to the imperial government that the legal prohibition against amorous relations between Africans and Indians ran afoul of the stubborn reality that Indian women preferred to marry Black rather than Indian men, and that Black men married Indian women so as to have free children (Martin 1957, 99). While there may have been a certain element of pragmatism in these unions, mutual attraction certainly played a role. Colonial laws sought in vain to prohibit such marriages, as happened in Mexico in 1568 (Dusenberry 1948, 291).

Reliable figures for the sexual composition of Maroon communities are extremely difficult to find, but the following is a sample of what is available. In 1693 a captured Maroon from the Matudere (Matadure, Matubere, Matubre, Tabacal) settlement[5] in Cartagena reported that it consisted of ninety-nine people – fifty-four Black males, forty-two Black females and three Mulattos (Borrego Plá 1973, 86). In the Bahoruco (Le Maniel) settlement[6] on the Haiti–Dominican Republic border in 1785, the population comprised seventy-five males (forty-two Maroon-born) and fifty-eight females (thirty-eight Maroon-born).[7] In the late eighteenth century the male-to-female Maroon ratio in Guadeloupe was estimated at two to one (Gautier 1985, 231, 234). Fouchard (1972, 289) estimates the number of women in Haiti who deserted at about 15 to 20 per cent, but it is unclear whether he is referring to the number of women imported or those advertised as runaways. Figures for the United States during the eighteenth century are somewhat lower than those for the French colonies. In one sample of runaways in Virginia, 12 per cent were females, and in another sample of 134 runaways (apparently from South Carolina), 11 per cent were females (Blassingame 1979, 202). In Suriname, Hoogbergen (1993, 167) reports, the deserters were mainly "men, in proportion often reaching 90 percent". In 1843 in the province of Santa Marta, Colombia, 89.16 per cent of the runaways were males and 10.84 per cent females (Romero Jaramillo 1997, 185). Aguirre (1993, 248–49) indicates that of 121 Maroons in Lima between 1840 and 1846 for whom data are available, 71.9 per cent were males and 29.1 per cent females. Mullin (1992, 289–90) states that in Jamaica between the 1730s and 1805, women constituted 24 per cent of the total number of deserters (631, as compared with 1,981 men). In Cuba, in the Todos Tenemos (Bota) settlement around the mid-nineteenth century, there were at least as many women as men, and in El Frijol settlement in 1815 the number of women might have slightly exceeded that of men (La Rosa Corzo 2003, 107–8, 180). According to the testimonies of two captured Maroons, in 1733 and 1734–35 respectively, in the Windward settlement in Jamaica the women and children combined greatly outnumbered the men (Tuelon 1973, 22).

Often, sex ratios of those who absconded are based on the records of those recaptured. Though these records frequently indicate a higher percentage of women than men being recaptured, such was not always the case, especially in urban communities. Karasch (1987, 305–6), for instance, notes that between 1826 and 1837 in Rio de Janeiro one set of newspaper advertisements showed that 25.9 per cent of the runaways were females, but females constituted only 15 per cent of those recaptured. She surmises that women found it easier than their male counterparts to hide in the homes of protectors, a view that Donoghue (2002, 154–55) seems to corroborate in the case of the Danish West Indies.

The extent to which the gender imbalance in the wider enslaved population influenced the gender ratio of persons who absconded remains uncertain, but it must have played some role. Among the plantation societies, only in the southern United States and Barbados did females outnumber males. In the southern United States, the relatively large number of females did not affect the general trend of a higher incidence of male than female *marronage*. In Barbados the ratio is said to have evened out by the mid-eighteenth century, and the data for the early nineteenth century show a slight female pre-dominance (Higman 1984a, 116, 413). However, statistics on the sex ratio among runaways in that colony still show a great imbalance in favour of males. Mullin (1992, 289–90) indicates that between the 1730s and 1805 women constituted 34 per cent of the deserters (283 men and 148 women), while Heuman (1986, 98) suggests a figure of 36.5 per cent in 1817.

The low proportion of women in nearly all the Maroon settlements raises questions about their alleged wide-scale abduction by men. It refutes Patrick Carroll's suggestion (1977, 489) that once the men had obtained their free-dom the desire for women became a top priority. Clearly, if the men had been bent on such abduction, as both Carroll and Debien assert, they would have taken enough women to ensure that each of them had at least one. Carroll (1977, 500), in his study of the Mandinga-Amapa Maroons, notes that the male to female ratio of the settlement moved from four to one in 1743 (some eight years after its foundation), to three to one in 1769 (the date of official freedom), and only evened out in 1827. In very few settlements were there as many adult women as adult men. This is the clearest evidence that the inci-dence of abduction of women has been grossly overstated in contemporary and modern literature. Perhaps it also indicates, as Ulrich Fleischmann (1993, 573) suggests, that male Maroons were able to suppress their natural biologi-cal desires for the opposite sex because the self-preservation instinct is stronger than the sexual urge. He (1993, 573) takes to task Alejo Carpentier, who, in a short play entitled *Los fugitivos*, depicts Maroons as having basi-cally the same instincts as dogs: a Maroon chases a woman, while a dog chases a bitch; the Maroon reverts to the plantation to satisfy his craving for women and is finally caught.

Stories like these applied to the average Maroon were myths rather than realities. So is the view of Maroons' sexual promiscuity with the women in the *palenques*. Díez Castillo (1981, 50) buys into this myth without attempting to assess its credibility. He simply declares that marriage almost never existed among the Maroons in Panama and that polygamy was much more common than monogamy. He does not consider that for polygamy to be common, Maroon women would have had to outnumber men significantly.

Occasionally, Maroons abducted White women, as was the case with the Matudere and Palmares Maroons in Cartagena and Brazil respectively (Borrego Plá 1973, 81; Marcano Jiménez 2001, 53). In contrast to stereotypes about the sexual proclivities of Blacks, Kent (1979, 182) informs us that

Brazilian Maroons carried off White women only rarely and usually ransomed them without sexually molesting them. The celebrated author Edison Carneiro (1946, 108) found only one occasion on which the Palmarino (Palmarista) warriors were alleged to have raped some White women, as reported by Antonio Garro da Câmara, a Pernambucan soldier, in 1682. Patterson (1979, 286) could not find a single recorded case of rape throughout the history of revolts and *marronage* in Jamaica, though several White women were killed. This is not to suggest that no instances of rape occurred in that country, but such cases were rare. In other jurisdictions we sometimes encounter charges of Maroons raping both White and Black women. For instance, William L. Hill, head of a militia unit in Onslow County, North Carolina, complained in 1821 that the runaways had "ravished a number of females" (Schweninger 2002, 6).

Gautier (1985, 229, 235–38), while recognizing that enslaved women of almost all ages, colours, and maternal circumstances absconded, insists that the fact that there were fewer female than male Maroons had nothing to do with a less acute desire for freedom but rather with the special circumstances of their lives. Among these were the need to take care of their very young children, who might not have survived the rigours of the flight from slavery to freedom; the fact that men enjoyed much greater mobility than women, since they were assigned to work as messengers, fishermen, traders, dockworkers, artisans, military cohorts, scouts, baggage carriers and so on; the suspicion that would have attended a woman being seen alone in the bush or with very young children; the risk of being raped by men of all colours; and the difficulties of negotiating through certain kinds of terrain. All these impediments provide a sound, if not a comprehensive, explanation for the relatively smaller female than male Maroon population.[8] Gautier also believes that the practice in Africa of men ranging much farther than women from their home base to hunt and fish gave men greater confidence to venture into the unknown forests in the Americas. She suggests that women were more disposed to flee with all their family members when the destination was another country where they would be declared free (ibid., 230).

The received wisdom is that women were disposed to flee to urban rather than rural communities because they offered more opportunities of earning a living and the deserters could avoid the rigours of forest or mountain terrain. Higman (1984a, 389) implies this for Kingston, Jamaica, and states it explicitly for Bridgetown, Barbados, in 1817. Heuman (1986, 99–101), however, found that most female fugitives in Barbados during the nineteenth century went to rural destinations – and, interestingly, that most male runaways headed for Bridgetown or Speightstown, perhaps because many of them were skilled or semi-skilled. Newspaper advertisements of runaways in South Carolina indicate that the enslavers believed that about twice as many women as men were headed for some urban area, but, perhaps strangely, they also thought that more women were headed for a rural than an urban destination (Morgan 1986, 67–69).

We cannot draw any firm conclusions about the urban or rural disposition of female fugitives until much more work is done on the subject. However, we can say with greater assurance that many more enslaved women were Maroons in spirit than those who actually made a spirited attempt to escape the physical trammels of slavery. McFarlane (1986, 149), commenting on the enslaved persons who did not make a formal bid for freedom through flight, argues that "this did not efface the vision of freedom, but made its pursuit more complex and variegated". A dramatic episode comes to mind: an enslaved woman in Maryland, on learning that her overlord had willed that she should be set free if he died without heirs, killed his three children (Jordan 1968, 392). This sad event occurred because the slavery system caused her to perceive such an act as the only way out of her nightmare of bondage.

Some Maroon women stand out as much as men for their efforts to escape bondage and create free communities. Lise, a midwife and repeated fugitive in Haiti, fled wearing an iron collar and dragging a withered right leg (Fouchard 1972, 392). Sally, of the Danish West Indies, made her bid for freedom though "far gone with child" and with one ear severed because of a previous attempt at running away (Donoghue 2002, 150). Hazard, belonging to the same colony, though only twenty-two years old, was apparently a frequent rebel and escapee. She was advertised in the colony's *Gazette* as being lacerated "on her back with the whip in several places" (Donoghue 2002, 151). The overlord of Isabel, a fugitive in Guatemala, sold her, dubbing her a "crazy runaway" (Lokken 2004a, 47). Rosette, of Haiti, is perhaps the most frequent runaway on record. A doctor in 1783 declared that she had deserted for the hundredth time, brandishing a knife, though the number of desertions was most likely exaggerated (Fouchard 1972, 391–92).

The story of Zabeth, who constantly sought freedom, is worth repeating. Both sad and noble, it is a story of remarkable eloquence. What makes it all the more striking is that she was a Creole, a category of enslaved persons whom some writers consider to have been more reconciled to enslavement than people born in Africa. The events described here took place in western St Domingue between January and April 1768, by which time Zabeth had become a regular deserter. From very early childhood, according to her manager, she had lived the life of a fugitive, and with age had become more prone to flight. Her manager had chained her to prevent further escapes but had become anxious lest she die from having been in chains for a long time, and so he released her. Two days later she absconded again but was caught shortly after. On this occasion her manager let her off with a stern warning that if she should escape again he would put her back in chains for the rest of her life. She promised him solemnly that she would mend her ways, but in an instant she was off again. She was apprehended and returned to him shortly thereafter, but as she was not in a physical condition to undergo punishment, he decided to send her to a place called Brouillet where, according to him, some disabled Blacks lived in virtual freedom.

She absconded again within two days. When she was returned, her manager chained her in the sugar mill, where she remained for the next month, until three of her fingers were crushed in the rollers. He placed her in hospital without removing her heavy chains, but within eight days she had run off once again, having scaled a high fence that enclosed the hospital. Yet again she was caught and kept chained for about a month, until she appeared to be approaching death. Her manager conspired with some others to request that he remove her chains, which he did after having her grave dug – with her helping. She was soon off again. As before, Zabeth was apprehended, and, seeing that she was at the point of death, the manager indicated that he intended to chain her in the mill, where it would be more convenient for her to die than in the hospital. He felt that in doing so he would make her a salutary example to others who might try to abscond. He declared that she had been of little value to the plantation and of late had been treated virtually as a free person (Debien 1974, 434).

It is difficult to understand how from very early childhood a person could have developed such a strong urge for freedom. While the desire for freedom is ingrained in humanity, its expression through flight into unknown and hazardous terrain would not normally be associated with a person of such tender age. Zabeth's understanding of and need for freedom must have sharpened as she grew older and became more conscious of the brutalities of slavery. Clearly, the manager did not tell the whole story of why she became such a persistent deserter, or of the trauma that she might have undergone as a young child. Was she, for instance, raped, cruelly whipped or brutalized in some other way? Or did she observe such brutalities being meted out to her relatives? Whatever it was that triggered the urge to distance herself from the plantation on which she was born, it must have been traumatic. She had not honed her craft sufficiently, for she was always caught within a few days or weeks of escaping. However, she was determined to obtain her liberty or die trying, and it appears that she suffered the latter fate. The manager tried to present himself as humane, but the humane course would have been simply to let her go. However, like the wardens at other maximum-security institutions, he felt that no one should be allowed to escape from his plantation.

Zabeth was one of many runaways who were blessed with a vision of freedom but cursed with the inability to bring it into reality. Coobah and Sally, of Jamaica, found themselves in the same dilemma. Coobah, an Igbo who was purchased by Thomas Thistlewood in 1761 when she was just fifteen years old, was raped by him within a year and harassed, sexually and otherwise, on several other occasions. She contracted venereal disease within the next four years and was also afflicted by yaws. From 1769 she became a repeated runaway, absconding eight times in 1770 and five times in 1771, in spite of very harsh punishments, including being placed in the stocks, being whipped, being branded on the forehead and having a collar and chains attached to her for months at a time. Thistlewood deemed her to be unprofitable and eventually decided to sell her. She was transported to Georgia (Burnard 2004, 217–18).

Sally, a Congolese by birth, was another enslaved woman who refused to accept the fiat of slavery. Thistlewood purchased her in 1762, but from the outset she showed an indisposition to work either as a domestic or a field hand and resisted every attempt to persuade her to comply with the dictates of her overlord. From the early days Thistlewood raped her, doing so on at least thirty-seven occasions, which he recorded in his diary. She, like Coobah, became afflicted with venereal diseases and yaws. She first ran away in 1767. Beatings and other forms of punishment and abuse did not dull her appetite for freedom, or at least for some space of her own. On one occasion Phibbah, her overlord's servile mistress, stripped her naked and tied her hands behind her so that mosquitoes could bite her freely. Sally managed to escape but was apprehended and punished by being tied up in the bilboes for a night. On another occasion her overlord raped her as a form of punishment. Almost every year she ran away a few times – on at least three occasions, after her overlord had sex with her. Each time she was brought back or returned of her own volition. It is unclear why she returned, but one view is that she became so demoralized that she could not make the psychological break with the plantation and the bondage that had become so much a part of her life. Thistlewood's diary records that she became completely deviant as the years passed, stole repeatedly from any- and everyone, refused to do any work, and was a social pariah even among other enslaved persons. He finally sold her out of the country in 1784 (Burnard 2004, 218–21).

These examples make it clear that, like their male counterparts, enslaved women chafed under the burden of slavery and sought ways of escaping from it. Those who managed to do so became part of a community that recognized them as human beings rather than chattels, and sometimes accorded them important leadership roles. Female Maroon leaders (who were also often major religious figures) included Romaine la Prophetesse, Marie-Jeanne and Henriette Saint-Marc in Haiti (Fouchard 1972, 365n1). García (1996, 61) states that in Barlovento, Venezuela, the lists of Maroons include a number of women who participated actively in resistance to physical and moral injustices, calling into question the view that enslaved women were submissive.

http://www.moec.gov.jm/heroes/nanny.htm

Figure 6. Grandy Nanny

Perhaps the most outstanding female Maroon leader was Grandy Nanny, who so influenced the Windward Maroons of Jamaica that to this day their headquarters bears the name Nanny Town.[9] Though a somewhat shadowy figure in contemporary European accounts,[10] she looms large in the oral history and legends of Maroon struggles in Jamaica. Her role as diviner and exorcist earned her the respect of senior male members of the community, who seem to have depended heavily on her for good augury and to ward off evil. The fact that the Windward Maroons, though often hard pressed by their antagonists, were never actually defeated in an engagement must in their own minds have had as much to do with Grandy Nanny's spiritual powers as with the group's military capabilities (Campbell 1990, 50–51). It remains unclear whether or not she actually participated in fighting, though some writers think that she did (Campbell 1990, 177–78;

Brathwaite 1994, 120). Thicknesse, the only British military officer who ever saw her, declared that she did not take part in the treaty negotiations and stated that she wore "a girdle round the waist and . . . nine or ten different knives hanging in sheaths to it, many of which I have no doubt, had been plunged in human flesh and blood" (Campbell 1990, 123).[11]

Other female Maroons played important non-combatant roles in aggressive and defensive activities. In 1733, many women went along on the Windward Maroons' attack on plantation Hobby to assist in carrying off the spoils (Kopytoff 1976a, 89). About the same time, expecting an assault from an expeditionary force, the Maroons left women to burn their settlement at Nanny Town if the male warriors, who had occupied various strategic positions, could not hold onto it (Kopytoff 1976a, 89). Around the end of the sixteenth century, in Cartagena, Pedro Ordóñez de Ceballos declared that in one engagement his men encountered 150 Black women who fought more valiantly than the men (Mathieu 1982, 88). In 1758 two women took part, along with thirteen men, in an attack on Thomas Bouchet at Nippes in Haiti (Gautier 1985, 232). There was also "rebellious" Sarah, enslaved by a Kentucky planter but determined to achieve her liberty at a high price to her enslaver. He described her as "the biggest devil that ever lived, having poisoned a stud horse and set a stable on fire, also burnt Gen. R. Williams' stable and stock yard with seven horses and other property to [the] value of $1500. She was handcuffed and got away at Ruddles Mills on her way down the river, which is the fifth time she escaped when about to be sent out of the country" (Blassingame 1979, 206).

In 1826 members of the Urubu (Vulture) *quilombo* in Bahia, comprising about fifty men and a few women, attacked and killed a number of Whites and were themselves eventually attacked by a detachment of regular soldiers. All the Maroons fought fiercely, though using much more rudimentary weapons than their enemies. One of the heroines of this deadly encounter was Zeferina. Reis (1993, 55–57), who researched the incident, reported that Zeferina had resisted, though she had only a bow and some arrows. During the contest she displayed great leadership skills, urging on the fighters and keeping them on line. The provincial president, in a sudden outpouring of praise, alluded to her as "Queen".

A number of Maroon settlements were named after women, including Magdalena, María Angola and María Embuyla (Colombia); Guardamujeres (Cuba); Nanny Town, Molly's Town and Diana's Town (Jamaica); and

Mulatto Girl's Town and Bucker Woman's Town (United States). Though some of these names may have been symbolic, it is likely that several of them reflect the significant role that Maroon women played in the particular communities. Summing up his discussion on gender, Fouchard (1972, 289) asserts that the role of women in *marronage* was as important as it was in colonial life in general.

MAROON ETHNICITY

Various writers have argued that Maroon communities were organized largely along ethnic lines. Contrary to what John Thornton (1998a, 201–5) and some others suggest, Maroon societies, unlike slave societies, were not built on ascriptive ethnic, colour or class criteria. Thornton notes that enslaved persons on the plantations often married or otherwise associated largely with their own ethnic (or national, according to him) groups, formed ethnic associations that elected "kings" and other important figures, participated in ethnic festivals and so on. He also states that in some countries these festivals grew in importance, especially in urban centres.[12] However, he pushes his argument about ethnicity too far when he suggests that Maroon communities commonly organized themselves according to ethnic groupings. While he proves his viewpoint about ethnic associations (if not ethnic exclusiveness) on the plantations and in the urban communities, he fails to do so in relation to Maroon communities.

He cites two examples in support of his belief: one of the runaway communities around the city of Cartagena in the late seventeenth century, which opted for a polity based on Akan ethnicity, and Palmares, which, he maintains, opted for an Angolan one (ibid., 201–2) . There was also a *palenque* near Cartagena in the late seventeenth century, containing an estimated 110 people, allegedly comprising only Creole Blacks (Borrego Plá 1973, 33). However, the relatively few examples of ethnic polities are insufficient to validate Thornton's claim about Maroon societies, given the thousands of them that are believed to have existed during the slavery period. It is also debatable that Palmares, while a *predominantly* Angolan polity, can be viewed as an exclusive one (Flory 1979, 123; Anderson 1996, 565). Another Maroon settlement that existed along Colombia's Prata River in 1809, while predominantly Hausa, nevertheless contained other ethnic groups (Reis 1993, 43).

The weight of the literature suggests that, commonly, individuals and small groups from various ethnicities coalesced to form viable Maroon entities.[13] Campbell (1990, 3) writes, for instance, of the Jamaican Maroons that "we have fragmentary evidence to suggest that there was ethnic plurality within most bands, although one group might be in a dominant position based on demography or military capacity". The Matudere *palenque* in the late seventeenth century comprised several ethnicities (Mathieu 1982, 111), while another *palenque,* thought to have consisted of some 250 souls, was far more diverse in its ethnic composition (Landers 2000a, 39). Likewise, El Portillo in Cuba contained mainly Congolese but housed persons from other ethnic groups (La Rosa Corzo 2003, 50–61). La Rosa Corzo (ibid., 180) observes that in Cuba no one ethnic group was predominant in any of the Maroon settlements, except perhaps in the Palenque de los Vivís. In every other settlement there were apparently a number of ethnic groups. Aguirre (1993, 257–59) informs us that the majority of bands that operated in the vicinity of Lima around the mid-nineteenth century were multi-ethnic, and occasionally included Whites, Indians and a few Chinese. Navarrete (2003, 37) notes that the Brazilian *quilombos* appear to have included Creoles and Africans from different ethnic groups. Karasch (1987, 312) states that they often included "deserters from the military services, foreign soldiers and sailors, free criminals and vagrants, freedpersons, and Indians".

It would have been virtually impossible for individual or small groups on the run to seek out specific ethnic settlements. Barbara Kopytoff (1976b, 37) argues that Maroon ethnic groups were more fluid than their counterparts in Africa; otherwise, they might not have survived. Clearly, the logic of Maroon existence and the imperatives of survival forced the vast majority of them into inter-ethnic alliances, which included Indians where they were present. In fact, it was quite common throughout the Americas for Africans and Indians to forge various kinds of relationships, from alliances of interdependent communities to integration within a single polity. The common predicament that they faced in the frontier societies of the region often made such relationships necessary, though they might not have been easily forged. These occurred from the earliest contacts between the two peoples.

We must, of course, acknowledge that while writers often refer to Africans as a monolithic group, in reality they were segmented into a wide variety of ethnicities, sometimes contending for space and precedence in their home countries before they were transported to the Americas. Such ethnic conflicts did not end when they were introduced to colonial situations and enslave-ment in the Americas. There were, for instance, ethnic conflicts between Akan (Minas) and Creole Maroons in Cartagena in the late seventeenth cen-tury; Akan and Madagascan in Jamaica in the early eighteenth century; and Akan and Congolese ("Bantu") in Berbice in the mid-eighteenth century.[14] Ethnic conflicts were sharp at times, and the arena for conflict was enlarged through the juxtaposition of European, African and Indian cultures in the Americas. Nevertheless, as a rule Maroon societies placed less emphasis on ethnicity and more on such imperatives for success as fidelity, hard work and ability. The fact that most Maroon societies displayed a strong Black/African element was incidental rather than deliberate.

African societies in the homeland were accustomed to incorporating vari-ous ethnic groups into a particular polity. For instance, the Asante forbade anyone to speak of the ethnic origins of enslaved persons introduced into their empire (Rattray 1923, 43–44). In the nineteenth century groups from as far afield as South Africa (for example, Zulu, Basotho and Swazi), and West Africa (for example, Ibadan and the Delta states) were incorporating other groups into their polities and allowing for political elevation based to a great extent on abilities rather than ethnicity (Davenport 1997; Akintoye 1971; Jones 1963). In all these cases, the instinct for survival took precedence over the desire to maintain ethnic purity. Maroon communities seemed to have been forged on a similar instinct.

Relatively few White people joined Maroon societies because they were already free, they held pejorative notions about Blacks, and it was anathema to most of them to submit to Black rule.[15] But there were always White fugi-tives, outlaws and others who, for one reason or another, fell out with the authoritarian rulers and found it politic to have Blacks as their bedfellows. The most obvious examples are military deserters and indentured servants (especially in the early days), along with buccaneers, corsairs, freebooters and pirates, as they are variously termed in the contemporary literature.[16] There were also anti-slavers (especially in the last days of slavery) who rejected the slavery system; and poor Whites who were not slaveholders, particularly in the sprawling rural areas of the United States, Brazil, Colombia and Mexico. These groups often joined or assisted Maroons for economic, political, reli-gious, moral, humanitarian, ideological or other reasons. Again, the slavery system in the Americas was filled with contradictions, and there were uphold-ers and opponents of the system on both sides of the racial and colour divide.

In 1549 a small group of Maroons in Peru, which included two Spaniards, was harrying both urban and rural areas (Bowser 1974, 188). The United States experienced a number of attacks by Black and White coalitions against the slaveholding interests. In the 1780s a White robber led a group of about fifty White and Black people, with whom he was causing havoc in the state of Virginia; in 1818 in that same state thirty Black deserters, in league with a group of White men, were harassing Princess Anne County. In 1861 a group of Black runaways was said to be acting in concert with two Whites along the Comite River in Louisiana; in 1863 White deserters from the Civil War linked up with runaway Blacks in Alabama; in 1864, five hundred Union men, deserters and Blacks were said to be carrying out raids in the vicinity of Gainesville, Florida. In the same year, in North Carolina, gruesome tales were told of some five hundred to six hundred runaway Blacks who had taken advantage of the chaos caused by the Civil War to rove around the country and wreak havoc, largely on White settlements. There was strong evidence that White deserters from the Confederate Army were associated with them in their depredations (Aptheker 1979, 153, 157, 164–65). White enslavers were befuddled at the idea that members of their own ethnic group could be sleeping with the enemy; ironically, they did not find it strange that they themselves were doing so.

It seems to have been much easier in the United States than in most other jurisdictions for White and Black deserters to forge alliances. Buckley (1998, 225), however, tells us that British soldiers who deserted also sometimes joined Black Maroon groups:

> One might suppose that white men would not leave the rude but familiar ways of military life for a crude and dangerous existence among jungled hills teeming with insect life. The fact that they did dramatically underscores the soldiers' fear of the garrison as a deathtrap. Nor would one today suppose that Europeans would throw in their lot with desperate Maroon groups once they had deserted. The official record also shows that captured groups of runaway slaves included white deserters. Moreover, a number of these men roamed the interior of West Indian islands for years with marauding Maroon bands of men and women. In so doing they added their military knowledge to the developed extraordinary skills of the Maroons as guerrilla fighters.

Buckley (ibid., 226) explains that while ethnic and colour differences might have made White deserters and Black runaways unlikely companions, they soon forgot their differences, because their alliance resulted from their mutual resistance to the deadly social and physical environment in which they were compelled to live – the plantation for the Blacks and the garrison for the Whites.

Two British nationals, Alexander Arbuthnot and Robert Ambrister, joined the Seminole Maroons in 1817 on the Suwannee River. Arbuthnot was a trader who supplied the Maroons with weapons, in addition to other goods. Ambrister was an ex-lieutenant of Marines, who took on the job of training six hundred or more of the Maroons and who stated that he had come to seek redress for the Blacks (Porter 1951, 267). American forces caught these White adventurers during the First Seminole War and executed them (Porter 1951, 266–67; Mulroy 1993, 15–16).

In the 1650s, following the British invasion of the island, Jamaica witnessed a combination of Spanish and African guerrilla forces fighting to expel the invaders. However, the Blacks were not fighting for the Spanish cause; rather, they were fighting to assert and maintain their independence from the British (Patterson 1979, 253). But Maroons were not always enamoured of alliances with White soldiers. On one occasion the Windward Maroons of Jamaica taunted soldiers who had been sent against them, saying that they had no fathers or mothers, and that if one of them should die the others would walk all over him (Campbell 1990, 122). In Berbice (Guyana) in 1763, White soldiers were dispatched from Suriname to assist in quelling the Black uprising. Some of them mutinied and tried to make their way to Venezuela. When they encountered the Black insurgents, they sought to forge an alliance with them. However, the insurgents, considering them to be spies, put most of them to death and forced the rest to work for them, including repairing firearms (Stedman 1988, 77; Thompson 1987, 166; Hartsinck 1770, 424–28).

On a few occasions Whites did not actually join Black Maroon groups but provided critical support for them in the form of shelter, food, firearms and so on. For instance, in 1830 the slaveholding interests in North Carolina discovered firearms secreted in the house of a White woman who lived in a secluded area. The woman's son also led them to a place where meat was stored secretly and informed them that his mother prepared meals daily for four to five runaways (Aptheker 1979, 160). It is quite likely that, given the woman's age and straitened circumstances, she was able to earn her keep by facilitating the needs of the Maroons.

Of the non-Africans who formed or were incorporated into Maroon communities, the most common were Amerindians. In Cayenne (French Guiana) in 1707, a Maroon community was reported to contain several Indians (Debien 1979, 108–9). Fouchard (1972) provides examples of ethnic intermixing between Africans and Indians in the border areas between Haiti and the Dominican Republic. Other examples can be drawn from the United States, Suriname, Dominica, Mexico, St Vincent, Brazil, Venezuela, Peru, Cuba, Nicaragua and Belize. Huachinango Pablo, originally from Yucatán, was leader of a *palenque* in Cuba in the late eighteenth century (Pérez de la Riva 1979, 57). In the 1550s Indians joined the African Maroon Miguel in establishing a settlement in Venezuela and attacking the mining community of Barquisimeto (Franco 1979, 36). In Mexico, from the earliest days Black and Indian Maroons established strong links and fought against a common enemy. According to Davidson (1979, 91, 99), by the 1560s deserters from the northern mines were terrorizing the regions from Guadalajara to Zacatecas, forging alliances with Indians and raiding ranches. In one instance, Maroons from the Guanajuato mines joined the Chichimec Indians in a brutal war against the settlers. Indian support was critical to the success of some Black revolts and made suppression much more difficult.

In 1641 Africans who had settled, along with Whites and other groups, on Providencia (colonial Providence Island, off the Nicaraguan coast), fled in the face of a destructive Spanish assault on that settlement, took refuge on the Central American mainland and gradually intermixed with the local Miskito Indians. Other Africans, seeking refuge as deserters from neighbouring European settlements or from shipwrecks, increased the numerical size of the population and built up a community that remained free from slavery, though placed on the lowest rung of Nicaraguan colonial society (Gordon 1998, 33, 35, 42).

One of the most well-known instances of miscegenation occurred among the Caribs of St Vincent from the late seventeenth century, through unions between runaway Africans and the local island peoples. In time the African elements became dominant – hence the name Black Caribs. In the eighteenth century, first the French and then the British fought a number of battles with them to divest them of their lands and establish colonial rule over them. During formal British occupation of the island, which began in 1763, two brutal wars took place – in 1772–73 and 1795–96. The Black Caribs eventually capitulated, and most of them were forcibly transferred to neighbouring Caribbean islands and later to Honduras, where they are generally referred to today as Garifunas or Garinagus.[17]

As noted already, ethnic tensions existed and sometimes flared not only between but also within Maroon communities (Kopytoff 1976b). Though unfortunate, this was not altogether surprising, given the linguistic and social differences between various individuals and groups when they first came together. New groups or communities generally go through four basic processes on the way to achieving unity – forming, storming, norming and performing.[18] The early history of most Maroon communities would fall into the second category. In the least stressful circumstances, it would have called for a great degree of tolerance and understanding for such diverse individuals and groups to forge a common bond. Although settlements sometimes housed individuals whose respective ethnic groups in Africa were at logger-heads with each other, Maroon communities were not born primarily out of the desire of ethnically and culturally homogeneous groups to re-establish cultural and kinship systems similar to those that they had left in Africa, but rather to defeat a common foe. Zips (1999, 63–64) notes that the experience of enslavement and *marronage* had radically changed their identities, and that

> [i]t was crucial to develop communal norms and means of communication that would allow various languages, cultures, and customs to fuse into one collective culture that would function as a bearer of an independent Maroon identity. Synthesizing various African heritages, behavioral patterns, legal and political ideas, and social structures resulted in a meaningful co-existence of people who had found their way into one another's lives coincidentally by having lived through a common experience. The resultant culture, which was actively shaped by the Maroons, did not become a mere aggregation of elements, but evolved from group interactions.

While ethnic tensions existed, especially in the formative years, few communities ruptured because of ethnic divisions. For most of them ethnicity became a secondary factor as they forged new kinship loyalties through miscegenation and cultural syncretism. In time, the more durable Maroon communities developed quite separate identifies or ethnicities, as would also happen notably among the Zulu, Basotho, Swazi, Ibadan and other African polities that emerged out of brutal warfare and forced migration during the nineteenth century.

In several instances contemporary (and occasionally present-day) writers refer to the large groups as "tribes", suggesting that they had acquired the profile of distinct ethnic groups. The large and powerful entities sometimes vied with each other and the slaveholding states for physical space and material resources, and occasionally fought to the death to eliminate each other. One of the most notorious examples was the part that the Ndjuka (Auka) Maroons played in destroying the Aluku (Boni) Maroon settlements in Suriname in 1793 (Hoogbergen 1990). By that time the Ndjukas had undergone over thirty years of "pacification" following their treaty with the colonial authorities in 1760, and were being used, not for the first time, by the Whites to eliminate the much more militant Alukus, who were a thorn in the side of the plantocracy. But the Ndjukas had their own grievances with the Alukus, who apparently posed a threat to their spatial integrity. For the same reason the Ndjukas attacked a number of groups that had begun to establish themselves along the Cottica River and Sara and Surnau creeks in the post-treaty era (Thoden van Velzen 1995, 128–29).

Other groups had various conflicts. In the unsettled circumstances of the late seventeenth century, several groups that had fled during the British invasion of Jamaica distrusted each other, and this distrust persisted for many years after the British had firmly established themselves as the new colonial authority. Patterson (1979, 258) views this circumstance as partly accounting for the return of several runaways to their overlords. However, by the early eighteenth century many groups were forging alliances with each other, based both on their material needs and on acceptance of the stubborn reality that it was only through such alliances (and sometimes even political integration) that they would be able to resist the increasingly large military forces being sent against them. Still, tensions and sometimes clashes occurred between different groups, the result of territorial notions and of treaty arrangements with the authoritarian state.

Suspicion of treachery between Maroon groups was not without some foundation. This was the cause of the clash between the Juan de Bolas Maroons, who had accepted a treaty with the British that required them to apprehend runaways, and the Karmahaly (Carmahaly, Vermejales, Vermaholis, Vermahalles) Maroons under Juan de Serras, in the late seventeenth century. The same reason prevailed when the Windward Maroons assaulted the small group, led by Three-Fingered Jack, that was troubling the Jamaican planters. The Leeward Maroons also considerably harassed a small group under Captain Gummor (Goomer) in the 1730s, apparently because the latter was viewed as trespassing on the Leewards' territory (Campbell 1990, 24–25, 93, 158). In Suriname, runaways led by Amawi and Nelo attacked the more peaceful Paramakas, who were under the protection of the more powerful Ndjukas. Ndjuka tradition asserts that the Amawi and Nelo had become bold enough to ambush Ndjukas on Wane Creek, a vital link connecting the Maroni with the Cottica River. The result was Ndjuka retaliation against Amawi and Nelo, decimating their numbers and killing their two leaders (Thoden van Velzen 1995, 128).

One of the most striking features of insurrection in the anglophone Caribbean is the dominant role of the Akan. This is said to have resulted from the more warlike organization and spirit of their polities, especially the Asante (Ashanti),[19] who built one of the largest and most respected empires in the West African forest region. Akan, Ewe and related ethnic groups of the Gold Coast sub-region have come down to us in popular literature as Koromantin (Coromantees) because this was the main port of exit for various hinterland peoples on their way to the Americas. They are believed to have formed the most substantial element among the enslaved peoples of the English-speaking and Dutch-speaking Caribbean because of the large number of forts and factories that the British[20] and Dutch had on the Gold Coast. It is therefore not surprising that Akan (or at any rate Gold Coast) peoples played the major role in revolts and *marronage* in these colonies.

However, the degree of slave insurgency in other plantation states such as Cuba, Haiti and Brazil, comprising Yoruba (southwestern Nigeria), Ndongo (Angola), Ardras (Dahomey), Hausa (northern Nigeria) and a host of other ethnic groups, severely undermines the thesis that the Akan were more warlike than other African groups. In South Carolina, Africans from the Bight of Biafra were more disposed to run away than those from the Gold Coast, Senegambia and Angola (Morgan 1986, 62). Palmares, which existed for most of the seventeenth century and constituted by far the largest Maroon polity that ever existed in the Americas, consisted largely of Angolan peoples; Congolese were also prominent, while Akan seem to have been largely absent. In 1835, it was mainly the Hausa peoples who plotted the aborted revolt in Bahia (Reis 1993).[21] Likewise, the Congos (called "Franc-Congos" in Haiti) played the major role in servile resistance in Haiti in the late eighteenth century, and constituted at least half the total number of runaways advertised in the press. This finding refutes the myth about their docility. The same source indicates that in that country Creoles stood fifth in the line of deserters, above Nagos, Bambaras, Mandingos and others, which also negates the view that Creoles were reluctant to decamp (Fouchard 1972, 438). In Fouchard's (ibid.) opinion, the numbers of various groups brought into Haiti at different periods was the most influential factor in the ethnic contour of flight.

Planter perception and preference had a lot to do with the alleged aggressiveness or docility of particular ethnic groups. For instance, planters in the British Caribbean liked Gold Coast (really Akan) workers because they were said to be nobler in bearing, better workers and more faithful to those who treated them well, but fierce and implacable enemies to those who mistreated them. Although they were at the centre of most instances of revolt and *marronage* in Jamaica, an initiative in the island's legislature to ban their entry into that colony failed to garner sufficient votes (Long 1774, 2:470). On the other hand, Moreau de Saint-Méry, a contemporary writer, asserts that the French purchased but did not think highly of Gold Coast workers (in French terminology, those from the whole area from Dahomey to Nigeria): "The Negroes of the Gold Coast are, in general, well made and intelligent; but they are usually criticized for commonly being deceitful, artificial, dissimulating, lazy, roguish, flattering, greedy, drunk, and lewd" (Stein 1988, 49). Some British planters also disliked the Calabar peoples (of southeastern Nigeria), deeming them intransigent (Donnan 1930–35, 1:108).

The Yoruba (called Lucumi in Cuba) were regarded in Cuba as indomitable and commanded the greatest respect among the other ethnic groups in the island (Ortiz 1975, 30–48). Strangely enough, the Cubans considered the Mandinga among the most docile and trustworthy groups, though they were deemed great rebels and fugitives in parts of Spanish America during the early days of colonization (Hall 1971, 55; Franco 1973, 9). They had a long tradition as great empire and state builders in West Africa, dating back to centuries before the beginnings of the transatlantic slave trade, and had important warrior classes. The Brazilians developed the myth of docile Angolans, although Palmares was fundamentally (not exclusively) Angolan, and the Angolan word *mocambo* was used commonly for runaway settlements in Brazil (Flory 1979, 123; Anderson 1996, 558).

African historians do not attribute a more martial spirit to the Akan peoples than to any other group in West Africa, nor for that matter did the Akan build more powerful empires than several other groups, including the Oyo Yoruba, Kongolese and Bini, at their height at various times between the fifteenth and eighteenth centuries (Law 1977; Birmingham 1975; Ryder 1969). Clearly, in the turbulent times of slave trading and empire building in western Africa, some soldiers must have been captured and transported to the Americas. There was conflict between Akan groups throughout the period – for example, the Asante and Fante (Wilks 1975, 1985) – but this is not a reason for asserting a significantly greater warrior element among people transported from the Gold Coast. If we wish to support the thesis of a warrior class among those transported, a much stronger case can be made for warrior classes being transported from Yorubaland, where extensive intra-Yoruba fighting took place during the late seventeenth and the eighteenth centuries and became far worse during most of the nineteenth century (Law 1977; Akintoye 1971). A similar case can be made in respect of the Kongolese and Angolans, who arguably experienced much more inter- and intra-ethnic turbulence than did the Akan during the period of rampant slave trading. We have to conclude, therefore, that ethnicity had nothing to do with the warlike or docile nature of any particular African group, and that it was rather demography or some other local factors that explain the dominance of a particular ethnic group in the struggle for freedom in a specific slave society.

PART 2

Origins and Development
of Marronage

The large number of *cumbes* that were in existence [in
Venezuela] at any one time indicates an untiring rebellious-
ness, expressed not in the form of organized wars but rather
in the founding of communities that became centers of liberation for the most ill-treated slaves.

– Miguel Acosta Saignes, "Life in a Venezuelan Cumbe"

CHAPTER 3

The Imperative of Freedom

ROUTES TO FREEDOM

Enslaved peoples had only two basic routes to freedom – being given it by their oppressors or taking it themselves. Included under the first option was self-purchase or purchase by a third party (with or without the consent of the enslaver, but always with the consent of the authoritarian state); receiving freedom as a gift from the enslaver, usually because of familial relations, personal liking or some special service rendered by the enslaved person;[1] manumission by the state for exemplary "national" service, which usually meant betraying revolts or Maroon hideouts, joining special corps formed to subdue Maroons or defending the state against internal or external aggression; and legal abolition of the institution of slavery. The forcible methods of attaining freedom ranged from armed uprisings on the plantations to desertion, often involving the establishment of Maroon communities.

Large-scale internal conflicts, caused by either civil war or external invasion, provided enslaved persons with the greatest opportunities of deserting in large numbers, with every hope of making good their freedom. This happened during the British invasion of Jamaica (1655), the French Revolution and the subsequent wars that spilled over into Haiti and other parts of the French Caribbean (1789–1804), the American Revolutionary War (1776–83), the American Civil War (1861–65), the Mexican War of Independence (1810–21), the Cuban Ten Years' War (1868–78) and the many wars of independence in Latin America in the early nineteenth century. During these periods enslavers lost tens of thousands of their servile charges, who either went off quietly to make a life on their own or participated in the wars in return for the promise of freedom by either side. Many Blacks lost their lives in these wars and commonly suffered discrimination after victory was achieved, even from those with whom they had allied. Nevertheless, many of them achieved physical freedom and clothed themselves in glory by their courage, martial abilities and sometimes the medals and citations that they earned.

During the so-called abolition era in the nineteenth century, the number of runaways increased appreciably. Among the contributing circumstances were the example of actual revolution in Haiti; agitation by abolitionists; the enslaved persons' conviction that the imperial authorities had abolished slavery and the enslavers were maintaining the system illegally; a rising incidence of armed servile unrest in many parts of the Americas (closely linked to desertion); the increasing reluctance of the state authorities to sanction Maroon-hunting expeditions; and the spur that abolition in one territory gave to enslaved persons in other territories to agitate for freedom. In the last years of slavery in the Americas, thousands of enslaved people in Venezuela, Puerto Rico, the United States, Cuba and Brazil simply deserted their overlords and declared themselves free.

In extreme instances the desperate desire for freedom drove enslaved persons to commit suicide. According to Fernando Ortiz (1975, 359), this was the supreme recourse of all oppressed peoples. He goes on to state that the practice had become so common in Cuba that it was invested with the character of an epidemic, and that in that country between 1855 and 1857 there were almost twice as many suicides as homicides – at least one-third of the total carried out by enslaved persons (and another third by Chinese indentured immigrants).

Suicide often became an act of war, intended to deprive the enslaver of a valuable labour resource; at the same time it was believed that committing suicide would facilitate quick return to Africa (Ortiz 1975, 360; Oldendorp 1987, 199; Bastide 1978, 81–82; Pérez 2005, 34–53). The records contain several cases of individual suicide and a few of mass suicide. When Palmares was eventually destroyed in 1695 by a military expedition sent against it, as many as two hundred of its inhabitants are said to have committed suicide by hurling themselves from a high rock rather than returning to slavery (Kent 1979, 187; Freyre 1963, 39n5).[2] Many Bahian *quilombolas* (*calhambolas* or Maroons) and other insurgents committed suicide rather than be apprehended following their attacks on White settlements in 1814 (Reis 1993, 47). One of the most well-known cases of mass suicide occurred in St John, Virgin Islands, in 1733, when more than thirty insurgents threw themselves off the top of a hill rather than allowing themselves to be captured (Dookhan 1995, 169). In Jamaica, it is alleged that in the 1730s many of the Maroons of Nanny Town did the same thing (Harris 1994, 47).[3] In 1760, following Tackey's revolt in that same country, many of the insurgents committed suicide rather than suffer capture and brutal execution (Campbell 1990, 155–56). Several instances of mass suicide were also noted among enslaved persons in Cuba in the 1840s after aborted revolts; on one occasion in 1843, as many as forty hanged themselves (Hall 1971, 56–60).[4]

In an attempt to prevent future suicides, enslavers often severed the body parts of those who died by their own hand, to impress upon the living that if the dead made it back to their homeland it would be in mutilated form. The fact that their actions had little impact on the incidence of suicide should have taught them that they had only a vague understanding of the African world view. While some Africans undoubtedly viewed self-inflicted death as facilitating the return of the body to its homeland, most of them believed the passage involved primarily the soul or spirit. Oldendorp (1987, 199), a Moravian missionary in the Danish West Indies, was one of the few White people who understood this:

> This belief in the migration of souls has a very harmful effect on some Negroes. Thus, when slavery in the West Indies becomes too hard for them, they take their own life in the hope that their soul will wander back to their homeland and be reincarnated there in a newborn child.

A number of enslaved persons saw *marronage* as the winning ticket in the lottery of life characteristic of slave society in the Americas (Hoogbergen 1993, 165). Enslaved persons could and did revolt, but this often happened within the framework of the plantation – that is, they took over the plantation as their military base. While some of these revolts were successful in the short term, such as those in Jamaica in 1760 and Berbice in 1763, only in St Domingue (modern Haiti) between 1791 and 1804 did the insurgents manage to overthrow the slavery system (and colonialism at the same time). Enslaved persons found it very difficult to sustain and sometimes even to stage armed insurrection because of geographical, military, demographic and other factors. Indeed, in some territories, such as Puerto Rico (Soler 1970,

201), there never was a large-scale servile revolt. Such revolts generally gave the plantocracy time and opportunity to marshal their forces for counter-assaults that put the insurgency down, often with much bloodshed. However, as noted already, these revolts helped to sustain Maroon communities, since many enslaved persons seized the opportunity to run to freedom.

La Rosa Corzo (2003, 230) acknowledges the severe limitations of armed revolts on the plantations when he states that they occurred in short, unconnected periods and were quickly and violently quashed. He goes on to say that the establishment of Maroon communities increased opportunities for insurgents and had broader and more lasting temporal and spatial connections than plantation revolts. Whereas the authoritarian state used its regular repressive machinery to quell revolts, it created a special administrative machinery and specialized human and material resources to locate and destroy Maroon compounds (ibid.). It was these factors that made *marronage* more lethal in the long term than armed revolt on the plantations. In all territories that had significant numbers of enslaved persons, *marronage* held the most promising prospect of freedom and constituted the major form of servile protest and challenge to the enslavers. But the two major forms of insurgency, taken together, struck genuine terror in the hearts of enslavers.

While figures have not been compiled for any jurisdiction on the comparative incidence of manumission and of long-term *marronage*, few scholars are likely to disagree that the latter constituted by far the greater avenue to freedom. That is why the enslaved persons took it. *Marronage* was cheaper, more immediate and less uncertain, and offered a relatively easier way of life and possibly a longer lifespan.

Maroon children stood a better chance than other Black children of being brought up in a wholesome environment and being cared for directly by their parents. Pregnant and lactating mothers, and those whose children were ill, must have enjoyed greater freedom from work. This was in stark contrast to the situation in slave society, especially in the period before the late eighteenth century, when most enslavers and managers felt that it was cheaper "to buy than to breed" working hands, so mothers and pregnant women were allowed little or no special consideration. Pregnant women were often worked in the fields up to the last day or two before the expected date of childbirth, and were sent back into the fields shortly after delivery. When they were whipped, their distended bellies were placed in a special hole in the ground.

Stedman (1988, 495) recorded an almost unbelievable instance of brutality in Suriname on a woman who had broken a crystal tumbler. Although she was eight months pregnant, her overlord caused her to be whipped until her intestines protruded through her body. Many miscarriages occurred because pregnant women were whipped severely, placed in stocks, kicked in their bellies and subjected to other brutalities. Women were allowed little time to nurse their infants, who were usually removed from them and placed under the care of nannies (generally superannuated women) during the day. The worst part was that children born to enslaved mothers legally belonged to their overlords, who could dispose of them as they saw fit, by either sale or gift, without the parents' having any recourse to the law to reclaim them. This situation existed until late in the slavery period, when in some jurisdictions the separation of families by enslavers was deemed illegal.[5]

Naturally, a large number of children were born in Maroon settlements, especially in those that remained in existence for several decades. Moreau de Saint-Méry (1979, 140) mentions that among the Bahoruco Maroons there were men sixty years old who had never lived anywhere but in the forests where they had been born. According to Gautier (1985, 231), the demographic profile of the settlement in the 1780s showed that 80 of the 133 inhabitants were born there. The Curuá *mocambo* in Brazil, which a military enterprise subverted in 1877, was said to include among its inhabitants children and grandchildren of deserters, who had been born there (Conrad 1983, 392–93). Thus *marronage* provided parents with the opportunity not only of raising their children in a slave-free environment but of producing children who had never been branded as someone else's property. Moreover, it allowed both parents to play a greater role in the child's upbringing than was possible on the plantations, especially when the parents belonged to different plantations. Of course, none of this should be taken to mean that adult Maroons never abused their children.

The mechanisms by which deserters sought to gain their freedom were varied and sometimes quite ingenious. Deserters usually left quietly during the night or in the early hours of the morning; on long weekends or during festivals, when they were allowed much greater mobility to visit friends and relatives on other plantations; when they had been sent on errands or during expeditions that they joined to apprehend Maroons. They went on foot, on horseback, by boat; along roads, and through swamplands and thorn bushes. Blassingame (1979, 200) says that deserters in the southern United States who took the Underground Railroad to freedom mailed themselves in boxes, hid in the holds of northbound ships, disguised their sex, paid poor Whites to write passes for them and, when literate, wrote their own passes. They stowed away on steamboats, pretended to be so loyal and obedient that their overlords risked taking them to the North, where they absconded, or passed for White. He also tells of an enslaved person who was so trusted by his over-lord that the latter sent him in pursuit of one of his runaways, only to realize some days later that the so-called faithful Black had probably taken flight himself (ibid., 204–5). A Cuban Maroon testified that he had run away and joined El Portillo settlement in the Sierra Maestra but was captured by Andrés de Guevara, who subsequently purchased him from his overlord and promised him his freedom if he would spy on his former companions. He agreed to do so, but when he was sent out he decided to join the settlement once again (La Rosa Corzo 2003, 50–51).

The escape of William and Ellen Craft of Georgia was ingenious in its planning and brilliant in its execution. The woman, who was an illiterate quadroon, acted the part of a rich male enslaver who was hard of hearing, which prevented anyone from conversing with her (him), and carried her right arm in a poultice that prevented her from signing her name. Her hus-band acted the role of her servant, who was accompanying her to Baltimore where she was going for medical treatment. They both travelled first class on the train and made the journey to freedom without mishap (Craft 1860).

THE INDIAN AS PROTOTYPE

In dealing with the subject of *marronage,* we need to remind ourselves that it was Indians, not Africans, who constituted the first Maroons in the Americas, and who set the pattern for what was to follow years later when Africans were introduced in large numbers (Pérez de la Riva 1979, 49–50). Much has been written in the annals of Maroon expeditions about the role of Indians as Maroon catchers and bounty hunters. It is true that these people often played important, and at times crucial, roles in such expeditions, and more generally in the surveillance of areas in which White troops were not stationed and perhaps could not be stationed without endangering their lives (Pérez de la Riva 1979, 51; Bowser 1974, 201; Thompson 1987). Stedman (1988, 76) referred to those in Suriname as natural enemies to the Blacks and friends to the Europeans. Contemporary records are replete with references to their role as Maroon hunters in Suriname, Guyana, Brazil, Mexico, Venezuela, Colombia and Peru, and the "gifts" (which some writers view as a form of tribute) that the authoritarian states paid them for scouting the land in search of fugitives and for their larger military contributions in the hinterland of these countries.[6]

What is less known is that there were numerous instances of cooperation between Indians and Africans, and that some Maroon settlements comprised members of both groups (see chapter 2). Pinto Vallejos (1998, 184), for instance, states that the Indians in Brazil who mounted a sustained resistance to European aggression often found useful allies in the African runaways. Schwartz (1979, 214) points out that numerous instances are recorded of Indian villages incorporating Africans and Afro-Brazilians into their ranks, causing much concern to the Portuguese colonial authorities. The Indians revolted everywhere against European atrocities, especially in the Portuguese, Spanish and British/United States zones. They fled to remote areas; established Maroon settlements; carried away food, other goods and occasionally women (including White women); and in numerous other ways proved to be a thorn in the sides of their oppressors, forcing the latter to send out large expeditions against them (Pérez de la Riva 1979, 51; Sharp 1976, 158; Esteban Deive 1989, 29). The following brief sketch of what happened in the Dominican Republic, Mexico, Colombia and Cuba gives an idea of the kinds of Maroon activities in which the Indians engaged.

Maroons in the Dominican Republic founded the first settlements in the Bahoruco Mountains in the early sixteenth century. They were divided into several groups, joining forces temporarily as the exigencies of the situation demanded, and returning to rebuild after periodic expeditions laid waste their settlements (Esteban Deive 1989, 37, 74). Perhaps more expeditions were dispatched against this group of Maroons than any other in that country. In 1519 Enriquillo, the famous Indian Maroon leader, and his followers were located there. He attracted numerous Blacks to his *palenque* and, according to Esteban Deive (1989, 29), for the next fourteen years the Dominican Republic was in a state of turmoil. In 1523 the authoritarian state was forced to declare war officially on the Maroons and sent a military detachment against them, the cost of whose rations was to be borne by a special tax on the neighbouring White settlers. Neither this expedition nor succeeding ones managed to dislodge the Maroons permanently from their strongholds, although soldiers reported killing several and wounding others; but the Spanish also sustained heavy losses, both in the field and in Maroon attacks against the plantations. In desperation the government sought to recruit Black auxiliaries to track down the Maroons more effectively, but the settlers protested, fearing that they would join the Maroons.

In 1528 the scope of conflict was considerably enlarged by the revolt of other Indian leaders – Tamayo, Ciguayo, Murcia and Hernandillo – and their followers. The ravages they wrought in various places, from La Vega to Puerto Real and Santiago, forced many settlers to abandon their urban and rural properties and seek refuge in the capital. In 1530 the government forces, comprising trained White soldiers and Black cohorts, secured important gains over the Maroons, killing several of them, but this did not put an end to Maroon activities. Wider social unrest from the growing number of Africans being introduced into the colony as enslaved persons, and the continual flight to freedom of many of them, caused the colonial authorities to fear, no doubt exaggeratedly, that the entire island would be lost to the insurgents. The governor proposed making peace with Enriquillo, the most dominant of the Maroon leaders, offering him a pardon and his freedom, but this proposal drew strong opposition from the Audiencia and so he continued to look for a military solution to the problem.

In 1532 the imperial government named Francisco de Barrionuevo as captain-general of the war against the Bahoruco Maroons, with the mandate to bring the Indians and Africans into submission either peacefully or violently, and destroy the settlements. Barrionuevo opted for a mediated solution to the problem and struck a peace with Enriquillo in 1533, granting him a full pardon with the understanding that he would round up Indian and African Maroons.[7]

In Mexico, just three years after the destruction of the impressive Aztec empire by the Spanish *conquistadores,* Spanish records noted that African runaways were joining forces with the Zapotec Indians in Maroon communities. Over the next decades the communities increased in size and in their capacity to hurt the Spaniards. In the early days, because of their relatively small numbers, they focused mainly on attacking travellers in such places as the Veracruz–Mexico highway (Martin 1957, 120), an activity they never quite gave up during their long history of resistance. In time, they were also able to deliver lethal blows to the plantations, mines and urban centres. In 1576 their frequent attacks on the newly built town of León, from their base in Cañada de Negros, became a matter of serious concern for the colonial authorities.

Some of the Maroons were said to have become bold enough to appropriate land that was marked out for the White settlers there, and to be indulging in other "insolences". The authorities tried to capture them, but most of them escaped to other areas in the country (Martin 1957, 123).

In 1648 in the Chocó, Colombia – which was to become a principal haunt of both Indian and African Maroons in the province of Cartagena (Borrego Plá 1973, 6) – the fight was carried to the Spanish by over a thousand Indians, joined by a dozen or so African Maroons (Sharp 1976, 158). The Indians kept up their struggle for a long time, until their numbers were devastated by White military expeditions and new diseases brought by the invaders. In Cuba in 1802 two Indians were creating problems for the Whites in Filipinas, west of Havana. The colonial authorities set a much higher reward than usual, of 400 pesos, for each of their heads. However, up to 1804 one of them still remained at large, leading a small group that included Indians from Mexico and eight Blacks. In that year the colonial authorities placed 2,250 pesos on his head. The records uncovered to date are silent on what eventually transpired (La Rosa Corzo 2003, 88–89).

Even when Indian and African Maroons did not forge a unity, Whites feared that they would do so. In Belize in 1817 a magistrate expressed the view that enslaved persons would join the Mayas in the interior and that they would soon overpower and destroy all the British subjects (Bolland 2002, 55).

Indian–African Maroon activities were widespread throughout the Americas. This reality reinforces the point, made in chapter 2, that while some ethnic consciousness existed among Maroons, it was not the main factor in their relations with each other; what mattered most was their common struggle against their oppressors. Realizing this, in the latter half of the sixteenth century the Spanish imperial government repeated its decree, published earlier in Venezuela, Mexico and other Spanish domains, that no Blacks, Mulattos or Mestizos should be allowed to live among the Indians (Veracoechea 1987, 81; Dusenberry 1948, 291).

AFRICAN MARRONAGE

The story of African *marronage* is writ much larger than that of their Indian counterparts. Large-scale African enslavement in the Americas was associated almost everywhere with the establishment and development of the plantation regime, producing a variety of staples for the export market in Europe, especially sugar, cotton, cocoa and coffee. In some colonies, such as Mexico, the Dominican Republic, Colombia, Peru and Brazil, the gold- and silver-mining economies were also important users of African labour. Sugar was the crop of choice, as Europe looked abroad for a cheaper sweetener than honey. Sugar cultivation was made cheap, not simply through the ease with which the sugarcane could be grown but, more importantly, through the import of cheap labour drawn mainly from Africa. Sugar was, of course, a much higher consumer of labour than other plantation crops, but yielded profits that made the wastage of human life worthwhile to the plantocracy in financial terms. While the debate persists about whether or not the European actions against their enslaved charges constituted genocide, the fact is that in very few plantation jurisdictions in the Americas (notably in Barbados and the Southern United States) did the slavery system reproduce itself demographically over the almost four hundred years that it lasted. Eric Williams (1964, 27) muses that sugar, something so sweet, could have produced such crimes and bloodshed. W. Akroyd (1967) entitled his book on this subject *Sweet Malefactor*; Maurice Lemoine (1985) named his book *Bitter Sugar*; and Nobel laureate Vidiadhar Naipaul (1974, 62, 119) calls the crop "a brutal plant", "an ugly crop" that produced "an ugly history".

The countries with the most brutal labour histories and the most Maroon communities were all sugar-producing ones; the relationship was fundamental, but this does not mean that only countries or regions producing sugar witnessed *marronage*. Although, from the anglophone perspective, Barbados is generally regarded as the home of the "sugar revolution" in the hemisphere, the earliest major production centres were Mexico, the Dominican Republic and Brazil. These countries witnessed the earliest large-scale revolts of enslaved persons and the establishment of the first Maroon communities.

Brazil had a particularly thriving economy in Pernambuco, in the northern part of the country, until the wars with the Dutch and the Maroons knocked it on the head (Boxer 1965). It also witnessed by far the largest and most sophisticated Maroon state in the Americas, often referred to as the Republic of Palmares,[8] a *quilombo* located in the huge forest on the Ipanema River in the interior of Alagôas and Pernambuco. Substantial *quilombos* also mushroomed in Minas Gerais, Mato Grosso, Goias, Bahia, Maranhão, Sergipe and elsewhere. The country became an important haunt of Maroon communities from the first years of Portuguese colonization. The number and size of these communities began to grow appreciably during the period of warfare between the Portuguese and Dutch (1630 to 1654), and *marronage* remained a major problem for the enslavers until the last days of Brazilian slavery.

In all plantation societies in the Americas, the slavery system led to extreme tensions between the enslavers and the enslaved. What Richard Price and Sally Price (1988, xiv) say of the situation in Suriname in the late eighteenth century is apposite to all mature plantation societies, *mutatis mutandis*: "[T]his was a maximally polarized society – some three thousand European whites . . . living in grotesque luxury off the forced labor of some fifty thousand brutally exploited African slaves." By that time Suriname had reached a crisis stage due to Maroon assaults – a condition at which Haiti had arrived around the same time, Jamaica in the 1730s, and Brazil somewhat earlier. In all these places except Haiti, the Whites managed to keep the slavery system intact but at tremendous personal and official (state) cost in terms of money, human lives and social liberties. As noted in chapter 1, slave resistance and revolt led to appallingly draconian legislation and brutality in the attempt to exercise control over other humans. But the enslaved persons' often equally violent reaction to the brutalities of the slavery system bred a pervasive fear among the enslavers and their families. Both predator and prey were affected by the dehumanizing influence of slavery.

Thousands of Maroon communities must have existed, and hundreds of thousands of enslaved persons must have fled from their overlords in various parts of the Americas, during the period that the *encomienda* and slavery lasted. Fouchard (1972, 174–75) examined the advertisements published in Haiti between 1764 and 1793 and calculated a stunning total of forty-eight thousand runaways in that country alone, located principally in Plymouth in the south and Le Maniel in the southeast. He makes what he considers an informed guess that only about 25 per cent of the runaways were caught (ibid., 34–39). However, David Geggus (1986, 114–17) takes him to task on this score, suggesting that he grossly over-represented the number of runaways by counting some runaways three times or more. Geggus suggests that "the number of runaways jailed is the best guide we have to the extent of marronage in Saint Domingue", although he notes the grave imperfections in such data, including the fact that on numerous occasions slaveholders did not bother to give notice of runaways or returnees. Philip Morgan (1986, 57) may be correct in suggesting that advertisements of runaways in South

Carolina (with application to a number of other slaveholding societies) constituted only "the most visible tip of an otherwise indeterminate iceberg". In Brazil, Whites tended to view the *mocambos* established by runaways as "African malignancies" (Flory 1979, 124).

The structure, durability, political and social culture, and internal and external relationships of Maroon communities were influenced by a number of factors, including the geographical size of the White colonial state; topography and ecology; the relative sizes of the different population groups (Indian, African and European); the spread of European settlement; the nature of the economic (generally plantation) regime; the various African societies in which the Maroons originated; the length of time individuals had been enslaved and their specific experience of enslavement; and both general and specific reasons for which individual Maroons absconded.

Maroon societies that were founded in the early days of plantation settlement had more space in which to range, because of the restricted nature of the plantations. But they also were probably forced to depend more completely on their own resources and ingenuity to provide goods that would have been more readily available in a fully developed plantation economy, such as firearms, tools and household utensils. The older Maroon societies, enjoying presumably a greater measure of autonomy (or at least freedom from European assault) and a longer period of evolution, would have developed stronger and more stable political, social and other structures than more recent settlements. Therefore, over a period of time, Maroon communities reflected important differences in both physical and social organization. The gravity of the problems that they presented to the enslavers was expressively summed up by a British officer in Jamaica who spoke of them as "the enemy in our bowels" (Campbell 1990, 21). Contemporary official and private correspondence in Jamaica repeatedly refers to the Maroons as the "intestine enemies" (Campbell 1990, 58, 75, 83, 84, 99 passim).

URBAN AND MARITIME MARRONAGE

African Maroon communities sprang up from the very early days of Black slavery in the Americas and were as ubiquitous as slavery itself. They became a significant problem in both the large and small territories, though in the latter case more in terms of the loss of labour value than of attacks on White society. Whether in small or large slaveholding states, under plantation or non-plantation regimes, a significant number of enslaved persons sought freedom through flight. However, the problem of space to manoeuvre, if not peculiar to, was at least exacerbated in small islands.

As the plantation system developed in places like St Kitts (St Christopher), St John (part of the Danish and later US Virgin Islands) and Barbados, the bush cover became more sparse, so Maroons had less space and cover in which to hide. While this did not decrease the incidence of desertion, because of the growth in the size of the enslaved population and the increased rigours of the slavery system the deserters had to contrive other means of maintaining their freedom. Some of them gravitated towards the towns, passing themselves off as freed persons, and working for Whites, free Coloureds and free Blacks who did not ask too many questions about their legal status. Bridgetown, for a long time the main port city in the British Caribbean, provided opportunities for runaways to ensconce themselves among the free Black population (Mullin 1992, 38; Handler 2002, 2, 13). The Free Gut and Water Gut areas in St Croix offered the same kind of protection, forcing the colonial government to pass laws prohibiting enslaved persons from living among freed persons who occupied these areas, though the law was not rigorously enforced. Freedmen actually married fugitives, and in one instance a person who harboured runaways declared that he had done nothing wrong since it was common practice to do so (Donoghue 2002, 115, 154–55; Hall 1992, 126, 161).

In Guatemala, the shipbuilding activities of colonists on the Pacific coast in the early seventeenth century greatly facilitated desertion (Lokken 2004b, 47). In the Danish West Indies, the islands' proximity to the Spanish settlements at Vieques, Culebra and Puerto Rico proved to be an attraction that many enslaved persons could not resist, especially since they were assured that the Spanish authorities would not send them back. In fact, in 1714 Governor Don Jan de Rivera offered several of them asylum and helped them to establish the San Mateo de Cangrejos settlement there (Donoghue 2002, 82). The colonial authorities in the Danish West Indies, rebuffed in their efforts to secure an extradition agreement with their counterparts in Puerto Rico, adopted several measures to arrest the flow of maritime Maroons. These measures included requiring all "canoe" or small-boat owners to register their vessels with the appropriate department; prohibiting the building, sale or other transfer of ownership of such vessels without official permission; and preventing the rental or sale of such vessels except in designated harbours (Donoghue 2002, 156–57; Oldendorp 1987, 36; Hall 1992, 127–29). Although the laws were periodically renewed and refined, and the sanctions against delinquents were increased, these measures had little or no effect on the incidence of maritime *marronage.*

The situation in Bermuda was somewhat different. Its small size – only twenty-one square miles – and its high concentration on seafaring activities that employed many enslaved persons theoretically gave many of them the opportunity of absconding. Like the Danish West Indies, Bermuda had a comparatively less rigorous system of slavery than the plantation colonies, and also stringent laws and measures to prevent fugitives seizing boats in the harbours to make good their escape. However, the relative geographical isolation of the Bermuda islands seems to have been the main factor that prevented large-scale desertion from that colony (Packwood 1975, 21–38).

It is perhaps appropriate to interject here that the plantations and small farms also offered the runaways shelter among the Blacks, free Coloureds and Whites who lived there. Here, too, farmers found their labour useful for a variety of purposes, including cultivating their fields, tending their cattle and engaging in domestic chores. Moreover, they did not have to invest high-risk funds in purchasing labour hands, especially in volatile situations of extensive *marronage*; they did not have to pay head taxes; and they hired this kind of labour dirt cheap, precisely because they held a sort of Damocles sword over the fugitives.[9] All this, of course, had to be done surreptitiously, but to many employers it was worth the risk because the potential financial savings were huge.

It was not only in the small island communities that rural-to-urban (and sometimes urban-to-urban) flight was common. Jamaica, Cuba, the United States, Haiti, Mexico, Peru and Brazil, among others, were greatly affected by what the authorities perceived as an urban menace. Indeed, urban Maroons were prevalent in all slavery jurisdictions in the Americas and drew the attention of lawmakers, who passed stringent laws against harbouring such people. In Mexico, Mestizos, Indians and Blacks increasingly jostled for space in the small and large towns, and by the early eighteenth century the free Black and mixed populations had become so large, due to manumissions and natural reproduction among free persons, that the urban Maroons could live among them with little chance of detection (Pereira 1994, 96). The situation was not so different in nineteenth-century Rio de Janeiro, Brazil (Karasch 1987, 304,

310). Haiti provides an outstanding example of a small to medium-sized country where Maroons embedded themselves in the urban centres and passed for free with relative ease (Fouchard 1972, 33–40). Deschamps Chapeaux (1983, 14; see also 17–18, 53–54) writes that the outer suburbs of Havana constituted an immense *palenque* to which many deserters fled. Wade (1968, 104, 105) explains how the phenomenon of "undisciplined low life" in the southern cities of the United States lent itself very readily to urban *marronage*:

> In the metropolis the worlds of bondage and freedom overlapped. The line between free blacks and slaves became hopelessly blurred. Even whites and blacks found their lives entangled in some corners of the institution of slavery. No matter what the law said or the system required, this layer of life expanded. Though much of it was subterranean, at points it could be easily seen. The mixed balls, the numberless grog and grocery shops, the frequent religious gatherings, and the casual acquaintances in the streets were scarcely private. Physical proximity bred a certain familiarity that most residents came to expect.

In these cities, as in many others, hiring out of enslaved persons or placing them on self-hire (hiring them out to themselves for a sum of money) was common, despite the unavoidable risk of their desertion – and many of them did desert. Even in more cloistered circumstances they found means of escaping. In Lima, Peru, an enslaved female in the convent of Santa Clara disguised herself as a male and slipped out among the construction crew that was working on the building (Bowser 1974, 189). Thus we find a curious situation in which people fled both to and from the urban areas to escape slavery. But, as we shall see shortly, they also fled to and from certain slavery jurisdictions for the same reason.

An interesting feature of rural-to-urban and sometimes urban-to-urban *marronage* was the emergence and development of the Underground Railroad[10] in the United States to transfer runaways surreptitiously from the southern slave states to the northern free states and Canada. The uniqueness of the Railroad lay not in its conception but in the degree of organization, the scope of the network, and the dedication of a large number of Whites, Coloureds and Blacks, who risked their freedom and often their lives to ensure the freedom of enslaved persons, in defiance of state and federal laws relating to the sheltering of fugitives. They encouraged enslaved persons to flee from their overlords; organized rest houses along the escape route; provided clothing, food and money for those who needed it; and often found new homes and employment for them. In other words, it was a network that did not see its job completed until the runaway was at least partially rehabilitated, mainly through the vigilance committees (usually arms of the Black church) with which it was closely associated and which were organized mainly by free Blacks (Quarles 1969, 99, 102).

The organizational and leadership core were largely Quakers, many of whom, from the late seventeenth century, were staunchly opposed to slavery, which they considered to be an abomination in the sight of God. They were in the forefront of the movement for abolition in Britain and also deeply influenced the movement for abolition in the United States. They drew the ire of the southern enslavers, many of whom regarded them as emissaries of the devil.

The Railroad seems to have begun its work in the late eighteenth century, but 1804 (or at least the early nineteenth century) is usually considered its founding date. The organization is believed to have engaged more than thirty-two hundred active workers and to have helped one hundred thousand fugitives to freedom in the northern United States and Canada between 1810 and 1850 (Franklin 1980, 190–94). As the Railroad became known in the North, whole communities in such places as Pennsylvania and Ohio voiced their support for its work. Quakers and others raised funds and often provided their own funds to meet the expense of running the Railroad.

The history of the Railroad is peopled with an array of personalities of all colours and classes. Among the Whites were the Quaker Levi Coffin, nominal president of the Railroad (Quarles 1969, 79), who helped more than three thousand people to escape; Calvin Fairbanks, who transported a large but undetermined number of people across the Ohio River, and was jailed twice and placed in irons for his part in assisting escapees; John Fairfield, who was once shot attempting to help escapees but continued his work; and John Brown, who led out a multitude of captives and became so immersed in the cause of liberation that he led an unsuccessful revolt of enslaved persons, for which he was later executed (Franklin 1980, 192–94, 202–3).

The most celebrated of the "conductors" was Harriett Tubman, a runaway who made it to freedom and who in turn led as many as three hundred people out of bondage, and also worked as a spy and informant for the Union Army. Periodically, she would work as a domestic to obtain funds to help the cause. Other Black people involved in the Railroad included Jane Lewis, who

ferried runaways across the Ohio River; Josiah Henson, who escaped to
Canada with his wife and two children and later devoted his life to helping
fellow fugitives; and Elijah Anderson, a tireless worker, credited with helping
more than a thousand people gain freedom before he lost his own, dying in
prison for the cause. There was also John Mason, himself a runaway, who was
once caught while working as a "conductor" and re-enslaved but managed to
escape. He is credited with helping to free some thirteen hundred enslaved
persons (Franklin 1980, 191–94; Quarles 1969, 78–80).

When the US Civil War broke out in 1861, the Railroad lost its importance, since enslaved persons found numerous opportunities to flee *en masse*
to the Union side. More than one hundred thousand of them, according to
William Freehling (2002, 2–3, 11–15), joined the Union Army and played an
important role in the victory over the South. People of all ages and sizes fled
to the nearest point of refuge.

Debien (1979, 125–26) asserts that in the French Caribbean, *marronage* was
more common among urban Creoles (perhaps proportionately) than among
plantation hands, since the former had much greater mobility and skills that
were needed. They fled from one town to another and sometimes lived close
to the ports, which afforded a great measure of anonymity to many transient
labourers congregated there. He stresses the complicity of those port employers who did not inquire too closely into the legal status of their new employ-
ees and provided them with more secure hiding places than the thickets and
hills, or embarkation to another destination. Given the widespread practice
of enslavers failing to report those who had absconded, it is difficult to con-
firm the accuracy of Debien's statement. His perception of the relative safety
of the urban Maroon compared with his rural or maritime counterpart is not
persuasive, unless we adopt his perspective that the typical rural Maroon lived
a vagabond life, preying on the small free Black and Coloured farmlands (a
view put forward by enslavers who lost their servile charges in this way).

Contrary to Debien's idea, most writers suggest that flight into the deep
recesses of the hinterland or to an overseas political jurisdiction beyond the
skyline afforded Maroons a greater and more meaningful freedom than hiding in urban tenements. In fact, arguably, the most common form of desertion for urban enslaved persons was what some writers call maritime
marronage – that is, taking jobs on board ships leaving the islands, paying
ship captains to spirit them away to foreign lands, forcing owners of small
vessels to do so, or stealing small vessels found anywhere along the coast and

striking out for the most secure nearby haven. Others joined maritime marauders – pirates, buccaneers, filibusters, corsairs and so on, as they were variously termed.[11] In the early days, Puerto Rico was a primary destination for maritime Maroons from the British and Danish West Indies, Cuba for those from Jamaica, and Trinidad, St Vincent, Martinique and St Lucia for those from Barbados. It took several years before the colonial powers were able to conclude treaties, especially with Spain, to extradite such Maroons (chapter 9).

Northern and western Hispaniola, Tortuga and other places that offered relatively secure havens became the haunts of these people, who knew allegiance to no country (Lane 1998, 97–102). In the first half of the seventeenth century, Dieguillo el Mulato, a runaway from Havana, in alliance with Dutch privateers, became the greatest scourge of the Spaniards along the Central American coast. He established himself on the Bay Islands off the Honduran coast and attacked Trujillo, Santo Tomas de Castilla, and other trading posts in the Golfo Dulce (Lake Izabal). A Spanish attempt in 1638 to come to terms with him failed, and in the 1640s he formed an alliance with the French privateer Jean Gareabuc (Juan Garabú). Years before and after Dieguillo's time, many runaways ensconced themselves in and around the mountains of the Golfo Dulce region, and, along with their Indian allies, became thorns in the sides of the Spanish settlers (Lokken 2004b, 47–49; Landers 1999, 20–21).

It is clear, as this chapter has demonstrated, that runaways took any and every route to freedom that lay open to them and created openings where they did not seem to exist. Urban *marronage* was an important dimension of the struggle for freedom, but in spite of the large numbers, especially of women and skilled persons, who found the cities as an appealing way out of their bondage, arguably they lived too close to the edge of slavery, too close to the enslavers, which placed them in the position of offering the enslavers secret service, sometimes bordering on servitude. Many of them were exploited by their employers, who paid them very little for their labour because they recognized the fugitives' vulnerability and dependency on them, and could turn them out or, worse still, turn them over to the judicial authorities at any moment. In contrast, although life in Maroon settlements in the deep recesses of the forests or mountains held far more rigorous challenges than in urban environments, the rural dwellers had a greater sense of freedom and independence and were free from the subtle or open exploitation to which their urban counterparts were usually subject.

CHAPTER 4

Establishment of Maroon Communities

CREATING A LIFE OF THEIR OWN

Marronage defined most clearly the conflict between Blacks and Whites, the struggle between the forces of freedom on the one hand and bondage on the other. Some writers suggest that the plantation's nemesis was the *palenque*, the first a death-dealing institution and the second a life-giving one, though others regard the contrast as being somewhat overdrawn. Nicolás del Castillo Mathieu's (1982, 89–90n106) observation that *marronage* became more or less endemic in Cartagena from 1570 is equally applicable to all the large plantation societies in the Americas, though with differing time frames.[1] David Nassy (1788, 1:87) declares that especially in the second half of the eighteenth century Suriname became a theatre of continuous warfare as a result of Maroon activities and Maroon-hunting expeditions organized by the authoritarian state. Guillermo Baralt (1982, 31–45, 158–59) notes that Bayamon in Puerto Rico became notorious for desertions (though relatively few Maroon settlements actually developed anywhere in the island). A common view is that where opportunities existed for large-scale *marronage*, such as in Mexico, Cuba, Brazil and Suriname, revolts based on the plantations were less common. This view has some merit, but Jamaica provides the outstanding exception; there, *marronage* and revolt on the plantations were both common and large scale. This is why that country gained such notoriety for insurrections, at least within the British circuit of slavery.

Under slavery Blacks were led as sheep to the slaughter, but the enslavers were to realize that many of them were really wolves in sheep's clothing. The so-called docile, malleable labourer was now transformed into a fearsome militant who stood on equal terms with the enslaver. Under the bondage of slavery he would mimic his overlord during festival occasions such as Christmas; under the freedom of *marronage* he would taunt his former overlord at any time, but especially during military encounters. As an enslaved person he was relegated to a subhuman being; as a Maroon he claimed equality with all human beings. Under slavery his overlord reserved the right to name him; under freedom he chose the name that pleased him, even if it was that of his former overlord. Purchased as a cheap commodity under slavery, he became a very expensive one, through both the depredations[2] that he carried out against the enslavers and the cost of the military expeditions to apprehend him. In these and many other ways the Maroon showed that he was not prepared to accept the enslaver's definition of him, but would define himself as he saw fit. Some writers see him as a "slave" transformed under freedom, but really he was a freedom fighter who had been kept in the prison of slavery for a while. This perception led Michael Craton (1982, 25) to assert that there was no really docile enslaved person.

It is almost entirely guesswork to determine the number of Maroon communities that existed at a given time in a particular country. Most authorities seem to agree that there were a number of small groups involving a few dozen people in all the large slaveholding states, as well as several medium and large aggregations. Small islands such as Barbados and the group comprising the Danish West Indies also possessed Maroon settlements, especially in the early years of colonization, before the bush cover was removed. In Barbados, the many gullies and ravines in the parish of St Thomas provided sanctuary for quite a few Maroons for a long time (Handler 8–9), while in the Danish West Indies the hills of St Croix were known Maroon habitats (Donoghue 2002, 115). It is generally believed that most of the small groups tried, as far as possible, to ensconce themselves in remote terrain, to live in quiet harmony with the surrounding fauna and flora, and to pass into oblivion as far as the slaveholding state was concerned. But there were also medium-sized and occasionally large groups that did not harry the Whites, preferring to farm the land and rear livestock, and sometimes carry on a secret trade with European interlopers. The Maroons and their descendants in Bluefields and Pearl Lagoon, Nicaragua, were two such groups, though they had to guard constantly against British and Spanish attempts to ensnare them and return them to slavery (Gordon 1998, 37–38).

Periodically, military expeditions accidentally came across or were told about Maroon settlements, containing upwards of fifty people, that they never knew existed. Two of these groups in the Dominican Republic in the early seventeenth century contained around seventy people each (Esteban Deive 1989, 70–72). In Cuba, it was fairly common for regularly dispatched Maroon-hunting expeditions to locate such settlements (La Rosa Corzo 2003, 124, 180 passim). The Todos Tenemos *palenque,* which an expeditionary force stumbled upon, contained between one hundred and two hundred souls (La Rosa Corzo 2003, 200–201). But there were other groups that adopted a more militant stance, ravaging plantations, outlying settlements and urban areas, and leaving destruction behind them. These were the Maroons who were most feared, the ones against whom the authoritarian states sent out frequent search parties – which cost considerable sums of money – and with whom the authorities had sometimes to seek a peaceful accommodation.

This is not to suggest that the enslavers were usually prepared to let live any Maroons – in small or large, new or old settlements – who were willing to engage in peaceful dialogue with them. Far from it: the fact that enslaved persons could and did drift from their assigned place in the hierarchy of human society was anathema to the authorities. This is why the authorities often searched out and attacked small, obscure, out-of-the-way settlements, such as those in the rugged, densely forested river valleys of Grão-Pará and Maranhão in Brazil (Conrad 1983, 386), which were usually more interested in peaceful coexistence than confrontation.

EXAMPLES OF MAROON COMMUNITIES

As noted in the introduction, this study will not provide a detailed or chronological history of the vast number of Maroon communities. Instead, it will discuss a few of the main communities in the context of their emergence and the problems they posed to the slaveholders. Succeeding chapters will elaborate several of the themes that will arise in this chapter.

The Spanish had the earliest and longest experience of *marronage.* They were the first European inhabitants of the hemisphere, they instituted the earliest regimes of enslavement of Indians and Africans, and they were virtually the last to abolish slavery, doing so (in the case of Cuba) only two years before the Brazilians abolished the institution in 1888. In a real sense, Spanish America provided the prototype of the slavery system – the laws introduced, the punishments exacted and so on – for both plantations and Maroon settlements, and of the kinds of interactions that occurred between Maroons and other groups within the region. Arguably, the Maroons etched their names and deeds more deeply into the body politic of Spanish-American society than was the case in other European jurisdictions, although the heroism of the Jamaican, Surinamese, Brazilian and Haitian Maroons may loom larger in the popular literature of the region than that of the Spanish. While Spanish America might not have thrown up as many dynamic Maroon polities or colourful personalities as did their European counterparts, the deeds and daring of the Spanish Maroons still spring to life on the pages of history, and seem to have forcefully embedded themselves in the psyche of all ethnic groups within Spanish America. Certainly, one gets the impression that the physical landscape testifies widely to the Maroon heritage through place names. Significantly, it was Spanish America that gave the term *cimarrón* to the activities of the groups that became known as Maroons when other European linguistic groups later adopted and modified the term.

The year 1503 marks the first recorded case of African Maroons in the Americas: fugitives in the Dominican Republic (Hispaniola) (Bryant 2004, 12). In 1513 flight and attacks by *ladinos* (Africans brought from Spain after some period of residence there) introduced into that colony had become so disturbing that the colonial treasury asked the Crown to restrict licences to import them. Ironically, at the outset the Spanish were reluctant to import *bozales* (Africans brought directly to the colonies from Africa) since they were regarded as non-Christian, uncivilized and likely to corrupt public morals. As a result of the unrest created by *ladinos,* however, voices were increasingly raised to import *bozales* instead, on the basis that they would be more tractable and uncontaminated by the evils of civilization. But the *bozales* revolted and ran away too, demonstrating that it was neither civilization nor its lack that led to flight but rather the harsh conditions of slavery in a Spanish colony where sugar was already becoming an export commodity (Esteban Deive 1989, 24–29, 33–36; Toletino 1974, 179). Few Spaniards heard the message, and most eventually concluded that all Africans were wild and uncivilized.

In time, some notable African Maroon states emerged in the Spanish zone: in the Dominican Republic, Mexico, Venezuela, Panama (part of colonial Colombia) and Colombia. From the late sixteenth century, the colonists in the Dominican Republic were anxious about the build-up of Maroon communities in the northern area of the colony. By the early seventeenth century, the depredations of the northern band of Maroons had placed the colony in a state of extreme deprivation and misery. Exports had practically ceased because of the collapse of the cattle trade, so the government had to mint money to pay for imports and the salaries of the bureaucracy and military (Esteban Deive 1989, 69). However, a stepped-up government policy of attrition, accompanied by offers of peace, led to a considerable reduction in Maroon activities, and within a few years they had ceased to be a major problem to the colonial authorities. But the area soon became a haven for buccaneers, many of whom the Spanish had driven out of St Kitts. These welcomed runaways and others who for various reasons sought their company, and soon became a new menace to the Spanish. Blacks became an integral part of buccaneer "society", whose members, according to Derby (2003, 20), were intensely loyal to one another. Some of the buccaneers moved on to the small island of Tortuga, where they multiplied rapidly and gave the island notoriety as the prime settlement of maritime outlaws from all nations. Derby (2003, 16) refers to the island as the "acropolis" of these renegades who roved the seas, extending their activities to Cuba, Hispaniola, Puerto Rico, Jamaica, Cartagena and Veracruz. In 1634 the Spanish sent a strong expedition, consisting of four hundred soldiers and mariners, to root them out. The Spanish killed several and captured 195 Frenchmen and Englishmen in addition to other prisoners, including thirty to forty Blacks. The rest of the band sought refuge with their brethren on the northern coast of the main island (Esteban Deive 1989, 75–76), but later regrouped and re-infested Tortuga.

Government attention turned once again to the Bahoruco region, where the Maroon population had become larger and more menacing than ever. The governor, Gómez de Sandoval, decided to take the field against them, along with a few other government officials and a significant number of White soldiers and Black auxiliaries. The governor's presence signalled his personal commitment to wiping out the sanctuaries that had aggregated, and his own personal bravery served as an inspiration to his followers. The journey was rough, especially through the steep and lofty mountains, and the scuffles with the Maroons were dangerous, but the governor and his party proved equal to the task. Several Maroons were killed or caught but the majority escaped. At Sandoval's death in 1623, the Maroon "problem" in that area still remained unresolved (Esteban Deive 1989, 74–75).

For much of the eighteenth century the Bahoruco Maroons, consisting mainly of deserters from the French colony, struck such fear into the hearts of the planters in Haiti and the Dominican Republic that eventually the French and Spanish colonial authorities decided to send a joint expedition against them. The expedition comprised at least 180 French fighting men and an undisclosed number of Spanish. The French later sent further reinforcements, but after spending some three months chasing after the Maroons through very difficult terrain, and at one time being forced to drink their own urine, the members of the expedition decided to retreat, with a much reduced complement of only eighty men. The cost of the expedition was estimated at 80,000 *livres*. The "border Maroons" (130 of them) were only quieted in 1785 through an *entente* between them and the Spanish government, which the French government in Haiti supported (Moreau de Saint-Méry 1979, 136–40; chapter 9).[3]

In Panama, especially during the sixteenth and seventeenth centuries, a large number of *palenques* emerged along the Charges River and in the dense forest that surrounded the main Spanish towns. The best-known *palenques* were Quita Fantasia, Matachín, Puerto Faisán, Pacora, Barbacoas, San Juan de Pequení, Palenque de Bayano and Gorgona. King Bayano (Bayamo), as he is often called, was the most celebrated Maroon leader in the country. He became the scourge of the White colonists in the mid-sixteenth century. He attacked the Spanish caravans that travelled to Nombre de Dios loaded with gold, silver and precious stones for shipment to Spain. The Spanish commander, Pedro de Orsua, experienced great difficulty in subduing him. Eventually, the government reached an accord with him and recognized his settlement as an autonomous unit (La Guardia 1977, 85–91). As noted previously, sometimes the Panamanian Maroons allied with French and British interlopers to rob the Spanish of their wealth, just as the Spanish were robbing the Indians. They used the forests to make pursuit difficult, especially for European forces untrained in fighting in such terrain (Díez Castillo 1981, 31–43; Campbell 1990, 8; Andrews 1978, 140).

In Cartagena province, by the late sixteenth century a number of Maroon settlements had emerged in the northern, central and southern massifs. Among the most well known were San Miguel, Matudere, Arenal, Palenque Cimarrón, and Palenque del Norosí. In the early seventeenth century the most famous *palenque* was Matuna, led by Domingo Bioho (King Benkos), some twenty leagues[4] from Cartagena, until he was captured and hanged in 1621. Other important *palenques* proliferated in the neighbouring province of Santa Marta and elsewhere.[5]

In the sixteenth century, especially with the growth of sugar plantations in Mexico, Maroon communities began to mushroom in Pachuca, Huaspaltepec, Alvarado, Guanajuato, Misantla, Tlalixcoyan, Huatulco, Coatzacoalcos, Tlacotalpan, Zongolica, Huatusco, Rinconada, Río Branco, Orizaba, Antón Lizardo, Medellin and Cuernavaca (Franco 1973, 20). The slopes of and low-lands between Mount Orizaba and Veracruz, along with Córdoba and Jalapa, became the most renowned Maroon haunts in the country (Davidson 1979, 92–93; Carroll 1991, 89–92; Bryant 2004, 12–13). In Cuba, also, substantial Maroon communities emerged, especially from the seventeenth century, par-ticularly in the eastern area, where the topography sheltered their settlements and made it difficult for the Whites to ferret them out. These communities established the first alliances between Indians and Africans, fighting against the common European enemy. Some of them also established alliances with the British, French and Dutch interlopers.

The most well-known of the Maroon wars, as they were called, took place in Suriname in the second half of the eighteenth century. That colony had a long history of *marronage*, going back to the period when the British first settled the colony in the early seventeenth century.[6] When the Dutch took over the colony as a result of the Treaty of Breda (1667), they discovered that a substantial group called the Conde (Condi) Maroons, under Chief Jermes, who had first settled on the Para Creek (a tributary of the Surinam River), and later on the Coppename River, were posing a serious threat to the plan-tations. In 1684 the colonial government made a peace treaty with them (Hartsinck 1770, 649), and this considerably reduced the assaults for some years. However, other Maroon settlements gradually built up on other rivers.

In 1690–93, in the wake of aborted revolts, several enslaved persons took to the forests and established settlements on the Saramaka River; they were later called the Saramaka Maroons. Further to the east, the Ndjukas were gradually building up their group of settlements, also profiting from aborted revolts and numerous runaways. By the mid-eighteenth century these Maroons had become a major problem for the plantocracy. As De Groot (1977, 523) notes, the situation evolved into guerrilla warfare between the authoritarian state and these groups. Other, smaller groups, such as the

Mwintis (Kofimakas) and Matawais, also existed, but these received less attention from the authoritarian state. In 1738 the number of Maroons in the "bush" was estimated at six thousand (De Groot 1977, 522–23). The government was finally forced to make peace with them: the Ndjukas in 1760, the Saramakas in 1762, and the Matawais in 1767. The Maroons scrupulously observed the terms of the treaties as far as raids on the plantations were concerned, and they periodically became cohorts of the colonial government, scouring the forests and rivers to apprehend and return runaways for bounties, as specified in the treaties (see chapter 10). However, they were neither systematic nor thorough, and gradually new Maroon establishments took root and older ones grew once again.

The most famous of these groups was the Aluku (Boni) Maroons, who existed at the time that the 1760s treaties were signed. However, the colonial government deemed them so insignificant that it did not bother to offer them treaties. Within a short time, because they now offered the most attractive haven to runaways, and due to the elaboration of plantations along the Cottica and Commewijne rivers, their numbers swelled rapidly, and by the early 1770s they were a dreaded force in the eyes of the plantocracy. They had settled behind the plantations whose life they were gradually sucking out through depredations against them and welcoming deserters into their ranks (Stedman 1988, 27–29; Price and Price 1988, xxi–xxii).

Faced with this situation and the repeated failures of military expeditions against the Maroons, in 1772 the government decided – amidst the fears of many White colonists and strong opposition from a few of them – to form a free corps of Black soldiers (variously referred to as *Korps Kwarte Jagers, Redi Musu, Neger Vrijcorps* and *Corps Vrije Negers*), generally known in English as Black Rangers. They also hired mercenaries from Europe to fight against the Maroons between 1772 and 1777. They forced many of the Aluku to take refuge in the border colony of French Guiana, but they had not got rid of their dreaded enemy. This only happened in the early 1790s – in what is popularly referred to as the Second Boni War (1789–93) – with the help of the Ndjukas, their new allies, who killed Boni, the Aluku leader, and together with some twelve hundred professional European soldiers drove the bulk of his followers across the Marowijne River into French Guiana. In 1860 the government finally recognized the freedom of the Maroons in Suriname, just three years before the official abolition of slavery in that colony (though abolition was followed by a ten-year period of "apprenticeship").

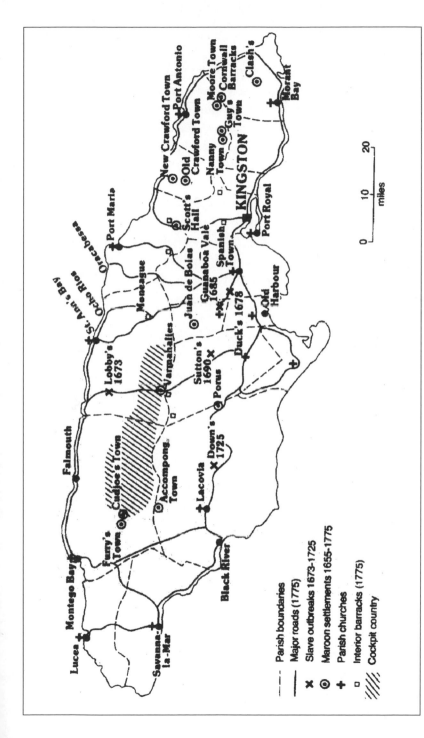

Figure 7. Jamaica: The Maroon phase 1655–1775. From *Black Rebels: African–Caribbean Freedom Fighters in Jamaica*, by Werner Zips; trans. S.L. Fisch (Kingston: Ian Randle, 1999). Used by permission of the publisher.

Jamaica provides another outstanding (and earlier) example of the triumph of Maroon societies against the odds. The origins of large-scale *marronage* in that country have been traced directly to the British onslaught against the Spanish in 1655, encouraged in part by the Spanish, who sought to use the enslaved persons as military allies to rebuff the alien invasion. However, many of the enslaved persons had the foresight to opt out of the system altogether, and were not quieted until about three-quarters of a century later, when the British made peace with them.

Throughout the late seventeenth century and until 1739, various Maroon groups wrought havoc on the White settlements. The most famous of these were the Juan de Bolas, Karmahaly, Leeward and Windward groups. Numerous expeditions dispatched against them failed to do any significant material or bodily damage to them, while a number of trained soldiers and civilians suffered deaths and wounds at their hands. Sir Thomas Modyford, governor of the colony, actually drew up Articles of War in 1665.[7] In 1687 the government was bewailing the creeping mortality of certain parishes and outlying settlements as a result of Maroon depredations. In that year the legislature noted that the settlements in St George were among the most vulnerable nodes, and that unless financial assistance came from the parish vestries to maintain a standing expeditionary force, most of the settlements in that parish would be taken over by the Maroons and adjacent settlements threatened. Further, the whole area was likely to prove a great attraction to prospective runaways, thus endangering the welfare of the colonists in the island (Campbell 1990, 41, 55).[8] The penury of the island's treasury was a frequent complaint of the governors and colonial legislature.[9] The British eventually signed treaties with Juan de Bolas in the late 1660s, and with the Leewards and Windwards in 1739.

Cuba was different from Mexico, Venezuela and other Spanish territories, for although *marronage* commenced from the early days of enslavement the colony did not witness large Maroon settlements before the nineteenth century. It also had most of its early problems with small groups of so-called vagabond runaways and bandits who lived largely by brigandage. According to La Rosa Corzo (2003, 42), it was only in 1747 that the first known expedition against a Maroon settlement took place, against El Portillo (Cabo Cruz, El Masio), which had snuggled undisturbed for twenty years in the Sierra Maestra massifs. The settlement consisted of only nineteen adults and two children at that time. The inhabitants deserted the settlement on the approach of the expedition, but eleven of them were captured. The others reoccupied the settlement after the expeditionary force had departed, and the *palenque* survived other assaults (La Rosa Corzo 2003, 42–66, 73, 227).

The vast majority of *palenques* (and almost all of the large ones) emerged in the eastern region of the island during the early part of the nineteenth century and became a lethal force in that area; they ceased to be a major problem in the 1850s. Their preferred habitat was the Frijol Mountains, which showed a much higher concentration of groups than elsewhere. The most important factor there was the steepness of the mountains, which made ascent extremely hazardous and enabled the inhabitants of the *palenques* to observe the terrain for miles around without being detected (La Rosa Corzo 2003, 117–67). La Rosa Corzo (ibid., 85, 95–97, 145, 169–222 passim) provides the most rational (if not completely persuasive) explanation to date for the great reduction in the number of *palenques* in the eastern region from the 1850s.

First, from the late eighteenth century military expeditions sent against the Maroons were extremely well organized and coordinated state-authorized and state-financed expeditions. They usually involved four or more groups of at least twenty-five armed men, commanded by a high-ranking officer, moving simultaneously into a given area and scouring the entire land, so as to reduce the Maroons' room to manoeuvre. These expeditions often lasted as long as two months and were usually led by professionals who had acquired a good knowledge of the terrain. Second, the strategy included returning to Maroon settlements that previous expeditions had sacked, in order to ensure that they were not rebuilt. Third, the spread of plantation settlements closer to the mountain ranges over time made the areas far less isolated than they had been previously, a critical factor in the location of Maroon settlements.

Very few of the expeditions in Cuba killed or captured significant numbers of Maroons, but they harassed them considerably, driving them from pillar to post and destroying their houses and sanctuaries. These factors combined to shatter Maroon confidence in the utility of large groups occupying permanent strongholds. The most favoured large settlements had become well known to Maroon-hunting expeditions by the mid-nineteenth century, and the colonial authorities had considerable information about them gleaned from the expedition leaders' detailed statements and diaries. Many Maroon groups responded to the frequent attacks by creating smaller roving bands, dedicated more to brigandage than to agriculture. The evidence was found in the steady growth of robbery on the highways and in the urban communities, and the concomitant reduction in both the number of permanent settlements and the frequency of state-authorized Maroon-hunting expeditions.[10]

Another reason for the reduction of hunting expeditions – though not clearly delineated by La Rosa Corzo – was the growth of anti-slavery sentiment that frowned upon them. In any event, the first Cuban War of Independence, which began in the eastern region in 1868, led to the revolutionary leaders declaring all Maroons free persons and inviting them to join the revolutionary forces, which many of them did. By the time that this first war ended in 1878, many enslaved persons had been set free in the eastern region. The next few years before slavery was abolished throughout the island witnessed its vast reduction as an institution, as planters reverted to a system of indentured servitude through the importation of large numbers of poor people from Spain, the Canary Islands, China and Yucatán.

La Rosa Corzo (2003, 227) lists eighty-two known settlements in the eastern part of the island from 1740 to the end of slavery, but some of these might have been counted more than once (since he lists the settlements by time period rather than by name). However, his list does not include "vagabond runaways" or armed bands (see chapter 2). This, plus the groups that existed in other parts of the island, and those in the eastern part that the hunting expeditions never located or of whose existence they were unaware, must at least be borne in mind when trying to determine the extent and impact of *marronage* on Cuba. Among the main eastern groups that he identifies are El Portillo, Palenque de la Cruz, Bumba, Maluala, El Frijol (Moa), La Cueva, San Andrés, Todos Tenemos, Calunga (Kalunga), No Se Sabe, El Cedro, La Yagruma and Bayamito. He believes that the last of these was the largest, with some 160 inhabitants (ibid., 248).

The United States generally did not possess large Maroon communities, though an increasingly large number of enslaved persons became runaways. Apart from the Underground Railroad, scholars on *marronage* in that country focus mainly on the activities in Spanish Florida, and especially the First and Second Seminole Wars. These wars came as a sequel to the infiltration of the area by Black fugitives, which began to cause problems for the enslavers in British Georgia and the Carolinas from the late seventeenth century. By the 1690s their presence, though still numerically small, had come to

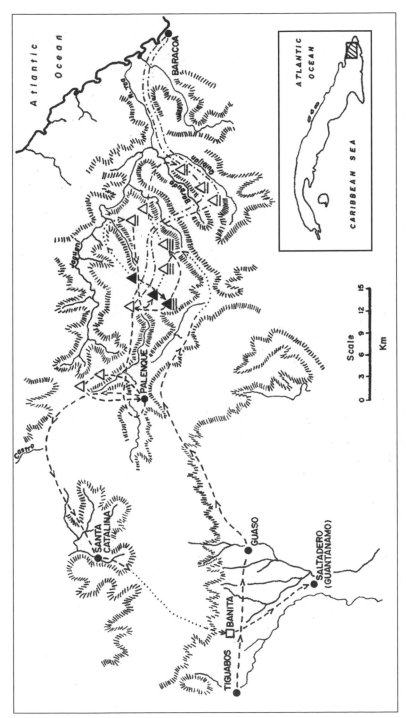

Figure 8. Route of Miguel Perez's Maroon-hunting militia in 1848. From *Runaway Slave Settlements in Cuba: Resistance and Repression*, by Gabino La Rosa Corzo; trans. Mary Todd. English language translation © 2003 by the University of North Carolina Press. Used by permission of the publisher.

the attention of the Spanish imperial government through dispatches by colonial officials who granted them asylum on the basis that they had sought to become Catholics. They had baptized several of them and given them land on which to settle. In 1693 the imperial government translated these *ad hoc* arrangements into official policy by decreeing that such fugitives should not be returned to their overlords (Landers 1998, 362). In 1704 Governor José de Zuniga y Cerda declared, in respect of the Apalachee Province, that any Black people in South Carolina, regardless of religion or status, who found their way into the province would be given certificates of freedom and would even be allowed to move on to other places without hindrance (Mulroy 1993, 8).

The British colonists in South Carolina complained of their loss of property and also alleged that the Spaniards used the runaways, along with Indians, to plunder their plantations. The situation continued unresolved well into the nineteenth century, with increasing numbers of runaways finding refuge in the Spanish borderlands. In fact, especially after the imperial government renewed its decree in 1733 against the extradition of runaways (Landers 1998, 365), the situation became worse as far as the British settlers were concerned. Groups as large as twenty fled South Carolina, sometimes killing Whites on the journey. In one incident in 1739, a group of fugitives sacked that colony and burnt the armoury in Stono. They made their way towards Florida, attacking all the plantations on the route and killing twenty or thirty Whites before a militia company routed them (Blassingame 1979, 206–7). Only occasionally, depending upon the disposition of a particular Spanish governor, did disgruntled settlers receive either the runaways or financial compensation for their loss (Landers 1998, 362–65).

The situation was exacerbated when the Spanish colonial governors, unable to deploy enough of their regular forces, began to use the Maroons as military allies. In 1726, for instance, the government made the fugitive Francisco Menéndez head of the Black militia, and in 1738 created a new town for them called Gracia Real de Santa Teresa de Mose, at which they built Fort Mose. It is known as "the first legally sanctioned free Black community" in the United States. The Maroons' commitment, bravery and great service, both on land and at sea, in the wars that followed fully confirmed for the Spanish the wisdom of the policy that they had embraced. The settlement came to an end when the British captured Florida in 1763. The Spanish did not regain control over the territory until 1784. Meanwhile, the imperial government resettled a number of the Maroons in Matanzas, Cuba, but a

Figure 9. Artist's reconstruction of Fort Mose. Courtesy Florida Museum of Natural History.

few found their way to Havana. Some of them may have relocated to Florida following the Spanish recovery of sovereignty over the area. Throughout this period the early Maroons became increasingly racially mixed, mainly through marriage with Indian women, and adopted aspects of indigenous culture, especially in their diet. They were also deeply influenced by Spanish colonial culture, notably in religion (Landers 1998, 366–77).

The next major episodes in Spanish Florida's border relations had to do with the now independent British North American colonies (the United States). African fugitives made their way once again in large numbers into the Spanish zone. Contemporary records suggest that some Indians, especially the Choctaw and Chickasaw, kept them in conditions of slavery similar to those on the American plantations, but other Indian groups treated them as free persons or held them under a light form of servitude. For instance, the Seminoles – meaning "runaways", according to Porter (1932, 323) – who were latecomers to the area and themselves victims of war and oppression that led to their forced migration, are said to have held Blacks in a form of bondage that was hard to distinguish from freedom.[11] This encouraged Blacks to abscond to Florida and take their chances with the Seminoles, even if that meant reduction to the form of enslavement practised by their new hosts.

Whatever the early situation, the Blacks belonging to the Seminoles increasingly developed symbiotic relations with them, marrying Indian women and assuming positions of authority within the various communities. In time, many Blacks became powerful figures in Seminole society. Blassingame (1979, 211) reckons that by 1836 there were some twelve hundred Maroons in the various Seminole towns, and states that by the mid-nineteenth century the Indians and Africans had become so intermixed that they were often indistinguishable from each other. Mulroy (1993, 2, 4, 17–19 passim) rejects this view, arguing that the Seminole Maroons, as he chooses to call them, usually occupied different land spaces and retained fairly distinct cultural forms from their Indian brethren. He (1993, 5) brilliantly sums up their impact on contemporary society:

> The maroons' history of origins, plantation slavery, Spanish and Native American associations, Florida wars, and forced removal to the Indian Territory culminated in a Mexican borderlands mosaic embracing slave hunters, corrupt Indian agents, filibusters, revolutionaries, foreign invaders, Apache and Comanche raiders, border outlaws, and Buffalo Soldiers. What emerges is an epic saga of slavery, flight, exile and ultimately, freedom. Theirs is a success story.

In 1814, during the war between Britain and the United States, the British built a fort (later called Negro Fort) at Prospect Bluff on the Apalachicola River in Florida and garrisoned it largely with Black runaways. After the signing of the Treaty of Ghent between the two combatants, the British departed in 1815, leaving the fort and a considerable amount of arms and ammunition, including six cannon, in the hands of a few Indians and more than three hundred Blacks under a Black Maroon leader called Garçon, who proved to be a thorn in the sides of the White settlers. The fort attracted a growing number of fugitives, whose fields extended fifty miles upriver (Porter 1932, 330).

The United States therefore decided to transgress border protocols, just as their British predecessors had done. In 1816, during a period of "friendly" relations with Spain, they sent a considerable force, including gunboats, into what was then Spanish territory, provoked the Maroons into a war and destroyed the fort. In one encounter with the gunboats, the Maroons initially had the upper hand, but their adversaries were eventually able to blow up the fort's magazine. About 270 men, women and children were killed in this action, and another sixty-four were apprehended, most of them burned or otherwise maimed for life.[12]

Porter (1951, 278) sums up the activities of Andrew Jackson, leader of the American forces in the Florida enterprise in early 1817, as "attacking and destroying Indian and Negro villages, court-martialing and executing British subjects, capturing Spanish forts and deposing their commander", all of which "revealed the impossibility of Spain's resisting any serious demand by the United States for the annexation of Florida". Jackson actually expelled the Spanish governor, established his own garrison in the area and claimed the territory for the United States. Finally, on 19 February 1819 a treaty was signed by which the Spanish agreed to cede the territory to the United States, which formally annexed it in July 1821. Many of the Maroons relocated to the Bahamas, where they established settlements at Nicholls Town, Mastic Point and Red Bay (Jordan and Litwack 1991, 187–88; Mulroy 1993, 14–15, 26). With the cession of Florida, flight to Mexico became a much larger problem than before, especially after that country became independent of Spain in 1821 and abolished slavery in 1829.

The American assaults did not deter the other Maroons in the vicinity of Florida. In fact, they began to make plans for reprisals, engaging in frequent drills. Their numbers increased in the next two years by some four hundred to six hundred deserters, who joined them in carrying out extensive raids on American plantations in which many White people were killed and enslaved persons were either abducted or, more likely, joined their ranks voluntarily. These offensives and counter-offensives led to what is usually called the First Seminole War (1817–18), which the Americans eventually won, though the

Maroons and Indians fought desperately, losing many of their comrades in the process. The remainder fled into the nearby swamps, making it very difficult for the Whites to pursue them (Porter 1951, 249–80; Mulroy 1993, 14–15).

The war was not yet over, as runaways continued to swell the ranks of the Seminole Maroons. During the next two decades they engaged in desultory warfare against the American forces, who found it extremely difficult to track them down. The Whites wanted the Seminoles off the neighbouring fertile lands and into reservations where they could control them more easily. Seminole Indian chiefs agreed in 1832 to move from Florida to Indian Territory west of the Mississippi River. However, the Seminole Maroons, in particular, resisted such attempts and, according to Mulroy (1993, 28), the opposition of the Maroons clearly laid the foundation for the Second Seminole War.[13]

This war, which began in 1835, was precipitated by the abduction of one of Chief Osceola's wives (the daughter of a Black Maroon woman and a Seminole chief), and his capture and imprisonment for a short time when he demanded her return (Porter 1932, 338). This young Seminole leader was determined to requite the wrong done to him. He led the attack on a group of American soldiers, killing about one hundred of them. The war that ensued lasted until 1842 and united Indians, Africans and their mixed offspring against the Whites. The inception of the war saw some 1,650 Indians and 250 African Maroons pitted against the state forces. Although, as on most occasions, the battle was unequal in terms of men and military equipment, the Africans in particular were said by a contemporary writer to be "the most formidable foe, more blood-thirsty, active, and revengeful, than the Indian. . . . Ten resolute negroes, with a knowledge of the country, are sufficient to desolate the frontier, from one extent to the other" (Porter 1932, 347).[14] General Thomas Jesup referred to the conflict as an African rather than an Indian war. He also stated that the Blacks were the most active and committed fighters, and they seemed to have a controlling influence over the Indian chiefs (Mulroy 1993, 29).[15] The Americans realized that the Maroons would pursue the war to the death rather than be returned to slavery.

The war finally ended with an agreement that the Maroons should be relocated to more remote areas in southwestern Florida (Blassingame 1979, 214). The conflict cost the United States twenty million dollars and the lives of fifteen hundred White civilians and soldiers. As usual, casualty figures for the Seminole Indians and Maroons are lacking, but they must have been substantially larger. The result of such bloodletting was that millions of acres became available to White settlers (Jordan and Litwack 1991, 227; see chapter 10). Eventually, beginning in 1850 a number of Seminole Maroons and Indians trekked from Indian Territory, where they had been transferred, across Texas and into Mexico. Other runaways joined them over the next few years. The Mexican government recognized them as free persons and gave them land in return for military assistance. On several occasions Texan and other White and Indian slaveholders pursued them across the border in determined but largely unsuccessful attempts to re-enslave them (Porter 1932, 349–50; Mulroy 1993, 58–89).[16]

Mulroy (1993, 3) vividly captures the role of the Seminole Maroons in the international shuttle game that was being played out in Florida, and later Indian Territory, Texas and Mexico in the nineteenth century:

> From the beginning of the nineteenth century to the outbreak of World War I, to further group goals, the maroons fought for Spain and Britain against the United States; for Mexico against Indian raiders and Texan filibusters; and for the United States against Indian bands and border outlaws. Along the way, they would engage American forces in the most expensive "Indian" war in the nation's history as allies of the Seminoles. Often pawns in bigger games, these maroons adopted sophisticated border agendas and strategies of their own and struggled bravely to secure their fate from the wishes and whims of others.

The role of these Maroons as military cohorts to various American and European powers allowed them a considerable degree of freedom, including owning property, carrying arms, and cultural autonomy (Mulroy 1993, 2–3; Landers 1998, 357–78).

POPULATION SIZES OF MAROON COMMUNITIES

Figures that contemporary writers (several of whom were colonial adminis-trators and/or planters) recorded of actual runaways/Maroons, given either as absolute numbers or relative to other segments of the colonial state's pop-ulation, are notoriously unreliable. Modern writers believe that they were usually inflated, but they give some indication of the climate of fear, some-times bordering on panic, which resulted from notions of great, marauding hordes. In 1542 Archdeacon Alvaro de Castro of the Dominican Republic estimated a (perhaps exaggerated) Black colonial population of 25,000 to 30,000 enslaved persons,[17] and 2,000 to 3,000 runaways. Another source four years later put the Maroon figure at more than 7,000 (Franco 1979, 38–39; Esteban Deive 1989, 43). In 1570 Mexico was thought to have 20,000 Blacks, about 2,000 of whom were Maroons (Martin 1957, 130). Suriname is believed to have had a Maroon population of about 7,000 in 1786 or roughly 10 per cent of the enslaved population (De Groot 1969, 6; van Lier 1971a, 58). Various estimates for Guadeloupe give figures of 600 in 1726, 3,000 in 1816, and between 1,200 and 1,500 in 1830 (Debien 1979, 109; Gautier 1985, 231).[18] Concerning Venezuela as a whole, Pedro José de Olavarriaga, a seventeenth-century official, put the figure at 20,000, while Acosta Saignes, a much more recent writer, estimated that at the end of the eighteenth century the figure stood at about 30,000 – that is, about half of the enslaved population (Marcano Jiménez 2001, 57). The total Maroon population of small slave colonies amounted to no more than a few hundred. For instance, one modern writer estimates the Maroon community in Dominica in 1785 at 300, and in 1814 at 578 (Marshall 1976, 27; Marshall 1982, 34).

Similarly, figures for specific Maroon groups vary considerably, but most modern writers believe that the largest settlements generally had between 100 and 300 persons, with relatively few exceeding that number. Diego de Ocampo's and Lemba's groups in the Dominican Republic in the mid-sixteenth century are said to have had around 100 and 140 respectively; another group north of Bani in the same country in the mid-seventeenth century was estimated to have more than 200 (Esteban Deive 1989, 48, 50, 80–81). In the 1670s Juan de Bola's followers in Jamaica were said to be about 150. Among the Windward group, also in Jamaica, the male warriors of Guy's Town in 1733 were estimated at around 200, while Nanny Town around the same time was said to have about 300 warriors.[19] In 1739 those from the Windwards who submitted were officially listed at around 470 (an unknown, but apparently much smaller, number refused to be party to the treaty and hived off on their own) (Campbell 1990, 50, 119; Patterson 1979, 254). In 1694 the Colombian government estimated the population of the San Miguel *palenque* at around 450 souls. When the members of an expeditionary force entered the settlement, they discovered the remains of 140 burnt houses, the inhabitants having fled before their arrival (Borrego Plá 1973, 107). If we assume an average occupancy of between two and three people per house, this would give a total population of between 280 and 420 – still a fairly large settlement even if the lower figure is accepted. The Matawais are said to have had around 300 in 1767 (Thoden van Velzen 1995, 113), while Le Maniel, on the Haiti–Dominican Republic border, comprised about 130 inhabitants in the last quarter of the eighteenth century (Moreau de Saint-Méry 1979, 140).

There are also more debatable figures, such as a group estimated at 200 that was located in the marshlands near Huara in Peru in 1545 (Bowser 1974, 188). In 1736 the main Leeward Maroon town in the parish of St James, Jamaica, was thought to contain about 1,000 inhabitants; there were also several outlying Maroon towns and villages in the parishes of St George and St Elizabeth, and more than 300 people in other outlying areas (Patterson 1979, 270). However, at the time of the treaty with the British in 1739, the number who submitted (which seemed to be the vast majority) amounted to only about 470 (Campbell 1990, 119).

The most impressive figures, which few writers dispute, are the 15,000 to 20,000 estimated for Palmares at the height of its power in the early 1670s (Kent 1979, 185; Carneiro 1946, 85). Mattoso (1979, 139), a recent writer, actually states that its population had reached 30,000 at the time of its destruction in 1694–95. In 1643 Cerca do Macaco, its capital, was said to contain fifteen hundred houses, and in 1675 an expedition encountered a well-garrisoned large city with more than two thousand houses (Mattoso 1979, 139; Conrad 1983, 370). This "republic of warriors" was really a confederacy of many settlements owing allegiance to a king. The Ndjukas and Saramakas follow, with much more modest figures of 2,500 and 3,000 respectively at the time of their treaties with the Dutch colonial government in 1760 and 1762 (Thoden van Velzen 1995, 113); then comes the 1,000 attributed to the Quilombo Grande in Brazil around 1759 (Pinto Vallejos 1998, 195).

DEPREDATIONS CRISES

Robert Conrad (1983, 359) alludes to the fact that in 1818 an adviser to King João IV of Portugal declared that the relationship between Brazilian overlords and their servile charges was one of domestic warfare.[20] While Gilberto Freyre (1956) may dispute this assertion, one can hardly read the record of Maroon assaults in that country and elsewhere without becoming aware that periodically, and sometimes frequently, the White communities experienced depredations crises reminiscent of warfare (McFarlane 1986, 132, 134). On many occasions Maroon assaults on White urban and rural areas became so deadly and rapid that the enslavers despaired of ever bringing the perpetrators to heel. A contemporary writer declared that

> [t]he inhabitants of Alagôas, Porto Calvo, and Penedo were constantly under attack, and their houses and plantations robbed by the Blacks of Palmares. The Blacks killed their cattle and carried away their slaves to enlarge their *quilombos* and increase the number of their defenders, forcing the inhabitants and natives of those towns to engage in fighting at a distance of forty leagues or more, at great cost to their plantations and risk to their own lives, without which the Blacks would have become masters of the captaincy because of their huge and ever-increasing numbers. (Conrad 1983, 370)

Maroon settlements were located in all the main plantation and mining areas of Brazil – Pernambuco, Alagôas, Sergipe, São Paulo, Minas Gerais, Rio de Janeiro, Mato Grosso, Goias, Pará, Maranhão and Rio Grande do Norte – and created major problems for the slaveholders through their ability to attract new runaways and the depredations that they often carried out against their former overlords. By the last quarter of the seventeenth century the inhabitants of Alagôas, Porto Calvo, Derinhaem and Rio de San Francisco (Penedo) are said to have become greatly impoverished by wars first against the Dutch and then the Palmarinos. Expenditure on these wars was estimated at well over a million *cruzados* (Carneiro 1946, 60). It took between sixteen and thirty-five Dutch and Portuguese expeditions (based upon the estimates of different authors) between 1644 and 1695, led by some of their bravest and most experienced warriors, to destroy Palmares.[21] The invading forces suffered heavy defeat on several occasions. They also won several partial successes, destroying many outlying settlements. In 1678 they managed to sack the main cities, forcing the king and some of his leading men to accept the offer of a peace treaty (Conrad 1983, 370–72), but it was a treaty that did not last long (see chapter 10).

In some jurisdictions, such as the Dominican Republic, Jamaica and Suriname, the colonial authorities believed that Maroon activities would lead to the total ruin of the colony. José Franco (1979, 47) declares that the Cuban government was concerned mainly with persecuting the Maroons and destroying the *palenques*. The island had an Office for the Capture of Maroons from the late eighteenth century, and special Maroon prisons.

Campbell (1990, 79) cites a member of the Jamaican legislature to the effect that the insecurity of the country had become so great, and the robberies and murders on the roads so frequent, that the settlers were unsure what the next day would produce. That island's government actually proclaimed martial law in October 1734 (Campbell 1990, 91–92; Patterson 1979, 269). Franco (1979, 44) declares that in the first half of the nineteenth century the White inhabitants of Santiago de Cuba, and perhaps other places in the island, lived in constant fear, and the plantation owners panicked at almost any news about Maroons. They would seek help at the drop of a hat because they dreaded the retribution from the oppressed people against whom they had committed barbaric acts. Davidson (1979, 98) tells us that the violence associated with servile insurrections, especially *marronage,* in the eastern slopes and northern mining areas kept Mexico City in a constant state of anxiety. Aguirre (1993, 257) asserts that brigandage not only represented a permanent source of conflicts and fears, but was also a central issue of political and social debates. He goes on to say that famous leaders such as the Negro León, Salomé Lacunsc, "Perjuicio", Juan de Mata, and León Escobar were synonymous with terror for travellers, landowners, merchants and colonial officials; that the newspapers augmented their fame and they acquired mythical status (ibid., 261). Porter (1932, 346) cites the following statement from a contemporary writer on the Seminole Maroons: "Ben, 22, Jacob, 24, Muredy, 20, most intrepid and hostile warriors." Carneiro (1946, 13) declares that the heroic deeds of the guerrillas of Palmares made them legendary, causing them to appear to surpass the limits of human strength and ingenuity.

The enslavers in the United States had their own share of difficulties. Davidson (1979, 99) speaks about the fear-ridden slaveholders, while Aptheker (1979, 153) cites an earlier writer concerning the fear and terror that the Maroons under Sebastian aroused among White settlers in South Carolina in 1711, before an Indian tracked down and killed their leader. He (ibid., 159) also cites another person writing in 1823 about Bob Ferebee and his men, who kept the inhabitants of Norfolk County, Virginia, in constant fear and anxiety. Stedman (1988, 80–81) wrote about the "abiss [abyss] of difficulties" that the Aluku Maroons created in the Cottica River area in the late eighteenth century, causing fear and consternation among the White inhabitants, most of whom expected a general massacre to take place any moment. Many of them therefore fled their plantations and crowded into the capital, Paramaribo. Debien (1979, 108, 109) opines that the pillage of a few provision grounds or sugarcane fields or the theft of a few cattle created fear of nocturnal attacks and of entire towns being burnt. However, strangely, he also asserts that it was only rarely that a colonist really believed that the Maroons posed a threat to his personal safety. The records are full of references to the widespread paranoia of the Whites and create the impression of slaveholding societies that were tension-ridden, most of all by the Maroon presence and depredations.

Around the mid-sixteenth century the Bahoruco and Vega regions had acquired reputations as such fearsome Maroon haunts that individual colonists ventured into those areas at their peril. One of the Maroon groups, led by a Black leader named Diego de Guzmán, had recently raided a nearby town, burnt part of a sugar mill, and locked swords with the Spanish. The colonists were thereafter afraid to venture forth except in groups of at least fifteen people. Though the danger temporarily passed shortly afterward, when Guzmán and some of his followers were killed by a military expedition sent against them, further dangers lay ahead in the rapid recruitment of new Maroons for the settlements in the area (Franco 1979, 39–40).

The enslavers and other citizens in outlying areas relatively close to the Maroon settlements, and also in urban areas within whose vicinity roving Maroon bands operated, developed a siege mentality. They became jittery at any news about Maroon assaults, often exaggerated the numbers of the Maroons in the bush or the hills, saw Maroons where they were not, and at times attributed to Maroons acts committed by others. Burdened by fear, many planters sold out and ran for their lives; others migrated to those urban centres where vulnerability was lower due to the relatively higher density of the White population and the existence of more organized military and police forces. Several rich landlords decided to remove themselves altogether from the arena of conflict, taking ship to Europe where they could bask, not in the sunshine of the luxuriant tropical climate, but in the riches that their attorneys sent home to them. All writers agree that insurgency on the part of enslaved persons and Maroons played a major role in determining both the numbers of White residents and the quality of life they enjoyed in the slave societies.

In 1693 an official in Pernambuco rued the fact that the colonists had established no new ranches but instead had retired from some of the livestock farms that they had erected in areas close to the *mocambos*, because of the great damage that they had experienced at the hands of the Maroons

(Carneiro 1946, 54). This affirmation of despair was echoed around the same time by another writer, who waxed emotional at the thought that many inhabitants stood in jeopardy of losing their lives, honour and property to the Maroons who repeatedly seized their goods, carried away the women and virgin daughters and killed the parents and husbands (Carneiro 1946, 55). But let us consider this bit of whining by enslavers whose tyranny had resulted in a servile revolt in Bahia in 1814:

> They burned more than a hundred houses, even killing innocent children, and the evil now continues in other places. In Iguape, Cachoeira, and Itaparica, the blacks of Gonçalo, Marinho Falcão, Rodrigo Brandão, and Francisco Vincente Viana have run away and revolted, and all these owners of sugar plantations have fled to this city, where they now are. Every day blacks run away from this city. (Conrad 1983, 404)

While the larger Maroon groups had the potential to inflict much more damage than the smaller ones, the latter also did substantial damage, especially in the urban and suburban areas. The extant records attest to numerous raids on towns and plantations by relatively small groups, though they are sometimes identified as belonging to large settlements. Conrad (1983, 361), for instance, informs us that in the 1820s some of Brazil's major cities were virtually encompassed by clusters of Maroon settlements whose inhabitants preyed on unwary travellers. In Peru, the colonial authorities around the mid-sixteenth century reported that small groups of fifteen to twenty Maroons went about robbing travellers and Indians, and were impudent enough to enter the city day or night; they also attacked farms and other properties. In 1549 a group of about twenty-three Maroons was reported to be committing robberies and murders against Indians and other people (Bowser 1974, 188). James Lockhart (1968, 189–90) mentions a group of about fifteen Maroons in the Piura region of Peru in the 1540s who attacked Indian villagers and travellers, killing the men and abducting the women. For a while they brought commerce between the highlands and the coastal Indians to a complete stop. Indeed, the Maroons created so much bother for the Peruvian authorities that putting them down, or "under", occupied a considerable amount of time and expenditure by successive governors and colonial councils (Bowser 1974, 187–221).

In Mexico in 1560 a small Maroon band of some fifteen to twenty people carried out a series of deadly raids on Spaniards in Guanajuato, Pénjamo and

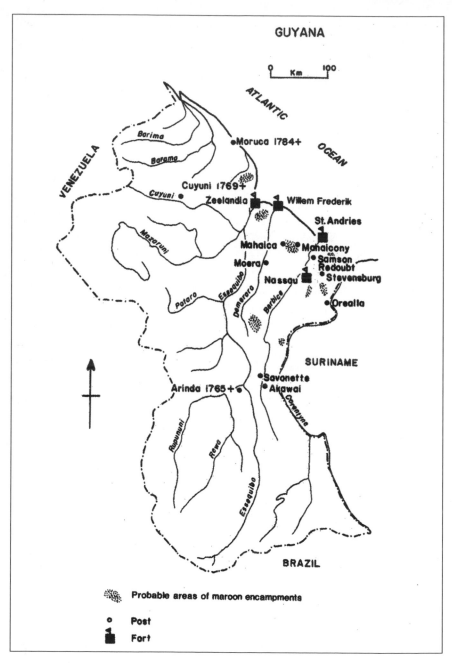

Figure 10. Guyana Maroon settlements in the early nineteenth century. From *Colonialism and Underdevelopment in Guyana 1580–1803*, by Alvin O. Thompson (Bridgetown, Barbados: Carib Research and Publications, 1987).

San Miguel. So perturbed was the viceroy that he ordered the local magistrate to have them wiped out by any means (Palmer 1976, 123–24). In 1606 the viceroy reported that there was a large number of Maroons in Vieja and Nueva Veracruz, Río Blanco and Punta de Antón Lizardo, and that they were bolder than before. They had begun to visit the town of Tlalixcoyán, robbing homes, carrying off Black domestics and setting fire to the Spaniards' houses (Davidson 1979, 93).[22] Gaspar Yanga, an African, originally from Gabon, who led a revolt in 1570 and shortly after established the Cofre de Perote *palenque*, justified assaults on White persons and property as a means of compensation for what the enslavers had taken from them over the years (Palmer 1976, 129).

Maroons in Cuba travelled up to twenty and even forty miles, over hills and through forests, to attack plantations to obtain clothing, firearms and other goods (Pérez de la Riva 1979, 57). It was this strike range that unsettled a number of White settlers, since the remoteness of a Maroon settlement did not guarantee their protection from assault. Guillermo Rivas's community in Ocoyta, Venezuela, in the 1770s provided an outstanding display of this kind of aggressive warfare. It was said that he frequently raided the towns and plantations far and wide, seizing arms, which he cached. Acosta Saignes (1979, 66) refers to his *palenque* as a core area of resistance and attack. He also states that Guillermo was accustomed to travel from Ocoyta to Chuspa and from Ocumare to Barcelona, in order to maintain close contact with the various communities and organize raids on the plantations and towns. He stole great quantities of cocoa, which he sold to White merchants (Acosta Saignes 1979, 64, 66–69).[23]

In Colombia, in the early sixteenth century, a group of Maroons set fire to the city of Santa María. In the early seventeenth century Domingo Bioho, Maroon leader of the San Basilio *palenque* in that country, created havoc among the White settlements. According to Escalante (1979, 77), he was a fiery and daring person, who once plunged with thirty male and female followers into the forests and marshes of Matuna and easily defeated a group of nearly twenty enslavers who had been tracking them. Such reckless bravery was replicated often in the history of Maroon warfare. In the next few years Cartagena, Tolú, Mompós, Tenerife and other areas felt the might of the growing community of warriors. They sacked and ransacked plantations, cattle ranches and other holdings. Even after its founder's death in battle in 1621, the *palenque* remained a scourge of the outlying White settlements until it signed a peace treaty early in the next century (Escalante 1979, 77–79). In the

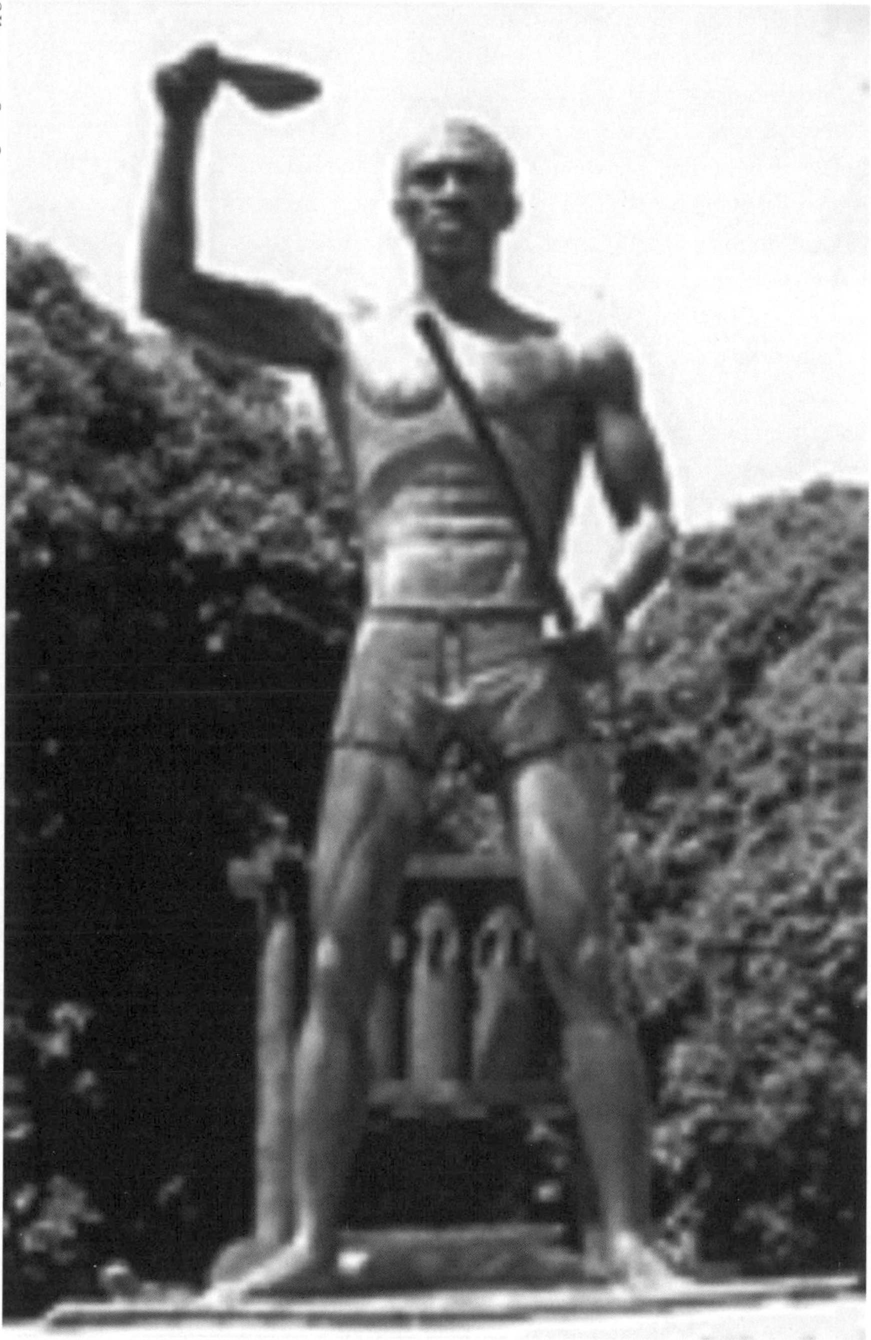

Figure 11. Gaspar Yanga

late seventeenth century, Maroons occupying the northern, central and southern massifs harried Cartagena. Among the most famous *palenques* were those of San Miguel, Matudere, Betancur, Santa Bárbara, and Norosí. Military expeditions largely wiped those settlements out in the 1690s, but in the first half of the following century new and equally militant groups succeeded them, among them the much-feared Castillo *palenque* led by Jerónimo (Borrego Plá 1973, 75–109; Escalante 1979, 76).

One method by which the governments tried to protect the colonists from Maroon depredations was to establish forts and other military installations at strategic points. The Suriname government built a *cordon pad* (military cordon) between the Boni Maroons and the plantation areas to protect them from what they regarded as a plague (Price and Price 1988, xxiv; Hoogbergen 1993, 181). In Venezuela in 1734, in response to the depredations of Andresote, the government erected a fort at the mouth of the Yaracuy River, capable of mounting eight to ten cannon (Brito Figueroa 1985, 210). In 1795 the Demerara government built a line of military posts along the west coast to improve security there (Thompson 1987, 145). Likewise, in Jamaica the government increased the number of forts and barracks, and beefed up security on the outlying plantations by deploying soldiers there. In that colony, and no doubt elsewhere, individual planters considerably strengthened their defences. Dallas (1803, 1:27) tells us that their houses were placed to command the entrance to the main plantation works and slave quarters, and were often constructed with flanks and loopholes to facilitate firing upon assailants as they drew near. In most instances such fortifications proved ineffective or, at best, only partially effective in restraining the Maroons.

In some instances the enslavers debated, inside and outside the governing councils, the issue of establishing garrison communities to protect the White population against Maroon attacks. This debate addressed several options, including creating a corps of free Blacks and free Coloureds who would be forced to live in designated areas in return for their freedom; granting certain Maroons their freedom, relocating them to strategic areas, and employing them as a surveillance corps; and bringing in poor Whites in significant numbers and settling them as small farmers in similar areas (Stedman 1988; Esteban Deive 1989; Campbell 1990; Pereira 1994).

The extensive attacks by Maroons on the highway between Nombre de Dios and Panama in the mid-sixteenth century caused colonial officials to consider creating a buffer community between the insurgents and the other settlements in the area, comprising about fifty or sixty men, half of whom would be their most trusted servile cohorts, whom they would set free. However, they did not translate this thought into action, perhaps because wiser opinion prevailed. The Maroons were estimated at several hundred (as many as eight hundred according to one source), and were allied with the Indians (Marcano Jiménez 2001, 18).

In 1617 Córdoba was established, with this end in view, along the Puebla–Veracruz highway (Pereira 1994, 98), which had become a happy hunting ground for Maroons who fell on the hapless traveller. It was only very partially successful in its objective. Between 1735 and 1737 it experienced a number of assaults by insurgents, runaways and Maroons that devastated it and the surrounding area, and stretched the colonial forces in Veracruz to their limits. Thirty years after the events the economy of that region had not recovered from the depredations. A delegation of planters to the provincial government recollected the "seditious movement and general uprising of all the enslaved people in this district, that cost much money, drew much blood and ruined the country in such a way that it has not recovered up to today". Such "tempestuous and turbulent" events were a "plague and calamity" in the life of Veracruz (Naveda Chávez-Hita 1987, 135–36; see also 156, 159). The planters further explained:

> This unexpected and pernicious outcome . . . obliged the district to recruit and arm persons, seek assistance from neighbouring districts and even the help of the military convicts of the city of Veracruz. They were kept under arms for five months, and conducted several attacks on the blacks, who defended themselves fiercely. And although they managed to destroy the settlements completely, it was a costly affair and consumed much blood, many lives and much money, amounting to no less than 400 thousand pesos, and led to the almost total ruin of the district. (Naveda Chávez-Hita 1987, 136)

Similar settlements were considered for Jamaica, Peru, Brazil and Cuba but few, if any, were erected. The central challenge was to attract to these frontier areas a sufficient number of settlers who were hardy, experienced and perhaps foolish enough to risk their lives for a cause whose success was at best dubious, and who stood to gain little from it. Most of the other suggestions were never attempted because of the expense and difficulties in containing the ubiquitous Maroons. By far, the most successful method was using Maroons to catch Maroons, discussed in chapter 9.

A critical aspect of the tension within slave society in the Americas was the very close alliance between Maroons and free(d) persons and those still in slavery. Those who deserted to become Maroons usually left behind many friends, relatives and well-wishers who often acted as their eyes and ears and helped to ensure that they were kept *au fait* with what was taking place in the towns and on the plantations (Zips 1999, 90; Brito Figueroa 1985, 210). Without these informants the Maroons would have been a much less lethal force against the slaveholding interests, and expeditions might have wiped out far more of them.

In one instance a Maroon informed his White captors that nine enslaved persons in the city of Santo Domingo acted as spies for the Siete Cabezas (Seven Heads) Maroon group (Esteban Deive 1989, 86). Extensive contact and communication also took place between the Maroons in Cartagena and various enslaved persons on the plantations. In the late seventeenth century the *palenque* headed by Betancur enjoyed alliances with the Blacks on the farms of Domingo Barrera, Diego Durango, André Pérez, José de Mesa and Juan de Mesa (Borrego Plá 1973, 76, 82–87). In the early 1770s Guillermo Rivas of Venezuela could rely on Andrés Domingo and Juana Francisca, who were enslaved persons, and Uvaldo y Oviedo (José Eduardo de la Cruz Perera), a young White British plantation official, as his spies in and around the plantations. It was also said that the Mulattos, Zambos and free Morenos openly collaborated with him (Brito Figueroa 1985, 217–19). The Maroons in Peru in the mid-sixteenth century had spies among the enslaved population of Lima, and the same was true in Jamaica in the eighteenth century (Bowser 1974, 188; Campbell 1990, 80–81).

In 1820 the police chief of Rio de Janeiro, Brazil, bewailed the fact that the Maroons always knew ahead of time about expeditions sent against them, not only because of the alarm and confusion that always attend such an enterprise, but also through the extensive contacts that the fugitives enjoyed with residents of all colours in the city (Conrad 1983, 383). In one remarkable instance, in Bahia in 1814, Malomi João, a *quilombo* leader, had as his chief spy and agent an enslaved person known as Francisco Cidade, who not only maintained contacts with other cells throughout Salvador but also regularly collected money and food for the *quilombo*. It is said that on a visit to Itaparica Island, Cidade conferred the title "Duke of the Island" upon a person called David. Using his *quilombo* as his base and his extensive contacts with Cidade and other enslaved persons, Malomi João eventually led a revolt in the country, killing more than fifty people and destroying much property (Reis 1993, 47–48). According to Reis (ibid., 45–46):

> For several days at the beginning of 1814 a large number of slaves abandoned Salvador and converged at a nearby quilombo. On 28 February a force estimated at 250 attacked fishing marinas where they had allies. At a marina belonging to Manuel Ignácio da Cunha, a prominent figure among the Bahian economic elite, slaves killed the overseer and members of his family. They burned fishing nets, their instrument of work, then joined others coming from the quilombo and attacked other marinas and the village of Itapuã. . . . The insurgents cried out for freedom and cheered blacks and their 'king' while urging death for whites and mulattos. With this in mind, they marched off toward the Recôncavo, setting fire to many houses (more than 150 in one account) as well as to plantations along the way.

In 1802 in Elizabeth City, North Carolina, Maroons led by Tom Cooper were believed to be inciting enslaved persons to conduct acts of insubordination and foment plots against the enslavers (Aptheker 1979, 154). In 1830 a major plot was detected involving enslaved persons and Maroons in that state. It is said that they had firearms and ammunition hidden, that they communicated through messengers between Wilmington, Newbern and Elizabeth City, and that they had several camps at Gastons Island, Price's Creek, Newport River and Dover Swamp, and near Wilmington (ibid., 160). It is clear from these examples that many who remained within the slavery system played crucial roles in Maroon activities and in undermining the system. For obvious reasons Blacks in Cartagena, and no doubt elsewhere, were usually tight-lipped when interrogated about the Maroon settlements (Borrego Plá 1973, 85).

Jean Pierre (2000, 111) argues that part of the Maroon repertoire was psychological warfare that helped to instil fear in the minds of their enemies. A constant refrain in both contemporary and modern writings is the fear, anxiety and tension that Maroon activities engendered among Whites. Borrego Plá (1973, 30) refers to the permanent state of alarm in which the Colombian enslavers lived, while Navarrete (2003, 34) writes that in all parts of the New World where slavery was a fundamental institution the fear of revolt and the Maroon problem tormented both officials and colonists. This fear, bordering on paranoia, was perhaps best expressed by the contemporary Haitian writer Milscent, who stated in 1791 that where there were only three hundred

Maroons the Whites thought there were ten thousand (Manigat 1977, 498). Likewise, La Rosa Corzo (2003, 73) argues, in the case of Cuba, that fear led the Whites to exaggerate the Maroon threat. Their fears were engendered by the physical destruction that was occurring around them, the failure of regular troops to deter Maroon assaults, and the complete uncertainty about where the Maroons would strike next. The enslavers' fear was the obverse of their policy of oppression, creating in them a form of psychological bondage or enslavement. This was seen clearly in relation to the so-called slave laws. As Jordan (1968, 108) rightly observes:

> While the colonial slave codes seem at first sight to have been intended to discipline Negroes, to deny them freedoms available to other Americans, a very slight shift in perspective shows the codes in a different light: they aimed, paradoxically, at disciplining white men. Principally, the law told the white man, not the Negro, what he must do; the codes were for the eyes and ears of slaveowners. . . . It was the white man who was *required* to punish his runaways, prevent assemblages of slaves, enforce the curfews, sit on the special courts, and ride the patrols. Members of the assemblies, most of whom owned slaves, were attempting to enforce slave-discipline by the only means available, by forcing owners, individually and collectively, to exercise it.

The panicky response of the Jamaican government in 1670 to the attacks of the Karmahaly Maroons was seen not only in the placing of the island on a war footing for the second time but also in the passage of certain legal provisions that considerably restricted the movements of the free White population. It became an offence for any military or civilian person to venture out alone two miles or more without being armed. An alarm was to be sounded at any hour when Maroons were sighted, and all the inhabitants were compelled to repair to a specified place on such occasions to await further orders. Any person sighting Maroons and failing to sound an alarm was to be tried under the Articles of War, published in 1665 when the island was first readied for war. These orders were to be published throughout the island every time any company of the militia or soldiers met for exercise.

The colonists' fear of Ventura Sánchez (Coba, Cobas), leader of the Bumba Maroons in Cuba, was so great that the Spanish authorities broached peace terms with him, though they eventually slew him through treachery (see chapter 9). It was said that he had organized a large-scale operation involving hundreds of runaways (Franco 1979, 42–43). There was also

Guillermo Rivas of Venezuela and his group, who belonged to the Ocoyta Maroon settlement. He had a reputation as a fierce warrior with a tornado raging in his head, and was celebrated for his great daring. He became the scourge of the White planter community but ultimately fell to an expeditionary force sent against him; one account of his death suggests that there was more valour than discretion in his encounter with the enemy (Acosta Saignes 1979, 64–65; García 1996, 65–79). Guillermo's tenure as a Maroon lasted for only about three years, but during that time he became a Phantom-like figure dispensing his form of justice against enslavers. He is said to have occupied haciendas and liberated the enslaved people therein (Guerra Cedeño 1984, 29; Marcano Jiménez 2001, 37).

Several years before Guillermo there was Zumbi, the last king of Palmares, who brooked no compromise with the enemy; he led a successful conspiracy against Ganga-Zumba, his uncle and predecessor, because of the latter's capitulation to the Portuguese in 1678. Zumbi was lionized for his deeds and was even considered immortal, or at least god-like, by some of his followers (Carneiro 1946, 13).[24] A contemporary writer called him a person of outstanding valour, great courage and rare steadfastness, and went on to say that he was a model for others because of his diligence, sound judgement and fortitude (Carneiro 1946, 53). He became the main scourge of the White population in Pernambuco, and when he was finally defeated and killed in 1694–95 the inhabitants of Recife celebrated his death for six days (see chapters 5 and 10).

While fear of Maroon activities bred increased brutality against deserters (see chapters 1 and 5) and a battery of laws to control the movements of enslaved persons, it also caused the plantocracy to tread lightly in dealing with those who remained on the plantations, for fear that they would join the ranks of the deserters.[25] Especially in times of heightened Maroon activity, planters complained that their servile charges became far more insolent, did less work than usual and took other privileges that in "normal" times would have been punished with a whipping. However, in times of upheaval the enslavers had to be wary. According to one contemporary source, in the days that Guillermo was on the offensive, enslaved persons on the neighbouring plantations exercised unusual freedom, and neither the owners nor the overseers dared to discipline them for fear that they would abscond and join the Maroon leader (Acosta Saignes 1979, 67).[26] According to García (1996, 65), one of the many myths and legends that inform popular discourse about

Guillermo Rivas up to today is that enslaved persons used to say to their overlords: "If you continue to mistreat me I will tell Guillermo." Dutertre (1667–71, 2:498) notes that in the French Caribbean, even before sugar had become "king", planters were torn about disciplining their human chattels because of the fear that they would make off into the forest. One member of the Jamaican plantocracy expressed similar views in the 1730s, in the days when the Leeward and Windward Maroons were still rampant (Campbell 1990, 80). In 1825, George Hyde, a Coloured merchant in Belize, echoed the same sentiments (Bolland 2003, 73).

Aptheker (1979, 160) cites a complaint that Maroon activities contributed to slave insubordination in North Carolina, in Sampson, Bladen, Onslow, Jones, New Hanover and Dublin counties, from September through December 1830. Slaveholders complained that their enslaved charges had become virtually ungovernable, going and coming as they pleased, and, when anyone attempted to discipline them, absconding to the woods where they stayed for months, stealing cattle, sheep and hogs and committing other outrages.

As noted above, Maroon activities led to the complete abandonment of many plantations, especially those within the eye of the Maroon storm, and discouraged would-be planters and investors from undertaking pioneer plantations in some of the most fertile areas of the country. This was exemplified in Suriname and Jamaica, reinforcing planter views that Maroons were a plague on the body politic. Various governors of Jamaica wrote about the impact of Maroon depredations on the outlying settlements, some of which had become overrun by trees and bushes (Campbell 1990, 142). In 1734, for instance, the colonial legislature recorded that twenty-seven colonists were forced to abandon their lands in certain parts of the country because a large number of insurgent Blacks attacked them frequently, plundered and burned their houses, and wounded some of them and killed others (ibid, 60). Governor Hunter had warned the legislature a few years earlier that because of recent setbacks to military expeditions sent against the Maroons, the latter appeared to be growing in numbers and audacity, and were likely to pose such a threat that some of the settlements might have to be abandoned to them (ibid., 61). Occasionally, Maroons actually occupied abandoned plantations, as happened in Jamaica around 1733 when a group of them took over three plantations within eight miles of Port Antonio (ibid., 79).[27] The Jamaican experience arguably replicated, on a grander scale, the experience of other plantation colonies.

CHAPTER 5

Military Expeditions and Judicial Terror

COMPOSITION OF EUROPEAN MILITARY FORCES

So-called Maroon expeditions were commonly officered by White military or militiamen and included White subordinates, Indians and enslaved Blacks. An interesting variant to this pattern was the creation in Peru, Cuba and other Spanish colonies of a constabulary, or association of enslavers, called the *Hermandad* (Brotherhood), comprising Whites and free Coloureds, whose dedicated task was the destruction of Maroon settlements and apprehension of deserters.[1] Periodically, the authoritarian states dispatched bigger and more organized expeditions to deal with specific problems resulting from the build-up of large Maroon establishments, but the most elaborate expeditions were those involving great contingents of soldiers, commanded by high military officers, and engaging in warfare with various Maroon settlements over several months or years. For instance, in the 1730s the Venezuelan government dispatched some fifteen hundred troops against the Yaracuy Maroons under Andresote (Brito Figueroa 1985, 210).

The following excerpt from a letter written in 1824 by the police chief of Rio de Janeiro to his superiors in Lisbon sets the stage for a more detailed discussion of the difficulties that many military forces faced in destroying the Maroons.

> I have ordered assaults against some of these [neighbouring] *quilombos* with a
> police squad and another force whose assistance I asked for, along with soldiers

of the militia, but all has been in vain. Such attacks are never undertaken without a great deal of alarm and confusion, and when the assault begins the blacks (and the deserters who live among them) have already been informed and have abandoned the place where they were thought to be hiding out. As long as expeditions are launched with military fanfare, they will always be given this kind of warning. The reason for this is that, both day and night, the fugitives carry on a regular trade with tavern-keepers and other black men and women of this city, who transport and sell the stolen goods which the fugitives acquire from country houses and from highway robbery. Moreover, as long as they are carried out by ordinary soldiers, these attacks can never accomplish anything except to frighten the blacks and drive them away, because it is not practical for booted, uniformed, and armed men to penetrate into those steep, lofty mountain jungles, caves, and grottoes where the blacks hide out and move about with total freedom. (Conrad 1983, 383)

Hunting Maroons proved to be a harrowing experience for Stedman and his mercenary colleagues, many of whom died in the Suriname forests from a variety of causes, including disease and starvation, while others ended up as physical and emotional wrecks. Usually, the tactic was to wear down the inhabitants through a policy of attrition, involving frequent attacks in the dry season and the destruction of the houses and especially the crops, thus creating hunger and dislocation among them.

The basic strike force of most authoritarian states was the regular army, which was also responsible for the general protection of the state against external aggression. The citizen militias (and the mounted police in the French Caribbean[2]), usually including all able-bodied males roughly between the ages of sixteen and fifty – with the exception of high government officials, certain wealthy men and the clergy – were expected to assist in the internal defence of the state, but the common report concerning them was that, with few exceptions, they proved incapable of the task. Though they went through some sort of drill, they were never physically or mentally strong enough to endure Maroon-hunting expeditions for any length of time, and some were downright cowards. Governor Henry of Jamaica berated them as more a hindrance than an asset to the military expeditions.[3] However, a few of them gave outstanding service to the slaveholding cause.

In the large states, the military usually consisted of a standing European army with adequate weapons (certainly superior to those that the Maroons possessed) and uniforms, and were well drilled. However, a critical flaw in the planning of many expeditions was that the officers often made no secret of the fact that they were on special assignments against the Maroons, and the build-up of a large body of troops at a particular point usually signalled that a large-scale expedition was imminent. Moreover, soldiers trained in Western combat tactics rather than guerrilla or face-to-face warfare proved largely incapable of fighting in forests, in swamps, among rocks, in caves and in other unfamiliar terrain where they encountered their adversaries – and were often cut to pieces. Their usefulness was therefore considerably reduced in Mexico, Brazil, Venezuela, Jamaica and Suriname.[4]

The contemporary literature sometimes refers to large contingents of regular foreign soldiers (usually accompanied by local regulars and irregulars) who proved totally incapable of matching a few dozen Maroons in desultory warfare, though some of them distinguished themselves for bravery. Buckley (1998, 218) explains that the vast forests and mountain retreats that encompassed the camps appeared strange, impenetrable and even hostile to soldiers who were not trained to operate in such an environment. Besides, the woods were the haunt of the formidable Maroons, whose adroit use of the forest cover unnerved their unwary foes. Davidson (1979, 99) observes that in Mexico the military expeditions encountered major strategic and tactical problems, especially in operations against hideouts in the frontier regions.

The Maroons knew their habitats intimately, usually used a combination of natural and man-made defences, and often chose the time and place when direct confrontations would take place. The troops might surprise small groups of Maroons, as happened on some occasions, but were rarely able to capture significant numbers at one time. This caused great chagrin to the White officers, who often concluded that such expeditions were exercises in futility.

In the smaller or less developed plantation societies, the army was usually very small and sometimes virtually non-existent. This is true of most of the small islands of the southern Caribbean, with the notable exceptions of St Lucia and Barbados, which were the headquarters of imperial forces stationed in the region. In Suriname, as in other Dutch colonies in the late eighteenth century, the army appeared more like an irregular than a regular force. Stedman (1988, 82) wrote, concerning the members:

> The military in Surinam are composed of several very good and experienced
> officers and well innured [sic] to the service, but for theyr [their] private men I

can indeed say little to boast of, being a composition of scum – composed of all nations – ages shapes – and sizes & by chance wafted together from all the different corners of the globe.

In spite of this, he commends this motley group for outstanding bravery, "fighting like little Devils" and on many occasions offering "infinite service" to the colony. Most mercenary soldiers, however, did not see why they should allow themselves to be shot at, and worse still killed, for the pittance that they received as pay. Even the regular troops sent from Europe often suffered from the same malaise.

The ordinary soldier was often brutalized for trivial offences (including being given as many as fifteen hundred lashes sometimes, at least in the British army), received very low pay, was frequently accused of being drunk (as were members of the White militias), experienced high levels of morbidity and mortality within the first few months of arrival in the colonies, and generally chafed under the conditions of their assignment to the colonies. The officer ranks were only slightly better, though they too did not appreciate fully why they were sent to the ends of the earth, as far as they were concerned, to fight an enemy that was largely invisible and for a cause whose rationale they hardly understood and for which they cared even less. On more than one occasion the Jamaica Assembly reprimanded military and militia officers for incompetence and/or cowardice. On at least two occasions officers in that country were court-martialled for their conduct during military engagements.[5]

The militias that were made up of local citizens were usually segmented along lines of class and colour, rather than military experience and ability. Many of them, in the face of battle, simply ran away in the hope of fighting (or running) another day. Rich planters in Jamaica simply refused to perform militia duties, to pay the taxes that were necessary to keep the military installations in good order, and sometimes to allow their enslaved charges to work without pay on the military installations (Patterson 1979, 285). Some Brazilian slaveholders in Pernambuco did much the same thing, threatening to abandon their farms if they were forced to hand over their servile charges for state use as baggage carriers (Carneiro 1946, 100). To combat the widespread reluctance of the colonists in that country, the *capitães do mato* (see below) were authorized to impress them into service, regardless of their protests and objections (Pinto Vallejos 1998, 188). In contrast, some rich planters in Brazil went out on expeditions under state direction and even on their own volition. This was far more common in Cuba and the Dominican Republic, where high government officials went on expeditions and sometimes paid for their courage with their lives (Carneiro 1946; La Rosa Corzo 2003; Esteban Deive 1989).

Military expeditions had relatively greater success when accompanied by Black and Coloured "soldiers" or auxiliaries, though they were often not militarily trained, at least not in the European sense of the term. Their methods of fighting were completely unorthodox, but much closer to how the Maroons were fighting. Since guerrilla warfare is not instinctive but learned, the logical conclusion is that the Black soldiers were experienced in, or at least familiar with, similar warfare in Africa. Whatever the explanation, the records speak loudly of the efficient work that the Black soldiers performed in identifying Maroon habitats, locating the carefully camouflaged entrance points and the vulnerable nodes in Maroon defence and attacking their adversaries fiercely. Some of the tributes to these Black soldiers are so strong that several contemporary and modern writers have concluded that without them it would have been virtually impossible for the colonial states' forces to achieve any significant victories against the larger and more well-established Maroon settlements in such places as the Dominican Republic, Jamaica and Suriname.

Nevertheless, it is important not to overstate the point. Free Blacks and Coloureds, in particular, impressed into joining military expeditions with little or no hope of material or social advancement, often resented being called to arms. In 1731, at the height of the conflict with the Maroons, the Jamaican legislature resorted to the drastic expedient of requiring all free Black and free Coloured men between fifteen and sixty years of age to enlist in the Maroon-hunting militias. Failure to do so was to result on the first occasion in six months' imprisonment, on the second in twelve months' imprisonment, and on the third in loss of freedom (Campbell 1990, 61). People impressed into the armed forces this way could hardly be expected to show any *esprit de corps.*

Several authoritarian states established "roaming vigilantes", as Davidson (1979, 99) calls them, comprising Black, Coloured and White scouting parties, rural constables, and men variously called bounty hunters, Maroon hunters, Negro hunters, Negro catchers, slave catchers, runaway catchers and bushwhackers, sometimes operating separately and at other times incorporating all ethnic and colour groups – with the sole or main purpose of ferreting out Maroons. Such groups, for instance, existed in Mexico, Colombia, the Dominican Republic, Peru, Cuba, Haiti, Brazil and Suriname.[6] In Brazil, *capitães do mato (capitães do campo, capitães dos assalto:* "bush captains"), who were often free Coloureds, led mixed groups of bounty hunters – Indians, Mulattos, Mestizos and Blacks. They roamed the rural areas in search of prey. According to the police chief of Rio de Janeiro in 1824, they were able to penetrate the forest in Minas Gerais (and perhaps elsewhere) because they wore leather clothing that protected them from thorns and briars (Conrad 1983, 383). In the gold-bearing province of Minas Gerais, they were paid in gold for each Maroon that they captured (Boxer 1962, 170).

La Rosa Corzo (2003, 4) states that in Cuba, small private bands were permitted to hunt down "vagabond runaway slaves", while large slave-hunting expeditions consisting of militia and military personnel were assigned the task of scouting the haunts of Maroon settlements for up to three months at a time (ibid., 28 passim), and the same was basically true in Brazil (Lara 1988, 295–322). Usually, large expeditions could take place only with the specific permission of the colonial authorities. In 1794 the Royal Consulate or Board of Development was established in Havana to formulate policy and coordinate major activities against the Maroons throughout the island, but much was still left to the regional governments (La Rosa Corzo 2003, 4, 7).

Indians became indispensable in Suriname, Guyana and Brazil, and they were used frequently in Mexico, Venezuela and elsewhere. Though on the whole the Jamaican authorities placed less reliance on them, on a few occasions in the 1720s and 1730s they imported Miskito Indians specifically to seek out and destroy Maroon settlements. However, these hired hands were not very effective because – according to Governor Hunter in 1731 – they were accustomed to fighting in swampy rather than mountainous terrain. But Bryan Edwards felt that they had rendered important service to the colony (Campbell 1990, 55). One important thing that the White expeditionary forces learned from the Indians was the imperative of silence on their expeditions, which included refraining from shooting game on the way (Campbell 1990, 54–55).

Whites were always concerned that Blacks on expeditions would join the Maroon ranks, taking whatever military equipment they could seize, as happened frequently in Jamaica in the 1730s. On one occasion as many as one hundred Black Shots and baggage carriers, both drawn from the enslaved population, deserted.[7] In fact, Campbell (1990, 81) boldly asserts that no state expedition in the 1730s failed to experience desertion among the Black contingent. For this reason the Whites generally gave firearms, as distinct from less lethal weapons, only to the most trusted Blacks, but there was no telling who would turn out to be faithful when an opportunity to abscond presented itself. Still, because of the critical shortage of Europeans who could or would undertake the task of flushing out Maroons, the authoritarian state had to rely increasingly on Blacks to fight for them.

Black and Coloured scouts were much cheaper to maintain and often more effective than White ones (though White scouts were cheaper than regular soldiers). In some jurisdictions, especially as the number and size of Maroon groups grew with the spread of plantation culture, the state bought enslaved persons, promised them freedom, and organized them into special units to fight the Maroons. The Black Rangers of Suriname noted above (also see chapter 9) are an outstanding example. Stedman (1988, 81) declared that they were "*brave* men acting wonders above expectation in conjunction with the Colony or Society's troops whose strength alone was no longer thought sufficient to defend this settlement at present". He also stated that once they came within striking range of the Maroons "no subordination can possibly keep them back and . . . are as eager as a pack of blood hounds, fearless of danger only panting to rush upon their foe" (ibid., 204).[8] He asserted that in the Guiana forests one of them was preferable to six White soldiers, both for expertise in jungle warfare and for commitment to destroying the Maroons (ibid., 204, 396). Likewise, Moreau de Saint-Méry wrote about the Coloured people who commonly pursued Maroons and who displayed their tactical superiority over the regular soldiers by casting off their shoes, thus allowing them to climb jagged rocks and descend steep cliffs just as the Maroons did (Fouchard 1972, 367). The Black Shots of Jamaica, while notorious for desertion, included several individuals who were intensely faithful to their overlords and the anti-Maroon cause. The most notable of these was Sambo, who served so well that he was promoted to the rank of captain. As an exception to the general rule regarding the Black Shots, the government eventually freed him and his family (Campbell 1990, 83–84).

Apart from men, the colonial states used other devices to destroy the Maroons. Among these were dogs – usually bloodhounds or "Negro dogs", the term commonly used in the United States – trained specially to hunt them down.[9] These animals constituted an important part of the Spanish, and to varying extents the Dutch, British and French, arsenal of attack. The

Spanish used them from the early days of colonization to hunt Indians in Hispaniola (Dominican Republic). In the hinterland of Cuba, the Dominican Republic and the United States the dogs of war instilled terror in many Maroons. Some Maroons actually died from dog bites (Villaverde 1982, 107).

In 1815 Alfonzo Martínez, leader of an expedition against El Frijol Maroons, calculated that in order to overpower the settlement, estimated as having over two hundred warriors (a gross overestimate, according to La Rosa Corzo), he required two hundred men and thirty bulldogs (La Rosa Corzo 2003, 107–8). From the 1680s the Jamaican government began to import dogs periodically to hunt down Maroons. One early government act made provision for a large gang of dogs to be paid for out of funds from the respective parish churches (Campbell 1990, 37). The government also imported a number of them from Cuba in 1795, along with their *chasseurs* (handlers), to assist in putting down Maroon unrest in that year. The French employed two hundred dogs in the last phase of fighting against the Black revolutionaries in Haiti.[10] It is said that these hounds were able to sniff out the most sheltered *palenques* in Cuba (Franco 1979, 41). In the nineteenth century, as the sugar plantation economy expanded in that island and the number of Maroon communities grew, so did the organized bands of hunters equipped with trained dogs (Pérez de la Riva 1979, 57). Ortiz (1975, 366–67) cites Merlin, who stated that the canine species of Cuba was unique for its strength, its intelligence and its incredible aversion to Black runaways. He might also have said that this was not a natural aversion but one sedulously cultivated through training by Maroon hunters. In the mid-sixteenth century the Spanish loosed dogs on a group of captured Maroons belonging to the Palenque de Bayano in Panama, who refused to give up their religion and accept conversion to Catholicism, in spite of repeated exhortations by their captors to do so before being executed. The Spanish turned the mastiffs on them, huge dogs that had been trained to tear at the flesh of Blacks. The latter had only thin rods with which to defend themselves, which were quite harmless to the dogs but enraged them further, driving them to sink their teeth into their victims and tear away great pieces of flesh. Despite their extreme agony, the dying Maroons refused to recant (La Guardia 1977, 88–89).[11]

Marcus Rainsford (1805, 426–27) explained how dogs were trained to disembowel Blacks in Haiti:

Figure 12. Richard Ansdell, *The Hunted Slaves* (1861). Reproduced by permission of National Museums Liverpool, United Kingdom.

As they approached maturity, their keepers procured a figure roughly formed as a negro in wicker work, in the body of which were contained the blood and entrails of beasts. This was exhibited before an upper part of the cage, and the food occasionally exposed as a temptation, which attracted the attention of the dogs to it as a source of the food they wanted. This was repeated often, so that the animals with redoubled ferocity struggled against their confinement while in proportion to their impatience the figure was brought nearer, though yet out of their reach, and their food decreased till, at the last extremity of desperation, the keeper resigned the figure, well charged with the nauseous food before described, to their wishes. While they gorged themselves with the dreadful meat, he and his colleagues caressed and encouraged them. By these means the whites ingratiated themselves so much with the animals, as to produce an effect directly opposite to that perceivable in them towards the black figure; and, when they were employed in the pursuit for which they were intended, afforded the protection so necessary to their employers.

Runaways adopted various strategies to reduce the effectiveness of bloodhounds as trackers, including bathing or rubbing themselves with certain plants and using copious amounts of pepper (Zips 1999, 77–83). The Maroons generally preferred to elude the dogs, but when they were in groups they often stood their ground and attacked the animals fiercely, sometimes killing or wounding them severely (Franco 1973, 81; Villaverde 1982, 46, 56–57, 86). If the evidence from the diary of Estévez is typical, these animals had a high mortality rate as a result of Maroon retaliation and the strain of long treks, climbing hills and going without food for long periods (Villaverde 1982, 46, 71, 82, 93, 97 passim). Estévez certainly did not display much greater pity for his own dogs than for the Maroons whom he brutally hunted down.

Military expeditions sometimes reported that the mortality rates suffered by their adversaries were much higher than those of their own forces, and not infrequently that they had raided and destroyed the Maroons' dwellings and provision fields. But equally often they returned defeated, harassed, and drained in spirit and body.[12] Few of them wanted to revisit the scene of such unfamiliar warfare, in which the vast majority of their opponents managed to escape, returned to their previous locations and rebuilt their wrecked settlements. Maroons were often physically but only occasionally psychologically wounded, for they understood that they had to pay a high price for their freedom. Like the spider, when their web was destroyed they knew they had to rebuild it again swiftly. While Maroons might suffer heavily from the periodic expeditions, they were able to carry the war to their enemies by destroying whole plantations, killing some or all of the Whites found there and seizing booty. Maroon attacks were facilitated by the fact that their numbers often included members who once belonged to these plantations and knew their strengths and weaknesses well. They also had friends and relatives on the plantations who often assisted them secretly.

Successful and unsuccessful state expeditions against Maroon communities often resulted in terrible backlash on planter society. The destruction of Maroons' houses and crops and the killing, maiming or apprehension of their people inspired the survivors to exact vengeance on the White body politic as a fitting requiem to their fallen comrades (Blassingame 1979, 213–14; Campbell 1990, 39, 68). Ocampo and Lemba, for instance, on different occasions conducted reprisals against their attackers, burning refineries in San Juan, Dominican Republic, and leading away a number of enslaved persons. Similar reprisals occurred in 1649, when the Spanish attacked the Ocoa settlement (Esteban Deive 1989, 48, 50, 81); and in the 1650s, when the British killed a number of Maroons in Jamaica and destroyed their dwellings (Campbell 1990, 19). State expeditions tended therefore to ricochet on the state, in a continuous sequence of cause and effect. What strikes even the casual reader is the vast number of state or individually organized expeditions (literally thousands) and the equally large number of Maroon assaults on the plantations and sometimes the towns. Nothing short of the complete routing of a Maroon group or the signing of a treaty between the belligerent parties could break the vicious cycle.

BOUNTIES AND OTHER REWARDS

Bounties on captured and killed Maroons were an important aspect of the authoritarian state's strategy to destroy the communities. Around the mid-sixteenth century, the Lima city council established a special bounty fund to which all enslavers had to contribute on the basis of the numbers of enslaved persons that they held (Bowser 1974, 198). In the late eighteenth century the Superior Council of Guadeloupe established differential bounties on the apprehension of Maroons, based on the length of time since they had absconded, from less than two months to over one year (Moreau de Saint-Méry 1784–90, 1:128). In 1693 in Cartagena the government paid four pesos for the head of each Maroon killed and forty pesos for each one taken alive (Borrego Plá 1973, 80). The ranks of Maroon catchers expanded to include bounty hunters of various ethnic backgrounds. They were always on the prowl, roaming both the rural and urban areas in search of prey.

In the United States in the early decades of the nineteenth century, they operated even in New York and New Bedford, free northern territories where they were not officially allowed. They kidnapped and returned to their over-lords people who were supposed to be runaways (Douglass 1973, 106, 112). The Fugitive Slave Act, passed by the federal government in 1850, expressly sanctioned such activities. It also gave federal marshals the power to com-mand any citizen to assist them in apprehending runaways, thus requiring every citizen to become a slave catcher (Quarles 1969, 107; Fogel 1989, 341–42). Freehling (2002, 8) writes of this despicable act: "The despotic fea-tures included no judge for alleged fugitives, no jury, no writ of habeas cor-pus, and an unappealable judgement only by a one-case commissioner, who received $5 if he freed the supposed runaway, and $10 if he dispatched the accused to slavery." Many Southerners and other pro-slavery groups were bent upon enforcing the act, sometimes at great personal and financial cost. In one memorable instance in 1854, concerning the Virginian runaway Anthony Burns, who had made it to the so-called safe haven of Boston, President Franklin Pierce deployed the federal government's marines and artillery to ensure that, once apprehended, he was not snatched from the hands of the enslavers. The cost of returning this runaway to slavery was said to be over $100,000 (Freehling 2002, 9), though philanthropists later pur-chased his freedom for the relatively small sum of $1,300. The fact is that, especially after 1850, safe havens were not always what they were supposed to be. It was events like these that caused William Wells Brown (1999, 702), who managed to run to freedom, to condemn White-controlled society as rotten to the core: "[W]hen I thought of slavery with its Democratic whips – its Republican chains – its evangelical blood-hounds, and its religious slave-holders – when I thought of all this paraphernalia of American Democracy and Religion behind me, and the prospect of liberty before me, I was encour-aged to press forward."

Apart from the ordinary bounties paid for the bringing in of a hand, a leg, ears or the head of a Maroon (according to the laws in the various jurisdic-tions), which also went up periodically, special bounties were offered as the exigencies of the situation demanded. In 1571 the Spanish imperial govern-ment offered the sale price of any captured Maroon to the bounty hunters in the Dominican Republic (Esteban Deive 1989, 53). In 1574 in Mexico, captors were allowed to retain the captured runaways if no one came forward to claim them; otherwise they could be indemnified fifty pesos in lieu of retaining such captives (León 1924, 10). In 1665 the Jamaican government established staggered fees for the apprehension or killing of the Karmahaly Maroons:

£30 sterling for Juan de Serras, the leader; £20 for any of his officers; and £10 for any of his other men. Any men who located and assaulted the Karmahaly settlement would be rewarded with all the women and children that they should capture, in addition to whatever booty they should acquire (Patterson 1979, 255; Campbell 1990, 27).

In 1685 the governor general of Brazil agreed to allow Domingos Jorge Velho – a famous military leader with a private army, who wrought havoc in suppressing Indian uprisings – to keep as his property all Maroons whom he might capture in a raid on Palmares (Hemming 1978, 356). In Cartagena in the late seventeenth century, booty (apart from Maroons) legally belonged to the members of the expeditionary force (Borrego Plá 1973, 80). In 1717 the Suriname government offered 1,500 guilders for the discovery of two important Maroon settlements and 600 guilders for any other settlement (Hartsinck 1770, 756–57). In 1818 the North Carolina authorities offered a bounty of $250 for the capture of seven particular Maroons, and a separate reward of $100 for the apprehension of their leader, Billy James (Andey, Abaellino) (Aptheker 1979, 157). In 1795 the Demerara government offered a bounty of 400 guilders for each Maroon taken alive and 200 guilders for each right hand brought in (Thompson 1987, 145).

In those jurisdictions where there was little or no differential in the bounties paid for dead or live Maroons, bounty hunters often killed Maroons even when they could bring them in alive. Instead, they brought in their hands, ears or other part of their anatomy, as the different laws might specify.[13] Killing at times becomes irresistible to a predator and, of course, killing a Maroon was easier than bringing him in alive. A dead Maroon could not escape or give any trouble, and one did not have to worry about feeding him on the sometimes long journey from the Maroon settlement to the urban centre. However, humane considerations gradually emerged (along with the awareness that a dead Maroon could not work), and the bounty hunters were encouraged to bring Maroons in alive through payment of a much higher premium for a live than a dead one.[14] Slaveholders naturally resented the death or even mutilation of their human property, especially when they were required to pay the bounty,[15] but there was little that they could do about it.

The enslavers celebrated some leaders of expeditions against Maroons as heroes. In Brazil, Tibaldo Lins, Clemente de Rocha, Manuel Lopes, Fernão Carrilho, Domingos Jorge Velho and Andrés Furtado de Mendonça became famous in the later seventeenth century for daring expeditions against

Figure 13. Domingos Jorge Velho and his aide-de-camp (*O bandeirante Do mingos Jorge Velho*, by Benedito Calixto, 1903)

Palmares, sometimes at their own expense. In Cuba their counterparts were Ramón Cordero, Francisco Rivera, Andrés Rivera, Domingo Armona, José Pérez Sánchez, Francisco Estévez and Valentín Páez. In Colombia they were Juan Gabriel and Governor Marín de Cevallos Lacerda; and in Suriname they were David Nassy and Juriaan François de Friderici.[16] Some of these people were large plantation owners and high government officials. However, as noted already, the vast majority of Maroon catchers were recruited among White small farmers, free Coloured people and the social outcasts of society. Pinto Vallejos (1998, 184) declares that slave-catching proved to be

> a very convenient means for putting vagrants and brigands to a socially produc-
> tive use. . . . The vast majority of the *capitães do mato* [were] drawn from their
> ranks, partly in the not too unreasonable expectation that they would be better
> trained for bush warfare. Teixeira Coelho expressed this most succinctly in 1780:
> "these vagrants, who in other lands would be a curse, are useful here: . . . they
> make up the squads that go into the jungle to destroy the *quilombos* of runaway
> slaves, and that help the justice in capturing criminals".

According to Roberto Frijol (1982, 18, 21), Francisco Estévez was the ulti-mate Maroon catcher, "the Atila of the Vuelta Abajo palenques", whose ded-icated and self-declared objective was the total extermination of the Maroons.[17] Villaverde (1982, 28) refers to him as a semi-civilized peasant, a family man, an owner of a small coffee estate and a slaveholder. His diary gives the distinct impression of a man with a dark and melancholy mind. Franco (1973, 84) asserts that Domingo Armona distinguished himself by his cruelty, which seemed to rival, if not surpass, that of Estévez. In one night he hanged eighteen Blacks whom he had met on his search for Maroons, with-out bothering to ascertain whether or not they were fugitives.

Ortiz (1975, 363) warns us not to be duped by stories of the valour and ded-ication of bush captains and bounty hunters, or with the rhythm of the applause that most enslavers gave them. Many of those, he asserts, who ded-icated themselves to such a heartless profession were cruel men and real ras-cals. In his novel entitled *Romualdo: uno de tantos*, Francisco Calcagno (1881, 47) depicts the Cuban *rancheador* (Maroon catcher) in this way:

> The rancheador is another of the odious types of our society: he is a monstrosity
> spawned by slavery. . . . The maroon gives rise to the rancheador, as the political
> criminal gives rise to the hangman. On the same level with the dealer [in slaves]

Figure 14. A Brazilian capitão do mato with a captured Maroon. From *Voyage pittoresque dans le Brésil*, by Johann Moritz Rugendas; trans. M. de Golbéry (Paris: Engelmann, 1835).

that we have described, we cannot determine who is more ignoble: both are worse . . . than all other types.

Ortiz (1975, 363) cites a dispatch from Philip IV of 23 July 1623 to the effect that the bounty hunters whom the legal authorities had appointed to track down runaways used their authority to intrude into the premises of peaceful Black persons in Cuba and elsewhere, indulging day and night in great extortion with full abandon, carrying off their horses, farming animals and other necessary farming equipment. The dispatch therefore ordered the colonial governors to take measures to prevent such evil and mete out justice to the Blacks, so that the molestation and vexations of the slave-catchers would cease.

In Brazil the *capitães do mato* often seized Blacks who had been sent on errands by their overlords, and extorted payment from the latter before releasing them (Boxer 1962, 170). According to Mattoso (1979, 142), they often neglected their duties and sometimes hired others to do their jobs, and some made captured runaways work for them.[18] She goes on to state that they were often paid by a relative of the fugitive to look the other way.[19] In 1824 the police chief of Rio de Janeiro declared that the bounty hunters of that province were worthless and that there were daily complaints about them; that the title that the government accorded them provided them with a cloak to steal; and that many of them had been arrested for stealing enslaved people, whom they sold to Minas Gerais (Conrad 1983, 383). In order to combat the practice of *capitães do mato* availing themselves of the services of the captives, the authorities in Minas Gerais passed a law in 1722 forfeiting the payment of bounties to them if they failed to deliver the captives within a fortnight (Pinto Vallejos 1998, 180, 188).

PUNISHMENTS

Fuentes (1979, 9) states that in Puerto Rico the runaway or Maroon was a kind of political criminal according to the state law, but a freedom fighter according to natural law. It was the state law that the enslavers applied. Kenneth Stampp (1968, 51) accurately observes that if the authoritarian state did not confer on the enslavers the power to punish their servile charges, slavery could not have existed. Shahabuddeen (1983, 129) refers to slavery as a system of terror. Punishment, in fact, involved a number of components: terror, physical abuse, prolonged solitary confinement, separation from family, social degradation and humiliation. It could be as crude as physical mutilation, or as subtle as making the enslaved person eat dinner at the same table as the enslaver's family, as was actually done to a captured runaway (Stampp 1968, 52). It could involve the humiliation of assigning a non-praedial to a praedial position, or assigning a truant male to do "women's work", which entailed dressing in women's clothing (Stampp 1968, 52–53).

For Maroons, the price of capture was often very dear. Harsh punishments underlined the slaveholders' resolve to stamp out desertion by almost any means. The execution of the law often meant death for Maroons. This was exemplified in the proclamation that Governor George Robert Ainslie of Dominica is alleged to have announced in 1814, when he declared all-out war on the Maroons: that he had instructed his officers to take no prisoners but to execute men, women and children (cited in Cracknell 1973, 67). It is said that his superiors in London recalled him to answer for the exceptionally harsh measures (Honychurch 1975, 91). For a long time the authoritarian states in several parts of Spanish America routinely dealt with Maroons who had gained particular notoriety in their eyes by beheading them, dismembering their bodies and placing parts of the mutilated corpses along the highways and at the cities' gates (Mathieu 1982, 90; Esteban Deive 1989, 50; Arrázola 1967, 73, 180, 203). Such brutality acted as a deterrent to some enslaved persons, but the fact that desertion continued unabated until the official abolition of slavery shouts loudly and eloquently that many were quite willing to risk their lives to obtain their freedom. In this connection, Debien (1979, 109) rightly observes that regardless of the harshness of the punishments that the slaveholders inflicted on the Maroons, they never seemed to be a deterrent. Some runaways, such as Zabeth (see chapter 2), were determined that only death could prevent them from deserting.

In 1763 thirty-nine of the sixty-seven persons captured in the Buraco do Tatú (Armadillo's Hole) *quilombo* near Bahia carried the mark "F" (Fugitive), which signified that they had absconded more than once (Conrad 1983, 379). In 1610 the *procurador general* of the cabildo of Havana suggested that apprehended runaways should have an ear or the nose cut off so that they could be more easily identified and recaptured if they absconded a second time (Navarrete 2003, 31). In the late sixteenth century, the Colombian government decreed that any male runaway who absented himself for fifteen days should be tied up at the city's pillory in the morning, decorated with strings

Figure 15. A Suriname Maroon hanged alive by the ribs. From *Narrative of a Five Years' Expedition against the Revolted Negroes of Surinam*, by John Gabriel Stedman (London, 1796).

of bells, receive one hundred lashes, and be left in that position all day long for other enslaved persons to view (Escalante 1979, 74). A male who had absconded for more than one month was to be castrated publicly and have his genitals displayed at the city's pillory. Those who had run away for more than a year were to be put to death. Females were to receive two hundred lashes for staying away for more than fifteen days, but apparently were not to be put to death (Escalante 1979, 75).

Between 1571 and 1574 the Mexican government, faced with sharply increasing incidence of desertion and the formation of Maroon settlements, produced several tough pieces of legislation. These included for absence of more than four days fifty lashes; for absence of more than eight days, one hundred lashes and irons to be fixed to the deserter's feet for two months; and for absence of more than six months, death, though castration was sometimes substituted (Davidson 1979, 92).[20] In 1590 the law on desertion was tightened. It prescribed thirty lashes for the first offence by anyone staying away for more than one night, two hundred lashes and amputation of both ears for a second offence, the same number of lashes plus amputation of a leg for a third offence, and hanging for a fourth offence (Palmer 1976, 125).

The French *Code Noir* (1685) stipulated that any enslaved person absent for a month was to have his ears cut off and a fleur-de-lys branded on his left shoulder. If he ran away a second time, he was to suffer laceration of his knees and branding on his shoulder. On the third occasion, he was to be sentenced to death (Franco 1979, 38). Debien (1979, 114) states that in practice the death penalty was used more sparingly, for *marronage* that did not involve armed assault. No doubt, this was not from any humane consideration by the state but due to the financial loss to the slaveholders. However, Moitt (2001, 137–38) informs us that in 1724 the *conseil supérieur* of Martinique condemned a woman to death by hanging for a third act of *marronage*, and that while the sentence was being carried out the cord broke and the executioner decided to strangle her, in spite of pleas for mercy from the onlookers.

Legislation in Brazil in the eighteenth century followed basically the same lines as that in the French Caribbean, with branding, loss of a body part and death being prescribed for the first, second and third offences of desertion respectively. The Crown rejected the petition of some members of the slave-holding fraternity to institute severance of the Achilles tendon for repeated desertion, on the advice of the Count of Arcos, one of the more enlightened viceroys of the colony, who viewed the proposal as an attempt to introduce tyranny as a form of social control and a barbarity unworthy of persons who professed Christianity (Boxer 1962, 171–73). Though the enslavers intended branding with special marks or letters to be a sign of dishonour – punishment, identification and humiliation – runaways in Brazil wore their brands as emblems of honour, visible testimony that they had asserted their right to be free (ibid., 172).

The city council of Lima, Peru, promulgated perhaps the most draconian laws. In 1535 it decreed that any male who had deserted for six days would be castrated, and anyone staying away for longer would be executed (Bowser 1974, 196). The punishments emphasized how gravely the enslavers perceived even simple or *petit marronage*. In 1539 the Peruvian authorities underlined their view of the runaway as a criminal by offering a reward of ten pesos for anyone who was apprehended after a day's absence (Bowser 1974, 197). About a decade later, they lightened the punishments only slightly. It is not known whether the drastic measures were costing too many labour hands or the governor (whom they consulted) influenced their judgement. Whatever the reason(s), the council now decreed that any deserter who had not returned within ten days should forfeit his genitals to the administrator of (in)justice if he had absconded to tryst with a Black or Indian woman; otherwise he would lose a foot, in addition to further punishments if he should be found guilty of other "crimes". If he absconded a second time for less than ten days, similar punishments would apply, and if he did so a third time, he would be executed automatically – that is, without recourse to a trial. If a first-time deserter did not return within twenty days, he too would be subject to automatic execution. The council also prescribed punishments for people who harboured deserters, the harshest being imposed on enslaved persons: one hundred lashes for the first offence, castration for the second and death for the third. The council empowered every White person in the city to capture runaways and to kill those who resisted arrest. In either event they were entitled to specific bounties. This was very rough justice, if it can be called justice at all (Bowser 1974, 197–98, 200, 397n27).

Castration, or "gelding", as one Louisiana jailer put it, was not unique to Peru; it existed in Brazil, Mexico, Colombia, Barbados, Louisiana, Virginia, the Carolinas, Pennsylvania, New Jersey, Antigua, Bermuda and elsewhere.[21] In 1590 the viceroy of Mexico decreed that some Maroons who were troubling the inhabitants of Panuco and the large plantations of Chicimecas, Almeria and Tlalcotalpa should be apprehended and castrated (Palmer 1976,

125). Following the servile uprising in Barbados in 1692, the colonial government paid ten guineas to Alice Mills for castrating forty-two insurgents (Jordan 1968, 156). In 1697 the South Carolina Assembly decreed castration for three persons who had sought to abscond to the neighbouring Spanish settlement; in 1722 the law of that state specified that fourth-time runaways should be castrated (Jordan 1968, 154–55).[22]

Castration as a form of punishment overrode the early Spanish code, *Las siete partidas,* which was promulgated in the thirteenth century and was supposed to be the basis for the Spanish colonial laws on slavery. The code prohibited castration and the imperial government's edict of 1540 (Franco 1973, 8; Naveda Chávez-Hita 1987, 123; Bryant 2004, 15). Castration was a particularly harsh punishment (though execution was harsher) because it struck at the Maroon's manhood and self-esteem. It was clearly intended to add humiliation to his suffering and to signal to him that the authoritarian state possessed the power to make him, at least physically, less than a man. This punishment, like the others mentioned above, was not imposed on the Maroon for the crime of rape but for simply running away to gain freedom. For Jordan (1968, 156), the punishment reflected "a desperate, generalized need in white men to persuade themselves that they were really masters and in all ways masterful, and it illustrated dramatically the ease with which white men slipped over into treating their Negroes like their bulls and stallions whose 'spirit' could be subdued by emasculation". Jordan (ibid., 158–59) adds another dimension to this issue by noting that Black men were generally believed to have significantly larger penises than White men. Castration, therefore, was intended to have the triple effect of mutilating the Black in a most awful manner, cutting him down to size and cutting him off from his manhood. But even this awful punishment – neither the threat nor the implementation – did not stop enslaved Black men from absconding. In 1831 a Louisiana jailer issued an advertisement that he had in custody a runaway who had been "gelded" lately and had not quite healed (Stampp 1968, 61). It just goes to show that enslaved persons did not need genitals to flee. More seriously, it demonstrates the overriding virtue of freedom in the minds of this man and other runaways.

Solitary confinement was another method of torture, but the objective here was to break the runaway's mind and spirit, though physical disability might be a corollary. Human beings are by nature gregarious, and solitary living might thus be viewed as a kind of necrosis. We know that one of the cru-

Figure 16. Back of Black, brutalized. From *Harper's Weekly,* 4 July 1863.

elest punishments meted out to prisoners is to place them in solitary confinement for long periods. In South Carolina this form of torture was referred to
as confinement in "the black-hole of the workhouse" (Lofton 1948, 413). The
French dubbed such places "frightening dungeons" (*cachots effrayants*), which
Debien (1979, 119) explains were maximum-security cells, probably without
light. James Walker, a manager in Berbice, described those that he had built

as dark cells and went on to boast about the salutary influence of such confinement (Thompson 2002a, 213). From around the last quarter of the eighteenth century they were constructed on all plantations in the French Caribbean that had more than 150 enslaved persons (Debien 1979, 119).

As noted above, even the dead (or rather their bodies) were often subject to exemplary "punishments" by displaying them in public places. In 1695 the colonial authorities in Pernambuco cut off the head of Zumbi, the last ruler of Palmares, and stuck it on a pole in the busiest part of Recife, in order to intimidate would-be deserters. It was perhaps also a symbolic representation by the authorities that this widely acclaimed god of war was, in fact, a mortal being whom they could dispatch to eternity (Carneiro 1946, 53; see chapters 4 and 10). In 1533 Governor Manuel de Rojas of Cuba, having killed four runaways in the mines of Jobabo, took their bodies to Bayamo, where he had them cut in pieces and the heads stuck on poles (Ortiz 1975, 369). In 1612 the Audiencia in Mexico City decreed that twenty-nine males and four females should be hanged, and their heads removed and placed on poles until total decomposition had taken place (Naveda Chávez-Hita 1987, 127). In 1771 Guillermo Rivas's head and an arm were cut off and placed at the entrance and exit of Panaquire (García 1996, 77, 79). In the early seventeenth century Fernando Montero (Montoro) was executed, and his hands and head were cut off, taken to Santo Domingo and placed on poles at the entrance to the public square. The rest of the body was cut into pieces and placed along the highways (Larrazábal Blanco 1998, 146).

A more well-known example of brutality and vulgarity by the judicial authorities appears in the extant records concerning Lemba, a much feared Dominican Republic Maroon leader in the mid-sixteenth century, who was killed in one of his many encounters with the colonial troops. The colonial government directed that his head should be placed on an iron hook and displayed on one of the gates that opened out into the King's Savannah. For a long time that gate was remembered as "Lemba's Gate" (Esteban Deive 1989, 50; Larrazábal Blanco, 1998, 143).[23]

Certain judicial sentences are chilling simply to read about them. Consider the following sentences passed on two Maroons that the French colonial government apprehended in 1752.

> Copena, charged with and convicted of marronage; of bearing firearms; of invading and pillaging, along with other maroons, the house and plantation of Berniac from which they stole furnishing, silver and a musket, and carried off many of

his slaves; of mistreating him; and of committing other excesses. Copena is sentenced to having his arms, legs, thighs, and back broken on a scaffold to be erected in the Place du Port. He shall then be placed on a wheel, face toward the sky, to finish his days, and his corpse shall be exposed. Claire, convicted of the crime of marronage and of complicity with maroon Negroes, shall be hanged till dead at the gallows in the Place du Port. Her two young children Paul and Pascal, belonging to M. Coutard, and other children – François and Batilde, Martin and Baptiste – all accused of marronage, are condemned to witness the torture of Copena and Claire. (Price 1979, 319)

Some punishments, if not more physically exacting, were far more callous. In the French Caribbean certain overlords retaliated against people who had taken flight by placing in irons their near relations, such as their fathers, mothers, sisters and wives (or reputed wives). They were chained together in twos and worked under this constraint even on Sundays, and slept in the lockups until their relatives returned (Gautier 1985, 229–30). Captured women with small children ran the risk of seeing heavy chains being placed around the necks or feet of these infants, some only six years old, which weighed them down and, in the view of one government official, always led to severe bruising (Gautier 1985, 237). In 1832 magistrate Xavier Tanc of Guadeloupe observed "a little girl about six years old dragging this heavy and irksome burden with torment as if the crime . . . of the mother was justification for punishing this young child in such a barbarous manner. At that age, her fragile frame and delicate flesh were all battered" (Moitt 2001, 139). The vicarious punishment of women and children for the desertion of their male adult relatives was also not unknown in Belize (Bolland 2002, 57).

Although the colonial governments were themselves known to mete out extremely harsh punishments, they did not always concur with vicarious punishment. In 1846 the Royal Court of Guadeloupe imposed a fine of five hundred francs on Crosnier, a plantation administrator, for punishing Hermine and Belonie because their children had absconded. In 1827 the judiciary in French Guiana convicted the planter Achille Wermin d'Aigrepon of excessive cruelty for chaining the mother and sisters of runaways, and further punishing two of them, Marie Thérèse and Denise, with up to two hundred lashes daily until the runaway relatives should return. The elderly Denise had expired as a result of the punishment, but the perpetrator claimed that she had poisoned herself in desperation. To compound his crime, he had ordered that her head be severed and placed on a pole outside her dwelling, as had the head of her seventy-five-year-old husband, Jacinthe, who had previously been punished for *marronage*. The criminal received the relatively light sentence of banishment from the colony for ten years (Moitt 2001, 139).

The political authorities also occasionally handed down much lighter sentences than the enslavers expected. A case in point is that of Miguel Jerónimo, the famous Venezuelan Maroon leader. The Audiencia in Caracas sentenced him to twenty-five lashes because of his advanced age; some of his followers also received comparatively light sentences. Perhaps the Audiencia felt that the atrocities that the overlords had meted out to their charges were mainly responsible for the many acts of revolts and violence against them. However, the enslavers were very angry over this judgement and entered a joint protest against the sentence, demanding that Jerónimo should be executed because he was the ringleader of numerous insurgents who had ravaged their properties for some years. They submitted that he had become so famous that he was popularly known by the sobriquet of "Captain" (Brito Figueroa 1985, 241).

In a number of jurisdictions it was common to place iron collars with bells attached around the necks of captured runaways, but many of them ran away again in pursuit of freedom (Stampp 1968, 53; Blassingame 1979, 196). Others were handcuffed to heavy logs at night and chained to other runaways during the day, or had chains attached to both feet, but found ways of fleeing. Peter, a Louisiana runaway, was one of them. He was reported in the local press as having on each foot an iron ring with a small chain attached to it (Stampp 1968, 53).

The Maroons' response to punishment was perhaps the ultimate test of their resolve. They bore it with dignity, courage and sometimes scorn. No doubt many of them had developed their fortitude in Africa during their early teens, when they were subjected to scarification and circumcision rituals without anaesthetics, during which they were not expected to utter a sound or even whimper. Following Tackey's revolt in 1760, which the Whites and their recent Maroon allies from the Windward and Leeward groups put down ferociously, several of the insurgents were condemned to cruel deaths. Fortune and Kingston were hung alive on gibbets in the public square, lasting seven and nine lingering days respectively before dying (Campbell 1990, 156). The morning before Kingston died he experienced convulsions throughout his body. According to Long (1774, 2:458n) a post-mortem revealed that his lungs were attached so rigidly to his back that it required some force to separate them. The writer appears rather callous in his approach to the brutal state punishment: "The murders and outrages they had committed, were thought to justify this cruel punishment inflicted upon them *in terrorem* to others; but they appeared to be very little affected by it themselves; behaving all the time with a degree of hardened insolence, and brutal insensibility."

John Stedman (1988, 67) recorded many brutalities against captured Maroons (and other Blacks) during his stay in Suriname in the 1770s, including the following: "One man was hanged alive with an iron hook struck through his ribs upon a gibbet – and two others being chain'd to stakes were burnt to death by slow fire – six women were broke[n] alive upon the rack – and two girls were decapitated – through which tortures – they went without uttering a sigh." Eddie Donoghue (2002, 33) refers to a similar event that occurred in the Danish West Indies. He also cites several examples from that colony of enslaved persons who met their death with fortitude, some of them smiling as they did so. He tells us that Reimert Haagensen, a Danish slaveholder in the mid-eighteenth century, was so struck by this circumstance that he referred to them as "stonehard". These and many more had their epitaphs written in blood and bore their punishments without flinching. Outstanding among them was Amsterdam, leader of a Maroon settlement in Demerara in 1795. The following quotation is long but it is worth citing.

> He was sentenced to be burnt alive, first having the flesh torn from his limbs with red-hot pincers;[24] and in order to render his punishment still more terrible, he was compelled to sit by, and see thirteen others broken and hung; and then, in being conducted to execution, was made to walk over the thirteen dead bodies of his comrades. Being fastened to an iron-stake, surrounded with the consuming pile, which was about to be illuminated, he regarded by-standers with all the complacency of heroic fortitude, and exhibiting the most unyielding courage, resolved that all the torture ingenuity or cruelty might invent should not extort from him a single groan. . . .
>
> With the first pair of pincers, the executioner tore the flesh from one of his arms. The sudden infliction of pain caused him to recede, in a slight degree, from the irons; and he drew in his breath, as if to form it into a sigh, but he instantly recovered himself – his countenance upbraided him, and he manifestly took shame for having betrayed even the slightest sense of suffering – then, resuming more, if possible, than his former composure, he patiently waited the approach of the next irons, and, on these being brought towards him, he steadfastly cast his eye upon them, inclined a little forward, and with unshaken firmness of

countenance, deliberately met their burning grasp! From that moment he shewed himself capable of despising the severest pain. Not a feature was afterwards disturbed, and he preserved a degree of composure implying absolute contempt of torture and of death. (Pinckard 1806, 2:249–50)

Both symbolically and actually, the horrid stench that accompanied the burning of human flesh pervaded Stabroek, the capital town, and so sickened a number of persons that they lost their appetites for the rest of the day (ibid., 250–51). It is possible that such punishments often backfired. On the one hand, they may have intimidated some persons. On the other hand, they may have hardened the resolve of many others and made them more determined to avoid capture or, if that was not possible, to die fighting. Moreover, the punishments would almost certainly have provoked hatred, and a desire for revenge, among the relatives and friends of those punished. Wood (1975, 268) put it succinctly, "[T]he harder the hammer fell, the more likely it was to create further sparks."

The discussion of punishments would be incomplete without noting that many free and enslaved Blacks suffered, sometimes brutally so, through unfounded allegations about their involvement in Maroon activities. In times of crisis, such as intense Maroon assaults or major revolts, the authoritarian state's machinery of oppression indiscriminately cordoned off all Blacks, treating them as though they were rebels and equally to be blamed for the attacks. Many lost their freedom, while others either lost their lives by judicial executions, suffered severe whippings, or were banished or sold overseas, thus severing their long-established ties with friends and families (Hall 1971, 57–63; Reis 1993, 205–32). Even Maroon-hunting expeditions tended to treat with suspicion all Blacks that they encountered, to harass them and sometimes to apprehend them, much to the disgust of their overlords, who complained to the colonial authorities about such high-handed action (La Rosa Corzo 2003, 76; Boxer 1962, 170). But it was a problem that was not easily resolved in the jittery climate of the times. Thus the activities of both Maroons and Maroon-hunters, or rather the whiplash of the activities, at times abridged the freedoms not only of the Whites but also of all groups and classes within the society, though in different ways.

The "private tyranny", as Jordan (1968, 108) refers to it, that the enslavers legally exercised was supposed to be for the public good of both enslaved and free people. It was bad enough when private tyranny took place, but when tyranny occurred as a result of the public judicial process the situation was far worse, for the state was expected to function at a higher level of humanity than the individual, and to set appropriate standards of human conduct. However, given that the planters were essentially the state and vice versa, it was perhaps asking too much in respect of impartiality, equanimity and humanity. Pinckard (1806, 2:248), who had nothing positive to say about Maroons, nevertheless was outraged at the atrocities that the colonial authorities in Demerara perpetrated under the guise of just punishment. He opined that it was difficult to believe that any civilized government could have meted out such cruelty and refinement of torture, and that it was a shame to humanity. This statement calls to mind Paulo Freire's (1972, 32) observation: "As the oppressors dehumanize others and violate their rights, they themselves also become dehumanized." This was part of the boomerang effect of oppression. That effect was felt throughout the entire slaveholding state, and affected all classes and social groups negatively. It is appropriate to close this chapter with the words of Albert Memmi (1965, xviii): "[O]ppression is the greatest calamity of humanity. It diverts and pollutes the best energies of man – of oppressed and oppressor alike. For if colonization destroys the colonized, it also rots the colonizer."

Part 3

Maroon Organization

Freedom is not an occasion to behave as you like and do whatever you wish, but true freedom is about accepting the responsibility to do what is right.

– Junior Morgan, cited in "The True Musical Freedom", by Ricky Jordan, *Weekend Nation*, 3 October 2003

CHAPTER 6

Physical Organization of
Maroon Communities

THE LANDSCAPE

The achievement of physical freedom was a magical moment for each
Maroon individually and for the group as a whole. It created the necessary
space between them and their oppressors, and allowed them to use their freedom as they saw fit. But this might be viewed as elemental freedom, in the
sense that it is the kind of freedom that all living creatures seek. It is not
driven by any ideology or rationalization about striving for the common good
of the human collectivity. The task of those communities that had attained
this level of freedom was how to translate it into more than a survival mechanism, to cope with the rough realities of life in the *palenques* and to develop
meaningful human relations. This would take time, patience, goodwill and a
long set of other human graces. The Maroons could revolt, and they did
revolt; they could build a human society, but could they build a humane one?

Maroon life displayed many African features,[1] but it did not represent
simply a translation of African norms and forms into a new environment.
The culture was distinctly Maroon, built around the idea of freedom and survival in strenuous "laboratory" conditions that often had no real parallels in
Africa (or the Americas). Over time, because of the increasing creolization of
the enslaved population, admission into the communities of people of various ethnic and cultural backgrounds, and adaptations of material and social
forms from other cultures within the wider colonial societies, Maroon com-

munities came to be relatively pluralistic or multicultural, especially from the late eighteenth century.

Whether in small or large communities, Maroons often learned to survive in the most exiguous circumstances. The physical organization of Maroon settlements was usually carefully planned. Some settlements were large or significant enough to be described by leaders of military expeditions and contemporary writers as towns or capitals (see, for instance, Stedman 1988, 404; Bolland 2002, 57), but they were clearly not nearly as large as the White urban settlements. They were often regarded as the headquarters of a number of smaller settlements organized in a centripetal pattern (Franco 1979, 46). The Maroon states led by Miguel and Guillermo Rivas, both of Venezuela, Françisque Fabulé of Guadeloupe, Grandy Nanny of Jamaica and Boni of Suriname are examples. The same was true of Palmares in Brazil, the Bahoruco settlements in the Dominican Republic, and the small but no less complex settlements built around Bumba in Cuba.[2]

The landscapes of some of these towns were impressive, some because of the natural beauty of the rocky cliffs and others because of the Maroons' ability to shape the environment into elegance. Stedman (1988, 404) gave one such example. He described the Aluku (Boni) town at a distance as presenting the appearance of "an amphitheatre sheltered by the foliage of a few ranks of lofty trees, which they had left standing, the whole presenting a truly romantick [*sic*] and enchanting *coup doeuil*". La Rosa Corzo (2003, 155) tells us that El Cedro settlement in Cuba was "in a 'picturesque, leafy' valley that had a stream running through it and was surrounded by hills". Todos Tenemos was perhaps even more impressive by the standards of the time. Located in El Frijol Mountains, in the 1840s, according to La Rosa Corzo, it was carefully laid out in public squares and blocks. It contained fifty-nine "houses" and thirty-four "huts", simple buildings used as storehouses.[3]

Palmares was, by almost all accounts, an impressive state or confederation of states. Its physical contours spread over a wide area, estimated by Mattoso (1979, 371) at sixty square leagues, and contained settlements of various sizes and levels of sophistication. An anonymous seventeenth-century writer who took part in an expedition against Palmares in 1675–76 (and whose work was published by Pedro Paulino da Fonseca in 1876) has left us the following description concerning the largest settlements:

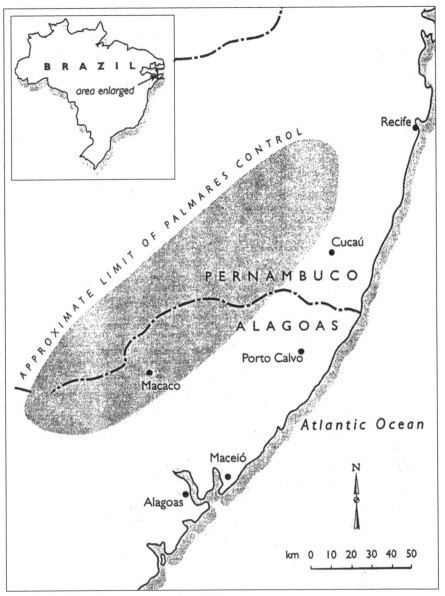

Figure 17. Palmares and vicinity. From "The Quilombo of Palmares: A New Overview of a Maroon State in Seventeenth-Century Brazil", by Robert Nelson Anderson, *Journal of Latin American Studies* 28 (1996). Used by permission of Cambridge University Press.

In a palm forest sixteen leagues northeast of Porto Calvo existed the *mocambo* of the Zambi (a general or god of arms in their language), and five leagues farther north that of Acainene [Arotirene] (this was the name of the king's mother, who lived in this fortified *mocambo* about twenty-five leagues northeast of Porto Calvo, and which they called the Acainene Compound, since it was fortified by a wall of earth and sticks).

To the east of these was the *mocambo* of the Wild Canes [Tabocas], and northeast of this one that of Bambiabonga [Dambrangaga]. Eight leagues north of Bambiabonga was the compound called Sucupira [Subupira]; six leagues northward from this the Royal Compound of the Macaco, and five leagues to the west of this the *mocambo* of Osenga. Nine leagues northwest of the town of Serinhaem was the compound of Amaro, and twenty-five leagues northwest of Alagôas the palm forest of Andolaquituxe [Adalaquituche], the Zambi's brother. (Conrad 1983, 369)

Bastide (1978, 85) – referring to the contemporary writer Caspar Barlaeus (Gaspar Barleus), who compiled his information from the Lintz and Baro expeditions – adds that the rural dwellers lived in huts thatched with *capim* grass, while the king owned both a town house and a country house. He also states that the palace seems to have been part of a complex of buildings in the capital that housed certain judicial and military personnel. Gilberto Freyre (1963, 39), in contrast, writes indiscriminately about Palmares as a place of mean and contemptuous dwellings: a "republic of shacks", and a capital "city of straw shacks".

Mucajubá, another *mocambo* in Brazil that endured for a long time, was situated on the banks of a lake and nestled among dense foliage in a remote area of the Amazon Valley. The settlement was said in 1856 to extend for two to three leagues, comprising a number of villages widely separated spatially. The British Consul, who wrote about its destruction in 1856, stated that it contained some large houses and that its population was estimated at one thousand to two thousand. It had large tracts of land under manioc cultivation (Conrad 1983, 390–91).

Apparently more notable still, in terms of its natural defences, was the Trombetas settlement, also in the Amazon Valley, in 1856.[4] Although we lack specific details of the hazards of the journey to the *mocambo* or how it was fortified, according to the British Consul, a captured Maroon reported that such difficulties and dangers attended the journey that thirty-three out of forty soldiers refused to follow their captain in search of the settlement. Up

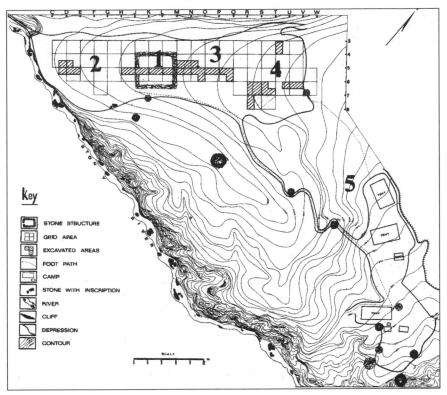

Figure 18. Nanny Town in post-treaty times. From *Maroon Heritage: Archaeological, Ethnographic and Historical Perspectives*, ed. Kofi Agorsah (Kingston: Canoe Press, 1994).

to that time no military enterprise had breached its defences and the enslaved peoples regarded it as an enchanted land (Conrad 1983, 391).

Campbell (1990, 47) describes the topographical features of the Maroon towns in Jamaica in greater detail:

> These were to be found in the mountains, with the outer towns relatively accessible at a lower declivity, the others becoming increasingly less so until the most strategic one, which was usually at an almost inaccessible point, was reached. Hardly any whites ever reached such a town. . . . The high elevation of these towns gave them a commanding view of the lowlands from whence the parties would approach.

Campbell describes the topography of the Leeward Maroons' habitats as mountainous country, intersected by a labyrinth of hills, valleys, rivers, deep ravines and awesome Cockpits (deep hollows), with narrow passes and countless caves (ibid., 10). She identifies the Blue Mountains and the John Crow Mountains as the preferred hideouts of the Karmahaly and later the Windward Maroons (ibid., 35, 50).[5] M.T.A. Ashcroft explored the John Crow Mountains in 1965; both decay and new verdant life were no doubt greater after two centuries of being uninhabited by Maroons. He wrote the following description of the area: "The John Crow Mountains must be the most deceptive in the world. Beneath a gentle and benign exterior they are harsh and implacable, utterly useless to man and exceptionally difficult to penetrate." The members of his expedition tried to cross from west to east, taking three days to do so and struggling "over crevasses in the jagged and unstable rocks, smothered in a tangle of rotting vegetation" (Fincham 1997, 218). M.R. Taylor, who explored the area in 1989, left an even more vivid description:

> It was the toughest going imaginable. . . . Frenzied vegetation spanned countless crevasses: we walked in a perpetual twilight, on roots and crumbly rock pinnacles well above the visible "ground". We had to map our way over the surface as we would have in a cave, in order to know where we had gone each day. When plotted on the topo, the day's map seldom agreed with our supposed route. (ibid.)

Dallas (1803, 1:39–41) offered an equally graphic description of the famous Cockpit[6] Country, the chief haunt of the Leeward Maroons:

> From the first Cockpit there is a succession of them, running from east to west, on a line in which they are passable from one to the other, though with more or less difficulty. There are also parallel lines of Cockpits, but as their sides are often perpendicular, from fifty to eighty feet, a passage from one line to another is scarcely to be found practicable to any but a Maroon. The northern aspect is commonly the steepest and often a solid perpendicular rock, so that if the opposite ascent were practicable, to descend into the parallel line would be impossible. This is the general character of these recesses, though they may in some degree differ in their direction.
>
> . . . . At this mouth, which looks like a great fissure made through a rock by some extraordinary convulsion of Nature, from two hundred yards to half a mile in length, and through which men can pass only in a single file, the Maroons, whenever they expected an attack, disposed of [*sic*] themselves on the ledges of the rocks on both sides . . . and lay covered by the underwood, and behind rocks and the roots of trees, waiting in silent ambush for their pursuers.

Some communities in Mexico, Haiti, Brazil, the Dominican Republic and Cuba were protected by a combination of rugged mountains and dense forests. Brazil was the country with the topographical features that best facilitated *marronage*. Its immense size, huge mountains, long and winding rivers and streams, numerous swamps, dense forests and prickly bushes made pursuit a truly formidable task. The main Maroon hideouts, located in Alagôas, Pará, Maranhão, Amazonas, Pernambuco, Sergipe and Espirito Santo, had some or all of these features. The first of these was home to the renowned confederation of Palmares.

In Mexico the famed Sierra de Zongolica, Sierras de Guerrero and Veracruz Mountains proved ideal hosts for Maroons (Pereira 1994, 97). Davidson (1979, 95) declares that the Cofre de Perote Maroons lived in a settlement that was ensconced in a lofty and rugged mountain range. This range lay behind the Veracruz lowlands, whose peaks rise to 12,500 feet on the south and 10,000 feet on the north and are covered with thick vegetation. In the centre lie the even more lofty peaks of Cofre de Perote and Orizaba, at 14,000 feet and 18,300 feet respectively. A strong military expedition sent against the sanctuary found that the Maroons had placed several impediments along the defiles of the treacherous slope. Many soldiers were wounded in attempting to overcome the obstacles (Davidson 1979, 96).

The Bahoruco, Higuey, Cotuy, Buenaventura, Samaná, Puerta Plata, San Francisco, Azua and San Juan de la Maguana areas were preferred sites for Maroons from the Dominican Republic and Haiti. The Bahoruco Mountains constitute some of the loftiest mountain chains in the Caribbean, and were steep and difficult to traverse. Naturally, therefore, they became the preferred place of refuge for Maroons from these two colonies (Esteban Deive 1989, 60).[7] Manigat (1977, 489) describes the western (francophone) section of Hispaniola, which comprises modern Haiti, as including "bushy savannahs, wooded hills, karst topography, with sinkholes, underground caverns or caves, and tropical-creeper vegetation in remote areas".

The Sierra Maestra Range, which many Cuban Maroons of the eastern region made their haunt, runs eastwards from Cruz Cape, is just over 150 miles long and contains most of the highest peaks in the country. The entire area is intersected by rivers whose courses are sometimes very steep, tumbling down to the sea. Most of the area consisted of primeval forest, with tracks that were too steep and narrow for pack animals to travel (La Rosa Corzo 2003, 45). Actually, the highest peak, at a little above 4,000 feet, is in the

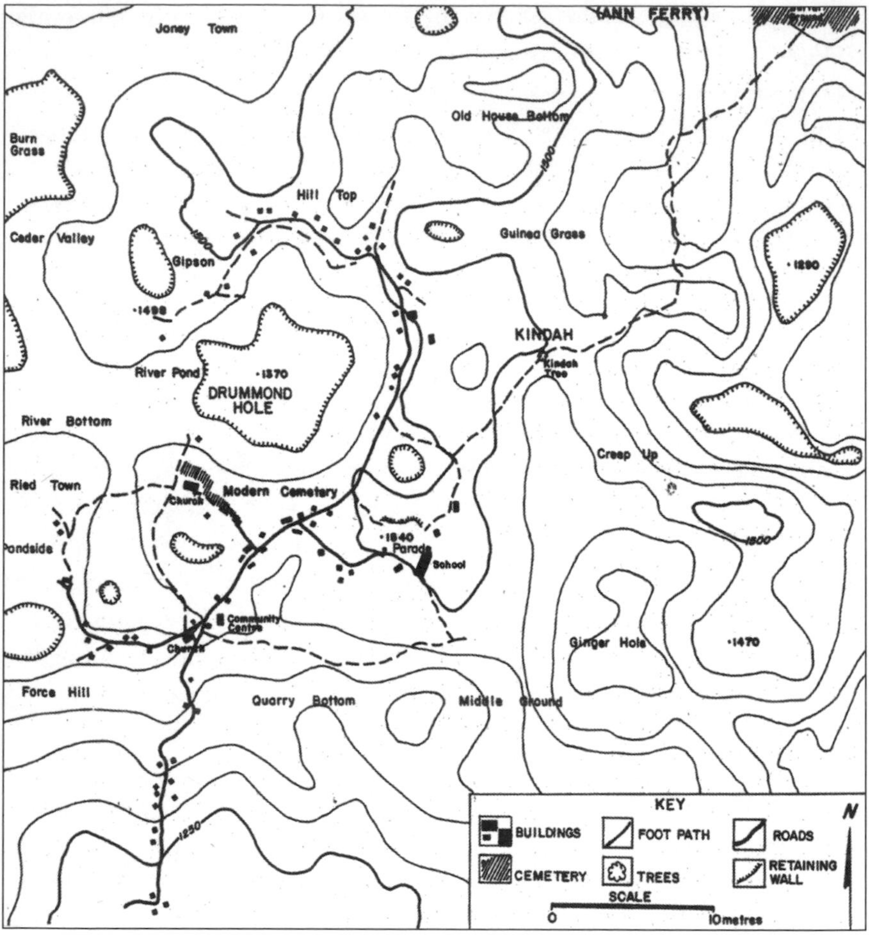

Figure 19. Accompong Town in post-treaty times. From *Maroon Heritage: Archaeological, Ethnographic and Historical Perspectives*, ed. Kofi Agorsah (Kingston: Canoe Press, 1994).

Grand Piedra Range, also a Maroon haunt (ibid., 99); while the Galán Peak (part of the Mal Nombre Range), which provided refuge to the inhabitants of the Vereda San Juan *palenque*, is some 3,200 feet high (ibid., 211).

The physical terrain in which Maroon settlements in Cuba were located made it more convenient, and certainly more sensible, for military expeditions to travel on foot rather than on horseback. Cuban bounty hunters became quite experienced in travelling this way, using horses only occasionally. One person described the approach to El Frijol (Moa) settlement as being devoid of any trails or paths, making it impossible to ride and forcing the expeditionary force to undergo extreme hardships transporting provisions on their backs (La Rosa Corzo 2003, 31; see also 29). The soldiers from Europe learned a tough lesson when they attempted to use horses, especially against the Jamaican Maroons.

Arguably, defence, or security, counted as the number one priority in selecting a site for a Maroon settlement. La Rosa Corzo (ibid., 228) states that the size of the settlement, the length of time that the runaways remained in it, its rehabilitation after assault, the size of the agrarian fields and crops grown, and the defence system were all determined by the safety factor.[8] He

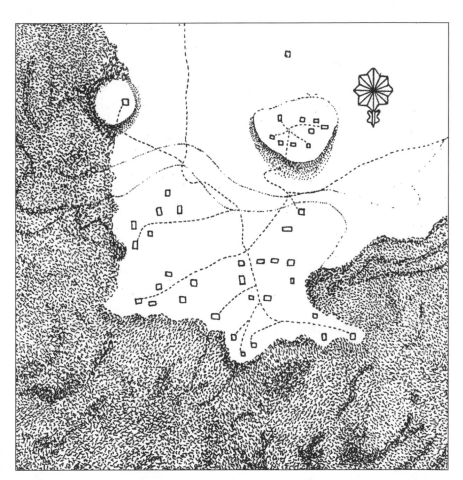

Figure 20. A Bahoruco Maroon community in 1785. From *Los Cimarrones dil Maniel de Nieba*, by Carlos Esteban Deive (Santo Domingo: Banco Central de la República Dominicana, 1985).

(ibid., 15, 225) notes three characteristics of Maroon settlements: isolation from populated areas, obscurity that made them difficult to locate, and difficulty of access for anyone seeking to enter them. He also remarks that the huts or houses were usually scattered in the settlements to make it difficult for expeditionary forces to surprise all the inhabitants at once and to permit unimpeded flight.

While water was abundant in or around many Maroon settlements, good drinking water was not always easy to find. In the Guianas and Brazil, with the many streams that chequered the landscape, Maroons often built their settlements close to those that offered a good supply of relatively wholesome drinking water. The best example is Palmares, by or through which many rivers flowed, including the Ipojuca, Serinhaem, Una, Paraiba, Mundau, Panema, Camaragibe, Porto Calvo and Jacuipe, with their numerous springs and tributaries (Carneiro 1946, 26). In Jamaica the Windward settlements were also well provided with water through the Rio Grande, Negro and Dry Rivers and the Jackmandoore Spring (Agorsah 1994, 168). For their greater convenience, or where water was less abundant, the Maroons employed their knowledge and technological skills to resolve the problem. For instance, an expedition sent against the Windward Maroons in 1730 reported finding a large cave with two troughs for holding water (Agorsah 1994, 169). In Haiti in 1717, a French officer on a military expedition discovered a settlement with a well forty feet deep (Moreau de Saint-Méry 1979, 135). The fields of Palmares were apparently well irrigated with canals (Conrad 1983, 369).[9]

Of course, apart from drinking, water was needed to grow crops and for other daily activities. Personal hygiene must have been an important feature of at least some of the communities. This is relevant, because part of the mythology of slavery is that Africans were naturally unclean. Historians have repeatedly noted the contradiction between that assumption and the fact that Black women were the main domestic hands in most White households, cooking, washing, cleaning the homes, looking after the children and occasionally breast-feeding them. The unclean conditions in which many plantation and other Blacks lived had a lot to do with their limited access to the tools of cleanliness and the state of knowledge about the spread of disease pathogens. In the late eighteenth century Stedman (1988, 409–10) recorded that the Maroons in Suriname used the dwarf aloes to make soap, evidence that they were concerned about personal cleanliness even in the trying circumstances of life in the bush and often on the run. In the 1570s Francis

Drake and his fellow corsairs, who encountered a group of Maroons in Panama, commented that they washed themselves regularly in the river and changed their clothes (Franco 1973, 26). Edward Long (1774, 2:379–80) realized that Blacks in Jamaica were in the habit of bathing in the river frequently,[10] but he put this down to their animalistic nature rather than to cleanliness, asserting that "cattle, wild beasts, and other quadruped animals, use it for their refreshment". He reasoned that Blacks preferred to build their dwellings close to the sea or rivers in order to reduce their walking time to these venues.

The shortage of water troubled many expeditions sent against the Maroons. On one expedition, against Le Maniel in Haiti, there was such a shortage of this precious commodity that the members of the expedition were forced to drink their own urine. A Spaniard who offered to guide them to the Maroon hideout advised them that it would be impossible to find water for the next five or six days, and so they were obliged to send to Port-au-Prince for water, which delayed the journey. Another expedition sent out in 1781 had to withdraw because of lack of water (Moreau de Saint-Méry 1979, 136–38).

A contemporary writer, referring to an early expedition that Captain Braz da Rocha Cardoso conducted with six hundred men against the Maroons in Brazil, stated that he encountered several hardships because the rough trails and the unfamiliar terrain made it almost impossible to transport equipment (Conrad 1983, 369). The writer apparently did not allude specifically to the shortage of water that must have been part of the difficulties. However, Hemming (1978, 356) mentions explicitly that a later expedition, led by Domingos Jorge Velho, the famous *bandeirante* or wilderness tamer, in 1685, entailed a gruelling trek across hundreds of miles of dry scrublands. According to one writer,

> [t]he march was made under the worst conditions of toil, hunger, thirst, and destitution that have been known and perhaps ever will be known in this sertão [wilderness]. . . . 132 persons died because of hunger, thirst and suffering; 63 died of sickness; and over 200 deserted because they could not stand such misery. (ibid.)[11]

Thus, limited (or overabundant) water resources could prove both a friend and an enemy to Maroon communities, though the Maroons themselves must have contrived ways to ensure that they did not usually suffer water shortages.

Among Stedman's descriptions of military warfare against these forest-dwellers are his observations on the non-human but equally formidable hazards that the expeditions encountered in the Guiana jungles, and what the retreat to the White settlement areas entailed after months of desultory fighting (Stedman 1988, 136, 138, 229, 392–93). The main microparasites included mosquitoes – particularly one species that he claimed almost devoured him alive – chigoes, sand flies, horseflies, ringworm, lice, wild bees, bats, spiders, scorpions and centipedes. Other dangers were serpents, alligators, tigers, and thorns and briars – all of which he called "cursed company".[12] Infection of one kind or another often resulted in dry gripes, fevers, the bloody flux and dropsy. He opined that the slightest scratch immediately turned into a running sore, and scratching became a daily preoccupation. Of the retreat to base, he (ibid., 157) wrote:

> [W]e continued our march till 8 o'clock when we arrived at the Society [Suriname government] Post *Soribo* in Pirica, in a most shocking condition, having waddled through water and mire above our hipps [*sic*], climb'd over heaps of fallen trees, creep'd underneath them on our bellies – scratched and tore [*sic*] by the thorns or macas that are here of many kinds, stung all over by Patat or Scrapat lice, ants, and *wassy-wassy* or wild bees, fatigued to death by marching in a burning sun, and the last 2 hours in hells [*sic*] darkness, holding each other by the hand, and having left 10 men behind, some with agues, some stung blind, and some with their feet full of chigoes.

According to Stedman (ibid., 230), after three months' campaign in the bush he and some others returned to base, leaving behind fellow soldiers who resembled "a gang of scarcrows [*sic*], as could have disgraced the garden or fields of any farmer in England".[13] Many who started out as soldiers of fortune ended up as soldiers of misfortune.

The military expeditions sent into the Cockpit Country and other Maroon areas in Jamaica often reported similar kinds of casualties. In 1730, for example, a party of over one hundred riflemen and baggage carriers was sent against the Windward Maroons of San Antonio, but was soundly defeated by a combination of environmental factors and their own ineptitude. According to the governor, they had become lost in the woods, and some of them had suffered badly from hunger, while others had drowned while attempting to cross the rivers and many had died from sickness, so about one-fourth of the expedition perished (Campbell 1990, 66).

Contemporary sources on the expeditions against Palmares speak of similar hazards and suffering: shortage of water; steep slopes; trees without fruits to sustain the soldiers; innumerable thorn shrubs; soldiers being forced to carry their weapons, powder, bullets, food, water and hammocks on their backs because carriages were useless in the terrain – all of which resulted in great suffering. The men were often forced to subsist for long periods on herbs and roots. These adversities caused many to die of hunger, thirst and sickness. A contemporary writer in Jamaica expressed the view that to dispatch men who were unaccustomed to operating under such harsh conditions was like cutting their throats (Campbell 1990, 66). Buckley (1998, 213), writing generally of European soldiers unaccustomed to the environmental conditions in the Caribbean, opines that it was an open grave for them.

DEFENCE SYSTEMS

The Maroons improved whatever natural defences the terrain offered through ingenuity and hard work. The variety and complexity of their habitats were evidence of their innovative responses to the ecological and security challenges that they faced. Wherever the topography was broadly similar, the defence systems that they developed were also similar. In every place in which large Maroon communities evolved there were forests, mountains or a combination of both. In forest or bush terrain, the defence systems entailed a combination of palisades, trenches or ditches, traps and stakes. The system of defence was predicated not only on making it as difficult as possible for military expeditions to breach the fortifications, but also to enable relatively quick and easy escape.

The defence system that the Dutch encountered in the capital city of Palmares in 1645 was very innovative. The western entrance, at which they arrived first, consisted of two gates, each surrounded by a row of palisades with thick crossbeams between them. Having demolished them, the invaders encountered a ditch filled with sharp-pointed stakes. On the eastern side were similar fortifications, and on the northern side was a swamp. On the southern side were huge felled trees, criss-crossing each other. The land behind the houses was studded with pointed stakes. A separate gate protected the centre of the city, which was estimated at half a mile long and contained a main street about six and a half feet wide, running from east to west

(Carneiro 1946, 76). During the next half-century, the threat to the integrity of the Maroon state had led to the evolution of a more sophisticated defence system. When the Portuguese made their final assault in 1694, they encountered a fence or stockade of 2,470 fathoms (4,940 yards), protected by trenches and sharpened stakes. Embrasures at intervals in the rampart accommodated guns, while flanks, redoubts and sentry posts also protected the site. The invading forces had to employ artillery to breach the defences (Carneiro 1946, 17, 45), and they still suffered heavy reverses at the hands of the Maroons.

The erection of double or multiple palisades was a common West African practice, exemplified by the following description:

> The town of Tamisso is a fortified place with a double fence of pointed posts. The space between the two fences, being some seven feet apart, is planted with thick forest and small sticks pointed and hardened by the fire, which render them as durable and as hard as iron. This is done in case the enemy should climb the first fence; they would meet an army of wooden bayonets, difficult to surmount as they are pointed not only upwards, but diagonally and horizontally. (Conneau 1976, 128)

In Guyana, George Pinckard (1806, 2:246–47) wrote, the typical Maroon settlement consisted of a circular area, cleared of trees, in the centre of which a few huts were built. A deep, wide ditch filled with water surrounded the area, and pointed stakes were placed into its sides and bottom. A bridge spanned the ditch but was located about three feet below the surface of the opaque water, so that the untrained eye would be unlikely to detect it. Leaves strewn all around the ditch further camouflaged its width. Openings that gave access to the bridge were created at several points around the ditch, so that the unwary intruder might be trapped – and perhaps impaled – once he ventured into the ditch. Other settlements were fortified by palisades or by fallen trees encircling the living area. These, in turn, were protected by sharpened bamboo stakes stuck into the ground. People wounded by these stakes often sustained grievous sores. In 1816 one writer noted that a settlement that existed in Belize, close to the Sibun River, was very difficult to find, and the area had many poisonous snakes (Bolland 2002, 56–57). Vaissière states that some Maroons in Haiti lived in settlements sealed off by palisades of liana and surrounded by ditches twelve to fifteen feet deep, eight to ten feet wide and studded at the bottom with pointed stakes (cited in Fouchard 1972, 425).

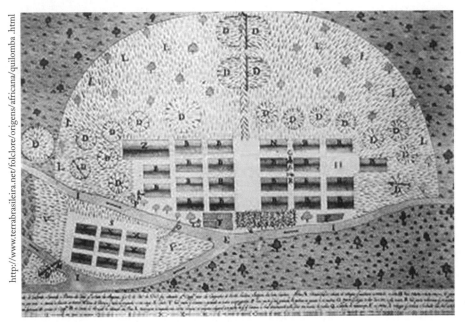

Figure 21. Plan of Quilombo Buraco do Tatú

The approach to the Buraco do Tatú *mocambo* in Bahia in the 1760s was treacherous, not only because of its location but also because there were numerous concealed pits filled with sharpened stakes (Conrad 1983, 380; see also 390–91). It had one of the cleverest and most complicated defence systems, based on palisades, caltrops and ditches. A swamp more than five feet deep protected its flank. Three sides of the settlement were protected by a labyrinth of sharpened stakes, driven into the ground and camouflaged so that they were not readily detectable. In addition, it contained twenty-one pits in which sharp stakes were embedded and covered with vegetation. The ostensible entrance to the settlement was a false path, camouflaged with spikes and traps. In fact, the settlement could be entered or exited only when the lookout placed planks over certain areas to make it accessible. When the Portuguese finally decided to assault it in 1763, they had to employ Indians not only as guides but also as a surveillance corps, and it is possible that these denizens of the forest pointed out the settlement's weaknesses (Schwartz 1979, 220–22).

Stedman, who spent the better part of five years as a member of a group of mercenaries hired to fight the Maroons in Suriname, left us several graphic sketches of life in the forest there, including the obstacles that the fighters had to negotiate in order to engage the Maroons in combat. He (1988, 84) described the clever fortification that the Aluku Maroons had erected. According to him, it was "strong" because it resembled an island that was naturally surrounded by a broad, unfordable marsh or swamp, which cut off all communication with it except by underwater paths known only to the Maroons. In front of the swamp, Baron, one of the leaders, had placed loaded swivel guns that he had seized from the neighbouring plantations. The settlement was further fortified by thousands of palisades on all sides that made it "no contemptible fortification".[14] Stedman (1988, 405) recorded an encounter with some Maroons in which their strategy entailed surrounding the field with large trunks and the roots of fallen trees, which were also placed at random on the field itself. These impediments considerably slowed down the progress of the intruders and placed them in great danger, since the Maroons lay hidden behind the fortifications, firing upon them from fairly safe positions. Stedman considered this strategy "excellent generalship".

The Cuban Maroons often dug trenches on the steep slopes and placed stakes and spikes in them at intervals, as was the case with the Arroyo del Fango *palenque* (La Rosa Corzo 2003, 126, 127, 165, 181). Pérez de la Riva (1979, 52) states that the Maroons in that country were accustomed to creating false accesses to their *palenques*, which they spiked with very sharp stakes of *cuaba* wood. Each stake was incised so that the top would separate from the rest of it whenever anyone pricked himself with it. It was embedded in the ground in such a way that it could not be removed except with a tool. Elsewhere (ibid., 57), he describes the defences as consisting of "pits full of forked poles of hard wood with very sharp points placed at short distances from each other".

Such fortifications must have entailed considerable skill, energy and commitment to the defence of the settlements. Antonio de León, military leader of an expedition against a group in the eastern province of Santiago de Cuba in 1830, described some of the difficulties that he encountered against the combination of natural and manmade hazards:

> I found myself in a ditch full of pointed sticks. However, we overcame this first obstacle without being heard. The second obstacle seemed insuperable: this was the climbing of a steep, rugged hill, covered with *tibisí*, which had two very narrow, winding paths that we followed endlessly. We had already climbed a good

third of the way, when at a turn of the path we encountered a Negro who, armed with a machete, attacked the first man in line. The latter having already loaded his gun, fired a shot, whose report was heard throughout the rocky area. . . . The sound of the shot caused the other Negroes on the hill to disperse. These then fled to the opposite side of the hill overcoming cliffs that have to be seen to be believed. (Franco 1979, 45–46)

There were several territories whose remote terrain was either flat or only slightly undulating and lacked dense forests or extensive bush cover. Coastal Peru, Barbados and the Danish West Indies are examples of territories without an abundance of good natural facilities. Nevertheless, Maroon communities developed in some of them and gave the slaveholders a good deal of bother. In coastal Peru, where the vast majority of the country's enslaved population resided, the runaways made the best use of what little bush cover was available and created quite a stir. From as early as 1544 they were said to be killing men and robbing farms just outside Lima and Trujillo (Bowser 1974, 187–88; Lockhart 1968, 189; Guillot 1961, 254–55).

Swamps or marshlands offered short-term shelter for small groups, but usually could not accommodate large ones, important exceptions being those in the United States, Peru and Cuba. Swamps sometimes presented serious problems for Maroon-hunting expeditions to negotiate. At one time, elevated spots in the 2,500-square-mile Dismal Swamp between Virginia and North Carolina were believed to offer sanctuary to about two thousand runaways (Aptheker 1979, 152). On the outskirts of Rio de Janeiro, runaways mingled with poor free(d) persons in shanties erected along the Aterrado, which once ran through a large, unhealthy swamp (Karasch 1987, 310). In 1545 in Peru, two hundred Maroons were living in the marshlands near Huara and so well fortified that a strong Spanish force had a very difficult time penetrating the settlement (Bowser 1974, 187–88; Lockhart 1968, 189). Another group, located in the mangrove swamps of Bahía Honda in Cuba, proved equally difficult to overpower. According to one observer, it housed seventeen runaways and was erected on piles over mangrove swamps and cattails, at a site that was so impassable that dogs could not reach it (La Rosa Corzo 2003, 246).

Individuals and small groups often lived in the numerous caves that are located throughout the Americas (Martin 1957, 120–24; La Rosa Corzo 2003, 101–2; Handler 2002, 5). Research by Alan Fincham and his colleagues, both in the field and in the literature, has resulted in the listing of 1,073 caves in Jamaica, many of which remain unexplored. A number of these caves are over three hundred feet long. Among them are Runaway Caves, Slave Cave, Nanny Cave, Liberty Caves and Retreat Gully Cave (Fincham 1997, 410–21). Archaeological work still needs to be done on these (and other) caves to determine how Maroons might have used them, but their names suggest a clear association with Maroon activities. M.T. Taylor, who along with other speleologists explored the caves of John Crow Mountain in 1989, declared that they "plumbed two dozen pits and several short horizontal caves" (Fincham 1997, 218). Archaeological work in Cuba has uncovered many Maroon caves, including Delfin, Raymundo, Guillermo, Huesos (also known as Garabatos), Palmas, Tocororo and Solapa de Zeo (several of them named after their modern "discoverers").[15] Montejo lived for a year and a half in a cave in Cuba, with snakes (not venomous, as he believed) and bats whose only audible form of communication he described as "Chui, chui, chui", which, of course, he never understood (Barnet 1996, 39).

Most Maroons were aware that they had to guard their freedom constantly lest a military expedition take them by surprise. For this reason, it is difficult to accept uncritically Díez Castillo's (1981, 51) suggestion that the Panamanian Maroons frequently got drunk and that their fiestas often ended in great brawls involving all the inhabitants of the settlement. He himself notes that such a practice threatened to compromise the integrity of the *palenques*. This does not mean that Maroons did not participate in festivities. Music, song and dance on social occasions, such as special days or events in honour of a deity, the planting and reaping of crops and the celebration of the new year, were common in Africa and were replicated in the Americas and documented by many contemporary writers. We know that such celebrations were a common feature of Maroon communities, but they were undoubtedly done with the greatest precaution, especially in areas near to White settlements. Nevertheless, being human, the Maroons sometimes let down their guard. Such a situation occurred on one occasion in 1753 in a *palenque* in the mining area of Los Remedios, Colombia, that was located deep in the forest. Some fishermen who wandered into the area heard the sounds of drumming and singing, and the *palenque* was detected and later destroyed (McFarlane 1986, 139).

An elaborate system of sentries, passwords, scouts and spies helped to forewarn the members of Maroon communities of impending expeditions

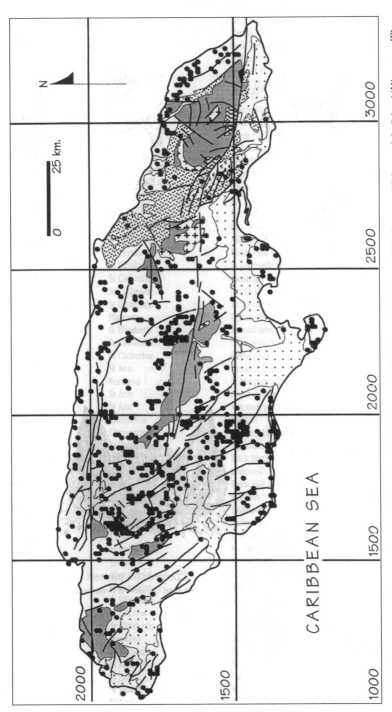

Figure 22. Locations of caves in Jamaica. From *Jamaica Underground: The Caves, Sinkholes and Underground Rivers of the Island* (Kingston: The Press, University of the West Indies, 1997).

against them. All the main Maroon communities are believed to have set up constant watch, not only at the vulnerable entry points but also over a wide strategic area so they could never be taken by surprise. These sentinels usually communicated through a combination of relay runners, horns, drums, and bird or animal calls to signal the approach of the enemy. However, on several occasions the military expeditions were able to breach these defences, and not only when they had former Maroons to show them the easiest and less guarded approaches to the settlements. This suggests that either some communities became complacent or overconfident, or the sentinels did not perform their jobs efficiently. Communities that had not been attacked for years and sometimes decades, usually because the White expeditionary forces had not known previously that they existed, must have been more prone to such complacency. On some occasions the freedom of at least some members was compromised by breaches in their security system. A case in point is the André settlement in French Guiana in 1748.

Louis (1979, 315–17), who belonged to the settlement, testified that the inhabitants had neither a password nor sentinels.[16] This was apparently because they naively believed that their settlement was impossible to find because of its remoteness and the lack of roads, tracks, plantations or other settlements close to it. They seem to have depended upon their ears to know when search parties were in the vicinity. They also seem never to have attacked any plantations; Louis testified that they never killed anyone.

Like the André settlement, La Cueva had never been attacked before, but an expeditionary force (aided by former runaways who had turned traitors) carried out an assault at 3 a.m. More Maroons were captured on this occasion than was commonly the case for expeditions in Cuba (La Rosa Corzo 2003, 101–2). The Palenque de la Cruz and the Calunga and Todos Tenemos settlements, all in Cuba, were entered at unguarded moments, though we do not know at what time of day these breaches took place (La Rosa Corzo 2003, 161, 180, 215). Early morning attacks, at 4.30 a.m. when the Maroons were still asleep, on the Matudere and Betancur *palenques* in Cartagena destroyed the first, though the occupants of the second had vacated the settlement some hours before the arrival of the expeditionary force, leaving behind only five people (Borrego Plá 1973, 79–81).[17] However, it seems that the locations of these last two settlements, and also that of San Miguel (sacked a year later) did not offer the best possible security. These *palenques* were situated at the foot of the Sierra de Maria, and though fortified with pointed stakes and

other traps in much the same way as other settlements, offered little resistance when the colonial state sent large and enterprising forces against them
(Borrego Plá 1973, 26–27, 79–109).

But even settlements that were well fortified and had been victims of
previous attacks did not always guard their approaches diligently. This happened notably in 1677 in the *mocambo* of Aqualtune, ruled by the Queen
Mother of the Palmares confederation. It was only after its defences had
been breached that the inhabitants realized that the enemy was at hand
(Carneiro 1946, 18, 97). A similar instance of carelessness or complacency
led to the demise of arguably the most formidable Maroon community in
Dominica, led by Balla. The settlement was located in an area that was quite
remote from the plantations. The expeditionary force had to travel all night
through wooded terrain, crossing rivers and steep mountains, before arriv-
ing at the settlement. The sentinels had not been put in place, although the
leader of the expeditionary force had attacked the settlement once before.
The settlement was located on a steep and rugged mountain, and the
Maroons had carved out a flight of steps to their dwellings in such a way as
to make it impossible for anyone to climb from stair to stair ("it being cut
into steps of a great height above each other") without assistance from
another person. According to a contemporary record, "These steps the party
were obliged to go up, one after the other, and to have their muskets handed
to them, the one on the upper, by him on the step below." This must have
taken some time and was probably attended with some noise. However,
while all this was happening the Maroons were making preparations for
dinner, and they only realized that their security had been breached when
death stared them in the face. In the sequel, not only did the expeditionary
force kill a number of them and capture their women and children, but also
Balla was eventually tracked down and killed (Atwood 1971, 246–47; Honychurch 1975, 74–75).

In the case of the Cofre de Perote Maroons, there is some debate as to
whether it was overconfidence or too much trust in the Whites by Yanga, the
leader, that led to a massive assault on the polity. According to one interpretation, after repulsing a military force sent against him, Yanga sent back a
captive with a letter to the colonial authorities, detailing the wrongs that he
had suffered at the hands of the Whites and daring them to come and get
him. However, another interpretation is that he had sent back the prisoner
with details of the terms of a possible negotiated arrangement with the colo-

nial state that would ensure the freedom of his people. Whatever the truth, the authorities now sent against him a force of between 450 and 600 men (according to different sources) that had no difficulty in locating the *palenque* and breaching its no longer secret defences. His followers fled in all directions, relentlessly pursued by enemy forces, while the capital was burned. Still, the colonial forces were unable to capture any sizable number of his warriors, and in the end the two parties struck a peace treaty that ensured the Maroons' freedom, but with the proviso that they should return all new runaways.[18]

Carelessness, miscalculation, complacency and braggadocio were not the only reasons that the integrity of Maroon communities was breached. Maroon movements often left marks on the physical landscape that they could not erase. Tracks, for instance, created by frequent use, about which many of the settlements could do little or nothing, especially in unwooded terrain, constituted an obvious defect in Maroon security that allowed military expeditions to follow them and locate their hideouts (Conrad 1983, 387; Marchand-Thébault 1986, 40). Dallas (1803, 1:40–41) informs us that since the Maroon communities in the Cockpit Country in Jamaica had a single entrance, the path became so beaten through frequent use that once a track had been located it almost invariably led to the entrance to the settlement. However, it proved almost impossible to assail the Maroons because of the remarkable natural fortresses in which they had chosen to locate their sanctuaries. In Guadeloupe, the tracks to Maroon hideouts were fairly well worn and well known, though Maroon-catchers were often faced with difficulties similar to those that their counterparts experienced in Jamaica. An extant map from 1807 (shortly after slavery was abolished) showed several of these tracks (Dubois 2004, 40). Expeditions in Cuba routinely sought out such tracks and were able to find many settlements of whose existence they had previously been unaware. Heavy rains, especially those producing floods, often proved a blessing to the Maroons in this respect since they obliterated their tracks[19] – and sometimes, to their detriment, the Maroon-catchers found themselves on the wrong side of the tracks.

In jungle terrain it was more difficult to find tracks, but trained African and Indian guides often detected them from broken twigs and branches. Still, it must have been an arduous and frustrating process to locate some settlements, since the Maroons deliberately took many detours on the way to them. Louis (1979, 315), of the André settlement, related (in his deposition to the government interrogator) the tortuous process by which newcomers were taken to his settlement near Lead Mountain. They were taken to this remote settlement by numerous detours, so that once they arrived there they were unable to find their way back. Escape from it would be a matter of pure chance, and any escapees risked dying of hunger before reaching a place where they could receive assistance.

MILITARY STRATEGIES

Many contemporary stories were told about fleet-footed Maroons who "appeared to be like ghosts of the landscape" (Brathwaite 1994, 123). Maroon communities, regardless of the nature of the terrain, were adept at hit-and-run, surprise and other such tactics (Dallas 1803, 1:29). Sometimes the Suriname Maroons attacked their enemies by firing at them from the tops of palm trees, descending and fleeing so rapidly that their antagonists were unable to hit them. They also generally ran in zigzag fashion, making it more difficult for the enemy to take careful aim at them (Stedman 1988, 402, 414, 561). They attacked and killed several soldiers when the latter were traversing swamps. The soldiers were particularly vulnerable at that point, since the water often reached up to their armpits, forcing them to lift their guns above their shoulders to keep the weapons dry. This prevented the soldiers from firing more than once or reloading their weapons without wetting the locks (Stedman 1988, 107, 402).

The Jamaican Maroons also worked out highly clever and unusual strategies (Dallas 1803, 1:42; Campbell 1990, 74). Long (1774, 2:348–49) declared, "Their manner of engaging with an enemy has something too singular in it to be passed over." In referring to an exercise that the pacified Leeward Maroons demonstrated before the governor in 1764, Long commented on their speed and "amazing agility": they discharged their firearms "stooping almost to the very ground", and immediately threw themselves "into a thousand antic gestures, and tumble over and over, so as to be continually shifting their place", thus making it very difficult for their adversaries to get a good aim at them. At first he classified their manoeuvres as an "evolution" of tactics with which the regular soldiers were unacquainted. Unfortunately, in his usual deprecatory manner, he concluded his observations by stating that "In short, throughout their whole manoeuvres, they skip about like so many monkies [*sic*]." These Leeward Maroons, when they lived in the Cockpit Country before signing a treaty with the British in 1739, chose entrances that required people to pass through them single-file for a considerable distance, built footpaths on steep eminences that people unaccustomed to the Maroons' traverses could not negotiate safely, camouflaged themselves by using the surrounding flora as part of their dress, imitated the sounds of birds and animals when communicating with each other, and threw rocks on their enemies (Carey 1997, 195–96; Campbell 1990, 71; Zips 1999, 77–83).

Apparent flight was often the prelude to a more aggressive strategy. On one occasion the Maroons of Guy's Town (part of the Windward group), whose headquarters were located on Carrion Crow Hill, faced with an apparently sudden attack by an armed expedition, "ran away", leaving about fifty women to burn the town before evacuating it. The expedition, oblivious of the fact that doom lurked down the road, entered the partially burnt-out town and found evidence of sudden flight. But they were in for a huge surprise. The Maroons had previously piled up on the hilltop large stones against which they had placed props. As the expeditionary force moved closer to the spot, the Maroons removed the props and sent their own form of brimstone raining down on their enemies. The official report on the expedition recorded that many soldiers were killed, others fled in panic leaving their arms and ammunition behind, and the Maroons captured three of them (Campbell 1990, 71). Carrion Crow Hill had, at least on this occasion, lived up to its name, as the birds no doubt took care of the rotting carcasses.

The Maroons of Nanny Town executed an even cleverer manoeuvre. According to the contemporary chronicler, who was a senior officer of the expedition sent against them, the Maroons feigned a retreat that suggested that they had scattered pell-mell when they heard that a military expedition was close to their quarters. About every half mile, the expedition found produce from the Maroons' gardens strewn all over the place, and shortly afterwards they came to a settlement where they found food being cooked, including several wild hogs on grills, left by their cooks in apparent haste. The invaders concluded that if they hurried they would rout the party and clear the way for an assault on their headquarters. However, to their dismay, they found that the Maroons had allowed them to pass through the entrance to the ambush and then cut off their retreat. A number of them were killed, and most of the rest were forced to flee in all directions (Campbell 1990, 120–21).

When it was clear to the Maroons that they could not beat off the invading forces, they sought safety in temporary flight or retreat, if that was possible (La Rosa Corzo 2003, 19–20, 40). Although their houses and gardens were usually destroyed, they generally rebuilt the settlement, or moved to another spot if they felt that their defence and security systems had been irretrievably compromised. A practice among some of them to limit their losses, especially of vital supplies, was to build hidden storage dumps in various places (Thoden van Velzen 1995, 127; Louis 1979, 316–17; Zips 1999, 89–90).

When forced to retreat, the Maroons often did so in a way that suggested that they had worked out their plan thoroughly. A Maroon group in Suriname carefully camouflaged their retreat and prevented the soldiers from killing them by setting their dwellings on fire just before the soldiers entered the settlement. By the time the smoke cleared, they had managed to evacuate their women and children and many of their prized possessions. To add to the soldiers' chagrin, they discovered that their pursuit was hindered by a deep marsh that surrounded the settlement (Stedman 1988, 405–6). In an even cleverer operation, the Suriname Maroons outwitted a military expedition that had discovered their settlement and was preparing to attack them on the following morning. A night attack was out of the question since the expedition, though it included Black soldiers, was unable to make its way in the darkness through the maze of bush and swamp that surrounded the settlement. The Maroons kept up a constant noise throughout the night, shouting, singing and firing rounds of ammunition. This noise camouflaged their preparations for retreat, which involved cutting off the enemy's access to the passes and preparing food for the evacuation. The whole night the women and children were engaged in preparing rice, yams, cassava and other provisions. On the following morning, all that the members of the expedition found was a lifeless settlement and evidence of the hasty preparation of food, to their great and "inconceivable astonishment" (Stedman 1988, 410–11).

Protection of the women and children was a cardinal aspect of Maroon strategy. In times of quick retreat, it usually meant hiding these members of their community in specially prepared hideouts, but this had as its main drawback the possibility, and even likelihood, of the children crying or making some other noise (Mullin 1992, 51). They often had to adopt other innovative means to cope with sudden attacks, sometimes at great risk to the warriors themselves. An outstanding example was the strategy adopted by the Seminole Maroons, under attack by the Americans in 1818. They detailed some of the men to ferry the women, children and belongings across the river, while the warriors, in alliance with a few Indians, remained behind to safeguard their retreat. In the battle that took place, the Maroons were at a great disadvantage because the glare of the sunset was in their faces, and the enemy were much more numerous and possessed far superior weapons. However, they won precious time, which allowed the women and children to reach the nearby swamp. Some of the men were killed or captured, but most of them managed to reach the opposite shore in safety (Mulroy 1993, 16).

When more time was available to evacuate their families, they were able to take them farther away to more secure hideouts. The Todos Tenemos settlement in Cuba had one of the best plans; it entailed retreating to another settlement specially prepared for protecting the women. The settlement, known as Guardamujeres (Protect Women), was strong enough to resist the only attack so far found by historians against it. It was surrounded by ditches filled with pointed stakes and in an area that allowed for superb defence. Several members of the expeditionary force that attempted to capture it were injured by the stakes and they eventually gave up the effort (La Rosa Corzo 2003, 182).

The development of fraternal relations across settlements allowed some room for manoeuvrability and succour in times of distress. Many autonomous communities remained in frequent communication with each other. They realized that guarding their freedom was a task that they could perform better jointly. They shared important information, acted as hosts to the members of other communities on hunting and raiding expeditions, perhaps combined their strength in such expeditions, and offered a place of retreat when enemy sorties forced Maroon occupants to flee their homes temporarily or permanently. This structure of relationships gave the Maroon communities a greater chance of survival than when they existed as isolated polities. They drew strength from each other, shared their resources, acted as each other's eyes and ears, and helped to ensure that they would not all be wiped out at once. La Rosa Corzo (2003, 231–35) has convincingly demonstrated the existence of such links in eastern Cuba.

It is said, probably incorrectly, that the captain of the allegedly exclusively Creole San Miguel *palenque* in the Sierra de Maria, Cartagena, in the late seventeenth century, did not admit runaways from other *palenques* or places in that province, in order to ensure the integrity of his people and himself as leader (Borrego Plá 1973, 78–79, 84).[20] This statement obviously cannot be taken at face value. He must have discreetly admitted other Creoles into his *palenque,* and other evidence suggests that at least a few African-born people lived in the settlement. Moreover, he seems to have maintained at least limited fraternal relations with Akan and other ethnic groups in other *palenques.* A captured Maroon from the Matudere settlement testified that they had developed a contingency plan, in the event of their settlement being destroyed, to repair (along with those Blacks of the neighbouring farms who wanted to join them) to the Sierra de Maria *palenque.* The crushing of the San Miguel settlement also sent its scattered followers rushing to the neighbouring *palenques* of Santa Bárbara and Quebrada del Cimarrón (Borrego Plá 1973, 26–27, 79, 87, 105–8), in much the same way it later happened with the Windward and Leeward Maroons.

In 1737, after their settlement in the hills around Córdoba, Mexico, was routed, the Maroons led by José Pérez and José Tadeo sought refuge in the Mazatiopan and Soyaltepec *palenques* (Naveda Chávez-Hita 1987, 135). The Bumba, Maluala and some other nearby settlements in Cuba enjoyed fraternal relations with each other. According to a captured Maroon informant in 1830, between Bumba and Maluala were three other settlements called Rincon, Tibisial and La Palma, which the Maroons used as resting places on their expeditions (Franco 1979, 46; La Rosa Corzo, 2003, 103–4, 127–28). When, a few months later, the Whites attacked and destroyed Bumba, many of the inhabitants found refuge in El Frijol (Moa) settlement (Franco 1979, 47). The Maroons in the Bahoruco mountain range in Hispaniola also seem to have enjoyed similar fraternal relations.

As noted already, some Maroon communities preferred to live in peace with the White inhabitants and engaged in warfare only when attacked. They took in runaways who came to them, but did not raid plantations for either people or goods. They engaged in trade rather than plunder.[21] According to the viceroy of Mexico at the end of the sixteenth century, the Maroons of the Pacific coast preferred to live in peaceful dialogue with the Indians who were just "a rifle-shot away". When the Spanish sent a force against them, they simply retreated into less accessible areas, where they lived in harmony with their neighbours during the next two centuries (Pereira 1994, 104). The ranchers in the area often employed them to round up their cattle. The major problem for the colonial authorities was that the Maroons, along with all other groups in the area, were not easily amenable to the straitjacket of colonial laws in this frontier society and defaulted, for instance, on payment of tribute to the Church (Pereira 1994, 104). Similarly, the Maroons of the Dismal Swamp in the United States preferred trade to plunder, engaging in regular but illegal exchange with the White inhabitants of the neighbourhood (Aptheker 1979, 152).

The Mandinga (later called Amapa) settlement, which was established in the Mazatiopa Mountains in Mexico around 1735 as a result of a series of servile revolts, changed within a relatively short time from hostile to peaceful dialogue with the neighbouring White communities, which found their services quite useful. They carried on fairly open trade with members of all ethnic groups. Don Andrés Fernández de Otañes, a merchant and senior magistrate of Teutila, used them as agents in dealing with the Indians who were involved in the vanilla trade, and they guarded the district's cotton warehouse. Carlos Ribadenyra, another wealthy man, employed them to drive away a group of Indians whose right to a certain piece of land close to his *hacienda* had been confirmed by the Audiencia. In 1762 the viceroy accepted their offer of assistance to repel an anticipated British attack and declared them free, though the slaveholders contested that freedom until 1769 (Carroll 1977, 494–98; Naveda Chávez-Hita 1987, 143).

The prevailing view, however, is that most Maroon communities were geared for aggressive warfare and took the fight to their enemies. Indeed, a few of them seem to have been fully dedicated to destroying the White settlements. Thus Ortiz (1975, 362) asserts that the Cuban Maroons dedicated themselves to acts of pillage in the countryside, compromising the security and property of many people. Gonzalo Aguirre Beltrán (1958, 12) declared that those in Mexico possessed a violent and aggressive ideology. Davidson (1979, 94–95) observes of the Cofre de Perote Maroons that "The settlement was by necessity a war camp, with its internal structure oriented to the needs of self-defense and retaliation." This observation might be applied to most of the settlements, in both their defensive and aggressive postures.

The Aluku Maroons in Suriname showed contempt for the White mercenary soldiers who had been recruited by the colonial state to wipe them out, sardonically referring to them as White "slaves" (Stedman 1988, 408–9; see chapter 9). As noted earlier, according to one interpretation, Yanga, leader of the Cofre de Perote Maroons, sent a defiant message to the Spanish government. After cutting to pieces several captured members of an expedition sent against him, sparing only one of them to bear the message, he explained that he and his followers had retreated to the Zongolica Mountains to escape

Spanish cruelty and treachery. They had attacked and robbed the plantations to requite the wrongs done to them and to obtain material compensation for their labour. He is alleged to have stated further that the Spaniards ought to come and test their strength against his, and so they would not plead ignorance of the route to his *palenque,* he was sending as a messenger a Spanish soldier whom he had decided not to execute, so that the man could serve as a guide and save them the job of searching for Yarga (cited in Pereira 1994, 99).[22]

Taunting was an art that Maroons practised against their enemies,[23] obviously to rattle them and give the Maroons a psychological advantage over them. Such taunting occasionally drove their enemies into ambushes. One notable instance of this occurred in 1761 in Haiti, when the Maroons defied their attackers by dancing. The latter became infuriated and rushed into ditches, the bottom of which had been filled with pointed stakes camouflaged with lianas and creeping plants; about fourteen of them were wounded (Moreau de Saint-Méry 1979, 136).

The passion for revenge was a powerful individual motive for Maroon attacks on the slaveholders. Many Whites who had settled down to a comfortable life lived in fear that they might not die in peace. Baron, a muchfeared Suriname Maroon in the late eighteenth century, was treated badly by his overlord and once whipped below the public gallows. From that time he took to the forest, swearing vengeance against all Whites and declaring that he would not rest until he had washed his hands in the tyrant's blood (Stedman 1988, 85). The Maroon Joli Coeur (Jolicoeur), also of Suriname, allegedly told his overlord why he was going to kill him: "[Y]ou O Tirant, reccollect [*sic*] how you ravished my poor Mother, and flog'd my father for coming to her assistance, recollect the shameful act was perpetrated in my infant presence, recollect this then die by my hands, and next be damn'd." He then severed his former overlord's head from his body with a hatchet (ibid., 271).[24] It is also alleged that Boni put two of his subordinates to death simply on suspicion that they had uttered a few positive words about Europeans (ibid., 453). It is important to bear in mind that revenge, in turn, constituted an important reason that some slaveholders joined Maroon-hunting expeditions (ibid., 360).

Bravery was an essential element in being a successful Maroon and certainly in being elected a leader (see chapter 7). The many hazards that Maroons faced in striving to maintain their freedom, against both the forces of nature and attacks by their enemies, meant that the warriors had to be stout-hearted and willing to look death in the face without flinching. They knew that in most large-scale encounters with their enemies they were likely to be at a major disadvantage in terms of weaponry, and that this could make the decisive difference in the conflict. Of course, Maroons did not simply lie down and die when faced with overwhelming odds. They fought and sometimes ran away in hope of fighting another day, though there must have been some cowards among them. The contemporary literature is replete with how Maroons – and enslaved persons generally – faced death with fortitude. Many chroniclers of expeditions wrote about their courage, but perhaps the noblest of these concerned a group in Mobile County, Alabama, in 1827, who, though poorly armed, withstood their attackers for a long while, "fighting like Spartans" (Aptheker 1979, 159). Dallas (1803, 1:122–23), no friend of Maroons, nevertheless extolled those in Jamaica for their military virtues:

> Some may be inclined to think a Maroon insurrection a petty warfare of unskilful Negroes; but I believe that the officers who served in this campaign will allow that the events of it, and the tactics opposed to them, if not so grand as those that fill the Grecian and Roman pages of history, were at least as singular and embarrassing. . . . A small body of negroes defied the choicest troops of one of the greatest nations in the world, kept an extensive country in alarm, and were at length brought to surrender, only by means of a subvention still more extraordinary than their own mode of warfare.

A rigid command system, often based on European military structures and titles (and in a few instances even uniforms), and certain death for betrayal were prominent features of Maroon communities. The adoption of European military features was possibly due to the Maroons' desire for recognition of their status as warriors among their own followers, enslaved persons and Whites, although such recognition might not always have been forthcoming. We know only partially what military training Maroons underwent, but it is clear that they had to acquire some skill in the use of their weapons, camouflage, retreat and so on. Soldiers would have been among the prisoners of war taken in African military engagements and sold into transatlantic slavery, and several of these must have formed the core of Maroon fighting forces.

Agorsah (1994, 171) mentions the term "military wing leaders" in the oral traditions of the Leeward Maroons, a reference reminiscent of a prominent feature of Asante military formation. Zips (1999, 55) suggests that since many Maroons had already performed initiation rites in their homelands, they would have been well acquainted with African techniques of warfare. He also states that at least some Maroon communities began to train boys and girls at an early age (ibid., 85). It is said that the Leeward Maroons were trained in the use of the lance and other weapons based on similar practices in Africa (Kopytoff 1976a, 88). Military training was also averred in the case of Palmares (Hemming 1978, 355; Conrad 1983, 369; Kent 1979, 180). A document sent to the Overseas Council in Portugal in the late seventeenth century declared that the *quilombo*'s strong resistance was due to "military practice made warlike in the discipline of their captain and general, Zumbi, who made them very handy in use of all arms, of which they have many and in great quantity – firearms, as well as swords, lances, and arrows" (Anderson 1996, 560). Subupira, one of the *mocambos* that constituted the vanguard of the confederation's defence, was the training centre, but details are not available on the military exercises. This *mocambo* was apparently second in importance to Macaco, the capital. It was fortified by a wood and stone battery, and its defence was enhanced by trenches, pitfalls and caltrops (ibid., 554–55).[25]

Maroons who were recruited into the ranks of various colonial or national armies[26] received the most extensive training. Outstanding examples are the men recruited by the British to fight against the United States in Florida in 1812–14, those used by the Spanish government in Eastern Florida against the United States, and those employed by the independent Mexican government against both Native Americans and US forces. In all these cases they were well armed, either through their own initiative or by being given weapons by the recruiting governments. Two of several examples are worth noting. The first was during the so-called War of Jenkins' Ear, 1739–48, between Britain and Spain (which phased into the War of the Austrian Succession). The Spanish government gathered many American runaways into an armed garrison near St Augustine, called Gracia Real de Santa Teresa de Mose, which became a free settlement, with its own priest assigned by the government. Some 200 of the 965 troops that comprised the garrison were Blacks, who received the same pay and rations as the White soldiers. Among the troops in the Spanish counter-assault on Georgia in 1742 was a regiment of Blacks whose commanders were clothed in lace, bore the same rank as the White officers and enjoyed all the privileges attached to their status. The second instance was in 1817, when some six hundred Seminole Maroons were said to be under strict discipline, drilling and parading under their own officers and initiating new recruits who came to them daily (Mulroy 1993, 9–10, 15). Mulroy (ibid., 10) writes that "[t]he Spaniards allowed Africans to live apart, own arms and property, travel at will, choose their own leaders, organize into military companies under Black officers, and generally control their own destinies".

Weaponry

Maroon weapons were usually rather rudimentary by European standards. Although John Stedman portrayed the Suriname Maroon in the late eighteenth century as a man holding a rifle aloft, this was not typical of the weaponry that most Maroons in that country or elsewhere possessed. The machete, which they had used to cut cane and with which many of them fled, was their most common weapon of defence, offence and survival. With it they not only made war, but cut through the bushes on their way to safe havens and cleared vegetation to make way for cultivable land. It was thus the most appropriate symbol of their freedom. The Maroons under Felipe of Panama in the mid-sixteenth century are said to have employed innovative methods to make weapons. They made spears and bows of the hardest woods that they could find, and arrows of cane stalks. Their blacksmiths fashioned knives and arrow and spear tips from the collars and chains with which they had fled. They utilized the intestines of monkeys to make cords for their bows (La Guardia 1977, 78). Sometimes they dipped arrowheads in poison to make them more lethal (Landers 2000a, 40).

Firearms were, of course, the preferred weapons of offence and defence,[27] but both the contemporary and modern view is that most Maroon communities were desperately short of them, and probably only their leaders possessed them. For instance, in 1603 the insurgents who had formerly worked in the pearl fisheries of Riohacha in Colombia were armed with lances, shields, bows, arrows, knives, machetes, darts and swords (Navarrete 2003, 59). In 1826 the Urubu Maroons of Brazil put up a fierce fight against their adversaries using knives, razors, machetes, lances, swords, sickles, and small- and large-bore shot guns (Reis 1993, 56). The range of weapons clearly suggests a critical shortage of firearms. However, we know that some Maroon

Figure 23. A Suriname Maroon attired for war. From *Narrative of a Five Years' Expedition against the Revolted Negroes of Surinam*, by John Gabriel Stedman (London, 1796).

communities obtained firearms, gunpowder and bullets by purchasing them through the extensive underground trade network (Bastide 1978, 87; Conrad 1983, 380), and also by seizing them when they raided the plantations. The best-armed group of Maroons about whom we know were the Seminole Maroons, in the second decade of the nineteenth century. They had once been allies of the British who, on their departure, left them in possession of the fort at Prospect Bluff, with all the arms stocked in it, including four pieces of heavy artillery, six lighter ones, thousands of small arms and large amounts of ammunition. Apparently, these Maroons and their Seminole Indian allies were also customarily supplied with gunpowder, lead and other military equipment by Alexander Arbuthnot, a Scottish trader operating from the Bahamas (Porter 1951, 260, 266; see chapter 4). Belizean Maroons must also have been well supplied with firearms, since enslaved persons there were generally allowed to carry such weapons. They developed great facility in their use, much to the chagrin of those enslavers who felt that the situation had got out of control (Bolland 2003, 73–74).

The Matudere Maroons bought firearms in Cartagena through a Zambo intermediary, and gunpowder from a White person (Borrego Plá 1973, 84–86). The extant literature concerning the Leeward Maroons in the late seventeenth century speaks about them having good arms and a lot of ammunition (Patterson 1979, 258). A group of about two hundred Maroons in Peru in 1545 is said to have been equipped with huge quantities of Spanish arms (Bowser 1974, 188). The *quilombolas* (Maroons) led by Cris-Santo and Epiphano in Maranhão, Brazil, in the mid-nineteenth century are also said to have been well armed with a fair quantity of weapons and ammunition, which helped them put up strong resistance against an expeditionary force (Conrad 1983, 387–88). Baron's group in Suriname possessed an unspecified number of swivel guns plundered from their enemies (Stedman 1988, 84). It is also quite possible that the larger communities, such as those of Palmares, Bayamito and Todos Tenemos, possessed a good many more firearms than the known sources lead us to believe, but further research on this aspect is needed. Maroons sometimes were clever enough to manufacture fake guns, out of wood and other materials, with which they fooled plantation personnel. They used coins, buttons and pebbles when lead bullets were in short supply, though the substitutes were not nearly as lethal as real bullets. When short of flints for their weapons, they sometimes used the shards of water cans (Stedman 1988, 392, 409).

Figure 24. Dogon blacksmiths (Mali, West Africa)

Given the importance of firearms, the Maroons no doubt spent much time maintaining them, but firearms of that period (firelocks and flintlocks) were prone to become defective and needed frequent repairs. Few Maroon communities would have possessed the skill to repair them or the capacity to make bullets, and probably none would have been able to make gunpowder. The military deserters from Suriname apprehended by the insurgents in Berbice in 1763 (see chapter 2) were put to repairing guns (how successfully we do not know) (Thompson 1987, 166). The Maroons of the André settlement in French Guiana repaired their guns and always kept them in good condition for hunting and military purposes, but they often found themselves critically short of gunpowder and bullets. Sometimes they had to substitute tiny stones for bullets (Louis 1979, 315). Palmares had a wide range of artisans, among whom blacksmiths, the masters of all artisans in Africa,[28] figured prominently. The state made its own weapons, with the possible exception of firearms, though it probably repaired them (Bastide 1978, 82, 86; Kent 1979, 180; Hemming 1978, 355). In 1645 the Reijmbach expedition observed four smithies in the capital (Anderson 1996, 551). In 1671 Governor Fernando Coutinho opined that the *quilombo* possessed a blacksmith shop and other places in which they made weapons, and that the hinterland was so rich in metals and saltpetre that it provided them with everything they needed for their defence (Carneiro 1946, 45).[29] Lemba, a celebrated Maroon leader in the Dominican Republic in the mid-sixteenth century, on one occasion took as booty iron, steel and an enslaved blacksmith (Esteban Deive 1989, 50). A Maroon settlement in Suriname in 1765 was said to have a complete forge (De Groot 1977, 524).

What is certain is that the colonial forces almost invariably held an important and sometimes a decisive advantage over the Maroons in terms of weaponry. The leader of a military expedition against some Maroons in Santiago de Cuba in 1830 expressed the view that the *palenque* would be almost invulnerable if the Maroons possessed sufficient firearms to defend it (Franco 1979, 46). What the Maroons lacked in military equipment they often made good through their skilful use of the terrain, with which they became very familiar, and their commitment to maintaining their freedom.

CHAPTER 7

Maroon Government

STRUCTURE AND FUNCTION

Marronage provided the opportunity for the clearest expression of the leadership capacities of enslaved persons, in military, political and other terms. Although not admitting the legitimacy of Maroon warfare, the enslavers often gave grudging recognition to the Maroon leaders by accepting the designations of "captain", "general" and so on, written into several of the treaties that the two parties signed. The struggle threw up a gallery of military personalities that the enslavers had never believed existed among their servile charges.

Maroon societies were not governed by the same codes of law that maintained White slave societies in the Americas. The fundamental difference between the two kinds of societies was that one was born out of the quest for freedom, the other out of the quest for material gain that entailed enslavement of the majority population in many American societies. Some material and social inequities existed in the daily operations of Maroon societies, as is true of even the most communalist societies. In Maroon societies, the leaders commonly had the largest houses and gardens, and more than one wife, though there was a critical shortage of women in most settlements. Stedman (1988, 405–6) described the Aluku town of Gado Saby (Gado Sabi) in Suriname as having about one hundred houses, some of which were two stories high. Boni, the main leader, lived in a house that had "4 pretty rooms, and a . . . piazza inclosed with neat manicole palisades". The Bayamito settlement in Cuba contained forty-five houses, each with a living room and a bedroom (La Rosa Corzo 2003, 129–30), but it is unlikely that all its inhabitants enjoyed an equal measure of domestic comfort. Atwood (1971, 227) stated that the Maroons in Dominica built "good houses", but he did not leave us any description of them.

The ruler or king of Palmares lived in a palace in the capital and had a country residence. He had three wives, while one of his chief officers had two (both of whom were the king's daughters) (Bastide 1978, 85, 88; Kent 1979, 178–80). The capital comprised an administrative complex that also housed the priesthood, magistracy, council chamber, military headquarters and civic authorities (Bastide 1978, 85). Carneiro (1946, 11) declares that it was a "rustic republic" that was well organized "in its own way". It clearly represented the highest point of political and social differentiation in Maroon societies and cannot be viewed as the norm. However, even here the degree of inequality did not lead to a hereditary class structure; this was ensured partly by the fact that the monarchy was elective, though the criteria for this position and other high offices were different from those of the Europeans, being based on proof of military prowess or sagacity (Carneiro 1946, 11–12; Bastide 1978, 87). Conrad (1983, 368), however, asserts that leadership could become hereditary in *mocambos* that survived for a long time.

In Maroon societies generally, the disparity in access to privileges rarely got out of hand, and certainly did not create a class of people defined by wealth or extreme accumulation of material resources; nor did the pursuit of material gain take place at any cost and regardless of the material conditions of the more lowly members of society. The fact is that most Maroon societies commanded only a very small amount of material resources. This factor, plus the need to shift their physical locations frequently, created little incentive for individual accumulation of wealth.

Some writers focus attention, not on the material resources that the leaders commanded, but on the political and judicial powers that they possessed. Put baldly, much of the contemporary literature features Maroon governments as despotisms. Pinckard (1806, 2:241) declared that some Maroons were ruled by imperious lords who governed with a stiff hand, and so some of them returned to their overlords. Thoden van Velzen (1995, 114–15) states, on the one hand, that "Present-day maroons [in Suriname] in most cases envision maroon leaders of the eighteenth and nineteenth centuries as despots", and, on the other, that "Maroons today speak with admiration of their war leaders, shamans, and headmen". Clearly, there is some tension or ambivalence in these dual views – as Thoden van Velzen himself notes – unless we read into the text that the Maroons regarded their leaders as enlightened or benevolent despots. Maroon leaders were not angels, nor were they governing that breed of being. Because they were human, they were subject to all the frailties and failings associated with humanity. Thus, some rulers governed with a heavy hand and sometimes in a brutal manner. Others may well have been despots, but these do not seem to epitomize the majority of Maroon leaders. One thing is certain, as Franklin Knight (1999, ix) observes: "Maroon communities, especially in the formative stages, required extraordinary leadership to combat the constant assaults by superior military forces with superior military resources."

Among the many despotic leaders that turn up frequently in contemporary and sometimes modern literature are King Bayano of Panama, Lemba of the Dominican Republic, Cudjoe (Kojo) and Cuffee (Kofi) of Jamaica, Guillermo Rivas of Venezuela, Alonso de Illescas of Ecuador, and Boni of Suriname. La Guardia (1977, 87–88) cites a contemporary source from the mid-sixteenth century saying that King Bayano inspired such awe among his followers that they feared and obeyed him implicitly. Strangely enough, the same contemporary source informs us that in their bishop's celebration of their apparently Afro Catholic Mass, he always reminded the *palenqueros* of the need to revere their king, since he had to preserve and govern them justly and defend them against the Spanish, who desired to destroy them. Esteban Deive (1989, 50) states of Lemba, one of the famous Maroon leaders in the Dominican Republic around the mid-sixteenth century, that his 140 followers obeyed him blindly,[1] though implicit obedience might not necessarily have meant that he was a despot. Patterson (1979, 261) repeats the common assertions that Cudjoe could be ruthless and even brutal to his followers and on occasion was needlessly selfish towards his own warriors, and that Cuffee, the main negotiator of the Windward treaty with the British in 1739, governed his people with an iron hand and shot all defectors and other delinquents.[2]

Some Maroon leaders, such as Illescas, Guillermo Rivas and Boni, developed reputations in both contemporary and modern literature as bloodthirsty and exceptionally cruel warriors. Illescas, the main leader of the Esmeraldas Maroons, is depicted in contemporary historical records as a brutal, if shrewd, ruler.[3] Among his many barbarities, he is said to have assassinated a large group of Indians who had invited him to a banquet. He is also said to have enhanced his power base by his military and linguistic capabilities, and by marrying an Indian chief's daughter, with whom he had six children; he had possibly as many as fifteen other Indian wives, who bore him many children. He also married off one of his sons to the daughter of an Indian chief whom he had eliminated, and one of his daughters to a Portuguese named Gonçala da Villa, who had been his aide-de-camp. In these ways he was able to establish firm rule over a multi-ethnic community comprising Indians, Africans and mixed-race groups.[4] All this stands in striking contrast to the Ecuadorian government's decision, on 2 October 1997, to name him a national hero, but some critics may regard that as a politically astute move by the government that inaugurated an annual Black National Day on the same occasion.

Stories have been handed down about Guillermo Rivas killing one enslaved person and punishing another; threatening to kill his own overlord and robbing him before fleeing to become a Maroon; raping the wife and daughter of a White merchant and beating the man; and tying up a White corporal named Pedro Cazañas and whipping him in the town centre. It is also said that he had his own judicial officer in the person of José Antonio Rengifo (Acosta Saignes 1979, 65–67; García 1989, 68–79). García (1989, 69) explains Guillermo's harsh treatment towards certain enslaved persons by suggesting that they were allied with the forces of oppression. He asserts further that Guillermo stood out against oppression in any guise or form, and the oppressor's colour was incidental to him. He alleges that none of the extant testimonies of Maroons captured from his *cumbe* contains any mention of any maltreatment or punishment on his part.

Stedman (1988, 452–53) recorded the testimony of a captured woman from the Aluku Maroons. She said that nothing could compare with the discipline that Boni maintained among his followers, and that he was absolutely despotic. She went on to say that he did not trust any of his followers with firearms until they had served him in slavery for some years, proved their unquestioning loyalty to him and displayed bravery. Few of them met a high enough standard to be entrusted with guns. But perhaps Boni's screening was so thorough partly because of a critical shortage of firearms, which Stedman mentioned several times regarding his encounters with the Alukus. His informant also made it clear that Boni was more loved than feared because of his "inflexible justice" and great courage. In other words, according to the woman, Boni governed with a strict but just hand, and people understood why this was so. Another captured Maroon, a man, said that he had fled to Boni because of a cruel overseer, but that Boni had treated him twice as severely as his previous overseer and condemned him to slavery. He therefore had escaped from Boni and for the next two years had lived the life of a wanderer in the forest before being apprehended by the Rangers (Stedman 1988, 482).

The traditions that Thoden van Velzen collected from among present-day Aluku descendants cast Boni in an absolutely despotic, and sometimes sadistic, light, even to his own followers. One tradition asserts that his cruelty exceeded that of the planters, and soon his followers began to desert him (Thoden van Velzen 1995, 120). Boni is depicted as a great leader but one who was unable to feel contented, on any day, until he had killed a child from his own group (Thoden van Velzen 1995, 115, 120). As Thoden van Velzen (1995, 115) notes, this seems very strange, given that there were few children among the Maroons. He points out that ritual deaths were usually only associated with the elimination of witches. But rarely, in African tradition, were there a lot of witches to kill at any one time, and child witches were rarer still. Nor could the reported child sacrifices be interpreted as offerings to propitiate malevolent spirits, since that practice also bears no relation to African traditional religions. It is true that sometimes, in certain communities, when a great man died, some of his servile charges would be slain to minister to him in the afterlife. It is also true that the Bini (in southern Nigeria) sacrificed huge numbers of people in 1897 in a vain attempt to keep the invading British at bay (Webster and Boahen 1980, 147; Dike 1956, 158–59; Crowder 1968, 123). But such large-scale human sacrifices were rare, and so the rational decision is to consign the stories about Boni's daily slaughter of children to the realm of myth.

One of the stories among present-day Alukus concerning Boni is that his own son drowned him (Thoden van Velzen 1995, 119–21), though the historical record indicates that he was killed in an encounter with the Ndjukas. The Alukus' story cannot be interpreted as an attempt to purge their history of the evil that Boni is supposed to have represented by viewing the alleged patricide as a catharsis; the tradition, in fact, is that Boni's son was even more cruel. But the story emphasizes the point about myths creeping into the oral record.

If we accept that some of the stories about Boni had an element of truth, we still need to know why he displayed such extreme cruelty even to his own followers. In most instances, his violence seems to have been neither necessary nor structured. In the context of the time, however, many of these acts were common, even quotidian, experiences in slave societies, carried out by individual planters, managers and judicial officers. Did the brutalities that Boni and other oppressed people either experienced themselves or saw inflicted on their significant others, both on the plantations and during military expeditions against the Maroons, lead to their own wanton disregard for human life? Were they suffering from some form of paranoia or schizophrenia? We may never know the answers to these questions, but we must at least ask them. In the case of Boni, who was a Mulatto born in the forest, some authorities feel that the circumstances of his birth might explain his intense hatred for Whites (Stedman 1988, 655n457): his father may well have raped his mother.[5]

We must also bear in mind, when assessing Maroon governments, that the vast majority of them could not have equalled those of the plantocracy and the authoritarian state in cruelty and the denial of basic human rights, at least against enslaved persons. Zips (1999, 27) rightly classifies the government of the oppressors as a "shocking dictatorship", while Patterson (1967, 9) views slave society as a whole as "a monstrous distortion of human society". The only part that enslaved persons played in such government was as victims. They suffered a daily round of contempt, abuse and wrong at the hands of their overlords, including being barring from access to the law courts to requite those wrongs, and general denial of personhood except when the oppressors considered them to be felons. This is why, in fact, despite the many state offers of amnesty to runaways if they returned to their overlords, relatively few did so, viewing the Maroon communities as offering greater freedom, mobility and justice than the White settlements.

Perhaps it is apposite to point out here that part of the mythology about Maroons generally is that they were exceptionally cruel, much more so than their former overlords. An American officer, writing in the 1830s about the Seminole Maroons, declared that they were "blood-thirsty and cruel" (Porter 1932, 337). Dallas (1803, 1:45–46) said of the Jamaican Maroons:

> In their inroads they exercised the most horrid barbarities. The weak and defenceless, whenever surprised by them, fell victims to their thirst of [*sic*] blood; and, though some were more humane than others, all paid implicit obedience to the command of a leader, when that was given to imbrue their hands in blood:

but, murder once commenced, no chief ever had power to stay the hand of his meanest follower.

Even Stedman (1988, 526–27), who had much to say about the bravery of the Suriname Maroons and their fidelity to those who treated them well, and who also wrote scathingly about cruel overlords, used rather horrified language when speaking of the Maroons' cruelty. On one occasion he (ibid., 525) wrote:

> [T]heir abominable cruelties, as those of all barbarous nations are truly shocking. . . . [W]hole estates as well as private families have become the victims of their wrath & experienced their fatality, putting even to death scores of their own friends and relations, with the double view of depriving their proprietors of their best possessions and at once delivering those negro slaves whom they love best from under the lash of their tiranny [*sic*].

In other words, they killed their foes because they hated them, and their friends and relatives because they loved them!

This kind of alleged irrationality on the part of Blacks has found echoes throughout the years of European contact with them. Thus one official in Veracruz, Mexico, in the eighteenth century wrote that the fear, bordering on panic, that Blacks inspired in Whites was well founded on experience and knowledge of the fierce barbarity of the Blacks, who were incapable of responding to reason, and who became more infuriated and sanguinary in the presence of death (Naveda Chávez-Hita 1987, 142). Joseph Arthur (Comte de Gobineau), one of the most extreme racist White supremacists of the late nineteenth century, opined that the Black man was as careless of his own life as that of other persons. He was a human machine in whom it was easy to arouse emotions; he killed for the sake of killing, being willing to destroy even himself, and showed "either a monstrous indifference or a cowardice" in the face of suffering (Miller and Dolan 1971, 237–38).[6] Much earlier, in 1814, a group of enslavers in Brazil explained the bravery that they witnessed constantly among insurgent Blacks by suggesting that they were so savage that they had no fear of death, since they killed for pleasure in their homeland (Conrad 1983, 402).

Maroon killings of enslaved persons must have been done for various reasons: personal grievances against particular individuals (including those who were active supporters of the enslavers); to overcome resistance against

Maroon attempts to carry off goods and women; and accidents, or what is often termed today "collateral damage". Very few, if any, Maroons would have killed enslaved persons simply out of caprice or as a demonstration of their power, for they generally depended upon their brethren on the plantations for favours and could not have afforded to alienate them *en masse*.

Sufficient evidence exists to suggest that Maroon polities were generally administered on humane principles. Justice in Maroon states was sometimes harsh, but it was born out of the imperative of survival and, overall, was certainly not nearly as brutal for the average person as in the slaveholding states. All colonial states in the region were by their very nature authoritarian; in some the elective principle was largely absent, while in others it was restricted to an elite based on a combination of economic, colour and class criteria. Even after the achievement of political independence, it took a long time for most states in the Americas to institute electoral principles that embraced the entire adult population.

THE CONSULTATIVE PRINCIPLE

Although, as noted above, Palmares was declared to be a monarchy (the chief ruler being called "king" and his womenfolk "queens" and so forth), the office was elective. According to a contemporary source, the inhabitants elected one of their most courageous and intelligent men, who held office for life. Any Black, Mulatto or Mestizo possessing the necessary qualifications was eligible for election (Bastide 1978, 87). So democratic was this election, according to one contemporary chronicler, that it was done by open ballot on a majority vote of the electors, apparently without fear of accusations of miscounting or fraud by either the winner or any of the losing candidates (Bastide 1978, 87). Of course, the ordinary citizens of Palmares did not vote; universal suffrage was not practised here or in any other large polity in the world.

As soon as the elections were completed, everyone present did homage to the new king, and while he exercised considerable power and usually chose his chief officers, he could not do so arbitrarily. Palmares has been referred to as a confederation of towns with their outlying settlements, or a network of settlements and strongholds (Kent 1979, 178–79; Conrad 1983, 368). A contemporary writer and participant in the 1676–77 expedition sent against the confederation noted that all the cities were under the authority of powerful rulers who lived in them. He asserted that Amaro, the ruler of one of the federal states, was so powerful that he lived apart from the others, and was so renowned for his courage and bearing that many of his enemies feared him greatly. His *mocambo* was well fortified and contained more than a thousand houses (Conrad 1983, 369, 373). The last thing that the king would have wanted was civil unrest, which would surely have arisen if he had alienated such powerful rulers by flouting the rules of political and civil conduct. Maroon communities were much more likely to be torn apart from without by military expeditions against them than from within by fissiparous tendencies. It is instructive that while contemporary writers focused on many aspects of Maroon life, rarely did they mention large-scale conflicts within Maroon polities.

Perhaps because absolute authority did not reside in a single individual in this monarchical federal system, it is often referred to in the literature as a republic,[7] suggesting that the focus of government was not on the monarchy *per se* but on the wider council of powerful lords, which included judges and chief military officers. Notably, the highest military office did not reside in the king.

In spite of this system of government, Freyre (1963) dubbed Palmares "a 'republic' under a dictator". Carneiro (1946, 11) quotes Sebastián da Rocha Pitta who, in his work entitled *História da América Portuguesa* (1730), referred to the constitutional form of the confederation as "a central despotic government, similar to those of its African contemporaries, which could only be considered elective in the sense that it was always based on proofs of great valour or sagacity". At one point Carneiro (1946, 50) seems to be more perceptive, noting that King Ganga-Zumba availed himself of a council of chiefs for the most important deliberations concerning war and peace, and that the president of the council was Gana-Zona, his brother. However, he is really hardly more discriminating than Freyre or da Rocha Pitta when he declares that the most important decisions rested with the king, before whom all the guerrillas knelt, clapping their hands and bowing their heads in a gesture of vassalage similar to what was common in Africa (ibid., 41). He might have extended the comparison between the Palmarino and African practice of government to point out that African rulers sought consensus among members of their councils and that, while they generally had the last word on a matter, their decision was expected to reflect that consensus.

The elective principle was common in Maroon polities from the earliest period, as was the case around the mid-sixteenth century when the Maroons in Darien (Panama) elected Bayano as king (Franco 1979, 41). Both Campbell (1990, 25) and Pérez de la Riva (1979, 53) note that the military prowess of the individual had much to do with his elevation to the office of maximum leader of the Maroon community, at least in its formative stage. On the one hand, for instance, Campbell (1990, 46; see also 51–52) says that once Cudjoe came to power he governed his followers with an iron hand,[8] and she goes on to note that he divided the military high command between his two "brothers" (perhaps fictive rather than biological brothers),[9] Accompong and Johnny. On the other hand, she states that further loyalty was ensured through a system based on ability, particularly military prowess, and that this developed in the Maroons a strong competitive spirit and ambition to excel (ibid., 47). Patterson (1979, 260) believes that Cudjoe's followers probably elected him because he was bold, skilful, enterprising and adept in guerrilla warfare. García (1989, 70) states that among the qualities that made Guillermo Rivas a leader among his people were bravery, military prowess, intelligence and intimate knowledge of the terrain in which he operated.[10]

Pérez de la Riva is rather ambivalent about the degree of authority that the maximum leader in Cuba exercised. He (1979, 51) states that the first step in organizing a *palenque* was the election of a captain or chief, who was chosen because he was the most courageous, the most cunning, or the most familiar with the region. He suggests that the elected ruler was given unrestricted power (or, perhaps more accurately, took it) over the others in the *palenque* and acted as if he were its owner and master. At the same time (ibid., 51–52) he observes that the leaders usually operated on the basis of consultation and consensus with their senior men. After selecting the settlement, these leaders or captains proceeded to plan its defence. Patterson (1979, 253) tells us that the followers of both Juan de Bolas and Juan de Serras, feared Maroon leaders in Jamaica in the late seventeenth century, elected them. Campbell (1990, 25), while noting the hierarchical system typical of Maroon societies, states specifically that Juan de Serras governed his people by consensus. According to her (1990, 49–50) and Kopytoff (1976, 89), even the most senior officials among the Windward Maroons were subject to the laws that governed the communities and could be executed for serious crimes or otherwise deposed, though they do not say by what council or on whose authority. García (1989, 70) claims that the Ocoyta Maroons in Venezuela also practised consensual government under the leadership of Guillermo Rivas.

In the Cofre de Perote *palenque,* Francisco de la Matosa (Francisco Angola) held the military command, while Yanga held the positions of head of state and civil and political authority. It is sometimes alleged that because Yanga was too old to conduct the military campaigns actively, he appointed a military commander (Pereira 1994, 99, 100; Palmer 1976, 128; Naveda Chávez-Hita 2001, 159n5). But examples of a similar division of authority in *palenques* in Colombia and elsewhere suggest that his age had nothing to do with this separation of powers. The Matudere *palenque* in the 1680s had a war captain distinct from the leader of the group, in the persons of Francisco Arará (some sources say Pedro Mina) and Domingo Padilla, respectively. The *palenque* also had a diviner who played a major (the testimony of a captured Maroon from the settlement suggested *the* major) role in determining when attacks were to be executed against White settlements (Borrego Plá 1973, 83, 84, 107; Landers 2000a, 39, 41). A similar distribution of power existed in the Buraco do Tatú *mocambo* in Brazil (Navarrete 2003, 36; Schwartz 1979, 222), and probably in the Gracia Real de Santa Teresa de Mose settlement in Spanish Florida (Landers 2000a, 42). These examples suggest that in Maroon settlements power did not usually reside exclusively in any one individual but was shared by various senior personnel.

We dealt in chapter 2 with the politico-military role of several women in some Maroon settlements. Nevertheless, it is important to note here that the political system that Thoden van Velzen (1995, 122–23) found in his work among the present-day descendants of the Ndjuka Maroons almost certainly dates back to pre-treaty times. He describes each village as being, in great measure, a small republic, where daily matters were settled through long discussions. He goes on to say that a strong democratic and egalitarian ethos prevailed in village life. While he notes that it was mainly the older men who ruled in these palavers, he observes that the views of women and younger men were usually taken into consideration. He also notes that consensus was the principle on which the system sought to operate. In another place and time, namely Cartagena in the late sixteenth century, women captured in the Matudere settlement stated that they had no access to the decisions of the males in the *palenque* (Borrego Plá 1973, 85). However, it is unclear whether the statement meant that they did not participate in decision making or that they were kept totally in the dark about the decisions that the men made.

It may be argued, perhaps rightly, that the relaxed atmosphere in which discussions and decisions take place in the Ndjuka villages of today could

hardly have existed under the military conditions in which the pre-treaty settlements were established and maintained; and that at the centre or headquarters a more oligarchic – or at least less democratic – system must have
prevailed. However, there was no reason why such an oligarchic system
should have existed at the village level. We know that what Thoden van
Velzen describes could not have been patterned on European models existing
at any time in Suriname because no such models ever existed. It was therefore either *sui generis* or based largely on African models.

Numerous descriptions exist of traditional African models that parallel
what Thoden van Velzen saw, perhaps most notably among the segmented
(or so-called stateless) societies of southeast Nigeria – Igbo (Ibo), Ijo (Ijaw),
Efik – and the Delta from which many enslaved persons in the Caribbean
were drawn (Webster and Boahen 1980, 98–110, 137–40; Jones 1963; Dike
1956). The Ndjuka electoral pattern might therefore have closely resembled
what Africans had practised in their homeland. In these African societies,
elected rulers generally could not govern despotically, though they had a lot
of influence. All important matters relating to the community were expected
to be debated by the senior members of the community, and sometimes by
the full assembly of adult men. When the British tried to change the Igbo
system, which had lasted well into the colonial period, they encountered
numerous protests and a few riots (Isichei 1976; Ikime 1966, 559–73). We
know today that, in the majority of African societies, even the most powerful
rulers were constrained by checks and balances on their power, through tradition and religious taboos (see below), as was the case in Asante, Dahomey
and Oyo, main areas from which transatlantic captives were drawn.[11] We
therefore need to look more critically at the alleged transformation of the
elected ruler from a democratic to an authoritarian, and sometimes a
despotic, figure in Maroon communities, and at what factors accounted for
that transformation, if it indeed occurred.

At the highest level, the command structure of most Maroon communities, while often built on the military systems of the Europeans in the
Americas, nevertheless retained important African features, foremost among
which were the councils of government. How, and how much, these operated
in specific Maroon communities of the Americas remain uncertain, but there
seems to be emerging consensus that they operated to a greater or lesser
extent. The maximum ruler did exercise some degree of personal authority
and might even, in certain circumstances, order the banishment or execution

of a particular person. However, his authority generally had as much to do with his personal influence as with the office that he occupied. Where the Maroon system often appeared most draconian was in the summary execution of convicted criminals; however, Maroon societies were operating in circumstances that left little room for deviant or defiant behaviour that might undermine the social fabric. It was the collectivity rather than the individual that mattered most, and some leaders took decisions that would be viewed as seriously flawed by present-day standards.

It appears that Cofre de Perote, the Leewards, the Windwards and the groups led by Françisque Fabulé and Guillermo Rivas were somewhat like a confederation of autonomous communities, though on a much smaller scale than Palmares. It may, in fact, be that all large communities were divided into sets of "villages" or combinations of villages and "towns", depending on their demographic and territorial size, and governed by consensus. The Windward Maroons constituted a sort of confederation in which the (at least) six autonomous settlements cooperated with each other, sharing military, agricultural and other tasks (Campbell 1990, 25; Kopytoff 1975a, 89; Zips 1999, 58).[12] Patterson (1979, 260) says that each band of the Leeward and Windward polities was divided into several settlements centred on a main town or village. A Franciscan friar who had been sent among the Cofre de Perote peoples (obviously at their request) to baptize the children, but who also acted as a spy for the colonial state, reported after a month that he was unable to determine the number of people that lived in the *palenque,* since they were divided into several groups (Palmer 1976, 127). Françisque Fabulé of Guadeloupe is said to have had as many as four hundred followers, divided into groups of about thirty-five, but this is debated among scholars (Moitt 2001, 136). Guillermo Rivas operated generally from the Ocoyta *cumbe* but is said to have founded other settlements in Chuspa and Aramina that were also under his jurisdiction (García 1989, 67).

Maroons as Slaveholders

Another tension in the contemporary documents is the allegation that Maroons abducted and enslaved large numbers of their own kind. Indeed, the impression is given that they abducted far more males than females (see chapter 2). This may well have been the case, and the analysis that follows should not be read as rejecting the assertion. However, certain questions arise, based upon the view that Maroons were no less (and no more) logical than most other human beings. Given the grave shortage of women in Maroon settlements, why did they not abduct more females than males? The women would have met a number of biological, economic and social needs and would have helped, through their unique reproductive role, to swell the size of the Maroon population. Economics was also a factor, since recent studies have indicated that in a number of slave societies in the Americas the women did most of the agricultural work (Beckles 1989b, 1999; Bush 1990; Moitt 2001).[13]

A logical response to the question posed above would probably be that the men were needed, not as farming but as fighting hands. In that event, would it not have been counterproductive to kidnap them and hold them in bondage rather than encourage them to join the Maroon ranks voluntarily? Would such people have been committed to the Maroon cause? If it is true that enslaved males were abducted in large numbers, the result would certainly have been a house divided against itself, a case of *marronage* within *marronage*. However, as noted already, the records only rarely speak of any major disunity within a given Maroon polity, and this usually had to do with personality and leadership issues rather than revolt of the enslaved group against the new slaveholders. We need to reconsider the question of the large-scale abduction of enslaved persons (both males and females) from the plantations, working around the extant records – which were compiled largely by the slaveholding interests, most of whom might well have believed that their "well-treated", "docile" and "faithful" charges would never have deserted them but must have been abducted by Maroons.[14] They might even have been attempting consciously to "whiten" the record of their own conduct and "blacken" that of the Maroons. It is also true that Maroons who returned or were captured sometimes alleged that other Maroons had abducted them, in order to prevent the colonial authorities or their overlords from punishing them.

Perhaps we come closest to the truth, in the majority of instances, by adopting the language of one Brazilian official in 1782, who noted that Maroons had gone to the town of Macapá in hope of "inciting the slaves of residents to follow them" (Santos Gomes 2002, 486). Maroons in that district made it clear that they were not interested in forcing enslaved persons to join their ranks and that they "would only go of their own free will" (ibid.). This made perfectly good sense for reasons of both unity and security. Porter (1943,

395) advances the view that "To 'capture' when used in regard to Negroes, was a frequently employed euphemism for inducing, persuading, or assisting them to run away."

Hoogbergen (1993, 175) recognizes the problem for the modern historian in simply accepting contemporary White opinion about Maroon abduction of large numbers of enslaved persons. According to him, the only meaningful way to deal with it is to assume that whenever *all* enslaved persons disappeared with the Maroons after an attack, we should view what happened as collaboration, even if the contemporary records employ the terms "carried off" or "abducted". In his classification, it was an act of rebellion on the part of the enslaved persons. However, if the Maroons carried off only women and children, we should conclude that it did not amount to rebellion by the missing – and presumably abducted – people. Even if we accept his approach, there is still a wide grey area encompassing the many small groups who disappeared after Maroon raids.

A related problem is how to differentiate the various systems of servility within Maroon polities. Most writers have assumed a linear relationship between the Maroon and American plantation patterns, and no relationship to what obtained in Africa. Until we can be more discerning on these issues, we have to make tentative observations and conclusions. To the extent that Maroon societies held people in systems of unfreedom, this was a contradiction within the body politic and indicates the imperfect nature of Maroon societies and the pervasive nature of the slavery system in the Americas. At the same time, we know that in many instances such unfreedom was not permanent.

Maroon societies had to guard themselves against the ever-present danger of betrayal by those who had ostensibly embraced their cause. Thus, runaways taken into Maroon societies were received with extreme caution, because those individuals might turn out to be spies for the White authorities or social misfits. Those who were judged to be spies, refused to engage in battle or betrayed the cause in any way were likely to be executed immediately (Pérez de la Riva 1979, 52; Zips 1999, 65), while others deemed social misfits might suffer a like fate or be cast out physically (though this was dangerous, since they might later guide Maroon-hunting expeditions). A less severe treatment might be to put them to a regimen of hard work. Palmares, in fact, often meted out this treatment to all would-be members of its various settlements.

In 1704 Nieuhof explained that the Palmarinos had a practice that new-comers who had fled to the confederation on their own volition would become free immediately, but those seized in raids would remain enslaved until they had redeemed themselves by capturing another (Kent 1979, 180; Carneiro 1946, 39–40). It is unclear what measures were put in place to ensure that these people, who would have had to be taken on raids in order to seize other captives, would remain loyal to the confederation and not hive off on their own or, worse still, return to their former overlords and disclose information vital to the security of the settlements. Nieuhof's statement must, therefore, be viewed with a certain measure of scepticism. Presumably, the number of captives taken on raids would have had to be very small to enable their captors to keep an eye on them.

It is more rational to believe that newcomers, whether joining the confederation involuntarily or voluntarily, were given tasks to perform to show their willingness to *serve* their new hosts, and that during this period they enjoyed few rights or privileges. If we can draw any conclusion from Nieuhof's statement, it is that the so-called slavery in Palmares was temporary and much more discriminating in comparison with colonial slavery in the Americas. Moreover, Palmares drew oppressed people of all ethnic and social groups into its fold. Hemming (1978, 355) asserts that the confederation became an inspiration and magnet to all Blacks who experienced cruelties and oppression on the coastal farms. Its capacity to resist more than a dozen expeditions that the Dutch and Portuguese dispatched against it – including six costly ones between 1680 and 1686 (Hemming 1978, 355; Kent 1979, 186; Marcano Jiménez 2001, 52) – only served to enhance its reputation as a bulwark against White oppression.

The much smaller *mocambos* also took precautionary measures against newcomers. Those in the Grão-Pará captaincy allowed newcomers to leave the settlement only after they had spent at least a year there. After that, individuals would be allowed to leave only with the leader's express permission and only in company with his most trusted men. The system apparently worked well, for the settlements in Grão-Pará continued to attract significant numbers of runaways seeking to join friends and relatives or simply to escape oppression (Santos Gomes 2002, 486–88).

In contrast to many earlier writers, García (1989, 70) insists that no form of slavery existed in the Ocoyta polity in Venezuela. In his view, the Ocoyta *palenque* was a metaphor for freedom (in his own words: "they knew that freedom was called Ocoyta"), and fugitives from surrounding areas such as Capaya, Cupira, El Guapo, Aramina, Caucagua and Panaquire knew that to reach Ocoyta was to reach the city of liberty. Zips (1999, 65–66), too, does not accept that newcomers to Maroon communities in Jamaica were reduced to slavery, but states that they remained in a subordinate position until their initiation was completed. This initiation included political, cultural and psychological socialization into their new society.

Louis (1979, 314–18), who belonged to the André settlement in French Guiana, testified that the only people admitted into the settlement were those whom the three senior leaders brought back after periodic trips outside, and that the new recruits had to promise never to betray them or they would be hunted down and killed. He did not say whether any of them were abducted. He himself, along with his father Rémy, seems to have joined the settlement willingly. However, André, captain of the settlement, refused to allow anyone to leave it and return to the White settlements, obviously for security reasons. Louis testified that he knew of six people who had asked permission to return to their former overlords but that André had refused their requests and had kept them in the settlement by threat of violence.

According to Moreau de Saint-Méry (1979, 141), Le Maniel Maroons abducted people and enslaved them. He also states that they admitted into their polity only people who came to them voluntarily, and only after ensuring that they were not spies. On the least suspicion of infidelity, the Maroons would execute them. The author's statements are somewhat ambiguous, since, in a sense, abducted people were also part of Le Maniel's polity. What he says here is inconsistent with his earlier statement (ibid., 139) that Santiago, the maximum leader of the community, was a Spanish Creole whom Maroons of that same settlement had abducted forty-five years earlier. Santiago had no doubt passed the test of loyalty and demonstrated the leadership capacities that raised him to the acme of power among his fellow Maroons.

Pérez de la Riva (1979, 52–53) writes that the Cuban Maroons would not allow anyone to leave the *palenque* until he (or, presumably, she) had spent a minimum of two years there. Newcomers were often assigned to several senior members of the Maroon state, and their length of service depended upon factors such as their loyalty, abilities, dedication to hard work and capacity to win the confidence and favour of those whom they served. After that, they were usually assimilated into the ranks of the free members of the community, and some might eventually become headmen. This situation was not unlike what prevailed in the city-states of the Niger Delta in the nineteenth century (Jones 1963, 124). The rise of Jaja, an Igbo sold into Bonny as an enslaved individual but who rose through the ranks to become the most powerful man in the Delta in the 1880s, offers a striking example of the opportunities for social, political and economic elevation in that area (Isichei 1977, 376–77).

Maroon societies had to be ever vigilant against subversion from within, and they treated any sign of disloyalty severely. Nevertheless, Maroon history has recorded several examples of capitulation and even betrayal by former leaders (see chapter 9). When Princess Orika, daughter of Maroon leader Domingo Bioho (King Benkos), was caught assisting in the escape of Captain Alonso de Campo – her former White lover from before she became a Maroon – who had been captured during a military expedition that the Colombian government had dispatched against the San Basilio Maroons, she was tried and sentenced to death (Escalante 1979, 78). This decision must have been very hard for her father to make, but it underlines the fact that, at least in some Maroon societies, betrayal would not be condoned, no matter who was the culprit.

The need for caution in Maroon communities is exemplified by an event that occurred in the early seventeenth century. A group of seventy-three Maroons in the Dominican Republic took a distressed Frenchman into their settlement. The man, named Guillermo Pereyra, lived among the Maroons for four years after they rescued him from Cabo Tiburón, where British pirates had abandoned him without food after assaulting the boat on which he had been travelling, taking him prisoner and holding him for a year. The sources consulted do not indicate that the Maroons maltreated him in any way, though they may have monitored his actions. Eventually, he left (or escaped from) the settlement in a British ship that had arrived there to trade with the Maroons, and later boarded a Spanish vessel that took him back to the Dominican Republic. Whether he was incensed by the ruin of his intended trip to Cuba to engage in contraband trade, whether he fell out with the Maroons or he wished to ingratiate himself with Spanish officialdom, he gave the Spanish authorities detailed information that allowed them to locate and kill many of the British traders and to mount a successful assault against the Maroons in question, killing or apprehending most members of the community (Esteban Deive 1989, 71–72).

Generally, Maroons distrusted White people, and it is not apparent why they kept Pereyra for so many years, especially since there is no evidence that he was particularly useful to them. Was it because he was French rather than Spanish, because he had been a contraband trader, or simply out of human kindess that the Maroons took him into their home? Whatever their reason, it led to the destruction of their settlement.

RELIGION AS A POLITICAL FORCE

In all human societies religion is a powerful political force. In the context of slavery, charismatic leaders such as Denmark Vesey and Nat Turner of the United States, Boukman Dutty of Haiti, Joaquim Nigth [*sic*] of Cuba, Tackey of Jamaica, and Pacifico (Lieutan) and Elesbao do Carmo (Dandara) of Brazil often transformed religion (traditional African, Islamic and Christian) from a conservative into a revolutionary tool. But it also often served as a constraining force against the use of arbitrary authority by the leaders. Price (1979, 295) makes an important point about the role of religion in present-day Maroon societies in Suriname, which must have had its origins in much earlier times. According to him, the influence of the leaders was to some extent circumscribed by the role of oracles, spirit possession and other forms of divination in these societies.

Several examples can be cited along the same lines from any number of African societies during the slavery period, but here we shall note the situation among the Igbo and Yoruba. Among the former, the ubiquitous role of the Aro-Chuku oracle and its priests, constituting the final court of appeal in all matters spiritual or secular, was a serious limiting factor on village elders. In Yorubaland, the Ogboni secret society and priesthood served essentially the same function. Annual investigations into the administration of the Alafin or emperor of the Oyo empire in Yorubaland (through contact with his "spirit double") ensured that he did not govern arbitrarily. In extreme circumstances, such an investigation might lead to a decision to remove him, in which case he would be sent an empty calabash, indicating that he was required to commit ritual suicide. His rule was also constrained by the central role that the Oni (titled ruler) of Ife (the Yoruba spiritual centre) played in his investiture and the overall well-being of the Yoruba peoples. Thus checks and balances were factored into the system of government in these societies, as they were in Asante and other West African societies.[15]

Religion played a major role in the daily lives of Africans and formed the fundamental aspect of their world view. To them everything had a religious significance: they explained conception, birth, life, sickness, death and so on in terms of spiritual forces. It was therefore not surprising that they transferred these ideas into their New World environment and interpreted the circumstances of their enslavement in these terms.[16] Nor was it surprising that African societies in the Caribbean threw up a class of leaders who were recognized for their reputed ability to commune with their ancestors, discern maladies, prescribe remedies, create amulets and conduct rituals to make their clients immune to evil forces.

Bastide (1978) and Reis (1993) forcefully bring out this dimension of religious life in Brazil. There, African traditional religions, Christianity and Islam merged dynamically in the nineteenth century, and religious societies flourished. The contemporary literature speaks frequently to the critical role of the African "medicine man" or "medicine woman" in Maroon (as in slave) societies. In the André settlement in French Guiana, Couacou (alias Bernard), the local herbalist and spiritual leader, treated the inhabitants for various illnesses (Louis 1979, 314). When the Cuban military expedition captured the Maroon settlement near Patabano, among the items seized were "four large straw baskets with magical paraphernalia and other trivia" (Pérez de la Riva 1979, 52).[17] A small, out-of-the-way community in Colombia that an expeditionary force came across in 1753 had a church and an old man who was their leader and priest. The inhabitants declared that there were "saints who came down from Heaven, some by day and some by night, with thunder" to visit him (cited in McFarlane 1986, 140).

One of the striking features of African religions in the Americas (and arguably of all religions) is the almost complete control that the priest often exercised over his adherents, who seem to have put themselves totally in his power or, as some allege, to have been powerless to do anything but his will. One of the best examples concerns a Congolese man called Hans, who was not given any special position in the plantation hierarchy among the enslaved people in Berbice, but was recognized as the most powerful diviner by a large group of people on several plantations. In one of his spells, according to the court records of his trial for practising obeah, one witness testified that the Blacks acted as if they were crazy. Some cast themselves in the mud, while others jumped about. Another witness testified that "My head began to turn as if I were mad; don't know how occasioned this: the first dance she [*sic*]

ever saw, whose heads turned in such a manner that they fell to the ground.
. . . Had not, nor ever does drink rum. I could see and hear every thing, but
was exactly as if I were crazy."[18]

Stedman (1988, 521) wrote that both male and female religious leaders held
complete sway over their adherents, claiming to have powers of divination.
The female would whirl and dance around, and whatever she commanded to
be done was dutifully performed by those assembled; so the séances were very
dangerous because enslaved persons were often instructed to murder their
overlords and flee into the woods. He goes on to say that the Ndjuka and
Saramaka commonly performed these rituals, and that two White eyewit-
nesses had declared to him that they had seen them performed.[19] The same
kind of control is often witnessed in Afro-Christian religions in other parts
of the Americas – for instance, Lucumi (Cuba), Shango (Trinidad),
Mucumba and Candomblé (Brazil), Vodun (Haiti) and Kumina (Jamaica).

William Suttles (1971, 98) refers to African religions in the Americas during slavery as being aggressive and imperialistic; Roger Bastide (1978, 81)
asserts that they became the common catalyst for war; while Gwendolyn
Midlo Hall (1971, 37) declares that they caused enslaved persons to become
rebellious. Campbell (1990, 3–4) goes the furthest when she asserts that
"More than any other single factor, African religious beliefs gave the unifying
force, the conspiratorial locus, the rallying point to mobilize, to motivate, to
inspire, and to design strategies: it gave the ideology, the mystique, and the
pertinacious courage and leadership to Maroon societies to confront the mer-
cantilist society with its awesome power. Maroon leaders were expected to be
imbued with knowledge bearing on the supernatural forces."

The use of religion was evident in revolts and *marronage* in Haiti.
Makandal had the reputation of being able to transform himself into different animals (Franco 1973, 26–27). Boukman carried out vodun rites on the
eve of the slave revolt in 1791 (Fouchard 1972, 358).[20] The religious dimension
is also evident in the name Ganga-Zumba, the king who ruled Palmares
from 1670 to 1680. According to Lockhart and Schwartz (1983, 221), his name
was derived from the term *nganga a nzumbi,* which was the title of the
Angolan priest who was responsible for the defence of the *quilombos* or
armed villages in that African country. In 1826 when the Urubu *quilombolas,*
along with free and enslaved people, planned to overthrow the White government in Bahia, they grounded their plans in extensive rituals carried out
in secret. A search of some huts in the province's capital revealed religious

objects that they had used. Among the objects confiscated were shells, rattles, drums, a cardboard crown decorated with seashells, statues of cows painted red, a red hat with three feathers, and a variety of other clothing and objects in red. Reis (1993, 57) believes that the name of the *quilombo*, the colours used, and the various motifs suggest a *candomblé* derived from the Sango ritual, related to the Yoruba god of war. In 1835, also in Bahia, there was a far more extensive plot under the aegis of Islam but incorporating elements of African traditional religions, reinterpreted and syncretized in the Brazilian context (ibid., 73–159).

In the 1712 aborted revolt in New York City, those involved took an oath of secrecy by sucking each other's blood and rubbing on their bodies a powder prepared by a Black conjurer that was believed to make them invincible (Blassingame 1979, 216, see also 221). Similarly, Tackey, the charismatic insurgent leader in Jamaica in 1760, and the Kumanti priests of the Saramakas are supposed to have had obeahs that prevented the White man's bullets from harming them or their followers. Joaquim Nigth of Cuba was accused in 1843 of selling magical charms to make insurgents invincible, while in Haiti many vodun priests sold charms to make their followers invulnerable to the White man's weapons.[21] More dramatically, according to legend, Grandy Nanny, leader of the Windward Maroons in Jamaica in the 1730s, had the power to catch the enemy's bullets in her buttocks and to use the same as a propulsion machine to return fire with those bullets. Her position among the main leaders of these Maroons was due as much to her alleged uncanny spiritual powers as her martial capabilities.[22]

Several communities adopted elements of Christianity, such as erecting churches, placing icons in honour of Christian saints, and donning the garments of the Christian (usually Catholic) priesthood. In Miguel's *palenque* in Venezuela, the religious leader bore the title of bishop (Franco 1979, 36). In the Mariscal Castellanos *palenque* in the same country, a Maroon, dressed as a priest, baptized young boys (Veracoechea 1987, 79–80). The Cofre de Perote settlement had a small chapel containing an altar, candles and images. It is said that, during the attack that broke the back of his resistance, Yanga remained in the chapel along with the women, offering fervent supplications to ensure the success of his warriors. Later, one of the conditions of peace that he made with the Mexican colonial government was that only Franciscan friars would be allowed to minister to his people (Davidson 1979, 95, 97; Pereira 1994, 99–100; Palmer 1976, 129). Some years later, in 1769, the

Figure 25. The Dark Virgin of Guadalupe

Mandinga-Amapa Maroons, who also made a treaty with the Spanish government in Mexico, dedicated the town and the new church to the Dark Virgin of Guadalupe, in honour of the victory of Fernando Manuel over his fellow Maroons who had opposed the treaty (Carroll 1977, 498–99; Pereira 1994, 102–3).

Louis, referred to above, testified to the colonial authorities in French Guiana about his community's deep commitment to Catholicism, or the Maroon version of it. He (1979, 313–14) declared that Couacou baptized the people with holy water and recited prayers daily, and that prayers were recited every morning and evening in the Maroon captain's compound as they were on well-managed plantations; those who were ill recited prayers in their homes. The Maroons were able to determine what feast or holy day was being celebrated in the town of Cayenne by the cannon shots that they could hear from afar. During the feast of Corpus Christi, at the first cannon shot indicating that the Holy Sacrament had been conveyed outside of the church, they fell on their knees and formed a procession around their houses, singing hymns, the women bearing crosses. In 1848 the Todos Tenemos *palenque* in Cuba had a church in the centre, inside of which there was an altar and a wooden figure representing Jesus Christ (La Rosa Corzo 2003, 181). Much earlier, in Mexico in 1523, the first Black insurgents in the colony erected crosses to celebrate their freedom and to declare that they were Christians (Davidson 1979, 89).

The existence of Afro-Christian religions in a number of present-day New World societies might readily be explained in terms of syncretism in the post-slavery period. But how do we explain it during the slavery period, especially among Maroons? One view is that several enslaved persons, particularly in the Catholic countries, had received some degree of religious conversion or acculturation before fleeing from their overlords, as the testimony of Louis indicates. But there was also a growing number of enslaved persons who were taught Protestant Christianity in the British, Dutch and Danish colonies, especially in the nineteenth century. This was so even in the Deep South of the United States, where the slavery system remained entrenched until the 1860s. Religious conversion was more widespread among Creole than African-born enslaved persons. Another idea is that Africans, whose religious world view was polytheistic, readily incorporated previously unknown gods into their pantheons, and assimilated Christ and the saints to their own corpus of deities. McFarlane (1986, 144) suggests that "the slaveowners' religion contributed to both the slaves' notion of freedom and their image of life in a free community". If these gods could work for the Whites they could also work (or be made to work) for the Blacks.

Patterson (1991, 299, 320) emphasizes the perception of Jesus as saviour of the oppressed, declaring that he "freely established fellowship with an unusually wide range of people, sinners of all sorts, including the very dregs of society". Patterson points out that enslaved persons were among the earliest converts to Christianity and constituted a sizeable segment of some Christian communities, notably in Corinth, where most of the converts were or had once been in bondage. He also suggests that "Christianity, alone among the religions of salvation, made freedom the doctrinal core of its soteria" (ibid., 294). If this is so, it might well explain why some Maroon communities adopted Christianity and came to view physical and spiritual freedom as being inextricably intertwined (notwithstanding that many enslavers called themselves Christians). This idea was strikingly illustrated in respect of aborted revolts in the United States, led by Denmark Vesey in 1822 and Nat Turner in 1831. The first one, led by a freedman who is said to have made "considerable wealth" from his trade as a carpenter, was betrayed by enslaved persons a couple of months before it was due to begin, but it involved extensive planning, coordination of activities and storage of large quantities of weapons (Lofton 1948, 401–17).[23]

The second revolt actually got off the ground and turned out to be by far the most destructive insurrection that visited the United States. Turner, a Creole enslaved person in Virginia, embraced a militant version of Christianity and increasingly felt called to liberate himself and his fellow sufferers not only from the bondage of sin but also from that of slavery. Actually, he ran away for about a month but returned voluntarily, to the surprise of many of his colleagues. It is quite possible that it was during this period of solitude that he heard the call to arms and returned, like the biblical character Moses, from voluntary exile to deliver "his people". He later confessed that he "wrapped" himself "in mystery" and devoted much of his time to prayer and fasting, during which he received revelations from the Almighty, who had "ordained" him for "a great purpose" (Johnson 1966, 228–33).

He first set the date for deliverance on 4 July 1831 (US Independence Day), but due to illness he postponed it until 21 August 1831, on both occasions based on some favourable augury. His first target was Joseph Travis, his overlord, whom he declared to have been a kind person, but who nevertheless had to perish for the sin of having participated in the evil practice of slavery. Turner and his followers having dispatched Travis to heaven or hell, then proceeded to wreak havoc on his enemies, sparing not man, woman or child. By the time the slaughter was over, some forty-eight hours later, they had killed fifty-five to sixty Whites. The state troops fiercely put down the insurrection, causing him to flee in hope of resuming his mission later. Once an insurgent, now a Maroon, he managed to elude capture for about two months before being apprehended by a White man and subsequently executed by judicial sentence (Johnson 1966, 235–45; Franklin 1980, 155–56). Thomas R. Gray, to whom he offered a voluntary confession while in prison, called him "a complete fanatic" and wrote about the "calm, deliberate composure with which he spoke of his late deeds and intentions. . . . clothed with rags and covered in chains, yet daring to raise his manacled hands to heaven, with a spirit soaring above the attributes of man" (Johnson 1966, 244–45).[24]

Bastide (1978, 89) argues, in the case of Palmares, that the White superstructure of temples and other features were extrinsic elements in a religion that was deeply African. He insists (ibid., 89) that the religion of the inhabitants must be viewed as part of the phenomenon of cultural resistance and syncretism, and goes on to add:

> The Bantu, whose mythology was relatively poor, identified their spirits with the Catholic saints, and the statues found by their conquerors were simply images of the spirits they worshiped. . . . Rocha Pitta [a contemporary writer] is therefore closer to the truth when he says that all the *quilombolas* retained of Catholicism was the sign of the Cross and a few garbled prayers, which they mixed with words and ceremonies taken from their native religions or simply invented.

The slaveholding fraternity recognized the deep religious world view that informed African life, while at the same time they considered African-derived religions to be not only unholy but also politically dangerous to the welfare of the authoritarian state. Though they recognized that some Maroon communities had embraced various forms of Christianity (usually syncretic forms of Catholicism), they regarded these forms as polluted and therefore hardly less dangerous than the African religions.

The authoritarian states, therefore, often sought to subvert Maroon communities from within by sending clergymen to reside among them to teach them the "official" version of Christianity. These were classic examples of attempts to use religion as an opiate. Maroon treaties in the Spanish colonies often contained clauses requiring the Maroons to adopt Catholicism and allow a White clergyman among them. At other times clergymen offered their services to Maroon communities with whom the authoritarian state was in hostile dialogue. This happened, for instance, among the Cofre de Perote Maroons. In most instances the ploy proved ineffective. However, there were a few occasions on which it worked. In one instance, José Félix Valverde, bishop of Caracas, in a letter to the king of Spain in 1734, declared that since military and other measures had failed to achieve the pacification of the Maroons, he had placed two Capuchin monks in areas that the insurgents were known to inhabit. These monks, through their salutary preaching and religious zeal, were able to obtain the capitulation of 180 insurgents on a promise of pardon (Brito Figueroa 1985, 210–11).[25] However, the clergy did not always opt for a mediated peace. Sometimes they supported and even called upon the state to wipe out the Maroons by military force. This happened, for instance, in 1611 in Guatemala, where frequent calls issued from the pulpit "to conquer the Black and mulatto runaways because of the harm they were doing to Indians and other people on the roads and elsewhere" (Lokken 2004b, 49).

In the vast majority of cases, the adoption of elements of Christianity did not make Maroons less revolutionary than their counterparts who retained much more visible forms of African religions. Santiago, leader of the feared Le Maniel Maroons in the 1780s, using Christianity as a tool, developed a combustible theology. In Moreau de Saint-Méry's (1979, 141) view, taking advantage of their gullibility and using a tiny cross and a rosary, he soon overpowered his followers' feeble minds.

The present evidence suggests that a greater number of Maroons embraced Christianity in Catholic countries than in Protestant ones. Pereira (1994, 106) reasoned that Catholicism was far more "pervasive and hegemonic" than Protestantism. Catholicism, with its elaborate ritual expressions, proved more attractive to the Maroons (and to enslaved persons), and their saints fitted more neatly into the pantheon of African gods. More important, many Africans might have viewed Christianity as not specifically a European, but rather a universal, religion. They therefore saw no harm in identifying with it.

An interesting aspect of the subject is the African perception of Whites as devils. This is illustrated by reference to a boy, eight years old, who had been captured on a military expedition against the Alukus but who had never seen a White person. He was completely terrified when he first encountered one and retreated from the approach of White people. He had been taught that White people were devils (Stedman 1988, 453). The association of whiteness with the devil was not new to African religious ideology. In 1661 a Gold Coast king is said to have referred to the Danes as being white like devils (Hanke 1974, 11).[26] It was the converse of the perception of blackness in European religious/racial ideology and was found in many African societies. The Italian slaver Theophilus Conneau (Canot) (1976, 142) recorded that once when he went to an African village to obtain captives, the children ran away from him, terrified at his appearance, and he felt sure that many looked upon him as their "Satan". Once or twice he saw women pick up a handful of dirt and toss it towards him, uttering a short sentence. This, he thought, was done to repel the evil spirit. Weatherford and Johnson (1969, 543–44) tell us that to Africans who had never seen a European before, whiteness suggested the unsightly discolouration of a dead person who had been in water for a long time. Early African associations of whiteness with evil were no doubt reinforced in the Americas by the harsh conditions under which Blacks suffered at the hands of Whites. The concept of the Whites as devils might have encouraged Maroons to attack and kill them, thus at the same time, in their view, warding off an evil force.

The essential point is that Maroon practice or adoption of any particular religion or religious ideas constituted not only an elaboration of their world view but part of their political strategy to secure and maintain their freedom. Though their religious icons and amulets did not protect them physically, these objects had a powerful and positive psychological effect on them. The power of the gods was displayed when, in a famous incident in Suriname in 1772, they commanded that a Ranger whom one of Baron's men had captured should have an ear severed and his head shaved, and be whipped and sent back with a message to his White overlords (Beet 1984, 135–36). Maroon religious faith contributed significantly to the courage with which they faced their enemies and death, which often astounded White observers. The fact that many of their communities survived for a long time, sometimes for over a century (though often moving and regrouping), would have reinforced in their own minds the efficacy of their icons, rituals and gods in preserving their freedom. Montejo was convinced that the strongest gods were African, though he also felt that they were capricious and wilful, and he could not unravel their thoughts in permitting African slavery in the Americas (Barnet 1996, 9).

CHAPTER 8

Maroon Economy

INTERDEPENDENCE OF MAROON ECONOMY

The main occupational divisions that scholars have identified in Maroon communities, based on their dominant economic activities, are agricultural-ists, miners, fisherfolk, traders, manufacturers, livestock keepers, bandits, and service providers (in the urban centres). It must, however, be recognized that such divisions are not rigid, since many communities became heavily involved in more than one of these activities. Banditry, of course, is not usually classi-fied as an economic activity, but some scholars seem to think that since many small communities earned a living in this way, such a classification is suitable in this context. Also, urban Maroons cannot properly be termed a "commu-nity" in the same sense as their rural counterparts, for no evidence exists that they actually formed a cohesive group or even directly associated with one another.

Maroons added to the natural bounty of the lands that they occupied through hard and unrelenting work, though they also plundered the White settlements for certain goods. Many large Maroon communities possessed a wide variety of material goods. The *rancheador* Francisco Estévez once located a *palenque* that he described as containing all the necessities of life (Villaverde 1982, 126). Atwood (1971, 227) states that Maroons in Dominica in the late eighteenth century planted gardens, raised poultry, hogs and other small stock, fished in the rivers and sea, foraged in the forest, and traded with Blacks on the plantations, thus providing a comfortable living for themselves.

Santos Gomes (2002, 485) describes the economy of the *mocambos* in the Grão-Pará captaincy of Brazil as consisting of "salting meat, dying [*sic*] clothes, planting crops, herding cattle, and making bricks to build French forts". Carneiro (1946, 28) tells us that the people of Palmares found in the forests all the elements necessary for their livelihood. He writes of the diversified economy of that state that those from the rural areas cultivated sugarcane, maize and plantains; those from the urban areas were usually artisans and produced iron objects; and others devoted themselves to hunting, fishing, raising chickens, and manufacturing baskets, hats, bellows, pots and other vessels (ibid., 7–8). Runaways, of course, often fled with a number of tools and household utensils, such as machetes, hoes, axes and cooking pots (Mullin 1992, 39; Fouchard 1972, 284–87).

A few examples must serve here to illustrate what is frequently found in contemporary records of the contents of Maroon communities. In the late eighteenth century, when an expeditionary force overcame the community led by Balla in Dominica, they found that it was well furnished with provisions, quite a lot of clothing, expensive pieces of furniture and several other objects (Atwood 1791, 249). In 1662 Archbishop Francisco de la Cueva Maldonado wrote to the king of Spain that there were four large Maroon communities in the Bahoruco Mountains of the Dominican Republic that cultivated the land, possessed meat and agrarian products in abundance, and collected large quantities of gold from the river with which they bought clothes, beverages and other necessities (Larrazábal Blanco 1998, 147). According to Estévez, a *palenque* in Santa Cruz de los Pinos in eastern Cuba contained much beef, pork, and smoked rodents, twenty large baskets of bananas, a lot of male and female clothing, part of a woollen bedspread, numerous earthen pots and iron kettles, and two horns with powder (Villaverde 1982, 46–47). In the early seventeenth century, Padre Laurencio, who lived for a while with the Cofre de Perote *apalencados* of Mexico, had this to say: "The plunder that was found in the town and cabins of these blacks was considerable. A variety of clothing that they had accumulated, daggers, swords, axes, some arquebuses and money, salt, butter, maize and other similar things" (Marcano Jiménez 2001, 29).[1]

Padre Laurencio was wrong to assume that the possessions of the Cofre de Perote Maroons were purely the result of plunder. The Maroons usually obtained these goods from various sources, including trade, plunder and production by the members of their own communities. Moreover, Maroon raids on plantations and other White settlements were exacerbated, and sometimes necessitated, by the extensive destruction that military expeditions wrought to the Maroon settlements – especially to their farming areas, in order to starve them into submission.

As shown in chapter 4 (see also chapter 10), Maroon depredations caused White settlers to flee certain areas in search of safe havens, and this had a widespread depreciating effect on the settler economies. At the same time, in several instances the agricultural, mining and trading activities of the large Maroon communities considerably improved the value of lands that would have remained unproductive. These included not only lands that the Maroons themselves cultivated but also those possessed by Whites. Two main examples are the lands that the Maroons of Palmares and Le Maniel occupied, which were so productive that they became the envy of White settlers who could not wait to get their hands on them. This was one reason that they strongly supported the subversion of these polities (Carneiro 1946, 16, 26, 29; Debbasch 1979, 146, 148). Indeed, some writers believe that because Maroons often enjoyed a symbiotic relationship with certain non-plantation settler communities in Brazil, Cuba, Peru, the Dominican Republic and elsewhere (see below), they should be viewed as a fundamental part of the economic landscape in those areas.

These observations should strengthen the view that the economies of most Maroon communities were interdependent but not essentially parasitic and predatory, as some writers have suggested.[2] It is amazing that writers should view the economic activities of fugitives from the most draconian forms of slavery as parasitic largely on the slaveholders. These writers apparently forget the genuinely parasitic plantation and wider colonial economies that were built on the sweat of enslaved Blacks and Indians. Pinckard (1806, 2:241), for instance, painted all Maroon communities in the Guiana colonies indiscriminately with the same brush, in relation to their food economy: "[T]he lower orders of them (for there are distinctions even among run-away slaves) were compelled to toil in the night, by going out of the woods, in plundering parties, to steal plantains and other provisions from the estates." Richard Ligon (1976, 98) wrote of Maroons in Barbados around the mid-seventeenth century that they "harbour themselves in woods and caves, living upon pillage for many months together"; and again, "The runaway Negroes often shelter themselves in these coverts . . . and in the night range abroad the countrey, and steale pigs, plantins, potatoes, and pullin, and bring it there;

and feast all day, upon what they stole." Debien (1979, 123, 126) claims that enslaved persons, free Blacks and Coloureds were the greatest enemies of the Maroons because the latter raided their small gardens or pastures and carried off their goods. He depicts the Maroons as hungry runaways who established their settlements near the provision fields that they raided at night to steal livestock. He does mention that free Blacks and Coloureds sometimes also assisted the Maroons, but makes no reference to those Maroon communities that lived mainly off their own extensive farms.

What Debien wrote was perhaps true of the small communities. They often depended upon plantation raids to supply them with most of their necessities, practised little or no settled cultivation, had virtually no weapons with which to defend themselves, and were frequently on the move (Philalethes 1979, 60). Usually, their escape was spontaneous rather than carefully planned; they had not sought (or perhaps not made) contact with the larger, more settled communities before or during their flight. It was this kind of Maroon, who led a fitful existence, that the Whites often held up as the symbol of *marronage,* though state officials and those engaged in military expeditions knew otherwise. But many small communities grew a lot of the produce that they consumed, and also reared animals or hunted game. An expedition that raided a small Maroon community in Tulate, Guatemala, in the early seventeenth century noted that it was well organized. Though it consisted of only nine houses, occupied by about twenty people, the houses and a small granary were stocked with corn, chillies, squashes, sugarcane, plantains and cotton. The inhabitants hunted iguanas and caught abundant fish (Lokken 2004b, 51). More impressive yet, a community of twelve households comprising runaways from the Engenho Santana in Bahia was found in 1828 to have over six hundred manioc plants, a large quantity of manioc flour, and six thousand coffee trees, besides significant quantities of sugarcane, cotton trees and fruit trees. It also possessed machinery for processing manioc, and spinning and weaving equipment (Flory 1979, 121). This community might have been part of a confederation of small settlements, but the circumstance still emphasizes the point that small communities were not *ipso facto* predatory ones.

Agriculture

The varied Maroon economic activities give the lie to the pervasive stereo-
type of "the lazy Negro". At least one European official report (from Vines,
British Consul in Belem, Brazil, in 1854) mentions that the inhabitants of the
mocambos in the Amazon Valley were "industrious" in looking after their
material needs (Conrad 1983, 390). The more established Maroon communities could not have been more unlike the wandering, straggling groups of
runaways that could have been regarded as Maroon communities only in the
most superficial sense of the term. The large Maroon communities did not
usually suffer from a shortage of food. They grew large quantities of wholesome food, and their cupboards were never bare, except when military expeditions destroyed their supplies. In fact, it appears that they commonly
overflowed, in striking contrast to what obtained among enslaved persons on
the plantations (see below).[3] The extent to which abundant food supplies was
an attraction to would-be Maroons remains uncertain, but it must have influenced some of them to flee to greener pastures.

African-born Maroons, in particular, brought with them to the Americas
extensive knowledge of tropical soil conditions. They came from basically
agrarian communities. Oluwasanmi's (1966, 53) observation that around the
time of Nigerian independence some 75 per cent of the people engaged in
farming as their main economic activity is perhaps apposite to West Africa as
a whole. The Maroons had earlier practised in Africa a wide variety of farming techniques and three main fallow systems: shifting cultivation, rotational
bush fallow and rotational planted fallow. They also knew how to engage in
crop mixtures and to stagger crop production during various seasons, planting different crops at different times so as to make the best use of the climate. They engaged in crop rotation during a sequence of years that allowed
the land to recover from exhaustion caused by certain crops. They practised
bush farming, hillside farming, swamp farming (for example, for rice), and so
on. The Wolof of Senegal distinguished five different kinds of flood land,
based on soil types and preferred crops (Morgan and Pugh 1969, 72, 104–5,
125–27). While the Maroons had to translate and modify this knowledge to
suit the particulars of their new environments, the change would not have
required drastic modifications of the techniques learned in Africa. At the
same time, it seems clear that Maroons borrowed heavily from the Indians
with respect to the cultivation of certain indigenous crops, such as maize and

cassava, and also with respect to knowledge of local soil types, especially in the early years of African settlement in the Americas. It was the indigenous peoples who pioneered the diversification of crops in the Americas.[4]

Arguably, among the Maroons provision of food was secondary in importance to that of defence or physical security. In societies that enjoy a high level of physical security and freedom from warfare, food security is (or ought to be) of primary importance. Such societies, while adopting measures to maintain physical security, do not usually make it as much a conscious daily concern as societies under military arms. But Maroon societies rarely enjoyed such physical security and therefore had to spend a lot of time guarding the lives of their inhabitants and also their agricultural fields.

Since the Maroons' choice of land was constrained by the need for safety and security, they did not always cultivate the best lands available. However, in the larger jurisdictions they often had access to virgin soil, sometimes among the best in the country. In Jamaica, for instance, large stretches of excellent farming land remained unoccupied by Whites because of their fear of the Maroons, and, in fact, settlers abandoned several plots that they had brought under cultivation (Campbell 1990, 142, 145).[5] As did agrarian communities in pre-colonial Africa, Maroons collectively cleared the bush, cut down the trees and tamed the land. Sometimes they planted small plots that were allocated to single families, but they also planted some fields collectively.[6] The André and Matudere Maroons, in French Guiana and Colombia respectively, generally cultivated separate plots but divided the catch from collective hunting and fishing (Louis 1979, 315; Borrego Plá 1973, 83). Freyre (1963, 39–40) writes about "the near-socialist form of life and work which the settlement of Negroes in Palmares assumed" and its "parasocialist type of culture". He also pays tribute to that state, whose agrarian economy was "a forerunner of the diversification of crops in contrast to the predominant monoculture of the white planters".

African Maroons, of course, were not the first regional peasant communities; that distinction belongs to the Indians. However, many Maroon communities did establish autonomous and viable peasant communities. Sidney Mintz (1974, 152–53) refers to them as "runaway peasantries" but suggests that they were not "typologically" peasant societies, because their "economic integration with the outside world" was "impaired" by the military threats and operations of the slaveholding states, so that some of them were "compelled to maintain complete isolation".[7] The fact is that the large Maroon societies displayed all the normal features of peasant societies, growing most of the food that they consumed and using the surplus to barter for a variety of other goods, often through a wide network of trade, as we shall see later in this chapter. They occupied definite land spaces that they claimed as a right, either by conquest from the Whites or through appropriation of remote and unused terrain. The fact that the authoritarian state usually did not recognize their titles to these lands should not be used as a yardstick by which to judge their land rights, since they disputed European titles to these lands and since the Europeans themselves had appropriated, and would continue to appropriate, lands belonging to the indigenous inhabitants.

Some Maroon groups took over abandoned plantations or cultivated the fringes of large existing ones. In some instances they also encroached on or forcefully took over Indian farming lands, thus unfortunately abridging the freedom of another set of oppressed people and creating or exacerbating hostilities between the indigenous peoples and themselves (Pereira 1994, 97; Marcano Jiménez 2001, 33). They planted flat lands, hillsides and even stream beds. At times they intercropped – planted their crops interspersed with brushwood or tall trees that offered some protection from detection by military expeditions. They planted both annuals and perennials, and their cornucopia included the main plantation crops – sugarcane, coffee and cocoa – that as enslaved persons they had been forbidden to grow. Some of them also kept livestock, though not usually in abundance. Apart from the plantation staples, and depending on their location, among the crops that the Maroons planted were cassava (manioc), maize (corn), rice, bananas, peanuts, pistachio nuts, pigeon peas, sweet potatoes, yams, eddoes, squashes, beans, okra, pineapples, melons, oranges, chillies, taros, tobacco and cotton.[8]

The Saramaka agricultural fields included rice, maize, cassava, sugarcane, coffee, passion fruit, bananas, plantains, pineapples, peanuts, tanias, okra, sweet potatoes, pigeon peas, beans, hot peppers, cashews and pumpkins. Cultivation took place around their dwellings and in fields farther away; often each field was dedicated to a major crop, though sometimes the Maroons intercropped the fields. They made oil from at least five different species of palm. Their pharmacology embraced a large number of wild plants (Price 1991, 109–11).

The diversified agrarian economy of Palmares drew praise from some of its Dutch and Portuguese invaders. The Palmarinos planted maize, their chief crop, twice yearly, and also cultivated large amounts of beans, sweet potatoes, plantains and sugarcane. The Dutch expedition under Lieutenant Jürgens Reijmbach, which invaded the confederation in 1645, saw large plantations cultivated mainly with maize, and two sugar plantations spread over about two and a half miles. Reijmbach commented that they cultivated all kinds of cereals, and their lands were well kept and irrigated by streamlets. Years later, in 1677, when Fernão Carrilho invaded the confederation, he too was impressed with the food economy of the inhabitants, noting that they planted every kind of vegetable. He was convinced that, along with its security, its food economy was one of its great attractions for fugitives (Carneiro 1946, 41; Kent 1979, 178–79).[9] The Cofre de Perote settlement had a thriving agrarian economy producing corn, pumpkins, bananas and other fruits, beans, sweet potatoes, vegetables, tobacco, an abundance of chickens and a large number of cattle (Pereira 1994, 99). The Seminole Maroons also cultivated a wide variety of crops and in addition kept horses, cattle and hogs. One early nineteenth-century White observer wrote, "We found these negroes in possession of large fields of the finest land, producing large crops of corn, beans, melons, pumpkins, and other esculent vegetables. [I] saw, while riding along the borders of the ponds, fine rice growing; and in the village large corn-cribs were filled" (Mulroy 1993, 19).

In Cuba, several *palenques* possessed large cultivated plots. The Palenque de la Cruz in 1842 cultivated one hundred plots. In the same year El Cedro possessed forty-seven plots cultivated with sugarcane, bananas and other fruit, all of an extraordinary size. Among the items that Todos Tenemos contained in 1848 were 200 sacks of rice, 625 pounds of jerked meat, and 14 live pigs. It cultivated some 67 hectares (about 167.5 acres) with bananas, taro, sweet potatoes, yucca, yams, sugarcane, tobacco, corn, ginger, greens and fruit trees (La Rosa Corzo 2003, 155, 158, 180–82). The André settlement was richly cultivated with millet, cassava, rice, sweet potatoes, yams, sugarcane, bananas, cotton and other crops (Louis 1979, 317). The Guy's Town Maroons in Jamaica in the 1730s produced sugarcane, cocoa, plantains, yams, melon, corn, pigs, poultry and cows (Campbell 1990, 50).

In 1702 a group of three hundred Maroons in Jamaica had 100 acres well planted with food crops (Patterson 1979, 259). Even more striking, the head of a military expedition in that island in the 1670s declared that Juan de Bolas's Maroons cultivated some 200 acres, the island's largest single source of domestic food production at that time (Taylor 1965, 185–86; Patterson 1979, 254). Though the accuracy of this statement cannot be determined, the peace treaty that the colonial state struck with Juan de Bolas recognized the right of each of his followers eighteen years and over to 30 acres, and later the colonial government proposed a grant of 20 acres to each member of Juan de Serras's group (Campbell 1990, 24, 25). An eyewitness declared that in 1823 the Me No Sen You No Com community in Jamaica contained 200 acres (80 hectares) of fine provisions (Mullin 1992, 59). The Calunga *palenque* in Cuba had a similar-sized field in cultivation in 1849 (La Rosa Corzo 2003, 155, 158, 180, 182, 204). In Dominica in 1814 the governor reported that his forces had discovered provision grounds that were 300 acres (120 hectares) in size (Craton 1982, 143). More amazing still, in 1733 a British officer estimated the size of a Maroon field, cultivated mainly with plantains, at 640 acres (256 hectares) (Carey 1997, 177). Even allowing wide scope for exaggeration, the acreage must have been substantial.

Stedman (1988, 404, 410) was surprised to find some baskets that the Aluku Maroons had dropped in their flight, containing well-cleaned rice. Shortly afterward, the members of his expedition came across the most beautiful oblong field that he had ever seen, where the rice was already ripe for harvest. In 1810 Charles Edmonstone, a Demerara militia captain, came across fourteen Maroon houses filled with rice, besides several well-cultivated rice fields at various stages of maturity. He estimated that the rice was sufficient to feed seven hundred men for an entire year. In addition, he found large fields planted with ground provisions (Thompson 1987, 143). His observations are remarkable because, while the size of the Maroon population in that colony was never accurately determined, we can be sure that no single community contained more than one hundred souls. In 1846 an expedition that came upon an unknown settlement in Cuba estimated its membership at roughly thirty. What was extraordinary was the amount of food that they were producing: some three hundred banana plants, twenty fields of corn (mostly dry), twenty fields of "second harvest" rice, fields of taro in "extraordinary abundance", yams, sweet potatoes, peanuts, tobacco and fruit (La Rosa Corzo 2003, 177). Since it is doubtful that the Maroons were cultivating these provisions as cash crops, we must assume that they intended to store the surplus for long-term use. Carrilho in 1677 stated explicitly that the Palmarinos stored their surplus grain against "warfare and winter" (cited in Kent 1979, 179). According to Armando Fortune, the Bayano Maroons in Panama had houses, pits and silos full of every kind of food that they caught or raised for their sustenance (La Guardia 1977, 86). Such activities were in

Figure 26. Leonard Parkinson, Jamaican Maroon captain.[10] Courtesy Bristol City Council.

keeping with pre-colonial practices in Africa, where some granaries held food for up to three years in case of emergencies (Suret-Canale 1971, 235).

Rice was one of the primary staples. It could be stored for long periods, the ecological conditions allowed for its cultivation on a large scale, and it was grown commonly in certain parts of West Africa, especially modern Sierra Leone, Gambia and Guinea (Bigman 1993, 34; Lewicki 1974, 33–37). Yam was another important staple amenable to long-term storage. This crop was widely planted in West Africa and was the most important food item of the forest peoples (Morgan and Pugh 1969, 85). Richard Price (1991), who consulted the extant work of Schumann, the late-eighteenth-century Moravian missionary among the Saramaka, and supplemented his understanding with fieldwork and oral information gathered from among present-day Maroons, has produced perhaps the best statement regarding the diversity of the Maroon economy in Suriname. Apart from mentioning the wide range of crops that they produced (see above), he notes that they cultivated numerous varieties of rice (Richard and Sally Price counted seventy varieties in the 1960s), fifteen of banana, twenty of cassava, seven of yam, fifteen of tania, four of maize, ten of hot pepper, six of watermelon, fifteen of okra, twelve of sweet potato, and four of sugarcane.

The Maroons supplemented these food crops by gathering from the variety of wild plants near their settlements, and fished and hunted for most of their animal protein. Game and fish were abundant on the mainland but less so on the islands, though Maroons engaged in coastal fishing. Price (1991, 114–117) gives a fairly long list of the fish and animals that the Saramakas caught, and the techniques that they used to snare their prey. The animals that they hunted included monkeys, armadillos, agouti, rabbits, lizards, opossums, porcupines, deer, anteaters and peccaries (wild hogs). Some kept chickens and occasionally cows, sheep and pigs. Grassy plains and freshwater and saltwater resources provided the Gracia Real de Santa Teresa de Mose Maroons with a rich supply of deer, buffalo, wild cattle, rabbits, squirrels, raccoons, turtles, wild fowls and a large variety of fish (Landers 2000a, 48). The Tulate Maroons in Guatemala had sufficient iguanas and fish not only to supply their needs but also to conduct a lucrative trade in those products with far-off settlements (Lokken 2004b, 51). The Jamaican Maroons, with much less abundant fauna, nevertheless hunted extensively for game and set traps covering some twenty miles to snare wild hogs (Campbell 1990, 38–39). Some communities that were located a good distance from White settlements kept large quantities of livestock, including cattle, horses, hogs and chickens.[11] Cattle raids on the plantations by the communities close to them were common. The Maroons also kept dogs, both for hunting and to alert them to the approach of strangers.[12] On one occasion a runaway in the United States took with him a pack of hunting dogs (Mullin 1992, 39). Because of the shortage of gunpowder and bullets, the André Maroons used mainly dogs, bows and arrows, and traps to hunt wild animals (Louis 1979, 316). The Jamaican Maroons commonly used the *junga* or spear for such purposes, and it is still a symbol of pride, associated with religious rituals, among their descendants (Warner-Lewis 2003, 60–61).

People who went on military expeditions against Maroons often commented on their provision fields and stores, almost as much as on their innovative defence strategies. These comments may speak more eloquently than any others to the Maroons' determination to create a life of their own that was not parasitic on the plantations. In 1685 Governor Ayres de Souza de Castro suggested that all captured Palmarinos should be deported to

Pernambuco, lest they flee again to the *quilombo,* taking with them other enslaved persons whom they had inveigled with stories about the abundance in which they lived (Carneiro 1946, 49). In the early nineteenth century, an American surveyor described the Seminole Maroons (recently devastated by slave-hunting raids and a major war) as "stout and gigantic in their proportions . . . the finest looking people I have ever seen", with well-cultivated fields and large herds of livestock (cited in Porter 1951, 253). Rarely do we find mention in the contemporary literature of Maroons being emaciated because of lack of food, and when it does occur, the context is usually one of dislocation and wandering as a result of military warfare. Stedman (1988, 409) described the Suriname Maroons whom the soldiers had killed as "plump and fat", and declared that it seemed that when they were allowed to live peacefully they "want for nothing". Times of peace generally meant times of plenty.[13]

It was precisely because the authoritarian states recognized the ability of the well-established communities to feed themselves that they developed strategies to destroy Maroon agrarian plots at specific times. In the case of Demerara, the strategy was to do so around harvest time (Thompson 2002b, 132). In the case of Brazil, in 1687 the former governor, Juan de Souza, stated that the greatest hurt that could be inflicted on the Maroons was to attack their food supplies. He suggested the formation of a special corps that would not only limit the Maroons' incursions into the colony to obtain food and other goods but also prevent them from sowing or – as an alternative, reaping – their crops (Carneiro 1946, 42). There is, however, no evidence that this suggestion was implemented, perhaps because of the heavy cost in men and money to maintain such a military corps. In the previous year, the Crown, responding to a letter from Governor Souto-Maior, had ordered that the colonial state should use the Palmarinos' food resources to feed the four hundred troops that should be sent into their territory at harvest time (Carneiro 1946, 42).

La Rosa Corzo (2003, 15–16) cites Pérez Landa and Jústiz del Valle, who imply that at least some of the larger communities in Cuba practised a high level of labour specialization – some of the young men cultivated the soil, fished or hunted, while another set felled trees for building canoes, piles, mallets, stakes and palisades. The women generally cultivated the land and raised sheep. He is sceptical that such a division really existed, since he found nothing in the contemporary records that he consulted to support such a conclusion. Nevertheless, as noted earlier, the citizens of Palmares practised a high level of statecraft, even to having special courts of justice and blacksmiths producing their own weapons (Hemming 1978, 355; Bastide 1978, 82, 86). That community would hardly have been unique in the specialized deployment of manual skills; the impressive Quilombo do Ambrósio in the mid-eighteenth century in Minas Gerais seems to have boasted a similar division of labour (Pinto Vallejos 1998, 192). In the case of the Cofre de Perote *palenque*, Davidson (1979, 94–95) states that Padre Juan recorded a clear division of labour: half the population tended the crops and cattle, and the other half comprised the military guard and the guerrilla fighters. Labour specialization, of course, existed to a fair degree in the plantation societies of the Americas, and was even more highly developed in Africa, the original homeland of the majority of enslaved Blacks.

As noted, military expeditions concentrated on destroying the Maroon provision plots,[14] which were usually at different stages of growth. In fact, it appears that some expeditions in Guyana were dispatched at particular times of the year, to destroy the plots when the crops were likely to be ready for harvest. This was often a significant blow to the Maroons, since they would have to subsist mainly by gathering until they could clear and plant the land and reap another harvest. To reduce the impact of such destruction (and sometimes to make use of more fertile soils), some Maroon communities cultivated several plots, secluded at some distance from their dwellings.[15] It was possible to hide the crops effectively by interspersing them with the thick undergrowth. In one instance the André Maroons planted three fields about a league from the old ones. A military expedition that raided the settlement in 1748 failed to discover the new fields (Louis 1979, 317).[16] Food security was critical to the preservation of their independence, and occasionally Maroons turned themselves over to the colonial forces or sought peace terms when their provision grounds were destroyed and they risked death from starvation.

INDUSTRY AND MANUFACTURE

Apart from agriculture, fishing and hunting, Maroons carried on various industrial and manufacturing activities, but more extensive research needs to be done on this topic. We know that the mining of gold (and, in some areas,

Figure 27. Akan gold weight. From A*kan Weights and Gold Trade*, by Timothy F. Garrard (London: Longman, 1980).

precious stones) was an important activity in Colombia and Brazil, and to a lesser extent in Venezuela, Mexico, Cuba and the Dominican Republic. In the Dominican Republic, and perhaps elsewhere, both women and men were involved in mining gold from the streams (Landers 2000b, 4). In the late seventeenth century, about three hundred Maroons in the province of Cartagena took possession of some three hundred royal gold mines in the region between El Firme and San Lucas, chasing the Whites out of the area and naming their own mayors and lieutenants from within the *palenques* (Borrego Plá 1973, 109). In Brazil, Maroons exploited the mines in the province of Maranhão and other places. They were well established in the Maracassume mines in that province in 1853 (Conrad 1983, 387). Maroons in Cuba and the Dominican Republic also produced small quantities of gold (Pérez de la Riva 1979, 53; Albert Batista 1990, 39). The Maroons traded much of this gold for various commodities (see below), but it is likely that they fashioned some of it into jewellery and figurines, just as Africans had been doing in West Africa for centuries. The Akan of the Gold Coast, for instance, produced artistic gold weights and measures (Leyten 1979).[17]

The extent of iron-working remains unclear, though a number of Maroon communities manufactured a variety of iron weapons, and archaeological finds suggest more varied metallurgical activities. There is no evidence that the Maroons mined metals apart from gold, and so we have to assume that they acquired copper, iron and other metals largely through trade and plunder. In 1662 Archbishop Francisco de la Cueva Maldonado noted that the Bahoruco Maroons depended upon trade to obtain iron and that their ironsmiths were excellent workmen (Landers 2000b, 4). Elsa Goveia (1965, 163) notes that enslaved persons in Antigua carried on a "growing trade in stolen iron, copper, lead, and brass", which the colonial government attempted to arrest by imposing stiff penalties on delinquents. According to Terry Weik

(1997, 86), Maroons in Central America raided caravans carrying bullion that they exchanged with pirates for scrap iron and other goods. Studies in the United States indicate that a significant number of fugitives were blacksmiths and other metalworkers (Libby 1992). They represented 10 per cent of runaways listed in advertisements in the *Maryland Gazette* (dates not given) and 5 per cent of those in the *Virginia Gazette*, a much higher percentage than in the non-fugitive enslaved population. Salvador de Madariaga, a mid-twentieth century writer, concluded that the Maroons valued iron much more than gold (Franco 1973, 26). The need for metal tools for agrarian and other purposes suggests that metalworkers played a major role in the economy of Maroon societies. It is reasonable to assume that since these societies attracted a wide cross-section of Africans, those who had worked as coopers, bricklayers, masons, boat builders and so on continued to practise their craft in their new environment.

The most important Maroon manufacturing activity was the building of their houses. Their accommodation was typical of those of the poor Africans and Indians, though some of their dwellings were bigger and displayed some elegance. The diary of the Cuban *rancheador* Francisco Estévez distinguishes frequently between *ranchos grandes* (large dwellings or "houses"), *barracones* (barrack-like quarters), and *bohíos* (simple huts) (Villaverde 1982, 46, 50, 80 passim). Most dwellings apparently housed two or three inhabitants, but a few held substantially larger numbers. For instance, a settlement in Santa Cruz de los Pinos contained twenty-two "ranchos grandes", in most of which there were six or seven beds (Villaverde 1982, 46). The Me No Sen You No Com settlement in Jamaica in 1823 contained fourteen rectangular buildings, none of which was less than twenty-five feet long, and one of which was seventy feet long (Mullin 1992, 59). One document from Brazil in 1876 described the houses found in a *mocambo* as being made of coconut fibre, with walls of joined sticks (Conrad 1983, 385). Houses in the Guianas were usually made mainly from the manicole tree (like those of enslaved people), and the Maroons usually manufactured hammocks from silk grass. The use of these materials and the style of manufacture again indicate the strong Indian influence on certain aspects of Maroon culture. The hammock was a useful amenity, since it could be carried about readily and slung between trees, and it gave protection from biting or stinging insects. A different kind of housing was noted in the Me No Sen You No Com settlement. Some of its fourteen buildings had wooden floors and shingled roofs (Mullin 1992, 59). In most

Maroon societies, the quality and durability of their houses were constrained not only by the materials at hand but also by the need to move the community at short notice. They could easily rebuild their houses, which were often destroyed by military expeditions and occasionally by themselves (as a defence strategy).

As regards food preparation, Stedman (1988, 409–10) commented on the skills of the Suriname Maroons at meeting their dietary needs. Most of their techniques strongly reflect African influence, and occasionally Indian influence. Stedman wrote admiringly:

> *Game* and *fish* they catch in great abundance by artificial traps and springs, and which they preserve by barbacuing [*sic*], while with *rice, cassava, yams, plantains*, and so on, theyr fields are ever over stoked [*sic*] – *Salt* they make with the ashes of the palm trees[18] . . . or use red pepper. We even discovered concealed near the trunk of an old tree a case *bottle* with excellent *butter* which the Rangers told me they made by melting and clarifying the fat of the palm-tree worms and which fully supplies the above ingredients while I absolutely found it more delicious – The *pistachio* or pinda nuts they also convert in[to] butter, by their oily susbstance & frequently use them in their broths – The *palm tree wine* they are never in want of, and which they make in cutting deep insitions [*sic*] of a foot over square in the fallen trunk, where the joice [juice] being gathered it soon ferments by the heat of the sun, when it is not only a cool and agreeable beveridge [*sic*] but strong [and] sufficient to intoxicate – and soap they have from the dwarf aloes.[19]

The cultivation of sugarcane in Palmares, Quilombo do Ambrósio and other communities must have meant the erection of at least rudimentary processing mills. The erection of simple mills should have presented few problems to the Maroons since a number of them were accomplished artisans. The main problem would have been the acquisition of the requisite materials. Despite a dearth of solid information on this subject, Flory (1979, 120–21) is convinced that the equipment used in the Quilombo do Ambrósio to manufacture sugar and rum could not have been much less advanced than what was used on the European plantations. He states that the fugitives often carried away manufacturing equipment from the plantations, and quotes a member of an expedition who said that his men found "all that was necessary for the establishment of a new fazenda [farm]".

The preparation of foods such as cassava and oil entailed complicated and time-consuming processes (Price 1991, 111, 117). Knowledge of how to prepare cassava would have been acquired from contact with the Indians, whereas that of making oil would have been derived largely from West African societies, such as Igboland, Yorubaland, Dahomey and Asante, where palm oil (and palm wine) had been processed for centuries before the transatlantic slave trade.

The Maroons produced mortars to separate the rice grains from the husks, sieves for sifting grain, giant clay pots for cooking, clay jugs and pans for preserving water and wine, and ceramic cups, bottles, basins, dishes and other utensils. They also made candles from local wax, powder horns from calabashes (gourds), blowing horns from conch shells, and drums. Maroons often carved the calabash surface with intricate motifs, again indicating African influence.[20]

In Jamaica, Maroon women were the main pioneers of bark-lace and bark-cloth production. Steeve Buckridge (2004, 51, 52) explains that in that country lace-bark forests were found mainly in Maroon areas, and noted that the product resembled fine lace but could be mistaken for linen or gauze.[21] In time these products became widespread in Jamaica, among both enslaved and free persons. Since the laghetto or lace-bark tree was native to Jamaica, Hispaniola and Cuba, and since the cloth production was derived from West African precedents (Buckridge 2004, 50–52), it is logical to assume that production of bark-lace and bark-cloth was also quite common in these other Caribbean islands.

In the André settlement the women spun cotton, while the men wove it. They made skirts and loincloths, but it is not known whether the men or women did this task. They obviously used the small spindle common in West Africa at the time, since the Maroon Louis testified that the cotton material was woven in small pieces and then put together. According to him, it was "decorated with Siamese cotton thread", which could mean that the thread was acquired by barter or spun according to a Siamese pattern (Louis 1979, 317). Sally and Richard Price (1980, 54) have concluded that, among the Ndjukas, "although weaving has never been highly developed by Maroons, their textile arts form one of the richest and most varied areas of their material culture".

Maroons in the Amazon Valley of Brazil manufactured charcoal, canoes and other sailing vessels (Conrad 1983, 390). This last activity must have been fairly widespread, especially among Maroons who lived close to rivers or the sea. They also manufactured various ceramic objects (Carneiro 1946, 8). Maroons carried with them a wide range of manufacturing skills. It will be recalled that, apart from a small quantity of food and clothing, very few enslavers gave their charges any other material goods, household or otherwise. Enslaved persons on the plantations therefore had to develop a material culture built partly on the skills that they had brought with them from their motherland and partly on borrowings from Indian and European culture. In the slaveholding states Africans constituted the vast majority of artisans, including blacksmiths, metalworkers, coopers, furniture makers, carpenters, woodcarvers, bricklayers, masons and boat builders. The wide range of products, largely of wood, that present-day Africans (and especially descendants of Maroons in Brazil, Haiti, Jamaica and Suriname) manufacture speaks to the skills that their ancestors took with them to their secluded settlements. Palmares is said to have had many artisans, including blacksmiths, masons, carpenters, tinsmiths, weavers and potters. The tools and weapons that an expeditionary force found in the Quilombo Grande (Bomba) and the Quilombo do Gabriel in Brazil suggest that these communities also contained a number of artisans. These consisted of two swords, two axes and two scythes in the first *quilombo,* and a loaded hunting musket, axes, scythes, hoes, a fishing net and some carpentry tools in the second one. There is also evidence that the André Maroons of French Guiana, the Lemba Maroons of the Dominican Republic and at least one group of Maroons in Suriname produced a variety of iron implements.[22]

Preliminary archaeological work carried out on a number of sites, including Pilakikaha and Fort Mose (Florida), Culpepper Island (North Carolina), Seaman's Valley, Nanny Town and Accompong (Jamaica), various caves near Havana (Cuba), José Leta (Dominican Republic), and Ambrósio and Palmares (Brazil), are improving our understanding of the material (and social) culture of the Maroons.[23] The digs at José Leta (and a few other sites in the Dominican Republic) revealed a wide range of artefacts, including metal arrow and spear tips; copper-sheet plates of some technical refinement; various iron objects including parts of knives, lances, tongs and pincers; other metal objects of various sizes that were used as bracelets, fish hooks and so on; slag, which confirmed that metalworking had taken place at the site; clay pipes, some of which were incised; wooden mortars and pestles; wooden ornamental combs; fragments of ceramic water pots, vases and other utensils (some displaying Indian and European motifs); and ceramic bowls and plates displaying designs adapted from those introduced by early Spanish settlers. Some of the objects resembled those found in archaeological digs in Cuba (Arrom and García Arévalo 1986, 48–74). While some of these objects may have been seized from European settlements, the Maroons obviously manufactured quite a number of them.

Archaeological work in Jamaica on Nanny Town and Old Accompong Town has also revealed some interesting artefacts, including terra cotta figurines; clay pipe stems and bowls; tin glaze and Delftware; glass bottles for wine, alcohol and medicine; fragments of firearms; a range of objects made of lead and iron; stone implements including grinding stones and flints; Spanish coins; glass and stone beads and buttons; charcoal; and a few cowrie shells. As in the Dominican Republic, designs contain African, Indian and European elements (Agorsah 1994, 176–81).

Archaeological digs at Macaco and surrounding areas in 1992 and 1993 unearthed Spanish ceramic objects dating back to the thirteenth century, and also objects of French, Dutch, English, African (Angolan) and presumably Indian (indigenous) provenance. The archaeologists collected more than two thousand artefacts, of which about 90 per cent were ceramic. The artefacts were both small and large (especially vases), of aesthetic and utilitarian value, and some of them clearly had religious and funerary associations (Orser 1992; Funari 1995). Here, as in digs at Maroon sites in Jamaica, Mexico and elsewhere, it is debatable whether the Indian-style artefacts mean that the sites were previously occupied by Indians, that the Maroon communities included Indians, that the objects reached the sites as a result of trade between Indians and Maroons, that they were plundered from Indian settlements, or that they were African adaptations of Indian art forms. There is also some discussion as to whether the forms of Catholicism so visible in Palmares indicated a strong European presence there. Several recent writers have strongly promoted the view that Palmares attracted oppressed peoples of various ethnicities and cultures, and a few have even argued that the term *republic*, first employed in seventeenth-century documents, speaks to this multi-ethnicity and transculturation.

TRADE

Maroons carried on an extensive underground trade with all ethnic groups – Whites, Indians, Blacks, and Coloureds – on the plantations, in other rural areas, and in the cities. The extant records mention this traffic often, remarking on the friendly relations between Maroons and those who traded with them, and as well on the constant complaints by state officials that the trade hindered their efforts to eliminate the settlements. Most jurisdictions had laws specifically proscribing all trade with Maroons. In Peru around the mid-eighteenth century, the penalty for Blacks trading with Maroons was two hundred lashes and exile (Bowser 1974, 200). Plantation workers often depended upon Maroon supplies of goods to meet pressing needs. They therefore traded crops and poultry from their small gardens, or items that they had pilfered from the plantations. In the French Caribbean, the small Maroon communities that were deficient in food crops exchanged fish, game and other objects for manioc, peas and vegetables, in what Debien (1979, 111) calls a symbiotic relationship.[24] Although plantation owners suffered the loss of material goods through such trade, the trading relationship made it less likely that the Maroons would burn down or seriously damage their plantations, thus providing a kind of security.

The Maroons also sometimes traded in the urban centres, mingling with the free Black and Coloured population. It was common knowledge in Jamaica that many of them could be found on Sundays among the large crowds that gathered in the urban markets from various parts of the country to buy and sell merchandise (Campbell 1990, 60). The enslavers accused the Jews of Kingston and Port Antonio, in particular, of trading military supplies to the Maroons. Whether or not these Jews knew that they were engaging in forbidden trade, some of them could at least pretend that they were doing so in all innocence. One of the Maroon communities had abducted two White boys, whom they employed to write letters that purported to be from a senior military officer in the island, requesting to purchase powder from certain Jewish merchants (Campbell 1990, 73). In 1764 three members of the provisional government of Bahia wrote the imperial government in Lisbon, alleging that Maroons entered the city at night in order to obtain supplies of gunpowder, ammunition and other weapons, through Black and White contacts there (Conrad 1983, 380; see also 383). Navarrete (2003, 38) writes that the merchants carried on a thriving commerce with the inhabitants of Palmares, exchanging their wares for agricultural products and offering them information about expeditions that were being organized against them, for which they were well paid.

A *mocambo* located near the Maracassume mines depended upon the yield of the mines for its basic support. According to the president of Maranhão province, where the *mocambo* was located, its inhabitants carried on trade in Santa Helena and other places for food, ammunition and other goods. They maintained amicable relations with peddlers and persons who lived close to their community (Conrad 1983, 387).[25] In Cartagena province, Maroons exchanged the gold that they had mined from the rivers for firearms in the city (Borrego Plá 1973, 27). According to Father Zapata of Cartagena, the *palenques* in that province that were inhabited largely by African-born fugitives were pretty well equipped with firearms, whereas one *palenque* that allegedly contained exclusively Creole Maroons was thought to have only bows and arrows (Borrego Plá 1973, 77). The contrast in the kinds of weapons possessed by the occupants of the different communities is overdrawn, for we know from captured Maroons from the Matudere (African) settlement that they had a number of archers (Borrego Plá 1973, 83). Nevertheless, Zapata's information emphasizes the more aggressive role of the African-born Maroons in obtaining firearms through trade.

The underground trade in Mexico was noted from the very early days of *marronage* in that country. The colonial authorities complained frequently of the connivance of Africans, Indians and even Spaniards in that trade, despite frequent prohibitions and threats of harsh punishments against offenders. Not only petty merchants but also rich ones, some of whom were high government officials, fed the trade. As noted above, Don Andrés Fernández de Otañes, senior magistrate of Teutila in the eighteenth century, is said to have employed Maroons in his vanilla trade and to have supplied them with weapons (Naveda Chávez-Hita 2001, 143).

During the late sixteenth and early seventeenth centuries, the Maroons in the northern area of the Dominican Republic (comprising Blacks, Mulattos and Mestizos) carried on a lucrative trade in hides with foreigners (Esteban Deive 1989, 61, 71–72). By the late seventeenth century this Spanish colony had become integrated into a wide contraband network of trade, "one which provided ample space for former slaves to find upward mobility through a combination of smuggling and swidden agriculture and hunting, along with marooned shipmen and deserters, adventurers and runaway bondsmen who would try their fortune" (Derby 2003, 17). In Venezuela, the Ocoyta and Varacuy Maroons raided the cocoa and other plantations, seized a lot of the crops and sold them to Dutch and British traders, who supplied them with firearms, powder, lead and other goods (García 1989, 68–69; Brito Figueroa

1985, 209, 217). Such trade was contraband as far as the colonial regulations were concerned, not only because it involved the Maroons but also because it was conducted without licence and with the enemies of Spain, especially the British and Dutch.

Ventura Sánchez, chief captain of the Bumba Maroons and by far the most famous Cuban Maroon leader in the early nineteenth century, had a large following who sold wax and other articles in Jamaica, the Dominican Republic and Haiti through the medium of White merchants (Franco 1979, 42; Pérez de la Riva 1979, 55). Franco (1979, 43) tells us that in 1819 a colonial official uncovered one of these operations, carried out by Luis Rufo, an Italian, who would take a small boat filled with clothes, shoes, hats, machetes and other goods to Sagua on the coast, in order to trade with the Maroons. Manuel Griñán (Gallo), the leader of a *palenque* that existed there, used to deposit the money derived from this trade (and from the sale of crops that his followers cultivated) with Juan Sabón, another White trader from Santa Catalina who chartered boats to Haiti. The level of organization suggests that the covert operation existed for some years. Other Maroons in the area traded with Don Rafael Peregrín from Arroyo Seco, and still others with the Hacienda de Lagunita (Franco 1979, 46). Pérez de la Riva (1979, 53) states that such people were spread throughout the Cuban countryside and categorizes them as White people of doubtful reputation. The items that they traded included wax, honey and gold. In 1853 government officials in Maranhão province, Brazil, arrested Marcellino José da Costa Ramos, Isidoro Francisco de Oliveira, Theodoro Sudré, and Mariano Gil for carrying on trade with Maroons (Conrad 1983, 388).

Border trade and other economic relations were often extensive, as we have noticed above in respect of the Grão-Pará captaincy on the one hand and French Guiana on the other (Santos Gomes 2002, 485). Similarly, Le Maniel Maroons, along the Haitian–Dominican Republic border, carried on an extensive trade with the Spaniards, from whom they purchased arms, ammunition, tools and dogs (Moreau de Saint-Méry 1979, 141; Debbasch 1979, 144). The Spanish authorities indirectly supported this trade, by not attempting to suppress it, because of its great benefit to Neybes and Beate, which were the main settlements occupied by the Spanish border population. Debbasch (1979, 144) writes that the inhabitants of Neybes acted as spies for Le Maniel Maroons and received their pilfered goods. Whenever there was likelihood of an attack, they would warn the Maroons, mainly to protect their commercial interests. In Brazil, the Quilombo Grande and the Quilombo do Gabriel, which an official government report in 1876 described as being very old, for a long time carried on a lucrative maritime trade in firewood with plantation owners and others in and around Rio de Janeiro. Various people usually went to the Maroon settlements to purchase this wood, which was said to be the best that the urban dwellers could purchase. So important was this trade to the consumers that, like the inhabitants of Neybes, they would warn the Maroons of impending danger from expeditionary forces. The elimination of these *quilombos* in 1876 must have been a significant loss to the neighbouring White settlements (Conrad 1983, 385–86).

The trade conducted with the Miskito Maroons and their descendants in Bluefields and Pearl Lagoon, Nicaragua, was a much more open and elaborate affair. Its network extended far and wide, embracing through agents – especially from Providencia (Old Providence), San Andrés and Corn Island – other settlements in Jamaica and the United States, and Spanish colonies on the Central American mainland. Orlando Roberts, a trader in the 1820s, described the trade as involving different groups of Indians and Miskito men from all parts of the coast who brought tortoiseshell, gum copal, rubber, skins, paddles, canoes and various other goods to barter for duck, check cloth, cutlass blades and other articles (Gordon 1998, 38).

The transactions were usually conducted with extreme honesty, out of fear of Maroon reprisals for betrayal (Pérez de la Riva 1979, 54). However, on at least one occasion the European trading allies betrayed the Maroon cause, though in this instance they were threatened with judicial sanctions by the Guatemalan state if they did not guide the expedition to their usual meeting place (Lokken 2004b, 50–52). The trade was important in providing the increasingly wide range of products that the larger and more well-established Maroon societies required, not simply to survive but to enhance their comfort, and for ritual and aesthetic purposes. Some White people made a lot of money from the transactions. This, for instance, was the case with the Scotsman Arbuthnot, who sold Seminole Maroons and Indians gunpowder, lead, knives, paints, beads, blankets, rum and other goods, and who, according to Porter (1951, 266), realized that such trade was "a paying proposition". Apart from the financial returns, some merchants might have engaged in the trade because they were ideologically opposed to slavery or because they did not have any special connections with enslavers. In some instances they might also have been seeking to preserve their farms or other businesses from

Maroon assaults. The point is that they established a *modus operandi* and *modus vivendi* with the Maroons that served them well.

Flory (1979, 122) believes that both positive and negative interaction with Maroon economies transcended racial lines, though he emphasizes the positive or cooperative aspects of such interaction. Though he does not articulate it, he certainly implies that it was an important medium of transculturation. He (ibid., 121) even argues, though much more controversially, that "some Brazilian quilombo economies mirrored the White economies from which they sprang to such an extent that it is misleading to think of them as discrete entities rather than 'outlaw' parts of a single economy".

Part three of this study has clearly shown that, contrary to what the White enslavers chose to believe, the Maroons were capable of high levels of organization, and their settlements offered a viable alternative to the slavery system that dominated most colonial and early post-colonial states in the region. Physical security and food security occupy important places in the organization of all human societies. However, they occupied an inordinate degree of attention among the Maroons, who often lived under conditions of continuous warfare that threatened to abridge their hard-fought freedom and sometimes to divest them of life itself. Overall, the Maroons displayed innovative responses to their environment and put to good use the knowledge that they had brought with them from Africa, not simply to survive but to improve the quality of their lives.

PART 4

Accommodation or Revolution?

Whereas the violence of the oppressors prevents the oppressed from being fully human, the response of the latter to this violence is grounded in the desire to pursue the right to be human.

    – Paula Freire, *Pedagogy of the Oppressed*

CHAPTER 9

Negotiations and Treaties

COLLABORATION BETWEEN ENSLAVER AND ENSLAVED

We have noted already that *marronage* was both ideologically and practically opposed to the slavery system. It would seem, therefore, that there could be no middle ground between the two systems, and that their relations with each other would always be antagonistic. In practice, however, Maroons and slaveholders often found a middle ground that, if not entirely satisfactory to either party, tended to resolve future conflicts through negotiation, arbitration and compromise rather than by force. From the earliest days of Maroon activities, negotiations took place to eliminate or contain the Maroons. For convenience, we shall divide the negotiations into two broad categories: those that did not involve Maroons directly but sought to subvert Maroon polities, and those between Maroons and the slaveholding interests. The first category involved the enslavers' negotiations variously with enslaved persons, free Blacks, free Coloureds and the governments of foreign countries. The second category concerned negotiations with individual Maroons, specific people within a given Maroon settlement and the Maroon community as a whole.

Within the context of slavery, and often outside the discourse on *marronage,* there were always ongoing "negotiations" between the slaveholding interests and enslaved persons who displayed various tolerance levels to enslavement. They ranged from those who were prepared to accept freedom if it was offered to them but showed no particular urgency to agitate for it, to others who were disposed to pursue it actively through good works and fidelity to their overlords. The term *negotiations* must not be taken in its literal sense but interpreted as sufficiently elastic to include unwritten codes of conduct between enslaver and enslaved that would reduce the burden of slavery.[1] Thus, for instance, an enslaved person might expect his overlord to grant certain privileges – from badges to cash, and, at the furthest extreme, freedom – as a reward for meritorious service, through a mutually understood system of reciprocal service and rewards.[2] Such rewards were firmly built into the system of slavery from its earliest days.

A curious feature of the struggle for freedom and negotiated space is that sometimes it led to the abridgement of the freedom of others, among not only the oppressors but also the oppressed. The abridgement of the freedom of the oppressors is easily understood through the dialectic of class or racial conflict. Freire (1972, 32) understood this well when he wrote: "As the oppressed, fighting to be human, take away the oppressors' power to dominate and suppress, they restore to the oppressors the humanity they had lost in the exercise of oppression." In other words, the oppressors are forced to cede some of their freedom in order to restore their humanity.

When, however, as often happens in human societies, the oppressed practise oppression against each other for selfish reasons, it is an altogether different matter. One of the many unfortunate aspects of slavery in the Americas was the frequency with which enslaved persons betrayed planned revolts and Maroon activities. This was true of the aborted revolts in Berbice in 1763; Charleston, South Carolina, in 1822; and Bahia in 1835 (Thompson 1987, 173–74; Lofton 1948, 412–14; Reis 1993, 73–75). In Haiti, also, in 1758, Makandal, the feared Maroon leader, was betrayed by an enslaved female whom he had asked to kill her master (Gautier 1985, 226). Tackey's revolt in Jamaica in 1760 was put down with the assistance of the former Maroons of the Windward and Leeward groups, who also killed him (Campbell 1990, 155).

From the early eighteenth century, French policy in Haiti was to confer freedom on enslaved persons after three years of devoted service as members of the militia, captains or scouts (Fouchard 1972, 353n2). Those who were assigned the rank of captain must have enjoyed the authority and trust inherent in the position, and they must also have enjoyed material privileges comparable to those of the Black slave-drivers. Periodically, the colonial governments also recruited enslaved persons for specific kinds of commando missions, promising them freedom for devoted service. This happened to thirty Blacks whom the colonial government in the Dominican Republic recruited to ferret out Lemba, a much-feared Maroon leader in the mid-sixteenth century. They were chosen for their dexterity and abilities as trackers and are credited with slaying or apprehending most of Lemba's followers, one of them killing as many as nine of these Maroons over an eighteen-month span (Esteban Deive 1989, 52). In 1795, when Maroons in Demerara were attempting to forge alliances with the servile population, some of whom were growing restless and rising up against their overlords, the colonial state offered Blacks who would join the expeditionary force their freedom for faithful service (Thompson 1987, 145). The Black Rangers were one of the few servile groups that received their freedom (though provisionally) before undertaking service for the authoritarian state.[3]

While the slaveholding states commonly included enslaved persons as members of Maroon-hunting parties, they did not always promise them freedom. In the last quarter of the sixteenth century, the city of Lima purchased two enslaved persons, Pedro Galán and Francisco Jolofo, from their overlords, to act as rural scouts. The price was very high, since they were deemed to be among the best scouts and quite knowledgeable about the areas around Lima – particularly Galán, who had once been a Maroon leader. The town council believed that they would be valuable assets in understanding how the Maroons operated and detecting their hideouts. They were to be paid no salaries or bounties, unlike free people, who would have had to be paid both, and apparently no promise of freedom was held out to them. In the end, they turned out to be a bad investment, because they were often hospitalised as a result of the wounds that they suffered in encounters with Maroons, they used their authority to commit thefts and other crimes, and they were generally arrogant and inefficient. The city tried desperately to get rid of them, but up to 1598 Jolofo, at least, remained in the city's service as a scout (Bowser 1974, 205–6). The Black Shots of Jamaica were an outstanding example of servile cohorts who were not guaranteed freedom for faithful service. But many of them deserted, either joining established Maroon settlements or going off on their own (Campbell 1990, 69, 73, 81, 86).

Maroons hated Blacks who joined expeditions against them as much as they hated the White plantation personnel. Indeed, some writers claim that they hated them even more because they had broken faith with their brethren, had ransomed their integrity for their freedom at the expense of the Black community (see Porter 1932, 345) and sometimes joined the expeditions in order to plunder and take booty. Maroons regarded them as the scum of the earth, a view that they reciprocated. Stedman (1988, 408) wrote about the mutual vituperation and verbal blood-letting that took place one evening, each striving for a victory of words, before physical hostilities commenced on the following day:

> [A] most abusive dialogue ensued, between the Rebels, and the Rangers, both parties cursing and menacing each other at a terrible rate, the *first* reproaching the others as being poltroon, and betrayers of their countrimen, whom they challenged the next day to single combat, swearing they only wanted to wash their hands in the blood of such scoundrels who had been the capital hands in destroying their fine settlement, while the *Rangers* dam'd the Rebels for a parcel of pityful skulking rascals whom they would fight one to two in the open field, if they dared to show their ugly faces, that they had deserted theyr masters being too lazy to do theyr work, while they [the Rangers] would stand by the Europeans till they died; after which they insulted each other by a kind of war hoop [*sic*], then sung victorious songs, and sounded their horns in defiance.[4]

In this connection, it is appropriate to refer to Frantz Fanon (1967, 42) who notes that a phenomenon among oppressed peoples is that, since they find it difficult to overthrow their oppressors, they tend to vent their anger at each other in abusive language and physical assaults. This may well explain why the Rangers acted in the way that they did, and more generally why Blacks betrayed slave revolts and Maroon settlements to their White overlords.

Dealing more generally with Black-on-Black violence, Maroons hated Black slaveholders perhaps even more than they hated White ones, though some scholars believe that most Black slaveholders were not as imperious or brutal as their White counterparts. As noted already, Maroons also abducted enslaved women (and men), but this was a two-edged sword. On the one hand, such abduction had grave financial consequences for plantation owners, since women accounted for most of the agricultural workers in many plantation economies (see chapter 8). On the other hand, the husbands and other relatives of the abducted women must have been bitter and angry at the loss of their kin, which must have aroused hatred in some and led them to seek revenge. Hoogbergen (1993, 175) cites an example from Suriname where males on a plantation went after a group of Maroons who had abducted "their" women and rescued them. Some enslaved persons on the plantations suffered injury, death and loss of property during Maroon attacks. Sometimes they forcefully repulsed the attackers (Hoogbergen 1993, 174–75). Thus, plantation hands did not universally love Maroons, which must be why some of them took the field with the Whites against the fugitives. Still, the vast majority of enslaved persons must have given either passive or active support to the Maroon cause since, as indicated earlier, they developed a symbiotic relationship and enslaved persons frequently took to the woods and mountains to join Maroon groups. As for the relatively few enslaved persons who were allies of the slaveholders, though they might receive some rewards and sometimes their freedom for participating in such expeditions, the reward may not always have been their chief motive.

One of the main reasons that Black persons betrayed their colleagues was to avoid being imprisoned or executed as conspirators. This happened with a group of Maroons in Peru, in the late sixteenth century, who were threatened with execution for highway robbery unless they acted as spies and scouts for the slaveholders. As a result, the latter were able to capture a group of between thirty and forty Maroons, some of whom they executed and others they castrated (Bowser 1974, 201). It is always difficult to make a choice when one's life – and sometimes the lives of close relatives – is at stake. Some apprehended Maroons, of course, refused to yield up any information concerning their colleagues, even when they were subjected to extreme torture. These exceptionally brave men, however, probably did not represent the majority of captured Maroons who were placed under similar duress.[5] We know that the captors depended upon captives to supply them with vital information concerning the sanctuaries in which they had lived.

Not all individuals who supplied this kind of information or otherwise betrayed their colleagues were caught in a life-and-death dilemma; some – arguably the majority – did so to obtain personal freedom. One of the most notorious cases was that of Graman Quacy (Greatman Kwasi) of Suriname. He was proud that the imperial authorities had manumitted him and given him a lovely coat, a gold medal and a golden breastplate with the inscription *Quassie, faithful to the Whites* for service to the colony.[6] He served as a healer and diviner among the enslaved people and also, according to Stedman (1988, 582), on behalf of their overlords, for whom he did such an effective job that the latter were often able to exercise considerable control over their servile charges. For more than forty years he was the main intermediary between the colonial authorities and the Maroons. He served first as a scout and then a negotiator. He even lived among the Saramakas as a spy in the mid-1750s,

Figure 28. Graman Quacy. From *Narrative of a Five Years' Expedition against the Revolted Negroes of Surinam*, by John Gabriel Stedman (London, 1796).

then deserted back to the colonial authorities and led a large expedition against them, which resulted in the loss of an ear to the Saramaka chief's blade (Price 1983a, 153–59). He continued his activities for several years as a bounty hunter against the Maroons, for which the colonial authorities rewarded him with a beautiful house in the capital (Price and Price 1988, 666n581).

In his last days, he provided amulets to the Black troops fighting for the Whites, so that they considered themselves invulnerable and feared no danger, "fighting like bull dogs". It is not known what made Quacy an Uncle Tom from his early years, but the more the colonial authorities honoured him, the more dedication he showed to their cause. It was perhaps due to Maroon respect for his negotiating skills and his widely feared power as a *lukuman* (diviner) that they did not kill him.

Not all Blacks who sided with the White cause ended up honoured by the authoritarian state, as the case of Luís Xavier de Jesus illustrates. Brought to Brazil as an enslaved person from Africa, during the next thirty years he not only gained his freedom but worked his way up the social ladder (as far as Blacks were allowed) by acquiring assets worth more than sixty thousand milréis. In 1811 he was placed in charge of Maroon-hunting operations and honoured by the state with the title of captain (*capitão de entradas e assaltos*) for his outstanding service as a Maroon catcher. However, he was accused of treason in the aborted servile uprising in Bahia in 1835 and deported to Africa. Although friends, lawyers and family tried over the next few years to prove his innocence and redeem him from exile, it was all in vain. It remains unclear why the authoritarian state should have believed that he was a participant in the revolt. He himself believed that his downfall was due to his wealth and position of authority within Bahian society (Reis 1993, 221–22).

The most reprehensible cases were when individuals compromised their fellows' bid for freedom simply to gain favours within the system, short of actual freedom. Such favours usually included monetary rewards and a medal declaring their fidelity. This was, in fact, the most common response of the White community to such people, for only in extreme cases were they prepared to grant freedom for information that led to the putting down of servile unrest. After all, every manumission of a Black person meant a loss of value to the White enslavers – and (from their standpoint) a potential threat to the social order, through less than complete control of the Blacks. Other members of the slave community often ostracized those who betrayed revolts or joined Maroon-hunting expeditions (see Thompson 2002b, 234). In some instances enslaved persons preferred to remain in bondage, not only because they were old or infirm but also because they had become dependent on their owners, and their lot was less rigorous than that of their free counterparts (Jacobs 1999, 575).

Esteban Deive (1989, 52) argues that the decision of enslaved persons to serve as auxiliaries against the Maroons revealed their alienation and subordination, and the lack of group consciousness among them in confronting their servile condition. It is certain that, especially in the early slavery period in the Americas, the Whites were far more united in their efforts to deal with the social realities emanating from slavery and *marronage* than were the Blacks, though that unity would be increasingly fractured as more liberal and revolutionary ideas began to permeate European minds from the late eighteenth century.

RELATIONS BETWEEN SLAVEHOLDING STATES

As noted before, flight to other colonial jurisdictions was an important facet of the runaways' quest for freedom. In the early years of colonization, fugitives from Barbados and other southern plantation colonies fled to the largely uncolonized islands of St Vincent, Grenada, Dominica, St Lucia and Tobago. There they joined the indigenous peoples, sometimes being enslaved by them and at other times interbreeding with them, notably in St Vincent where they became known as Black Caribs. But as the French and British increasingly colonized these islands, especially from the mid-eighteenth century, they became a less popular destination. For a long time Puerto Rico offered sanctuary for Maroons from the British and Danish Caribbean; the Dominican Republic for those from Haiti and later those from Puerto Rico; Trinidad for those from Barbados and occasionally the Dutch Guiana colonies; Yucatán, Guatemala and Honduras for those from Belize;[7] Haiti, after achieving independence, for those from Puerto Rico, Jamaica, Cuba and elsewhere; Paraguay and French Guiana (the latter after emancipation) for those from Brazil; Cuba for those from Jamaica; Argentina and Brazil for those from Paraguay; Venezuela (sometimes called Orinoco at the time) for those from Grenada and the Dutch Guiana colonies; Florida for those from South Carolina, Georgia and Alabama; and, later, Mexico for those from Texas after that territory fell under US sovereignty. After the northern United States abolished slavery, many enslaved persons sought freedom in New York and other northern states, sometimes continuing into Canada. Throughout the Americas, states in which slavery was abolished from the early nineteenth century became increasingly attractive for runaways from states in which the institution remained intact. Slaveholding states that shared borders with foreign neighbours were particularly vulnerable, since fugitives moved to and fro across the borders, as was the case between Florida and Mexico, Haiti and the Dominican Republic, Essequibo and Venezuela, and French Guiana and Brazil.

There was always a lot of discussion among the governments of slaveholding states about how to contain the Maroons, and requests for the extradition of runaways from one jurisdiction to the other. Occasionally they signed treaties agreeing to reciprocal extradition of deserters. In 1732 and 1753, for example, the French and Portuguese governments signed treaties in respect of French Guiana and Brazil, while in 1713 the colonial authorities in Suriname and French Guiana did the same thing (Marchand-Thébault 1986, 41). The arrangements did not always work smoothly and were often sternly tested.

For a considerable part of the eighteenth century, relations between French Guiana and Brazil were soured by territorial claims along the contiguous border and allegations about harbouring fugitives that crossed over into each other's sphere, contrary to the treaties that their imperial governments had signed requiring the reciprocal return of such persons. The French were the main transgressors in this respect, because it was common for fugitives to ensconce themselves in the forested areas of Amazonia, Brazil, and periodically cross over into French Guiana to carry on trade or escape Maroon-hunting expeditions sent against them. The Brazilians further complained that the French raided the Brazilian areas and carried away their enslaved workers, and that they violated the treaty by imposing harsh punishments – even including the death penalty – on fugitives that the Brazilians returned to them.[8] The Grão-Pará captaincy, on the border between the two states, witnessed the phenomenon of *mocambos* being set up there but their inhabitants travelling frequently across the rivers into French Guiana to cultivate plots. They even made bricks for the French to build a fortress in Cayenne (Santos Gomes 2002, 478–86).

In the case of Suriname, from the 1770s the Aluku (Boni) Maroons, pressed by the Dutch military forces, began to cross over into French Guiana. The French were in somewhat of a dilemma as to how to handle the situation. The Maroons, considered dangerous, were too numerous and militant for the small colonial force to engage them successfully in running battles. Some people argued, though not convincingly, that they might add to the size of the labouring population at the disposal of the French. The colonial government took a pragmatic approach to the problem, recognizing the immigrants as free people and providing them with land on which to settle – all this against the terms of the treaty signed with the Dutch. The Maroons settled down to a largely peaceful life, apparently receiving few, if any, French fugitives and justifying the authorities' decision to grant them asylum. In 1860 a convention between France and the Netherlands recognized them as being under French protection (Marchand-Thébault 1986, 42–43).

It was not only fugitives from Brazil and Suriname that the French accorded shelter, but also those from Barbados and other southern Caribbean islands who ran to Martinique, Guadeloupe and other French islands. According to Governor Christopher Codrington of Barbados, they were lured by the greater number of holy (rest) days that the French allowed their enslaved charges, and the possibility that they would be recruited into the colonial military service (Beckles 1986, 88).

The French, however, intensely disliked the policy of non-repatriation when fugitives fled their colonies for foreign jurisdictions. The situation of the Haitian Maroons who fled to the Dominican Republic strikingly illus-trates this point. In the late seventeenth century Francisco Segura y Sandoval, governor of the Dominican Republic, declared free some seventy refugees from Haiti and allowed them to found the settlement of San Lorenzo de los Negros de Mina (San Lorenzo de los Negros Minas) (Larrazábal Blanco 1998, 152, 161; Landers 2000b, 4). In 1688 Jean-Paul Tarín de Cussy, governor of Haiti, complained to Andrés de Robles y Gomez, his neighbouring Spanish counterpart, against the latter's decision to recognize certain run-aways as free persons and make them land grants in return for service in the colonial forces. In 1689 a French fleet appeared before the city of Santo Domingo, demanding the return of these and other refugees who had fled from Haiti. The governor refused to return them and instead enlisted them into the free Coloured regiment. It will be recalled that it was not until 1697 that Spain signed a treaty officially recognizing France's right to Haiti, the western part of Hispaniola, into which the French had infiltrated some years earlier. In the wake of that treaty, the two imperial powers reached an agree-ment about the reciprocal return of refugees on payment of certain fees, but the Spanish honoured the agreement more in the breach than in the obser-vance during the next century. Much depended upon the disposition of the particular Spanish governor at any given time. As for San Lorenzo de los Negros de Mina, it remained in existence for a long time, in spite of allegations by several officials and other slaveholders that it was a nest of robbers and lowlifes, and suggestions that the government should destroy it. In 1740 its population was estimated at two hundred people (Larrazábal Blanco 1998, 152–64).[9]

Fouchard (1972, 427–28), whose work generally displays analytic depth, deals rather superficially with why the Haitian Maroons preferred to flee into the Spanish zone. He notes rightly that the contours and expanse of sparsely inhabited territory and the difficulties of the mountain terrain were pull factors, and also that the underdeveloped plantation regime offered comparatively easy work for many enslaved persons who were occupied in cattle ranching, certainly a less strenuous pursuit than plantation work. However, his suggestion, even if tongue-in-cheek, that enslaved persons usually ate the same food as their overlords is frivolous. His comments about cattle herding allowing for long siestas, the indolent life to which the Spaniards were accustomed, and the fluid social and class relations between enslaved and free persons are more imaginary than real. He caps his analysis by saying, "In brief, the Spanish part of Saint-Domingue [Hispaniola] represented in the eyes of the slave the closest image of the liberty to which he aspired." This is not to deny that a system of enslavement based on cattle herding had a much more relaxed atmosphere than one based on sugar and offered somewhat greater opportunities for Black social mobility. However, Spanish policy in the Dominican Republic and elsewhere was hypocritical in the context of the official brutalities meted out to runaways from Spanish overlords, and the *cédulas* explicitly excluding them from royal benefaction, regardless of their religious profession (Veracoechea 1987, 222).

Derby (2003, 12–20) implies that part of the problem related to "competing regimes of value" between the poor Spaniards in the Dominican Republic and the rich Frenchmen just across the (ill-defined) border between the two countries: the one lived largely through the growing of tobacco and cacao and the rearing of cattle; the other through the cultivation of sugar. The Spanish expressed their envy by encouraging desertion from the French zone, sometimes going so far as instigating desertion, and even abducting enslaved persons to sell in the Dominican Republic. Debbasch (1979, 144) goes a step further by asserting that Spanish francophobia in the Dominican Republic was the main reason for their strong support for Le Maniel Maroons – that they would have done anything to harm the French colonists. As noted above, the situation between the two colonies was exacerbated by boundary disputes, especially in the south, and prevented any serious effort to colonize that area (Debbasch 1979, 145).

The conflict between Haiti and the Dominican Republic was one of several episodes in Spanish relations with other colonial powers, and involved some of the most intractable problems in hemispheric and imperial relations. The Spanish havens usually offered all fugitives from neighbouring (especially Protestant) countries protection and freedom if they declared that they had sought asylum in order to be baptized into the Catholic faith. The Spanish government made this clear in dispatches to Venezuelan officials in 1680 and 1757, and to Florida officials in 1693 and 1733 (Veracoechea 1987, 222; García 1989, 20; Landers 1998, 362, 365). Rarely did the officials return runaways to their owners in foreign jurisdictions. In 1778, a resident of Petén, Guatemala, wrote the captain-general of the country, explaining that he had taken into his care four runaways from Belize and Jamaica who had sought refuge and baptism. The official advised him that the governor of the province could grant the refugees their freedom because of their quest to be baptized, in accordance with a royal *cédula* of 1739 (Jones 1994, 112).

The situation regarding the Dutch territories of Essequibo and Demerara in the late eighteenth century illustrates the kinds of problems that other territories faced with respect to desertion to the Spanish colonies. In 1772 Laurens Storm van's Gravesande, governor general of Essequibo and Demerara, informed the directors of the Dutch West India Company that the problem of runaways to Venezuela had become urgent and required official mediation to arrest it; without it, the plantations would be ruined. In 1775 the militia officers of Essequibo sent a letter to their colonial government, declaring that unless immediate action was taken, the constant desertion of their servile charges would lead to the total ruin of the colony. In 1784 their counterparts in Demerara voiced a similar concern, adding that not a week passed without significant numbers of their workers deserting to the Spanish colony. For several years the colonial authorities in Demerara and Essequibo and the imperial authorities in the Netherlands pressed the Spanish in vain to sign a mutual extradition treaty.

The officials in Venezuela and elsewhere maintained that it was a long-standing policy of their imperial government not to return runaways who sought asylum among them because they desired to become Catholics, unless it could be verified under oath that the fugitive had committed murder. The dispossessed planters, perhaps rightly, viewed Spanish action as emanating more from secular opportunism than religious conviction. The Dutch alleged that the refugees were baptized by Catholic priests but kept in slavery. The Spanish territories in question were less densely populated than those of their neighbours, and so their policy was a good way of attracting new labour hands. Certainly, Coro, Cumaná, Guayana, Caracas, Curiepe and other areas in Venezuela benefited substantially from the Spanish policy of welcoming such runaways (García 1989, 20). It is also said that because the plantation system was not as fully developed in these Spanish territories as in the British and French ones, Spanish slavery was comparatively less brutal, but this remains a moot point. A third factor was that relatively few fugitives from Spanish territories took refuge within the other European jurisdictions (Thompson 1987, 139–40; Debbasch 1979, 144; Fouchard 1972, 427n1). While aggrieved planters sometimes unilaterally exercised the right of pursuit, it led only rarely to the apprehension of the runaways and tended to exacerbate tensions between the countries. For a long time delegations and other approaches to the Spanish colonial government or the imperial government in Madrid commonly ran aground on diplomatic reefs.

In the case of Jamaica the situation was different, insofar as that colony did not share a frontier with Cuba, but the Spanish still smarted over the loss of Jamaica to the British in 1655 and clearly considered welcoming deserters to Cuba as a way of undermining British control of the island. In fact, the Jamaican colonists were convinced that the Spanish were plotting with the Maroons to recapture the island. Periodic rumour even suggested an imminent Spanish invasion. For instance, in 1730 the British Board of Trade and the Jamaican government became alarmed by rumours of Spanish-Maroon collusion, especially after a captured Maroon declared that one of his captains had visited Cuba and promised to assist the Spaniards if they should invade the island (Campbell 1990, 144). Though no such invasion ever materialized, the Jamaican colonists continued to dream from time to time of insurrections and Spanish-Maroon assaults.

From the mid-eighteenth century the Spanish relented, perhaps because of their own growing problems with Maroons or perhaps due to wider diplomatic concerns in Europe itself. Whatever the reason or reasons, they began to make treaties with their neighbours that entailed the reciprocal return of runaways. Such a treaty was signed, for example, with the British in respect of runaways to Puerto Rico in 1767, with the French in regard to refugees from Haiti into the Dominican Republic in 1776, and with the Dutch in relation to fugitives from Essequibo and Demerara into Venezuela in 1791.[10] The almost immediate result of the Franco-Spanish treaty was the movement of French farmers into the border areas, an act that completely upset the equilibrium of life among Le Maniel and other border Maroons and led to conflict between the two sides. Le Maniel Maroons began attacking the farms and carrying away implements and enslaved persons. The more timid settlers withdrew, but others remained in an area that became a hotbed of strife. According to Debbasch (1979, 146), those who stayed on carried out their tasks with firearms in hand. The settlers, however, realized that they could never develop flourishing plantations in the teeth of such resistance, and so they pushed for a treaty with the Maroons.

Generally, the treaties with the Spanish led to a temporary drop in *marronage* to the jurisdictions listed above, but this kind of desertion gained new life with the abolition of slavery first in Haiti, then in the British colonies, and so on. There was desertion, for instance, from Jamaica to Haiti, the Danish West Indies to the British Virgin Islands, Dutch St Maarten to French St Martin (the two colonies sharing the same small island), and Suriname to Guyana. In 1825, in a move that presaged a more forward-thinking policy on the issue of slavery, the British imperial government ordered its governors to end the policy of returning fugitives from foreign jurisdictions to their overlords (Ragatz 1977, 437).

NEGOTIATIONS WITH MAROONS

Negotiations between the enslavers and the Maroons were carried out at the individual, sectional (that is, involving particular members within a settlement) and community (involving all the members of a given polity) levels. At the individual and sectional levels, the main intention was to produce internal dissension within the Maroon polities, thus causing them to implode. The methods by which the slaveholding fraternity tried to do so included offering amnesty (sometimes with, and at other times without, freedom) to any fugitives who turned themselves in to the military or police authorities within a specified time; offering Creoles freedom provided they turned in their African-born brethren; offering freedom to people who had been in the settlement for a number of years but requiring them to hand over those who had joined it recently – that is, within a year or two; promising the leader and some of his close family and associates their freedom provided they handed over the other members of the community; guaranteeing individual Maroons their freedom if they brought in at least one other Maroon, and bounties if they brought in more than one; and agreeing to grant freedom to those who acted as scouts or spies or who would otherwise betray Maroon hideouts.

Usually, the initiative for such accommodation came from the slaveholders rather than the Maroons, which might indicate that the slaveholders felt a greater urgency to reach an amicable settlement. It was far more common for individuals or very small groups than for large ones to turn themselves in to their overlords or government officials. Such events perhaps should be discussed as part of *petit marronage* or perhaps day-to-day resistance.[11] At the level of the authoritarian state, it usually involved publication in the daily newspapers, and sometimes legislative enactments, offering amnesty to any deserters who returned within a stipulated period.[12] However, at times this offer was limited to those who were deemed not to have committed murder or another major criminal offence. Individuals wishing to turn themselves in might seek the services of an influential member of the White community, such as a rich planter, a member of a religious brotherhood or a priest, to mediate the conditions of their return. Except in the case of major offences, to rebuff the overtures of such a mediator, known in Brazil as a *padrinho* (godfather), was considered a great insult to him (Karasch 1987, 315).

Some petty civil officials took it upon themselves to negotiate with the runaways. In the 1570s rural constables in Peru often arrogated to themselves the power of mediating the return of runaways to their former overlords, without referring the matter to the judicial authorities. While this perhaps started as a quick, cheap and efficient way of resolving the problem of runaways who wished to return, it became a source of abuse by the constables, since their mediation came with a price to the overlord, depending upon what his purse could bear. Indeed, rumour was that the constables secretly detained the captured fugitives who sought to negotiate a return to their former overlords, until they received a solid negotiated price. In spite of official attempts to stamp out this practice, it was not easily suppressed (Bowser 1974, 206). There were also instances in which Peruvian constables and Brazilian bush captains allowed captured Maroons to go free in return for sometimes quite handsome fees (Bowser 1974, 215–16; Mattoso 1979, 142). It was all part of a system of colonial administration that was notorious for its graft and corruption, and these petty officials had no scruples about following the path of the more senior officials. In some instances Maroon-catchers encouraged individuals to escape and then apprehended them in order to receive bounties. More unscrupulous ones actually kidnapped enslaved persons and sold them to other overlords. It is said that some runaways willingly gave themselves up to Maroon-catchers to be sold to slave buyers instead of returning to their former overlords (Karasch 1987, 310, 315),[13] but this must have been quite rare.

Some writers gave curious reasons for Maroons' voluntarily returning to their former overlords. Dr George Pinckard (1806, 2:241), a British surgeon on duty in the region, opined that many of them had deserted to live in idleness but soon found that the work they had to do to maintain themselves in the woods was so much harder than on the plantations that some of them decided to return to slavery. He had affirmed earlier that the enslaved African did not understand the relationship between freedom and industry, and thus it would be wrong to expose him prematurely to the "vicissitudes of freedom", since he would be unable to make proper use of it (ibid., 2:206–7). This would be a form of cruelty, since it would force him to relinquish great comparative happiness for much misery and distress. The historian José Saco declared that many of them returned ill from the vagrant life that they had led as Maroons (Dusenberry 1948, 287). Another historian, Herrera y Tordesillas, asserted that some runaways became tired of living outside of subjection and so returned to their overlords (Palmer 1976, 122).

It is unclear whether Herrera y Tordesillas was referring to specific cases of amnesty in which the runaways returned to the fold of their overlords without punishment. However, the clear implication of his statement that they preferred enslavement to freedom, as erroneous as it sounds, has a large scholarly contemporary literature (see Thompson 1995, 93–119). Much of this kind of thinking was simply the Aristotelian doctrine of natural slaves, resurrected for the Africans as it had been for the Indians some years earlier.[14]

Offers of amnesty netted very few people because the Maroons preferred freedom to bondage. The offers were evidence of the authoritarian state's inability to apprehend Maroons, and even of desperation to reach an accommodation with them (see Thompson 2002b, 132–33; Arrom and García Arévalo 1986, 40n7). An outstanding example of the runaways' attitude to such offers was the case of those who had deserted their Spanish overlords in Jamaica during the British invasion and conquest of that colony in 1655. The British had encouraged the enslaved persons to revolt against their overlords and join with the invaders, but few did so, preferring to establish autonomous Maroon communities (Taylor 1965, 101–2; Campbell 1990, 17, see also 23, 24).

In the late seventeenth century Governor Martín de Cevallos Lacerda offered amnesty to the Cartagena Maroons which included the choice to return to their previous overlords without punishment, to be sold to other persons if they did not desire to return to their overlords, or to purchase their freedom if they had the financial means to do so (Borrego Plá 1973, 106). Even this offer was largely unsuccessful, and the governor declared war to the death against them. In retaliation, the Maroons determined to assassinate him, but some of their captured brethren revealed the plot, apparently under torture (ibid., 79–86).

Thomas Atwood (1971, 228–32) mentioned a curious arrangement between the Maroons in the island of Dominica and the French. According to him, when the French recaptured the island in 1778, during the American Revolutionary War, the new governor, Marquis Duchilleau, engaged the Maroons to assist in defending it. He supplied them with firearms, bayonets and other military equipment, and gave them the same provisions that the French soldiers received. To arm them, he seized the British settlers' weapons, and, as part of his arrangement with the Maroons, he allowed them to attack the British plantations. He refused to return the arms on request by the planters or to offer them any assistance against the attacks, which had escalated and become more flagrant, and he even threatened to bring down the full weight of the law on anyone who should harm his Black allies. As a result, many planters abandoned their plantations and sought refuge in the capital, Roseau. It was only after the British appealed to his superior, Marquis de Bouillé, in Martinique, who ordered him to re-arm them, that they were able to check the Maroon activities.

Michael Craton (1982, 143–44) reiterates the story that Duchilleau armed the Maroons but does actually mention the matter of the governor's incitement of them to attack the planters. Lennox Honychurch (1975, 70–71) also skirts the issue of the governor's open support of the Maroons. Basil Cracknell (1973, 66–67) writes that the French authorities disarmed the British and made little attempt to prevent the Maroons from destroying their plantations. Patrick Baker (1994, 74) accepts the conventional view that even before the French reconquest of the island, the enslaved persons and Maroons hated the British Whites much more than the French Whites, and that the latter often helped the Maroons to attack the British plantations.

But rather than critiquing the view that Duchilleau encouraged or incited the Maroons to attack the planters, Baker simply refers to Boromé's (1969, 55) caution that Atwood's interpretation cannot be taken at face value, though he also notes that Boromé (1972, 112) seems to be ambivalent on the matter.

It is clear that Duchilleau used the Maroons as his allies and the best recourse, in the circumstances, to fight the British. There was no love lost between the two European powers, which had fought many bitter battles over the Caribbean islands, and no doubt the governor and other French people still smarted at the loss of Dominica to the British in 1759 (ratified by the Treaty of Paris in 1763). However, caution is advised in accepting that Duchilleau openly encouraged the destruction of the British plantations. Certainly he may secretly have wished for that to happen, and he must have realized that disarming the planters would make them much more vulnerable to Maroon assaults. Atwood, of course, is not an impeccable source, for he was once British chief judge on the island, a strong upholder of the slavery regime and intensely hostile to the Maroons, as his book indicates. A more careful and detailed critique of the events of this period is necessary before we can make definitive statements about what actually happened.

It was not the last time that the French would make a play for Maroon allies in Dominica. In 1794, shortly after the French had proclaimed the abolition of slavery in their colonies, a French official sought to make an alliance with Pharcell, the main Maroon leader in the island, promising him support in the form of weaponry. However, John Orde, the British governor, neutralized the French influence by striking a treaty with the Maroon leader, by which he agreed to the colonial state's recognition of his freedom and that of the members of his household and twelve of his followers. In return, Pharcell and his men were to scout the terrain for runaways in return for a bounty and to assist the British more generally to preserve the internal peace and tranquillity of the colony, especially in relation to foreign invasion (Craton 1982, 226–27). However, other Maroon groups that remained outside this arrangement continued to create serious problems for the colonial authorities. They rejected Governor George Robert Ainslie's offers of amnesty and attempts at a peaceful settlement through treaties. The governor therefore adopted brutal and at times highly questionable measures to wipe them out, for which his superiors in London later called him to account. In 1813 Quashie, one of the main Maroon leaders, placed a bounty on his head (Honychurch 1975, 74, 90–91; Craton 1982, 145).

In 1790 in Santiago de Cuba, where roving bands were causing dismay among the colonists at a time of heightened tensions between Spain and Britain, the regional government decided to strengthen its fortifications and needed cheap labour to do so. It therefore offered all runaways who would turn themselves in an unconditional pardon, and promised that they would not be returned to their overlords. In return, they were to work on rehabilitating the fortifications. It remains unclear whether the government's offer included freedom for the runaways or meant that they would now be enslaved by the state. In any event, very few took up this offer (La Rosa Corzo 2003, 76). In the same country, Governor Eusebio Escuerdo once put forward a plan to grant Maroons amnesty and recognize their freedom (not through formal treaties, as in other jurisdictions) if they should agree to become a bounty-hunting band to catch their fellow Maroons. The experiment was tried with the Maluala Maroons but was not very successful (La Rosa Corzo 2003, 114), apparently since few of them liked the idea.

By contrast, in 1676 over one hundred Palmarinos returned to their overlords, presumably under negotiated terms, after an expeditionary force sacked several of their chief towns (Conrad 1983, 371; Carneiro 1946, 90). In 1734 in Venezuela, through the persuasion of two Capuchin clergymen, 180 Maroons gave themselves up on the understanding that a plea for amnesty would be forwarded to the Crown on their behalf. In that same country in 1774, following the death of Guillermo Rivas, several of his followers returned to their overlords (Brito Figueroa 1985, 210–11, 218). In 1816, after an attack on El Frijol settlement in Cuba, in which the expeditionary forces destroyed the houses and crops and made settled life almost impossible, eighty-nine Maroons eventually turned themselves over to the colonial authorities, but we are not told whether this was on condition of any form of amnesty (La Rosa Corzo 2003, 112). A similar event occurred in Dominica in 1785–86 involving the remnants of the devastated settlement led by Balla (Atwood 1971, 249). In 1834 in Suriname, fifty-three people fled from plantation Victoria because their overlord was about to sell them to another person. They returned to the plantation when they received news that the sale was cancelled and that they would not be punished (Hoogbergen 1993, 186). In 1820 an offer of amnesty in Belize to some recent runaways was also apparently successful (Bolland 2002, 55–56; Bolland 2003, 71).[15]

Some runaways actually preferred to live on the plantations than in the environmentally more challenging Maroon settlements, especially if they could negotiate less stringent conditions of servitude. An outstanding example of this is the case of the enslaved people of El Cobre in Cuba, who belonged to the king of Spain. In 1677, some 378 people fled temporarily to the mountains because of state attempts to transfer the most robust of them from the copper mines to work on the fortifications in Havana.[16] From there they negotiated with the authorities, who agreed not to remove any of them without their permission. In time they won other concessions, including the right to work for the king no more than two months yearly, reserving the rest of the time for themselves; to acquire freehold possession of land allocated to them by the state; to be recognized as a *pueblo* or community with its own *cabildo* or local government; to sit on the *cabildo*; and to have access to the law courts much more freely than was normally allowed to enslaved persons (Díaz 2000).

In 1763 a report on the Deshaies plantation in Guadeloupe indicated that nearly all its servile inhabitants had fled and that the land lay virtually uncultivated, producing only a few new plants that would not yield food for another year (Debien 1979, 131). Fortunately for this plantation, the change of management led to the return of most of the deserters within a short time, though their inability to cope with the rigours of forest life had as much to do with their return as the new managerial situation. They were reported to be in an extreme state of ill health and exhaustion on their return (Debien 1979, 131).

There is also the case of a group of deserters from a plantation near Ilheus in Bahia in the late eighteenth century. They managed to persuade their overlord to agree to a large number of conditions, including shorter working hours and safer working conditions; more food and clothing; Friday and Saturday for themselves (in addition to Sunday, the legal rest day); the right to plant rice fields in any marshlands that they deemed suitable for the purpose; provision of nets and canoes to carry out their fishing activities; facilities to ship their produce to Bahia free of freightage costs; and the sacking of the incumbent overseers and appointment of future ones only with their approval. These were radical – even revolutionary – demands in the context of slavery, reading more like demands put forward in the mid-twentieth century by the growing Third World trade unions. However, the overlord decided to agree to them because the flight of his workers had caused his plantation to remain inactive for two years with much resultant damage. Most of the workers returned to the plantation, but the overlord had apparently learned little. He reneged on his promise, sold many of them and had others cast into prison, including Gregorio Luís, their leader, who languished there for many years. As a result, the plantation never regained its former vibrancy (Conrad 1983, 397–400; Schwartz 1977, 69–81).[17]

Not only did few Maroon leaders accept amnesty, especially where freedom was not part of the terms, but also, as noted in chapter 6, they often taunted the authoritarian state to come and get them. Sometimes they did so even after suffering severe losses at the hands of their enemies. Others laughed to scorn such offers of amnesty, while still others used abusive and threatening language.[18] On one occasion, when Colonel Fourgeoud, the mercenary leader in Suriname, offered the Alukus amnesty if they surrendered, they

> replied with a loud laugh, that they wanted nothing from him who seemed a half starved Frenchman, already run away from his own country, that if he would venture to give them a visit in person, he should not be hurted, and might depend on not returning with an empty belly. They called to us [the mercenaries] that we were more to be pitied than themselves, who were only a parcel of White slaves, hired to be shot at, & starved for 4 pence a day, and that they scorned to expand [expend] much of theyr powder upon such scarcrows [*sic*] who had not been the aggressors by driving them in[to] the forest & only obeying the command of their masters; but if the planters and overseers dared to enter the woods themselves not a soul of such scoundrels should ever return. (Stedman 1988, 408–9)

In 1732 the Leeward Maroons invited the White members of an expeditionary force sent against them to come and dine with them, adding that they would barbecue the Whites (Mullin 1992, 49–50). In 1735 they showed contempt for a British delegation under Belvill Grenville, a military officer, who was dispatched to discuss peace terms with them. The emissary related that one of the Maroon leaders appeared to pity him and advised him not to return, lest he should be slain (Campbell 1990, 102–3). Sometimes the taunting was more subtle. For example, Maroons who had settled in Puerto Rico sometimes sent greetings to their former overlords in the Danish West Indies, telling them what a good time they were having in their new homeland (Donoghue 2002, 156).

On several occasions both ordinary Maroons and their leaders betrayed their comrades. Let us examine the cases of ordinary Maroons, reserving discussion of the leaders for the section dealing with the treaties that they signed (page 289). The authoritarian state usually offered generous terms to people who betrayed Maroon communities (or slave revolts). In 1574 the Mexican government passed a law that any runaway who handed over one of his comrades would obtain his freedom, and would be paid twenty pesos for each additional person whom he delivered. However, the law specified that any free Mulatto or free Black who protected a runaway and then turned him in to receive the reward would suffer the death penalty (Pereira 1994, 97; Palmer 1976, 125; León 1924, 10).[19] In 1665 the Jamaican government promised that any enslaved person who killed or captured any of the Karmahaly Maroons would be freed, and also offered both pardon and freedom to any Maroon who would bring in a fellow Maroon, dead or alive (Campbell 1990, 27).

The colonial authorities often subjected captured Maroons to extensive "debriefing", using torture to elicit information that would allow for more easy and complete subversion of the polities. There is sufficient evidence to suggest that torture with this end in view was widespread.[20] In this connection, Porter (1943, 396) writes, "One may be pardoned for wondering what methods of persuasion may have laid [*sic*] behind some of the communications so freely – nay, so eagerly – offered by Negro slaves and prisoners under examination by overseers and army officers."

In 1693 an expeditionary force tortured people found in the Matudere *palenque* in Cartagena to obtain information from them concerning the organization and demographic profile of the settlement (Borrego Plá 1973, 79–80). In 1749 the authorities in Caracas employed torture to elicit valuable information about an intended servile revolt (Brito Figueroa 1985, 212–13). Brito Figueroa (ibid., 217) also accuses the slaveholding authorities of subjecting four very small children to torture on one occasion in 1774, in order to obtain information about Guillermo Rivas's forces. In 1855 state officials in the Amazon Valley, who had found it impossible to locate some of the *mocambos* in that district, were finally able to find and destroy the Mucajuba *mocambo*, one of the largest, after coercing a captured Maroon to show them the best way through the lake on whose bank the settlement was located (Conrad 1983, 390). In 1795 Demerara government officials tortured several of the prisoners apprehended in a recent expedition, to get them to reveal details about a settlement that the expedition had failed to discover. In spite of it, the captives went to their deaths without supplying the information (Pinckard 1806, 2:248–51).

We therefore have to be suspicious of many of the instances in which prisoners were alleged to have supplied information voluntarily about Maroon communities. When Maroon women captured in Dominica in 1786, or Moses, a North Carolina Maroon captured in 1830, divulged strategic secrets of the communities to which they had belonged (Honychurch 1975, 74; Aptheker 1979, 160), did they do so under torture or voluntarily? Of course, at times Maroons fled their haunts for personal reasons, including conflicts with other Maroons, and became informants against their brethren. It was unwritten but standard policy in all jurisdictions that a Maroon who claimed that he held information that would serve the interests of the authoritarian state should be treated with the greatest civility and brought to the colonial authorities post-haste.

In 1737, after two years of deadly assault by Maroons under the leadership of José Pérez and José Tadeo, the colonial authorities in Córdoba, Mexico, finally managed to convince a Maroon called Fermín to betray the *palenque*. This resulted in the capture of the leaders and several of their followers. The leaders were subsequently executed, while those who remained at large sought refuge in neighbouring *palenques* (Naveda Chávez-Hita 1987, 133–35). In 1786, Petite Jacques, a confidant of the Maroon leader Cicero of Dominica, betrayed his friend, who was later executed (Honychurch 1975, 74).

In 1739 the defence network of the Leeward and Windward Maroons of Jamaica was compromised by former members of their communities, who led White military expeditions to their hideouts and showed them how to breach the defence systems. Among the defectors from the Leeward Maroons were Venus and Assiba, whose reasons for defecting are unknown; and Cuffee, Sambo and Zuashey, who declared that the Maroons had abducted them and that they had later made good their escape. Venus provided crucial information about the daily activities in which the Maroons would be engaged at that time of the year, while all five of them led expeditions to the Maroon towns. However, as usual, the expeditions captured very few Maroons. The belligerent parties finally agreed to peace terms, and the colonial authorities compensated Maroon defectors and other guides with freedom for giving meritorious service that led to the signing of the treaties (Campbell 1990, 107–15, 121–24).[21]

In 1815 the San Andrés and La Cueva *palenques* in Cuba (the latter unknown to colonial officials up to that time) were assailed as a result of information given to the authorities by Batista Bayona and his wife, former members of the San Andrés *palenque,* who absconded from the settlement, turned traitors and acted as guides to future expeditions (La Rosa Corzo 2003, 99–101).[22] The treachery of two of Pedro León's men eventually led to his death in 1841, after ten years of deadly assaults on the inhabitants of Lima and the surrounding areas. One of these traitors, José Rayo, made commander of the rural police by the authoritarian state, offered a reward of one thousand pesos and a pardon for any Maroon who would kill the "implacable enemy of public peace and security". Responding to this offer, Felipe Galdeano, one of the men in León's *palenque,* assassinated him as he lay relaxing in his home (cited in Aguirre 1993, 261).

A classic case of defection and betrayal with deadly consequences for the particular Maroon community – a major one in the Bahoruco region – occurred in the Dominican Republic in 1666. A Maroon had fled this *palenque* because he had lost a scuffle over a woman with Pablo, the leader of his settlement. The fugitive was eventually taken to Government House. The governor treated him as a guest of honour, and he responded by divulging information critical to the security of his settlement. This led to two major expeditions, quite close together, against the Maroons (the first headed by the governor), at the end of which they agreed to accept peace terms that required them to quit the Bahoruco region in return for recognition of their freedom (Esteban Deive 1989, 86–89).

An unusual event transpired among the Pajarito Maroons in Panama in 1768. A female whom they had abducted some time earlier managed to escape, and guided a military expedition sent against the *palenque.* Most of the occupants managed to escape initially, but not the leader. His captors prevailed on him to take them to the escapees' hideout, and as a result most of the Maroons were either captured or killed. The captives were later sentenced to death, and, since there was no official executioner, the authorities struck a deal with the Maroon leader by which he agreed to perform the function of that sad office in return for his freedom (La Guardia 1977, 104–5).

Interestingly, Campbell (1990, 60, 269n63) states, on the basis of Edward Long's unpublished manuscripts, that some planters in Jamaica made secret deals with the Maroons, paying them a sort of retainer to ensure that they did not attack their plantations and that they would protect the planter's property and person from assault by other Maroons. Long, himself a contemporary planter on that island, was in a good position to know what was going on, and so we must give serious consideration to his views. It is also said that some colonists in the neighbourhood of Palmares paid tribute to the Maroons in the form of tools, powder, lead, arms and other articles that they requested, in exchange for being allowed to cultivate their plots peacefully. Among those involved in this arrangement was Cristobal de Burgos, an appellate judge (Carneiro 1946, 56–58; Flory 1979, 126). There is likewise a letter by members of the provisional government of Bahia in 1763, reporting on the destruction of the Buraco do Tatú *mocambo* by an expeditionary force, which states that planters were forced to accommodate the Maroons because they were afraid that they would be assassinated or their crops destroyed (Conrad 1983, 380). The letter details the many kinds of assaults that the Maroons had been accustomed to carry out against the planters and other people.[23] These examples emphasize the degree of fear, frustration and feebleness that some planters felt in face of Maroon depredations. They also indicate the inability of the authoritarian state to ensure the safety of the colonists – or, at least, the planters' lack of faith in the state's ability to do so.

Maroon Treaties

By far the most significant negotiations between the Maroons and the slaveholding fraternity related to the recognition of Maroon communities as independent or autonomous polities, and often the confirmation of Maroon occupation rights to certain lands. Some negotiations also referred to Maroon assistance in maintaining the security of the authoritarian state against internal and/or external aggression. Mexico, Panama, Colombia, Brazil, Jamaica, Suriname, Essequibo, the Dominican Republic, Dominica, French Guiana and the United States all signed treaties that included such terms. In this section we shall deal with specific aspects of a few of the main treaties, and in the next chapter undertake a general analysis of treaties.

Treaties between Maroons and slaveholding states were forged as early as the mid-sixteenth century, if not before, with Maroon groups in the Dominican Republic and Darien (in Panama). The two treaties made in 1580 with the Darien Maroons, though not as wide-ranging as the later Mexican treaty with Yanga, recognized the freedom of Puerto Bello and Ballano, two *palenques* near Nombre de Dios (La Guardia 1977, 94–97; Campbell 1990, 8). These treaties contained several of the clauses found in later treaties. However, the Darien treaties also contained an important clause not common in the later treaties that the other colonial powers signed: the right of any enslaved person whom his overlord had maltreated to buy his freedom for the same price at which he had been bought (Franco 1979, 41).[24]

The treaty made with the Cofre de Perote Maroons contains many of the clauses that became common in later treaties struck by the British and Dutch. These included government recognition of the freedom of all people who had joined the settlement up to 1608, the refusal to admit newcomers, the obligation to return fugitives to their overlords for a fee,[25] the commitment to aid in the repulsion of any external invasion of the country, and a pledge to keep the peace and obey the laws of the colonial state. The government recognized the Maroon establishment in 1609 or 1630 (depending on one's interpretation)[26] as a free town with the right to have its own *cabildo* and a justice who was to be a Spaniard. Franciscan friars were to be allowed into the settlement and the government was to refurbish the church. No other Spaniards were to be allowed to live in the town, although they might come for short periods to conduct business. Yanga was to be governor for life, followed by his children and their descendants.[27] These Maroons settled down to a peaceful life, moving to the slopes of Mount Totutla in 1630, and later the town of San Lorenzo de los Negros, which they built. However, over time the erstwhile fearsome Maroons became victims once again of White settler politics. The settlers appropriated land that should rightly have belonged to the Maroons, while the colonial state did nothing to stop the practice (Naveda Chávez-Hita 2001, 131).

In Colombia, the earliest treaty seems to have been made in 1619 with the Maroons established in the Sierra de Maria, in a vain hope by the authorities to resolve the Maroon question. Peace talks in the 1680s with new groups fell through for various reasons, not least due to opposition by the slaveholders to such arrangements (Borrego Plá 1973, 28–41). The development of other communities in Cartagena and elsewhere presented serious difficulties for the authorities by the end of that century (Borrego Plá 1973, 25–26). After about a century of harassment by the Maroons of San Basilio, the colonial government finally sought a peace treaty through the mediation of Bishop Don Antonio María Casiani. This treaty was finally agreed upon in 1717, and from that time these Maroons became a pacific group in the country's history. An official document in 1772 noted that they had not mixed with other groups and had a distinctive language, though they commonly used a sort of pidgin Spanish. Their political leader, military captain and mayor had to be approved by the governor (Escalante 1979, 79).

Palmares under King Ganga-Zumba signed a treaty with the Portuguese in 1678, after the federation had experienced some serious reverses as a result of several well-organized expeditions dispatched against it (Conrad 1983, 371–77). The treaty represented a humbling of the proud inhabitants of Palmares. One contemporary writer summed up its terms in this way:

> that they agree to make peace with the king of Palmares, acknowledging his obedience; that they be granted the site where they would choose to settle, a place suitable for their dwellings and their farms; that they must begin to live there within three months; that those born in Palmares would be free; that they were to return all the runaways who had come from our populated places; that they would have commerce and friendly trade with the Whites; that they would acquire the privileges of the king's vassals; that they would remain obedient to the orders of the government; that their king would continue as commander of all his people; that the wives of the king and all the other rulers would be returned to them. (Conrad 1983, 376)

The king's two sons, who headed the delegation to the colonial government, promised to assist the authorities in suppressing any remnants of resistance among hardliners.

Jamaica was the scene of two important treaties with the Leeward and Windward Maroons in 1739. The Windward Maroons were much more militant than their Leeward brethren, who preferred to live a pacific life under Cudjoe, their leader, in hope that the colonial forces would leave them alone. In practice, while they were never immune to colonial military expeditions, they were certainly not targeted in the same way as the Windwards. They also proved to be more amenable to overtures by the colonial government to sign a peace accord, though only after they had suffered serious reverses at the hands of the colonial forces.

The governor spoke triumphantly of the treaty with the Leeward Maroons, noting that it constituted a great increase in the military strength at the disposal of the colonial state, and ensured the most useful allies in quelling any servile unrest (Campbell 1990, 119). He might have said the same about the Windward Maroons. The now "pacified" Maroons, as they were often termed,[28] or ex-Maroons, as they might more appropriately be called, lived up to expectations, not only becoming bounty hunters but also assisting in the suppression of revolts, notably that of Tackey in 1760.

There can be little doubt that Cudjoe's treaty with the colonial govern-

Figure 29. Cudjoe negotiating the treaty of 1739. From *The History of the Maroon*s, by R.C. Dallas (London: T.N. Longman and O. Rees, 1803).

ment seriously abridged the freedom of the Windward Maroons and also that of all other Maroon groups. The Leewards were now on the side of the British, returning runaways and attempting to subvert Maroon groups that refused to submit to the authoritarian state (Patterson 1979, 274). Cudjoe contributed a force of some fifty warriors to the military expedition against the Windwards. Still, these much more fearsome warriors were not conquered. In fact, in the main expedition sent to subdue them in 1739, they had by far the better of the encounter, killing a number of the invaders and forcing most of the soldiers and baggage carriers to flee for their lives. Shortly afterward, another expedition was dispatched, this time along with a captured Maroon who had explained to them the intricacies of the defence system. On this occasion the expeditionary force made it clear that they had come to parley rather than to fight. Perhaps it became increasingly clear to the Windwards that Cudjoe's treaty with the British had seriously compromised their own integrity, since they would now have to fight two antagonists instead of one. After a lengthy discussion and apparently some disagreement among the leaders (see chapter 10), they agreed to sign a treaty with the dreadful clauses that required them to return all future fugitives who came their way and hunt down all those who refused to submit to the colonial authorities (Campbell 1990, 120–25).[29]

Some proposed treaties were not signed or broke down for a number of reasons, including misunderstandings, distrust by the Maroons, disagreement with certain conditions laid down by the authoritarian state, and treachery. In 1662 negotiations with the Bahoruco Maroons – thought to constitute as many as six hundred families in four main communities (Landers 2002, 4) – that Archbishop Francisco de la Cueva Maldonado of Santo Domingo was to mediate fell through, apparently because the Maroons did not trust the Whites. The main Maroon leader had made this point very clear to the archbishop, but had nevertheless agreed to meet with him shortly to finalize the terms of peace. The archbishop's proposal had included the recognition of the Maroons' right to their freedom on condition that they agreed to relocate to a more accessible area that the government would assign to them, to become Christians and to track down future runaways. However, the Maroons had a change of heart and did not keep the rendezvous with the archbishop (Esteban Deive 1989, 84–85; Arrom and García Arévalo 1986, 83–84).

Treachery also played its part in the relations between Maroons and the

slaveholding states. In 1556 the colonial government of Panama agreed to recognize the freedom of a group of Maroons in Nombre de Dios, and required
them to send a number of "hostages" to ensure that all members of the community agreed to the terms of the "capitulation". However, the officials
shipped off the Maroon leader, who was one of the hostages, to Spain, where
he lived out the rest of his days (Marcano Jiménez 2001, 18–19). A somewhat
similar event occurred in the Dominican Republic in 1611, when a Maroon
leader and several of his followers were sold out of the country, contrary to
the stipulations of the agreement endorsed by the governor (Esteban Deive
1989, 70–71; see chapter 10).

In 1728 a small group of Maroons in the Chocó area of Colombia were
duped into believing that the colonial government was willing to discuss their
grievances under a flag of truce, but four of their leaders were ambushed and
executed, and the group apparently never posed any serious threat afterward.
In 1819 an outstanding case of breach of faith involved Ventura Sánchez,
leader of the Bumba Maroons in Cuba, who was to learn a mortal lesson on
this score. Trusting the colonial authorities who had approached him through
the intermediary of a priest, he journeyed to Santiago de Cuba to negotiate
the terms of the agreement but was ambushed by a group of Maroon-catchers. He committed suicide instead of falling victim to his enemies, and his
head was taken to Baracoa and put on public display in an iron cage at the
entrance to the city. Brigadier Escudero, who had sought the assistance of
the priest, couched his perfidy in the language of a victorious military officer,
declaring to the governor of the island that he had destroyed the main
Maroon leader (Franco 1979, 42–43).[30] However, Bumba survived this act of
treachery, and under new leaders joined with its sister communities of
Maluala and El Frijol (Moa) in striking fear into the Whites.

CHAPTER 10

Maroons and Revolutionary Struggle

REASONS FOR MAROON TREATIES

Contemporary White writers viewed treaties with Maroons variously as anathema, capitulation to barbaric hordes, the result of imperious necessity, and evidence that the once sharp edge of Maroon steel had become blunted. It is difficult to know exactly how Maroons viewed the treaties, but some must have felt that they signalled their triumph over the slaveholding regimes that badly wanted to enslave them once again. A number of present-day nationalist writers view the treaties as a sell-out, whereas others prefer to focus on the nobility of the Maroons' struggle rather than on the capitulation to the forces of oppression that some treaties suggest.

The shift from armed to peaceful dialogue and finally to treaties was born out of the perceived need for some accommodation on the part of both the Maroons and the slaveholders. Maroons had to fight continually to keep their polities from being destroyed by military forces; they often had to move their settlements to new locations; and they spent a lot of their time, resources and energy on defensive strategies. Even those communities that withstood military assaults for years could not be assured of a completely settled life as long as planter expeditions continued to be sent against them.

At least theoretically, treaties meant they no longer had to count their dead, dying and injured at the hands of military expeditions. It is debatable whether they were really materially better off, since most of the treaties prohibited them from ranging far and wide for game and other forest products. They also knew that they would no longer be able to profit from seizing booty as part of the spoils of war. In fact, after the treaties were signed, some communities became heavily dependent on the colonial state for basic supplies that they had formerly acquired by war and contraband trade. It might even be argued that the innovative spirit of these Maroon societies was dulled by the growing dependence on the colonial state for goods, whether viewed as tribute or gifts. Johannes King (1979, 301), a nineteenth-century descendant of the Matawai Maroons, remembered the wide range of goods that the government sent to his people every three years, according to the terms of the treaty: "salt and cloth, guns, powder, bullets, shot, beads, pots, knives, cutlasses, axes, gridstones, two types of adzes, razors, shovels, scissors, mirrors, and nails . . . , screwdrivers, tinderboxes and flintstones, large griddles for making cassava cakes and pans for cooking fish, cloth to make hammocks, hammers, cowrie shells, bells, cockle shells, barrels of rum, barrels of salt meat, barrels of bacon, and barrels of salt cod". Those ex-Maroons whose treaty arrangements involved the receipt of gifts at stated intervals sometimes complained about the officials' failure to send the goods on time, or about the amount specified or the quality of the goods. In spite of the restrictions that treaty arrangements were likely to impose on them, the Maroons who signed treaties must have reckoned that the positive aspects would outweigh the negative ones.

As for the slaveholders' position, Borrego Plá (1973, 40) makes the point succinctly and clearly that treaties were more than a concession to Maroons: they were implicit admission that the *palenques* could not be conquered by force. The treaties constituted a painful solution to a painful problem. The governments were forced to temper public rhetoric with private diplomacy, tacitly recognizing the Maroons' freedom in order to avoid continuing warfare.

Most slaveholders understood the need for accommodation, especially in relation to the large and long-established Maroon communities. Others were ambivalent, wanting and yet not wanting to reach an accommodation. On the one hand, they wanted to enjoy the peace and security sought after in these treaties, to be able to put their lives together again and get on with the business of making money and enjoying the good life in the idyllic world of the sugar, cocoa and coffee plantations. On the other hand, they knew that treaties meant the relinquishment of all hopes of regaining control over their servile charges or recovering the money that they had paid for them. As

Marchand-Thébault (1986, 38) notes in relation to the financial aspect, "The runaway slave was in principle a slave lost to the master." The enslavers also smarted over the thought that the treaties might send direct or subliminal messages to their enslaved charges that they were capitulating to superior physical and spiritual forces, and that the oppressed might be emboldened to abscond in hope that they too might be able to negotiate their freedom. The slaveholders' passion for revenge against Maroons who had killed their relatives and friends and destroyed their plantations would not be sated. How could the colonial state morally justify making peace with such "bloodthirsty savages"? How could it ask them to lay down their arms and accept the Maroons into "civilized" human society?

Despite such misgivings, the majority of White slaveholders wanted peace badly, to put an end to their fears and anxieties and the economic depredations associated with *marronage*. Borrego Plá (1973, 29) points out that *marronage* provoked distortions in the economy of Cartagena province, an observation applicable to all areas where large Maroon communities became established. As noted already, *marronage* was a very expensive business, especially to the planters. It entailed the loss of a number of their labour hands, often the most hardy and robust, and depredations against the plantations and sometimes the towns. The cost of military expeditions also ultimately had to be borne by taxes and other levies on the slaveholders. Such taxes could be extremely high at times, especially for small, struggling economies and settlers. Whether intended, coordinated or not, the collective activities of the Suriname Maroons in the late eighteenth century virtually brought the colonial state to its knees and led to a bankrupt treasury. One estimate indicates that during the most intense period of warfare against the Maroons in that country, from 1770 to 1776, it cost the colonial government eight million guilders (Schalkwijk 1994, 150).

The British colonial government in Dominica raised more than £50,000 in special taxes between May 1785 and May 1786 to conduct military expeditions against the Maroons. These taxes were levied on all produce, enslaved and free persons, mercantile and other businesses, rented houses, sales and so on (Atwood 1971, 237–40, 250–53). In Jamaica, financial expenditure on fixed and mobile defence systems frequently left the colonial cupboard bare, all in a vain effort to contain the Maroons (Dallas 1803, 1:27, 36–37; Campbell 1990, 37, 41, 60). The enterprises of small planters and businessmen often collapsed under the weight of the financial burden of suppressing *marronage* and other forms of Black insurrection (Donoghue 2002, 156). Maroon activities, of course, had not only financial and political impacts on the slave societies but also social ones. Along with other forms of resistance to slavery, they influenced the incidence of planter absenteeism and the number of White females who were brought out to, or brought up in, the slave colonies. *Marronage* thus helped to destabilize slave society in significant ways. It was not surprising, therefore, that planters sought accommodation with Maroon leaders.

Land-grabbing lay at the core of many of the European overtures for treaties and their lethal assaults on the Maroons. Land-grabbers, or potential land-grabbers, could be found almost everywhere that the Maroons had developed large tracts of land. Enslavers were surprised at the dirt-eating practices of enslaved persons, but they themselves displayed a peculiar kind of earth hunger that was very visible in Palmares, Minas Gerais, Jamaica, Haiti, St Vincent and the United States, among other places.

In the case of Palmares, its physical size was variously estimated in 1695 at around forty-five hundred square leagues and one thousand square leagues respectively (Carneiro 1946, 30). According to Carneiro (ibid., 16), from 1677 the campaign against Palmares assumed the character of a struggle for possession of the lands of the confederation, considered unanimously as the best in the whole captaincy of Pernambuco. As soon as the peace treaty was struck with King Ganga-Zumba in 1678, the Portuguese began to petition for large land grants in the area; Fernão Carrilho, one of the heroes of the campaign, was among the main petitioners. The colonial authorities distributed a large quantity of land that cost the recipients nothing (Carneiro 1946, 16). Likewise, in the 1690s the authorities promised Domingos Jorge Velho large portions of land in the area if he would undertake a successful campaign against the Palmarinos. Later, when the Maroons were defeated, he requested from the Crown the entire area that they had occupied, in his estimation amounting to one thousand square leagues. Disputes over the allocation of land to members of the various expeditions and other interested parties occupied the attention of the Overseas Council in Lisbon for several years (Carneiro 1946, 16–17; see also 29–30, 61, 165–80).

In Jamaica, the fertile lands in the parishes of St James and Westmoreland that were the stomping grounds of large numbers of Maroons were prime targets of settler attention. Philip Thicknesse, a military officer who played a major role in the peace negotiations with the Windward Maroons, declared in his *Memoirs,* with obvious exaggeration:

Such who are acquainted with that island will be surprised when they are told, that all the regular troops in Europe, could not have conquered the wild Negroes, by force of arms; and if Mr. Trelawny had not wisely given them, what they contended for, LIBERTY, they would in all probability have been, at this day, masters of the whole country. (Campbell 1990, 124)

More realistically, in 1739 Governor Edward Trelawny informed his superiors in London that the main reason the colony was not as highly developed as it might have been was that scarcely any good land existed in safe areas, and a large quantity was located in areas controlled by the Maroons. Some colonists who had received grants in those areas and had started plantations had been forced to abandon them because of the Maroon menace (Campbell 1990, 145). Trelawny also noted in 1741 that Titchfield, in Portland, contained only a few huts but possessed a commodious harbour and offered excellent prospects for trade, and had until recently been retarded in its development by the Maroon menace.

According to Trevor Burnard (2004, 22–23), in 1730 only an estimated 443 Whites and 7,137 enslaved persons lived in the parish of Westmoreland. However, after the treaty struck with the Leeward Maroons in 1739, lands in that area began to be widely available to settlers, and by 1768 the holdings there included sixty-two sugar plantations and ninety-six other enterprises, mostly cattle pens and small cotton, pimento and ginger farms. Burnard (ibid., 23) states that population and production expanded dynamically between 1730 and 1788. The White population grew by 237 per cent and the servile population by 145 per cent, while sugar production increased from 5,450 hogsheads in 1739 to 8,000 hogsheads in 1768. Westmoreland then became a very wealthy parish: the average value of plantations there in 1768 was 42 per cent higher than the average value in the whole island.[1]

In St Vincent, peace between the Black Caribs and the British was jeopardized by the colonists' greed for more land, especially in fertile areas where the local inhabitants resided. They used every ruse and the usual stereotypes about the savage and barbaric nature of these people to incite their government to take over their lands forcibly and herd them into reservations or transport them overseas. The fragile accommodation that existed between the two parties eventually broke down in 1772 through the machinations of the land-grabbers. War ensued, terminating in 1773 in an agreement that the Black Caribs would be allowed to retain about one-half of the island, including some of the most fertile spots, in return for recognition of British sovereignty over the island and the other usual terms found in peace treaties with local peoples and Maroons. These included the return of runaways, assistance in the defence of the colony, and the ultimate right of the colonial state to determine disputes in its law courts.

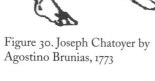

Clearly, the treaty was only a holding mechanism on both sides, since its terms did not satisfy either party, and the imperial government, under pressure from a land-hungry and angry plantocracy, would never allow the Black Caribs to retain so much territory. It was therefore no surprise that the treaty was not faithfully observed on either side. This eventually led to the more definitive war of 1795–96. Joseph Chatoyer, the Black Carib leader, refused to surrender to his aggressive enemies, but he eventually surrendered to the mortal wounds that he received at their hands. The British transported 4,338 Black Caribs first to the neighbouring island of Balliceaux in the Grenadines, but since this island was too small to accommodate them, they were transferred to the sister island of Bequia. The problems at this new location were the island's scanty food resources and its insalubrity, which led to the death of many of the exiles within a few months. The British therefore embarked the remaining 2,248 Black Caribs for Belize in 1797, though 200 of them died on the journey. The authoritarian state systematically tracked down and slaughtered most of those who remained hidden in St Vincent (Craton 1982, 147–53, 190–94,

Figure 30. Joseph Chatoyer by Agostino Brunias, 1773

204–6; Gargallo 2002, 9–11, 57–67; see also chapter 2).

As noted in chapter 4, in the second decade of the nineteenth century American military forces and armed planter bands carried out a series of invasions into Spanish Florida. Porter (1951, 254) states bluntly that the original impulse for these incursions was American expansionism, caused by the same land hunger that targeted Canada at that time, though the objective was later expanded to include securing the frontier against Maroon settlements and activities. Having taken formal possession of the Spanish territory in 1821 (following a treaty of cession signed in 1819), the American government moved fairly quickly to expel the Maroons by a policy of persuasion and coercion. In 1823, under pressure from the American government, the Seminole Indian leaders signed a treaty agreeing to the removal of their people from the fertile northern areas to an area below Tampa. Mulroy (1993, 27) informs us that most of the projected area for the reservation was uncultivable swampland, and that during the next few years many Maroons and Indians became wanderers, stealing cattle from White settlers in order to survive. Others refused to abide by the treaty and remained on the "ceded" land. The result was continued friction between Seminoles and White Americans, with further attempts by the latter to herd the Indians and Maroons into reservations in Indian Territory west of the Mississippi, and further resistance by the oppressed. This gradually set the stage for the Second Seminole War (Porter 1943, 390–421; chapter 4).

The situation relating to the fertile lands around Le Maniel was resolved in a somewhat different manner. The colonial authorities reached an initial agreement with the Maroon leaders in 1785, in many ways similar to the earlier Jamaican treaties, but with the important proviso that they would shift their settlement from their present location to another spot that the French would allocate to them. The French wanted to remove the Maroons because of concern that they would not be controllable in their present habitat, and that the Spanish settlers, who carried on a lucrative business with the Maroons, might influence them against the French. Debbasch asserts that this is exactly what happened, and that it led to the Maroons' refusal, in the following year, to relocate. However, although the Maroons rejected the proposed treaty, they declared that they would cease attacks on the French and return runaways to their overlords for a bounty. They kept their word, at least in regard to attacks against the colonists. In fact, the French considered their word to be so good that requests for land grants in the area multiplied rapidly. Debbasch (1979, 148) considered this as tantamount to a coup on the part of the French, since they were able to resolve the Maroon problem "without having to undergo the humiliation of a formal treaty".

Whites both opposed and supported treaties, because they could exploit the situation for their own benefit. Two examples illustrate this point. Several new farmers in the neighbourhood of the *palenques* in Cartagena strongly opposed a royal decision of 1691 to negotiate with the Maroon leaders with a view to recognizing the settlements as free villages. These farmers surreptitiously used Maroon labour on their farms, labour that they felt would not be as abundant, and certainly not as cheap, if the labourers should be declared free persons (Borrego Plá 1973, 90). In contrast, in 1748, Don Andrés Fernández de Otañes, senior magistrate of Teutila in Mexico, vigorously promoted the recognition of the Mandinga-Amapa inhabitants as free people, obviously to regularize his use of their labour (Pereira 1994, 102; Naveda Chávez-Hita 1987, 143–45).

Sometimes Maroons sought some form of accommodation with the authoritarian state, but more frequently it was the other way around. In spite of the circumstances that led to treaties, official correspondence often gave the impression either that the initiative for peace treaties came from the Maroons or that the authorities badly mauled them and forced them to sign such treaties. This comes out clearly in the dispatches of Governor Trelawny concerning the Leeward and Windward Maroons. Although the governor implied to the imperial government that the Maroon leader had first broached the issue of a treaty and was on his knees when the document was actually signed, Cudjoe's grovelling seems to have been more myth than reality. Mullin (1992, 50–51), quoting an excerpt from the journal of a member of the expeditionary force, shows clearly that Cudjoe executed a dance before Guthrie, the officer signing on behalf of the colonial government, which required him to kneel several times in front of the White officer, but not in a grovelling way: "Capt. Cudjoe danced and showed a great many antic tricks, fell at col. Guthrie's feet several times; hugged him, and had a long conference with him, and so parted." What seems more probable is that Cudjoe and Guthrie took an Akan-style oath, which involved the mixing of blood from both parties with other elements. By drinking this potion, the two sealed their friendship forever and agreed to abide by the terms of the treaty (Campbell 1990, 88–118; Patterson 1979, 271–75).

Unlike most offers of amnesty, treaties generally explicitly recognized the right of the members of the particular Maroon polity to their freedom and usually to the lands that they occupied. Some treaties also provided for the periodic granting of gifts to the Maroon leaders, considered by the Maroons and by some writers as forms of tribute. These aspects of the treaties are perhaps the strongest affirmation to those who argue that the Maroons had won the war. Others argue that the plantocracy had won the peace, in the sense that Maroon treaties almost invariably required them not to harbour any new deserters but rather to return them to the enslavers for a fee, and to assist in periodic expeditions to catch new deserters and destroy new settlements. In addition, some treaties required the Maroons to lay down their arms, obey the laws of the slaveholding state, receive a staff and other insignia of office from that state, and allow the state to place a resident representative among them.

In the Spanish territories priests became the dominant figures in the "pacified" Maroon polities. Romero Jaramillo (1997, 175) explains that in some cases the priests not only lived with the Maroons but also proved instrumental in establishing towns for them. In Suriname the postholder (*posthouder*) assumed the role of resident representative to the Ndjukas, Saramakas and Matawais. This official existed in all Dutch Guiana colonies, and normally his main tasks were to act as a rural paramilitary officer, cultivate amicable relations with the Indians and facilitate Dutch interests in the deep interior of the colonies. His role in respect of the ex-Maroons included attempting to use them as his allies to ensure rural peace and further facilitate Dutch interests (Thompson 1987, 186–90; Thoden van Velzen 1995, 113).

Gordon Lewis (1983, 232) equates the authoritarian state's legal recognition of Maroon polities to the creation of pluralistic states, but this is stretching the interpretation of the treaty phenomenon. Most treaties restricted the Maroons in a number of ways, including subjecting them to the jurisdiction of the authoritarian state in such matters as external relations and trials for capital offences. As Thoden van Velzen (1995, 113) observes, the treaties did not allow Maroons to conduct their own foreign relations. In fact, their operations were usually restricted to the areas in which it was agreed that they should reside, and they had to seek specific permission from the authoritarian state to travel farther afield. The state representatives placed in their midst generally played an increasingly large role in their lives. The secret functions of such White residential officials included spying on the Maroons to ensure that they remained "pacified" and did not harbour runaways. In Jamaica these officials, and the colonial government at large, contributed to the fissiparous tendencies within the now pacified and relocated communities of the Windwards and Leewards. The post-treaty era was marked by dissension, loss of respect for Maroon captains, and lack of central leadership among them. They frequently appealed to the colonial courts to settle their disputes, and even adopted the names of important government officials and plantation owners. Most of them had clearly lost their martial edge, and the situation was worse for the children born into the post-treaty settlements (Kopytoff 1976a, 90–102; Campbell 1990, 126–208).

MAROON DISSENSION OVER TREATY ARRANGEMENTS

It is important to note here that the prelude to treaties was negotiation not only between the slaveholders and the Maroon leaders but also between the Maroons themselves. It is doubtful that the terms of any of the treaties were acceptable to all the Maroons in large communities, for there were probably some hardliners who would have preferred to fight the Whites to the last man for both ideological and pragmatic reasons. Many of them also distrusted the word of the Whites who, they felt, had not kept faith with Blacks on previous occasions.[2] But the leaders also resented some of the terms proposed by the enemy, especially those restricting their movement within the colonial area and requiring the return of future runaways and sometimes recent recruits to the settlements. Again, the paucity of extant records prevents extensive exploration of this dynamic in treaties, but occasionally a gleam of light comes through – for example, when several Maroons hived off from the main body rather than submitting to the terms of the treaty. This happened especially when Maroon leaders negotiated treaties that required them to return some of their followers to bondage. A case in point is that of Diego de Ocampo, who accepted terms under which the colonial authorities recognized his freedom and that of three of his relatives, but he in turn undertook to return the rest of his followers to bondage. Between twenty-five and thirty of them hived off and joined another Maroon leader in the Bahoruco region (Esteban Deive 1989, 48–49; Franco 1979, 40).

There was also the case of Enriquillo, a celebrated Indian Maroon leader, whose *palenque* comprised mainly Africans and who plagued the plantocracy in the Dominican Republic. In 1533 he agreed to a treaty that guaranteed freedom only for the few members of his immediate family. He died in splendid comfort in 1535, but in 1547 the African Maroons, who had not forgotten their leader's treachery, killed his successor and nearly all the inhabitants of the small town of Azua that he governed. The dozen or so Indians who escaped fled to the Spaniards, promising to join them in wreaking vengeance on those who had destroyed their kinfolk (Esteban Deive 1989, 40–42).

Another case involved the (unnamed) leader of a group of seventy-three Maroons located in the mountains of the Dominican Republic, some seven leagues from the capital. In 1611 the leader offered to submit to the colonial authorities provided that his wife, his brother, the creole Blacks, the leaders of the Angolans who were part of the community, and he himself should be allowed to remain free. The rest would return to slavery under their former enslavers with the proviso that they would be sold to others if those enslavers should treat them harshly again. It is said that sixty-four Maroons submitted under these terms, while the remainder fled the settlement. Despite having agreed to the peace terms, the governor decided to sell the Maroons abroad for fear that they would serve as a bad example to other enslaved persons (Esteban Deive 1989, 70–71). It was not unusual for the authoritarian state to banish or sell outside of the country people who had not been convicted of grave offences, such as murder or armed robbery, but who had stayed away for several years, because the state considered it too dangerous to reintegrate them into the workforce.

As regards the Windward Maroons, some writers believe that there was some disagreement between Grandy Nanny and the other leaders about the signing of the treaty in 1739. Interestingly, she did not participate in the negotiations with the British officers who met the four senior male leaders at Nanny Town, but we should not infer from this that these men sidelined her. As the spiritual head of her community, she may have considered it more appropriate to advise the men on matters relating to the negotiations rather than to be present at the actual event. Another possibility is that she rejected the first overtures from the British because she distrusted them, but later became convinced that they genuinely desired to make peace and thus accepted the terms (Harris 1994, 47; Campbell 1990, 122–23, 177–78).

In several other instances, disagreements over treaties led to open conflicts among Maroon leaders – as exemplified by circumstances within the Mandinga-Amapa *palenque* in Mexico in the 1760s. The young Mulatto leader, Captain Macute (Makute), stood opposed to a negotiated settlement with the Spaniards, while the older Fernando Manuel supported it. In the power struggle that developed, Manuel triumphed, and was ungracious enough to deliver his younger compatriot to the Spaniards to be executed and several other Maroons to their former enslavers. Manuel reached an agreement with the Spaniards in 1769 under which the latter recognized his settlement as a free community on the usual terms, including the requirement to return future runaways.[3]

ROLE OF THE CLERGY IN TREATY-MAKING

The slaveholding states deputed clergymen, high military officers, senior civil officials, former Maroons, enslaved persons, and relatives of Maroons to mediate peace settlements with Maroon leaders. The role of the clergy, especially in the Spanish and French jurisdictions, calls for further comment. The intense religiosity of the Africans may have been one reason that the state appointed clergymen. The colonial officials apparently reasoned that the priests would enjoy greater immunity from attacks and at least be shown some measure of respect. It appears, also, that on some occasions Maroons approached priests, or priests seized the initiative, to discuss terms of disengagement. One outstanding example, from Santiago de Cuba in the early nineteenth century, was the negotiations with Ventura Sánchez (Coba), leader of the Bumba Maroons (Franco 1979, 42). Another was the overtures that Francisco de la Cueva Maldonado, archbishop of Santo Domingo, made to the Bahoruco Maroons around the mid-seventeenth century (Esteban Deive 1989, 84–85; Larrazábal Blanco 1998, 147). Such negotiations led some Whites, at least in the French Caribbean, to accuse the Jesuits of collusion with Maroons. According to Debien (1979, 118), "The important role the clergy played in the surrender of Maroons, and the negotiations they carried out in order to bring smaller bands back, led to the colonists' accusation in 1791 that they were in connivance with the refractory Maroons, that they were protecting them no matter what, that they were, indeed, 'accomplices of the rebels'."[4] In the Dominican Republic, Peru and perhaps other Spanish territories, many enslaved persons fled to convents and monasteries for asylum, and it is said that the clergy sought to uphold their claims to freedom against the authorities' efforts to return them to slavery (Esteban Deive 1989, 40; Bowser 1974, 168–71).[5]

In Peru, for instance, the clergy were frequently at loggerheads with the Audiencia and members of the plantocracy over their claim that enslaved persons had the right to seek religious asylum in their monasteries. In the 1630s conflict arose between the secular and religious authorities over two escapees from jail who had sought refuge in the cathedral in Lima but were apprehended there and hanged on the orders of the Audiencia. In a second incident an enslaved person, condemned for the murder of another enslaved person, sought asylum in the cathedral, and again the secular authorities entered the cathedral and dragged the accused away to prison. A major row ensued over the right of the secular authorities to enter holy ground and seize people without the permission of the religious authorities. The matter was referred to the Crown's attorney in the colony, and, though temporarily settled in favour of the secular authorities, similar cases continued to be a bone of contention between the two parties (Bowser 1974, 168–71). In 1585 the Audiencia of Peru expelled fifteen Dominican friars accused of wresting from state custody two Blacks being held for murder and robbery and spiriting them away to the Lima monastery (Bowser 1974, 169). Similarly, in Haiti the colonial authorities thought that the Jesuits were in collusion with Maroons and other insurgents and expelled them from the colony in 1764 (Leyburn 1941, 116).

Despite these conflicts, the priesthood in all jurisdictions generally upheld slavery, and the "established" churches in all of them – Catholic, Anglican, Lutheran and Dutch Reformed – owned plantations and other institutions that employed enslaved persons in large numbers.[6] They preached salvation from spiritual, not physical, bondage[7] until the late eighteenth century, when the dissenting (new evangelical) churches emerged, first in the British and then the other colonies, preaching against the evils of slavery as an institution.

RETURN OF RUNAWAYS

Several writers have indicted Maroon leaders on two specific charges relating to their treaty arrangements with the slaveholders: that they agreed to apprehend and return runaways, and that the treaties confirmed their lack of interest in attempting to overthrow the slavery system as a whole. These writers question the designation of Maroons as "freedom fighters". There can be no doubt that the return of runaways is by far the most contentious issue in the historiography of *marronage* in the Americas. Eugene Genovese (1981, 52–53) finds their actions with respect to the apprehension of runaways "maddeningly ambiguous". Campbell (1990, 13) dismisses the idea that "slave-catchers" could be viewed as genuine "revolutionaries or even reformers, seeking to transform the society from one of servitude to freedom". She states further that "this aspect of the Maroon story, which is so universal, must be one of the most perplexing" (ibid., 131). Thoden van Velzen (1995, 113) opines that "Particularly galling, and a cause of considerable friction later, were those articles of the treaty demanding that maroons deliver all later runaways into the hands of their former masters." He is convinced that the main effect of the treaties was to transform former foes into vassals.

As noted already, the vast majority of treaties with Maroons, following the Spanish precedent in the sixteenth century, incorporated some clause about the return of new runaways, and by the late seventeenth century this had become a *sine qua non* of such treaties from the viewpoint of the slaveholders. Similar provisions are found in the treaties made with the Maroons of Cofre de Perote in Mexico; Diego de Ocampo in the Dominican Republic; Juan de Bolas's group and the Windwards and Leewards in Jamaica; the Saramakas, Ndjukas and Matawais in Suriname; the Puerto Bello Maroons (relocated to Santiago del Principe after the peace treaty) in Panama; and the San Basilio Maroons in Colombia. Juan López Cepeda, president of the Audiencia, declared concerning the "pacified" Santiago del Principe Maroons that they served as a check against other Maroons (La Guardia 1977, 95; see also 96–97). In the case of Juan de Bolas, the Jamaican government recognized him as "Colonel of the Black Regiment" in that colony's militia, a semi-formal incorporation of him and his men into the pro-slavery forces (Campbell 1990, 23; Patterson 1979, 254). One British officer expressed the view that the new allies "are now become our bloodhounds . . . and they are in our behalf more violent and fierce against their fellows than we possibly can be" (Campbell 1990, 21).

It is difficult to justify Maroon agreement to return future runaways, and we cannot comfort ourselves that this aspect of the treaties generally remained a dead letter. The fact is that subsequent to the treaties, many groups actively pursued and returned runaways for bounties, material gains that replaced those that they had previously obtained through assaults on White properties. Worse still, some of them played major roles in putting down servile revolts and destroying new Maroon settlements. As noted already, the post-treaty Maroons in Jamaica played a signal role in quelling the large-scale Tackey revolt in 1760 and killing Tackey himself. They were also the chief antagonists of the new group that was developing under

Three-Fingered Jack, whom they also killed (Campbell 1990, 155, 158). The Ndjuka Maroons played a seminal role in the last phase of the Boni Wars from 1789 to 1793, in which the Boni Maroons were finally defeated (Thoden van Velzen 1995, 114).

Nonetheless, we must be careful not to go to extremes in assessing the post-treaty Maroons. Campbell (1990, 7) does so when she asserts that the willingness of the treaty Maroons throughout the region to ally with the slaveholding regimes was as pervasive as their resistance in former times. Taking the contrary point of view, Mullin (1992, 48–49, 293) asserts, in the case of Jamaica, that the policy of employing treaties to gain Maroon allies was a clear failure, and that Maroons should not be regarded as a sort of rural police apprehending runaways. He notes that the Whites always distrusted the treaty Maroons and feared that they would join the insurgents in servile uprisings. He states further that in spite of the assistance that the Leeward Maroons, in particular, gave in the suppression of the Tackey revolt, one colonial governor expressed the view in the 1770s that their behaviour during that revolt confirmed that they could not be relied on to defend the country in times of social unrest (Mullin 1992, 49, 293). When the Maroon uprising took place in 1795, several enslaved persons joined the ranks of the insurgents. Many Whites viewed the uprising as the confirmation of their fears that all Blacks, treaty Maroons or not, were a perfidious breed and could never be trusted fully – not, of course, taking into account their own failure to treat the Maroons with the respect due to them. It was hardly surprising that after the suppression of the uprising a large number of Maroons were exiled to Nova Scotia.

Clearly, treaties did not stop large-scale *marronage*; in fact, it is quite possible that they encouraged other enslaved persons to abscond and set up new communities, in the hope that they too would secure formal recognition of their freedom through a treaty. For this reason, some slaveholders stoutly opposed all negotiations by the authoritarian state with the Maroons.[8] Suriname provides an outstanding example of the escalation of Maroon wars after the battles with the Ndjukas, Saramakas and Matawais (the main threats up to that time) had ceased as a result of treaties in 1760, 1762 and 1767, respectively. The most extensive wars commenced around 1768 against the new and perhaps more fearsome Aluku (Boni) Maroons. The government was forced at one point to hire mercenaries – dealers in death, according to García (1989, 76) – to assist the regular soldiers and citizen militias, embodying the Black Rangers, and seeking the assistance of the now "pacified" Ndjukas.

"Pacified" Maroons accused the plantocracy of harassing *bona fide* members of their communities on the pretext that they were newly inducted members, and of placing impediments on their movement around the country as free people. Maroons in Suriname complained bitterly on this last score. For its part, the plantocracy complained that Maroons were harbouring new deserters, still raiding their plantations, failing to provide contingents for periodic expeditions, and engaging in other acts that undermined the stability of plantocratic society. According to Thoden van Velzen (1995, 124–25), a large number of runaways found refuge among the Ndjukas, Saramakas and Matawais, though they tried to hide the newcomers from the government officials who were resident among them. These officials did not prevail on them to return more than a few of the newcomers to their overlords, and the inhabitants usually denied that they had given refuge to any runaways. The Ndjukas likewise made alliances with the Paramakas (a small group of Maroons who emerged in the post-treaty period) and other small groups. In 1805 they offered sanctuary to a group of Black Rangers who had mutinied during the British occupation of the colony when imperial warfare was renewed (1803–14). They kept some of these, perhaps the most robust ones, as labour hands, often carefully hidden away on agricultural plots some distance from the living quarters. Eventually, the British signed a treaty with them that defused the situation and allowed the renegade Rangers to live among them. In time the descendants of the mutineers became an additional Ndjuka clan (Thoden van Velzen 1995, 114, 125–26; Schalkwijk 1994, 158).

In Mexico, too, the enslavers accused the Cofre de Perote Maroons, who had agreed to be removed to the town of San Lorenzo de los Negros, of not observing the treaty faithfully, especially with regard to harbouring runaways, but again the truth is that both sides honoured it only partially (Naveda Chávez-Hita 1987, 128, 140–41). Similarly, the treaty with the Bumba Maroons broke down because both parties kept its terms only in part (Marcano Jiménez 2001, 23). These examples are evidence that treaty Maroons were not always total vassals.

Nevertheless, few would question the view that the lowest points of treaty-Maroon activities, from an ideological or nationalist standpoint, were their hunting down of fugitives (however limited or extensive) and their participation in warfare against other insurgent groups. Patchy contemporary evidence suggests that other enslaved persons vilified them for doing so. A group of enslaved persons in Berbice in 1828 declared that while they had obtained medals from the colonial government for assisting in the apprehension of some Maroons eighteen years earlier, they were still cursed and ostracized by other Blacks for their role as Maroon-catchers (Thompson 2002b, 234).[9]

The bitterness between the Ndjuka and Aluku Maroons had to do not only with the Ndjukas' apprehension that the Alukus were trespassing on their hunting and roaming grounds, but also with the Ndjuka policy of returning at least some runaways to their overlords (Hoogbergen 1990).[10] Thoden van Velzen (1995, 127–28) writes that the Ndjukas raided new Maroon settlements because they believed that the people in them had moved too close to the "backwoods", where they were trespassing on the territory of "dangerous forest spirits" that they might unleash, to the hurt of the Ndjukas. In a world of strong belief in elemental spirits capable of doing great harm (or good), as was the case in Ndjuka and other polities, one can at least understand the Ndjukas' concerns, if not their actions.

The attitudes and actions of the Maroon leaders who signed treaties, and sometimes at the same time signed away their birthright, were no different from what has obtained historically among peoples of all races, ethnicities and nations. It is true, as some writers remind us, that Maroon polities were attempting to secure and maintain their freedom in difficult and sometimes revolutionary circumstances; and that each polity was often the primary (and sometimes the ultimate) framework of loyalty. Today, the nation-state is the focal point of loyalty, and its welfare is considered paramount. People defend it with their lives and are prepared to take preemptive measures against other nations to ensure its integrity. It may therefore be argued cogently that the foregoing observations provide a plausible explanation of why certain Maroon communities acted in exclusionary and sometimes hostile ways towards each other. However, to many scholars such an explanation is unsatisfactory.

In attempting to explain, if not justify, Maroon decisions to sign treaties involving the return of runaways, Zips (1999, 11–12) adopts the premise that *marronage* was ideologically opposed to slavery, and that "this paradigmatic assumption is not undermined by any evidence of breaks in solidarity, collaboration with the oppressors, and treachery within the [Maroon] ranks". Still, this perspective does not make the problem disappear. Zips realizes this, and so he poses the rhetorical question: "Shouldn't the Maroons themselves have felt abandoned, when after 85 years of armed combat they were still only a small minority, which was often fought and betrayed even by fellow blacks?" He also opines that this issue can only be addressed from a moral perspective, and "passing moral judgment from a chronological distance of 250 years is simply out of the question" (ibid., 67).[11]

The problem with Zips's approach is threefold. First, the same argument can be used when passing judgements about slavery, as Zips himself does in his 1999 book. Second, he is wrong to suggest that Maroons were an isolated group within African society in Jamaica. Again, his own study shows clearly the considerable help that the Maroons received from enslaved persons who remained on the plantations, and their continual absorption of new runaways into their ranks. If isolation occurred, it was after they signed the treaties agreeing to return runaways. Third, and most important, the people whom they agreed to return to the enslavers were those who sought their freedom in flight, not those who remained under slavery. In other words, these fugitives from injustice were acting precisely as the pre-treaty Maroons had done. Therefore, if morality were invoked, it should be to emphasize the imperative for these Maroons to give succour, not umbrage, to their fellow runaways. Perhaps the best explanation of the ambivalent position in which the treaty Maroons found themselves is that of Fleischmann (1993, 577n5), who states that Maroons owed their fame not so much to their morality as to their bravery.

A point that must not be overlooked is that it was the leaders who often betrayed the Maroon cause, by signing treaties with the authoritarian state that contained clauses prejudicial to the interests of the community as a whole. Some leaders went so far as to sign treaties that preserved their own freedom and that of their families and friends, on the understanding that they would hand over their rank-and-file members to the authoritarian state. This was similar to what occurred in Africa during the slave-trade era, when the ruling classes sold ordinary Africans into bondage overseas in return for European consumer goods (Rodney 1970, 253).

It must be stressed that some Maroon leaders refused to sign treaties that required the return of future runaways and/or members of their polities, while others simply refused to sign any sort of treaty. Jerónimo, leader of the Castillo Maroons of Colombia, flatly rejected a clause in the proposed treaty that required him to return new runaways, and this aborted the peace negotiations (Escalante 1979, 76). The leader of the San Miguel settlement, also in

Colombia, refused to accept peace terms that required him to exclude African-born Maroons from the agreement (Borrego Plá 1973, 105, 106). In 1764 Maroons in the Bahoruco Mountains of the Dominican Republic rejected a royal decree offering to recognize their freedom if they would leave the mountains and live a sedentary and peaceful urban life (Larrazábal Blanco 1998, 164). In 1816 the Seminole Maroon leader Garçon refused to enter into peaceful dialogue with the United States forces sent against him. In the sequel, about 270 of his men, women and children were killed when the enemy blew up the magazine in his stronghold, while another 40 were caught.[12]

The vast majority of the Maroon groups in Jamaica in the late seventeenth century rejected peace terms similar to those offered to Juan de Bolas, whom they regarded as a traitor to the cause of liberation (Campbell 1990, 24–25; Patterson 1979, 254). Long (1774, 2:339) explained that none of the Karmahaly Maroons under Juan de Serras accepted similar terms, but "[o]n the contrary, they were better pleased with the more ample range they possessed in the woods where their hunting ground was not yet limited by settlements". Patterson (1979, 273–74) argues that not only enslaved persons but all of Cudjoe's followers were bitter because he had sold out to the authoritarian rulers. He points out that as a result of the leader's treacherous action, angry members of his group as well as enslaved persons formulated plans to neutralize the effects of the treaty. Among these were some of Cudjoe's high-ranking men, who contacted enslaved persons on neighbouring plantations and incited them to revolt. Cudjoe dealt with his own dissenters severely and sent four ringleaders to the governor. The colonial judiciary condemned two of them to death, and sentenced two others to transportation. However, as an act of clemency they pardoned them and sent them back to Cudjoe, who in turn executed the first two and sent the other two back to the governor to have them exiled. The governor complied with his request (Patterson 1979, 273).

Palmares might have saved itself from crushing defeat and destruction had all its leaders and rank-and-file members accepted the treaty struck in 1678 between Ganga-Zumba and the authoritarian state. But the treaty was humiliating to a large proportion of the population, since it sought to return most of them to slavery. Many residents of the confederation, though born into slavery, had lived most of their lives as free people. More independent leaders, notably Zumbi, the king's nephew, who had refused to capitulate to

Figure 31. *Zumbi of Palmares* by Manuel Victor

the forces of oppression, utterly rejected the treaty. As it was, Ganga-Zumba was assassinated two years after the treaty was signed, and Zumbi, his successor, simply refused to carry out its terms (Mattoso 1979, 139). As noted earlier, in a series of military encounters in 1694–95 between the two inveterate enemies, the brave warriors of Palmares were overcome, their cities sacked and their inhabitants dispersed. In 1695 a former inhabitant of the confederation betrayed Zumbi's hideout, leading to his capture and decapitation by the authoritarian regime. It took two years for Domingos Jorge Velho to engineer the ultimate defeat of the confederation. In the final assault on the capital, some four hundred people are said to have lost their lives, and another five hundred were captured (Kent 1979, 186–87). It is clear that most of the twenty to thirty thousand Palmarinos who constituted the confederation were not killed or captured. Karasch (1987, 312n29) points out that the Palmares *mocambos* still "preoccupied" the attention of slaveholders in Pernambuco and Alagôas in the nineteenth century. This strongly suggests that either all the *mocambos* that made up the confederation had not been destroyed in the late seventeenth century or, perhaps more correctly, that refugees from the confederation established new *mocaombos* or rebuilt the old ones. Conrad (1983, 377) points out that folk festivals in various parts of Alagôas kept the memory, and perhaps some of the spirit, of Palmares alive into the twentieth century.

In 1655 a group of Maroons in the mountains of the Dominican Republic refused to accept the government's offer of formal recognition of their freedom in return for assisting in the colony's defence against a British force under Oliver Cromwell. They took this decision to their ultimate detriment, for a little over a decade later an expeditionary force wiped them out (Larrazábal Blanco 1998, 148). In the 1730s negotiations between the Colombian authorities and El Castigo *palenque* fell through because the *palenqueros* refused to agree to stop accepting new runaways and to allow a colonial magistrate to reside among them (McFarlane 1986, 135). According to McFarlane (ibid.), no evidence exists to suggest that Maroons in Colombia acted as state auxiliaries in the apprehension of runaways, and negotiated agreements between the colonial state and the Maroon polities were rare. In Suriname, in the late eighteenth century, Boni, Baron and Jolicoeur fought bitterly against the colonial government rather than capitulate to superior forces numerically and technologically, and have become major nationalist figures in that country today (De Kom 1971, 75). Thoden van Velzen (1995, 112) refers to them as "freedom fighters".

None of the Maroon groups in Haiti (as distinct from the Dominican Republic) signed a peace treaty, though Le Maniel Maroons came close to doing so. This, plus the fact that a large number of them participated in the War of Independence (see below), has spawned a strong school of modern, nationalistic Haitians who insist that the Maroon was an "avenger of his race", the *maquisard* (guerrilla) of Haitian proto-nationalist resistance to oppression (Manigat 1977, 485, 486).

We have perhaps belaboured the point about Maroon leaders who refused to make agreements with their enemies, in order to refute the widely held view that most of them capitulated when they had a chance to do so peacefully, even if this meant betraying their followers. The reality is that if we take the sum of all the Maroon treaties, these would have embraced only a relatively small number of the thousands of Maroons. The vast majority of Maroons lived and died without making such treaties, even at times when their opponents would have been keen to do so.[13] This considerably strengthens the argument of those who insist that, on the whole, the Maroons were freedom fighters.

MAROON REVOLUTIONARY CONSCIOUSNESS

The second charge levelled against the Maroons is that they did little or nothing to overthrow the system of slavery as a whole. While there may be some measure of truth in this assertion, the circumstance of Maroon existence would hardly have allowed the majority of them to think, much less to operate, in such global terms. Few, if any, Maroon communities were in a position to wage a general anti-slavery or anti-colonial struggle. Many found themselves in a constant state of fight and flight to maintain their integrity, sometimes against huge military odds. Most of them did not (and perhaps could not) forge the kind of relationship with their Black brethren that allowed for revolutionary action on a national scale. Richard and Sally Price (1988, xxii) inform us that "the Maroons against whom Stedman and his comrades fought consisted of a number of very small bands – at the height of their strength no more than a total of several hundred men, women, and children. Organized primarily according to the plantations on which they had served as slaves, these Maroon groups periodically banded together, split apart, and rejoined, depending on the immediate military situation and the shifting alignments of their leaders." Maroon communities generally lacked the weapons and organizational skills to wage all-out war on the slave-holding states. Even if several of the large communities had combined to do so, which would have been a feat in itself, they would have been largely ineffective.

While a particular slaveholding state might have been weak at a specific point in time, it could usually call upon the resources of its "mother" country or on similar slaveholding polities to assist it. This was demonstrated as early as 1548, when enslaved persons in San Pedro, Honduras, revolted against their Spanish overlords. The Spanish dispatched reinforcements from the neighbouring colonies to put down the revolt (Franco 1979, 35). In the 1560s and 1570s the combined assaults of Indians and African Maroons on the White settlements in Mexico had become so lethal that Davidson (1979, 91) describes the situation as one of anarchy. While this description is no doubt an exaggeration, the important point is that the oppressors were not driven out because of assistance from Spain. During the Berbice slave revolt of 1763, the colonial government received assistance not only from the neighbouring colony of Suriname and from the Netherlands (its imperial overlord), but also from Barbados and elsewhere (Thompson 1987, 163, 166, 172). Several such examples might be cited.[14]

It might be argued that some Maroon communities had a wider vision of freedom and made efforts to translate it into reality through a process of depredations and attrition rather than all-out warfare. We cannot be sure of this, because we usually perceive Maroon thoughts obliquely, through the prism of their adversaries, whose records are virtually the only extant ones. Until much more work is done on Maroon societies, it will be difficult, if not impossible, to trace the development of Maroon revolutionary consciousness in the Americas generally, or in any particular jurisdiction, over a long period of time. However, it seems that as time passed many Maroons developed a growing consciousness of the need not simply to strike a blow for their own freedom and sometimes that of enslaved persons on neighbouring plantations, but to overthrow the slavery system (and colonialism) as a whole. Certainly, recent literature on Brazil, Haiti, Venezuela and elsewhere suggests a growing revolutionary consciousness among Maroons (and enslaved persons) from the late eighteenth century. The extent to which they were aware of the growing opposition to and debates about the slavery system in Europe and the United States is unknown, but there was a curious parallelism between these debates and verbal attacks on the one hand, and the widening circle of Maroon physical assaults on the other.

In Haiti, the activities of the charismatic Makandal, for eighteen years around the mid-eighteenth century, have become legendary. He is alleged to have had a "school" of poisoners, to have planned to wipe out a large number of Whites by poisoning the water courses, and to have caused the plantocracy endless bother (Manigat 1977, 496; Hall 1971, 41). More significantly, legend states that on the eve of the servile revolution in that country in 1791, Toussaint Louverture established links with the notable Maroon leaders Jean-François, Boukman, Biassou and Jeannot (Fouchard 1972, 160). In fact, Fouchard (ibid., 358) asserts that the Maroons organized the rebellion, establishing the necessary liaisons with the various groups and distributing arms and passwords.

Some Venezuelan writers extol Guillermo Rivas as a Maroon leader who sought to free as many enslaved persons as possible and chastise the enslavers. Indeed, he was widely viewed as a liberator not only of enslaved Africans but also of oppressed Indians and free Coloureds, from whom he received material and military support. Among those who formed his leadership core were Juan Joseph, a free Zambo; Vincente Sosa, a free Moreno; and Isidro Rengifo, an Indian (Brito Figueroa 1985, 215–17).

Brito Figueroa (1985, 210) argues that the Maroon leader Andresote, also of Venezuela, had set his sword against slavery as a whole, and that was why he was so loved by the mass of the enslaved population; that was also why the colonial authorities were so determined to destroy him. The writer (ibid., 206) bewails the fact that most Venezuelan historians seem not to appreciate the critical link between the struggles of enslaved persons against both slavery and colonialism, and the later independence struggles at the national level. Acosta Saignes (1979, 67; see also 73) declares that the experience of these Maroons and their particular forms of resistance should be viewed as an important factor in the involvement of the masses in the national independence war. To him, Brito Figueroa, García and a few others, that link became (or should have become) evident when, shortly after the war began in 1810, numerous Maroon communities joined the other forces of national liberation.

A similar observation might be made in respect of the Mexican Maroons who joined the independence movement that began in 1810 and, after a long and intense struggle, ended in victory for the freedom fighters in 1821 and the abolition of slavery eight years later (Pereira 1994, 103; Naveda Chávez-Hita 1987, 154–56). Likewise, in Cuba many Maroons in the eastern region threw in their lot with the Liberation Army in the island's first war of independence from Spain (1868–78), the army leaders having recognized them as free persons (Franco 1979, 48; La Rosa Corzo 2003, 12). In all these cases the struggle for independence benefited both directly and indirectly from Maroon manpower, bravery and experience in guerrilla warfare. In the confused atmosphere of the times, it was difficult to distinguish clearly between actual Maroons and insurgents. It is useful to recall Patterson's (1979, 279) observation that *marronage* and armed revolt were inextricably linked in the history of the Americas.

The United States stands virtually alone in not recognizing the role that Maroons, and enslaved persons generally, played in the war of national liberation. Many slaveholders joined the revolutionary vanguard and never thought of liberating their enslaved charges. A few enslaved persons who fought on the winning side in the war received their freedom (Franklin 1980, 157; Quarles 1969, 56), but the slavery system actually expanded and intensified in the southern states in the postwar years. It is therefore not surprising that, up to the present, Maroons are not viewed as freedom fighters in the country that continues to honour slaveholders like George Washington and Thomas Jefferson, and Indian-killers like Andrew Jackson, as national heroes.

The wars of independence fuelled the cause of the enslaved population by giving new sharpness to their ideology of freedom, and by placing large quantities of firearms at their disposal that they could use after the wars were over. Most authorities seem to agree that the problem of *marronage* became more large-scale and urgent in the post-independence phase of the slaveholding state's history. In most jurisdictions, the wars had resulted in many enslaved person taking advantage of the dislocation, and sometimes chaos, that engulfed the society to make a bid for freedom. In vain did the slaveholders attempt to arrest this tendency when the wars ended, and to return the so-called fugitives to slavery. This happened, for instance, in Brazil, Venezuela, Mexico, Peru and Colombia. Moreover, the wide-scale insurgency associated with *marronage* and armed revolts on the plantations in the last phase of slavery helped in a significant way to redesign the political, economic and social landscape, and to bring the institution to its knees. It devastated certain geographical areas, adversely affected the economies of much larger areas, and resulted in the erosion of the social mechanism of control of the servile population,[15] thus forcing the pace of emancipation.

Fouchard, in his excellent book, refers to the Haitian Maroons as the "maroons of liberty". Esteban Deive (1989, 16), in contrast, rejects the notion that Maroons possessed a nationalistic and revolutionary consciousness. He argues that the economic, juridico-political and sociocultural subjugation in which the enslaved people were kept did not permit them as a social class to arrive at a broad and critical understanding of their situation. The state of dependency, as well as the values and rules of behaviour imposed by the dominant class and constantly reinforced by a subtle but conscious process of deculturation and socialization, prevented them from reaching a political understanding of their deprivation and of the revolutionary struggle.

In the case of Haiti, Esteban Deive (ibid., 16–17) submits that "the crisis of slavery" originated as a struggle between the rich Whites, poor Whites, free Coloureds and free Blacks for political, economic and social justice among the free people, and "the independence of the colony", but not as an assault on the slavery system itself. The enslaved people latched on to this process and were able to achieve their freedom. Moreover, military leaders such as Toussaint Louverture and Jean-Jacques Dessalines were regular combatants and not Maroons. This interpretation of the revolution is seriously at odds with that of a number of recent scholars, notably Fouchard (1972, 160, 358–59) who, as noted above, declares that the Maroons played the leading part in organizing its early stages.

While the free people struck the first blows in what was to become a titanic conflict leading to the end of colonial slavery and colonialism itself, it is clearly a stretch to suggest that these people actively pursued independence from France (though Esteban Deive might be using the term "independence" here to mean a measure of internal self-government). It was the enslaved people, now transformed into insurgents, along with the Maroons who moved the struggle into its independence phase and created a revolution in the former colony. Fouchard (1972, 359, 365n1) claims that five years before the revolt broke out, Jérôme, a Coloured person turned Maroon, was preaching independence to his followers and distributing batons made of lead. Indeed, he insists that long before the 1791 uprising, a large number of Maroon leaders had visions of partial or full independence for the country. This is what Fouchard (ibid., 455–56) has to say:

> We are not the ones who are doing the talking. These details emanate solely from the colonists' own reports in their correspondence or from the writings of their own colonial historians. It is only through these sources that, from the first rebellion in Bahoruco up to the general uprising of the slaves, we have seen file past, torch in hand, the maroons of liberty, and their bold and courageous leaders: 1679 Padrejean "whose intention was to cut the throats of all the whites in the North-West"; 1691 Janot Marin and Georges Dollot called Pierrot who "nourished the thought of massacring all the whites in the Port-de-Paix quarter, women and children sucking at the breast". 1719 the black Michel at Bahoruco, 1724, One-legged Colas. 1730 Plymouth, 1734 Polydor, 1747, Pompée who had the same aspiration of liberty for all. 1757 the black Médor who declared that he was organizing a mass poisoning with the same objective of "obtaining liberty". 1758 Macandal who "had agents in all points of the colony and projected the elimination of all the whites"; around 1775 Noël, Télémaque Canga, Isaac and Pyrrhus Candide in the North, Jacques at Cul-de-Sac. 1785 Santiague, Philippe, Kébinda, at Bahoruco. 1786 Jérôme called Poteau who at Marmelade "preached independence" and organized gatherings of blacks. 1787 Yaya at Trou or finally Boukman, the most glorious of the lot, who entered history through the decisive revolt in 1791.[16]

Though the record of Haiti is writ large, it is not unique in terms of Blacks' conception of a larger independence than what a few of them enjoyed. In Peru, as early as the mid-sixteenth century the Maroons were said to have appointed a king and to have planned to overthrow the Spanish government. Whether the idea was realistic is not germane here; the important point is that they were able to conceive of such a grandiose scheme. The colonial government took the rumour seriously enough to send against them a strong force of 120 men under the command of Juan de Barbarán, a former *conquistador*, to wipe them out (Bowser 1974, 188; Lockhart 1968, 189; Guillot 1961, 254–55). The Berbice revolt in 1763, though spontaneous, clearly demonstrated that at one point the insurgents were bent on taking over the entire colony (Thompson 1987, 158, 169–70; Lichtveld and Voorhoeve 1958, 81–84).

The aborted revolt in Venezuela in 1749 revealed a large-scale plot involving Maroons, enslaved persons on the plantations, and large numbers of Indians disaffected through having to pay tribute and being subjected to other exactions by the colonial authorities. Their intention was to overthrow the colonial regime in Caracas and neighbouring areas, abolish slavery and set up a government of the liberated people. The colonial authorities reckoned that the plot sought to embrace some thirty thousand to forty thousand enslaved persons. Under torture, a servile informant revealed that the enslaved persons intended to kill the White men and women, take over the royal palace and appoint Eusebio Guzmán, a Black man, as governor (Brito Figueroa 1985, 211–13).

In the case of Bahia, Carneiro (1946, 9–10) asserts that the eight Muslim-organized revolts, or plots to revolt, between 1807 and 1835 had as two of their main objectives to slay all the Whites and take over power. The Urubu *mocambo* uprising that took place there in 1826, in alliance with the enslaved people, indicated that extensive and careful planning had gone into the preparations. Zeferina, a captured female Maroon, testified after a military expedition had destroyed the *mocambo* that they had planned the uprising for Christmas Eve, when the Maroons expected several enslaved persons from Salvador to join them. They intended to kill the Whites, set free the enslaved persons and assume control of the regional capital. Maroons, enslaved persons and freed persons were all involved in the plan (Reis 1993, 55–57). In the Bahia uprising in 1835, a letter that the authorities seized indicated that the insurgents intended to kill "everyone in white man's land", which Reis (1993, 121) informs us meant not only Whites but also Mulattos and locally born Blacks; in other words, "those born in Brazil". In the United States, Jordan (1968, 114) declares:

> Nearly universally, Negro conspiracies were regarded (and perhaps there was some real basis for the view) as aiming not only at freedom but Negro mastery. Slave conspiracies were often said to have plotted taking over the entire locality for themselves and to have intended "utter extirpation" of most or all of the white people. The colonists seemed incapable of envisaging a Negro revolt which would end with the blacks gaining freedom and nothing more. A successful insurrection loomed as total destruction, as the irretrievable loss of all that white men had won in America – which, of course, was America itself.

While all except one of these plans (Haiti, 1791–1804) were aborted at either the planning or the early execution stage, they nevertheless demonstrate that it was quite possible for enslaved persons and Maroons to develop revolutionary consciousness at the regional and national levels. McFarlane (1986, 149) supports this view strongly when he asserts that some forms of *marronage* often envisaged not only a complete collective break from enslavement for those involved in flight, but also an end to slavery as the best guarantee of their own freedom. They therefore sought alliances with other enslaved persons in insurrections to achieve such an object. We cannot, therefore, accept *carte blanche* Esteban Deive's statements about the lack of revolutionary consciousness of enslaved people, or La Rosa Corzo's (2003, 24) assertion that the Maroons in Cuba never thought of overthrowing the slavery system – that their objective was to gain freedom but their condition "kept them from developing a collective awareness and social goals that were beyond their mission as a class". If by "collective awareness" he means an awareness that embraced all or nearly all enslaved persons, clearly he is correct. But this would reduce the issue to absurdity, since no revolution ever begins with such a level of awareness; rather, it starts with an awareness of a few people and, as it progresses, embraces a wider circle.

Conclusion

I paid my duty
To live here peacefully
Tell them slavery done.
I paid my duty
To practice my culture
Tell them slavery done.
I paid my duty
For my children's future
Tell them slavery done.
I paid my duty
To live here forever
Tell them slavery done.
  – Barbadian calypsonian Tony "Commander" Grazette (1985)

Conflicts between Maroons and slaveholders were just one mutation of the virus that ate away at the body politic of the slaveholding states. Relations between Europeans and other peoples in the Americas were characterized by violence born of systems of oppression and the reactions of the oppressed to those systems. Slavery, with *marronage* and the brutal hammer of civil strife as its corollaries, involved the wanton loss of human life. Military expeditions against Maroons saw Blacks shot down like animals and Whites slaughtered in revenge, both for maintaining slavery and for attacking Maroon settlements. The violence destroyed whole families on both sides. All of this happened because one group of people decided that another group should not enjoy the freedoms common to humanity, and oppressed them in the interest of Mammon. The inevitable unfortunate consequences of large-scale violence always leave deep scars on the body politic. But sometimes there is no route to freedom for oppressed peoples except through the portals of violence.

The uplifting aspect of the Maroons' story is that it describes a group of people who determined not to be killed off completely as a people and adopted numerous aggressive and defensive strategies, first to survive and then to improve the quality of their lives. Over time they created a culture of their own that, while bearing resemblances to those of Europe and Africa, was distinctly Maroon in its combination of features, including the triumphs, tragedies and mythologies that inform human societies.

The significance of *marronage* transcended the numerical size of the Maroon community as a whole, for Maroon activities had an impact on all groups and all aspects of life, especially in the slave plantation societies. It created more than a headache (Flores Galindo 1984, 117–18) for these societies. It was the prime instrument that moved the state authorities, on the one hand, to pass the most draconian pieces of legislation in the history of the Americas, and, on the other, to recognize Blacks (at least, some of them) as persons entitled to their freedom, not simply recipients of freedom through the largesse of the state or the slaveholder.

Maroons were thinking, planning people. They showed considerable ingenuity in the organization of their communities, which included defensive structures, agricultural plots, and political, judicial and social systems. They showed that enslaved people were not the inanimate, robotic creatures that Charlevoix tried to make them out to be: "[T]hey are robots, whose springs it is necessary to rewind each time that one wants them to move" (Fouchard 1972, 35). Certainly they needed no rewinding of their springs when it came to *marronage*. They won sneaking admiration from many a military leader who went up against them, not the least of whom was John Stedman.

A few writers have raised the question of whether the Maroons should be classified as "social bandits" – in the same way, for instance, that many have regarded the more mythical Robin Hood and Zorro, or the more flesh-and-blood "bandits" that operated in Cuba and other Latin American countries from the late nineteenth century.[1] Schwartz (1979, 212) apparently accepts that this view has some merit. He asserts that "in a slave society the ideological basis of social banditry varied from its classic form of archaic peasant protest" but "the reactions of Brazilian slaves and Brazilian peasants against oppressive social and economic order were strikingly similar". He also opines that Maroon depredations in that country "foreshadowed" the social banditry of the post-colonial period. Aguirre (1993, 264–65) accepts that Maroon attacks on members of the wealthy class resulted in the acquisition of jewellery, other valuable objects, money and a great deal of unwrought gold, and that these were instances of the poor robbing the rich, leading to somewhat less inequitable social distribution of material resources. However, he does not view Maroons as a group as social bandits. The fact is that many of them also divested poor Whites, Blacks, Indians and other oppressed groups of their resources, and they did not generally share their booty with enslaved persons, or only did so in exchange for other items. At the juridical level, the situation is less clear, since a number of Maroon leaders – most notably Guillermo Rivas of Venezuela – punished slaveholders for their treatment of their enslaved charges. In this sense they may be said to have been meting out a measure of social justice ("popular justice") that was largely absent from slave societies.[2]

Though he does not accept Schwartz's view, Flory (1979, 127) puts forward the equally interesting suggestion that, while the authoritarian states regarded Maroons as outlaws, various groups, depending upon their vested interests, might have considered them otherwise. He writes:

> It remains true that all quilombos existed outside the law and were potentially vulnerable to its sanctions. But in the Latin American context this need not have placed the "outlaw" in categorical conflict with the postulates of society. To be an outlaw in this sense simply meant that one was a prospective victim of arbitrary and selective enforcement determined by the class needs of those who controlled the legal system. The runaway slave community shared this vulnerability with drifters, squatters, and all the free poor who existed at the sufferance of their social superiors. With these obscure and ill-defined social types, it appears, the runaways also shared markets, news, ambitions and rivalries.[3]

Whether Maroons were outlaws or not, their activities had a major impact on the financial life of the slaveholding states and on individual slaveholders. As Freehling (2002, 7) observes, in a curious sense Maroons were runaway investments. Especially in the large states, the governments and planters repeatedly cried out against the cost entailed in catching or eliminating these runaways: the need to bivouac mercenary or specially posted government troops from Europe to give defensive and offensive support to the state; military installations that often included forts in strategic places; bounties that had to be paid for the capture of the runaways, and sometimes compensation to owners for others who were judicially executed; loss through death, injury, desertion and manumission of enslaved persons who joined the European-led forces as combatants, scouts and baggage carriers; loss of White personnel through military expeditions against Maroons and counter-attacks by the latter; reduced work output by enslaved persons who, the enslavers feared, would desert if they pushed them too hard; and extra taxes that often overburdened those plantations that were already tottering on the brink of financial collapse. Added to these costs were losses due to Maroons' seizure of enslaved persons on the plantations, or encouragement of them to desert; the destruction of plantation and other buildings, machinery, animals and crops (and also the carrying away of moveable items, especially tools, household utensils and firearms); Maroon occupation – even if temporary – of some of the outlying plantations; high levels of planter absenteeism; depreciating value of plantations, and difficulty in attracting purchasers; and reluctance of merchants to give credit to plantation owners whose property was deemed to be particularly vulnerable to Maroon attacks. Some governments declared that their treasuries were virtually or actually bankrupt, although they had taxed the colonists to the hilt to meet the exigencies of the Maroon wars. Individual planters declared bankruptcy and in the last resort put their properties into the hands of their creditors or simply abandoned them altogether (Davidson 1979, 98–99; Conrad 1983, 362).

Maroon communities clearly offered a much higher quality of life than that on the plantations, and, some scholars might argue, even than that enjoyed by the vast majority of free Blacks in the slaveholding societies. One thing is clear: the Maroons possessed a strong sense of pride in the freedom that they had recaptured through their own initiative. They were fully aware that this freedom was circumscribed by a number of factors, including the need to be always vigilant against military expeditions sent against them, and the fact that they could not move freely within the compass of the wider colonial state. On the other hand, they could order their lives without the daily round of abuse characteristic of slave society, practise their religion and other aspects of their culture with less hindrance and raise their children in a free environment.

However, the virtues of life in the *palenques* and *mocambos* must not be exaggerated. Maroon life was hard, and a few people quitted it and returned to their erstwhile overlords because they could not endure it. Moreover, most scholars seem to believe that the vast majority of Maroon settlements were destroyed at some point in their existence by military expeditions and, in fact, that they had a rather ephemeral existence. More careful work needs to be done in this area. A review of current writings on the subject leads to the conclusion that relatively few Maroons were caught in the numerous raids that the slaveholding fraternity carried out against the settlements, and that the displaced persons either found refuge in other settlements, repaired the ravaged ones or built new ones. La Rosa Corzo's study, while claiming that the colonial state in Cuba was largely successful in wiping out the Maroon communities in Cuba by the mid-nineteenth century, also makes it clear that there were a large number of small communities (with twenty or fewer inhabitants) that the expeditionary forces came across only by chance or through informants. We will never know how many eluded detection, and further archaeological work and the collection and analysis of oral traditions are necessary before it will be possible to ascertain the location of some that survived until the end of slavery. This is particularly true in Brazil (especially Amazonia), Mexico, Cuba, Venezuela and the United States.

Of course, for those Maroon communities that were wiped out or substantially disfigured by expeditions, life for their survivors had to start all over again. Many of them were re-enslaved, sometimes after being wounded in battle or being severely whipped or losing body parts though judicial sentence. Invariably, Maroon families were broken up during such encounters, through deaths, escape of only some family members, sale to various plantations or abroad and so on. Many Africans must have gone through at least three experiences of seeing their families separated – at the time of capture in Africa or sale in the Americas, during escape to Maroon settlements and at the time of recapture and re-enslavement. Slaveholders sometimes experienced an increase in their servile population as a result of capture, since the colonial laws regarded children born in Maroon communities as the property of the enslaver who "owned" their mother. At other times, when the maternity of the child could not be established, or when the authoritarian state made special arrangements with Maroon-hunting expeditions, the children (or any Maroons whose overlords could not be ascertained) were treated as booty belonging to their captors. The choice between re-enslavement and death with some measure of dignity explains why Maroons fought so hard to elude capture, and why many of them committed suicide, sometimes in large groups.

Runaways who made it to safe havens – usually states that had abolished slavery and refused to extradite them – immediately experienced a marked difference in their emotional and psychological condition, and often in their physical circumstances, even where they were forced to work as common drudges. In the first flush of freedom, William Wells Brown (1999, 713) exclaimed, "I was no more a chattel, but a man!"; and again, "The fact that I was a freeman – could walk, talk, eat and sleep as a man, and no one to stand over me with the blood-clotted cowhide – all this made me feel that I was not myself."[4] This is what Frederick Douglass (1973, 111) experienced when he arrived in New Bedford via New York, after escaping from slavery in Baltimore, Maryland:

> In the afternoon of the day when I reached New Bedford, I visited the wharves, to take a view of the shipping. . . . [A]lmost everybody seemed to be at work, but noiselessly so, compared with what I had been accustomed to in Baltimore. There were no loud songs heard from those engaged in loading and unloading ships. I heard no deep oaths or horrid curses on the laborer. I saw no whipping of men; but all seemed to go smoothly on. Every man appeared to understand his work, and went at it with a sober, yet cheerful earnestness, which betokened the deep interest which he felt in what he was doing, as well as a sense of his own dignity as a man. To me this looked exceedingly strange.

There is no denying that the free states were not characterized by the sound of the cracking whip; the cries of people being broken and disfigured for life; the sight of heads and other body parts displayed on poles along the highways, in the public squares and elsewhere; the agony of people being wrested from their families, never to be seen by them again; the apprehension of Whites who had to walk about armed and often in groups for safety; an atmosphere charged with tension and fear of both the known and the unknown. Freedom did not bring material or social equality to Black persons, for they were discriminated against in the free states in various ways. Post-emancipation societies experienced their own traumas and new kinds of revolts, riots and other forms of worker protest. But they did not have to face *marronage* with its troublesome consequences for everyone in the society.

In an otherwise very interesting article, Schweninger (2002, 19) comes to the strange conclusion that "If the great majority of runaways did not die at the hands of a group of White planters led by [a] slave (who later received his freedom for his betrayal) theirs was largely a futile effort." Her conclusion overlooks the lethal role that Maroons played in the ultimate overthrow of the system of slavery by making life miserable and short for a large number of enslavers. It is clear that without the continuous resistance of enslaved persons, of whom the Maroons were at the top of the class, the White abolitionists would have been largely ineffective, and slavery would certainly not have been abolished in the nineteenth century, even when the slave mode of production had become anachronistic. Slavery would have remained an important social system throughout the Americas. During the process of liberation, the enslavers moved from considering the physical elimination of the insurgents as the final solution to the Maroon problem to accepting treaties that guaranteed their freedom as the final solution. The pressure created by new groups of Maroons and other insurgents ensured that there could only be one ultimate solution: freedom for all enslaved persons.

Maroons wrote their names and deeds collectively, and sometimes individually, into the historical record. They left marks on the physical and temporal landscape as tributes to their struggles for freedom. Their persistence in the face of overwhelming material and technological odds speaks eloquently to the triumph of courage over steel and freedom over bondage. It was their love of life that caused them to face death with fortitude. Davidson's words (1979, 100), *mutatis mutandis* for other societies in the Americas, seem particularly appropriate:

> Slave resistance in Mexico is more than just another chapter in the Negroes' long struggle for freedom and justice. In the context of Mexican social history it illustrates the interplay of diverse races and cultures that makes that history one of the most complex and fascinating in the New World.

Notes

INTRODUCTION

1. Price and Price (1988, xxi); Price (1983a, 74–75); Escalante (1979, 79).
2. Actually, that honour probably belongs to Santiago del Principe, founded around 1580 (De la Guardia 1977, 94–97).
3. For further references to the Maroons as former enslaved persons see Knight (1999, vii) and Zips (1999, 11, 109).
4. As far as possible, this study employs the modern names by which the former colonies were known. For instance, instead of using "Hispaniola" or "Santo Domingo" I generally use "Dominican Republic"; similarly, instead of "St Domingue" I use "Haiti".
5. Brito Figueroa (1985, 205) also complains about the failure of Venezuelan historians to accord enslaved persons the place that they deserve in the social history of the country, not least in respect of their struggles for freedom.

CHAPTER 1

1. See chapter 5 for specific discussion of punishments meted out to Maroons.
2. Thompson (1987, 146); Price (1983b, 1–2, 14–15); Peytraud (1897, 343); Esteban Deive (1989, 64); Aptheker (1979, 158–59); Campbell (1990, 22, 27). Governor Mauricius of Suriname employed the term *hydra* to describe the emergence of new Maroon groups after the destruction of the old ones. Lockhart and Schwartz's (1983, 220) comment about Brazil is relevant for all slave societies: "[W]hen a village was destroyed a few survivors always seemed to escape and a new community would spring up, soon to be joined by additional newly escaped slaves" (see also Villaverde 1982, 99).
3. For instance, in 1580 the Audiencia of Panama spoke of the expedition of Don Gonzalo Ronquillo as "the war against the black Maroons" (De la Guardia 1977, 94, see also 96). Two officials in Brazil spoke about the conflict against Palmares as "a cruel war" and "a crude war" (Carneiro 1946, 54, 109).
4. Tannenbaum (1992, 100) wrote that "[e]ndowing the slave with a moral personality

before emancipation, before he achieved a legal equality, made the transition from slavery to freedom easy, and his incorporation into the free community natural".

5. In this instance, of course, it was all classes of the Coloured population (rich, middling and poor) who joined the fight for social equality.

6. According to Porter (1932, 319), Douglass was "the son of an unknown father and Harriet Bailey, a slave who had also some Indian blood".

7. Some writers see this as a "prophetic" statement concerning Toussaint Louverture, who became the chief leader of the Blacks during the Haitian revolt in the 1790s that eventually brought about an end to slavery and colonialism in the country.

8. Mathurin (1975, 24) also states that in 1791 the workhouse in Morant Bay, Jamaica, held a person described as "a little hump-backed old woman".

9. Freyre (1963, 131) goes on to explain that the others would have died or run away.

10. They were generally regarded as Africans, though some people thought that they were Indians (Larrazábal Blanco 1998, 164–67).

11. The term was first applied in Spanish America to cattle that had escaped into the wilds, and then to Indians who had absconded. The Spanish drew a distinction between "domesticated Indians" (*indios mansos*) and "wild or maroon Indians" (*indios bravos o cimarrónes*) (Knight 1999, vii; Peréz de la Riva 1979, 50). For further discussion of the origin of the term, see Arrom and García Arévalo (1986, 15–30); Esteban Deivc (1989, 11–12); Fouchard (1972, 381–82).

12. Zips (1999, 37), in an overall interesting study of the Jamaican Maroons, highlights the physical, psychological and emotional factors that impelled enslaved persons to become Maroons, and places too little stress on the sheer love of freedom that caused them to do so.

13. Fouchard (1972, 33–129) outlines the "classic causes" of *marronage*.

14. On the matter of a small elite dominating a large group of people for a long time, see Philip Mason's *Patterns of Dominance* (1970).

15. House of Commons, "Mr. Gannon's Report on the Condition of Apprenticed Africans", *British Parliamentary Papers*, 1826–27, 22 (355): 39.

CHAPTER 2

1. This is reminiscent of Fouchard's (1972, 151) statement about "an imperious desire for freedom" that many enslaved persons felt and that transformed them into Maroons.

2. It was first published under the Spanish title *Biografía de un Cimarrón*.

3. William Wells Brown (1999, 684) describes the whip with which his mother was punished in this way: "The handle was about three feet long, with the butt-end filled with lead, and the lash six or seven feet in length, made of cowhide, with platted wire on the end of it."

4. *Narrative of the Life of Frederick Douglass* (1845), and *My Bondage and My Freedom* (1855).

5. Some confusion exists about the Tabacal and Matudere settlements, and also the identities of Domingo Padilla and Domingo Criollo. Borrego Plá (1973, 86) and Navarrete (2003, 96, 103) agree that the two settlements were one and the same under different names; Landers (2000a, 38, 51n27) is less explicit on the point. Other writers treat them as separate settlements. Landers (2000a, 39, 41) states that Domingo Padilla and Domingo Criollo were the same person, that his father came from Angola, and that he was captain over the Matudere settlement, but other writers view the two names as belonging to separate individuals and sometimes place Domingo Criollo as leader over different settlements (see Romero Jaramillo 2000; Llano Isaza 2002; Friedemann 1998). According to Navarrete (2003, 97n169), certain documents refer to Domingo Criollo as Domingo Angola and state that he led the Magdalena *palenque*. It is possible that this confusion arises because the group of settlements in the Sierras de María might have recognized an overall leader in much the same way as Palmares, but this point has not been fully established. Navarrete (2003, 108, 115–16), however, asserts that Domingo Criollo was *caudillo* of the Sierras de María and Magdalena *palenques* (based on a statement to that effect attributed to a captured Maroon from one of the settlements), and that his authority probably extended to those of San Miguel, Arenal, Duanga (Luanga), Joyanca, Sanagual, Arroyo Piñuela, María Angola, María Embuyla, and Manuel Mula (Manuela Embuyla?).

6. There is some lack of clarity among various writers about the use of the term *Bahoruco*. Geographically, it relates to a mountainous area on the border between Haiti and the Dominican Republic. From the earliest days of colonization, Maroon groups made their homes in this area (Esteban Deive 1989, 12), but many writers referred to the most celebrated of the groups as Le Maniel. Unfortunately, most writers seem to employ the terms *Le Maniel* and *Bahoruco* interchangeably (see, for instance, Debien 1974, 1979; Debbasch 1979). The problem is compounded by the fact that the term *manieles* is sometimes used to refer to Maroon communities in general (Esteban Deive 1989, 14). Except when referring to the late eighteenth century (French records from that period consistently use *Le Maniel* for a specific group of Maroons), in the interest of consistency I employ the term *Bahoruco*. Another problem is that some authors speak of Le Maniel community as existing in St Domingue, whereas others locate it in the Dominican Republic. In reality, the group consisted almost exclusively of runaways from Haiti who lived in the largely un-delimited border areas between the two colonies, and who tended to cross over into the Dominican Republic to engage in trade and especially for safety when attacked.

7. The fact that people born in this settlement outnumbered those who had deserted indicates that it was becoming a self-perpetuating community.

8. See also Geggus (1986, 117–18); Karasch (1987, 307); Campbell (1990, 4–5); Moitt (2001, 134–35).

9. Old Nanny Town was taken and occupied by a British force between 1734 and 1735. After the treaty was signed with the British in 1739 a New Nanny Town (subsequently named Moore Town) was built at a different site (Campbell 1990, 164–65; Agorsah 1994, 174).

10. See Tuelon (1973) for a short discussion on this subject.

11. See also Kopytoff (1976a, 90). Campbell (1990, 123) believes that Thicknesse exaggerated her appearance, apparently in terms of the many knives that she wore.

12. Ethnic associations (called *cabildos* or *cabildos de nación* in the Spanish colonies) existed throughout the slaveholding states and were particularly prevalent in Spanish and Portuguese America. For further discussion on this subject, see Bastide (1972, 1978); Ortiz (1984, 1992); Reis (1993); Thornton (1998b); Warner-Lewis (2003).

13. They also united sometimes to plan and execute armed revolts. For instance, in a petition that the slaveholding interests in Bahia sent to the Prince Regent of Portugal in 1814, they pointed out that "[i]t is sometimes argued that they are of different nations and so unable to unite their forces. Well, the opposite has happened in the present revolt. . . . And so it must be, because the desire to free themselves is common to all" (Conrad 1983, 402).

14. Borrego Plá (1973, 39); Campbell (1990, 24–25, 93, 158); Kopytoff (1976b, 38–42); Thompson (1987, 168–69).

15. Fouchard (1972, 150) states that some White people in Haiti took to *marronage*. Pérez de la Riva (1979, 57) cites a Spanish official letter written around the late eighteenth century that indicated that although the *palenques* (*cumbes*) in Cuba consisted mainly of Black runaways, they also sheltered fugitives from justice, criminals, and pirates involved in smuggling and trading, and that in some instances the leaders of *palenques* were Whites or Yucatán Indians.

16. Many enslaved persons in Nombre de Dios, the Isthmus of Darien and Lima took advantage of the presence of enemy fleets along the Colombian and Peruvian coasts to revolt, and some actually assisted in the ventures. Noteworthy examples of this are Francis Drake's and Juan Oxenham's incursions into the Spanish Indies in the last decades of the sixteenth century, and those of William Penn, Robert Venables and Henry Morgan in the seventeenth century. In 1538 Maroons helped the French to sack Havana (Díez Castillo 1981, 4–12, 31–43; Franco 1973, 25–26; 1979, 37, 41; Borrego Plá 1973, 25; De la Guardia 1977, 92–93; Kapsoli 1975, 68; Arrom and García Arévalo 1986, 40n7).

17. Craton (1982, 63, 147–53, 190–94, 204–6); Gargallo (2002, 9–11, 59–67); see also chapter 10. According to Michael Craton (1982, 207), "Fanning out from unhealthful Rattan [Roatan] Island they now number more than 40,000 in twenty-five settlements in Honduras, Belize, and Guatemala, with smaller groups in three other Central

American countries." Their culture has remained deeply African up to the present (Gargallo 2002).

18. In this respect, see Kopytoff's (1976b) interesting article on the subject of Maroon ethnicity. See also Zips (1999, 57, 63–64).

19. See Schuler (1970); Campbell (1990, 156–57, 162); Patterson (1967, 271–73, 276); Long (1774, 2:470).

20. Strictly speaking, the term *British* should be used only from the early eighteenth century, when an Act of Union of 1707 united England and Scotland into a single kingdom. However, I have stretched the term *British* as far as possible to avoid confusion that might otherwise have crept into the text.

21. See also Kent (1970, 334–56).

CHAPTER 3

1. Occasionally, through their wills slaveholders manumitted large numbers of their servile charges – and in rarer instances, all of them. One outstanding example is John Randolph, an American slaveholder, who by will manumitted all his enslaved people, numbering more than four hundred, at his death (Franklin 1980, 158).

2. There is some debate as to whether they deliberately threw themselves from a high rock or fell off it accidentally (Kent 1979, 187). However, it is difficult to believe that such an accident would have happened to so large a number of people.

3. See also Carey (1997, 207).

4. See also Fuentes (1979, 13–14).

5. Thompson (2002b, 218–19); House of Commons, "Copies of the Record of the Proceedings of the Fiscals of Demerara and Berbice in their Capacity of Guardians and Protectors of Slaves . . . from the 1st January 1814," *British Parliamentary Papers*, 1825, 25(476): 13, 25–27, 36–37, 63, 66, 85. Harriet Jacobs (1999, 551) recorded seeing all seven children belonging to an enslaved woman being sold at once. In the woman's anguish she cried out, "Gone! All gone! Why don't God kill me?"

6. In Brazil, Schwartz (1979, 214, 216) writes, "The destruction of virtually every *mocambo* from Palmares to the much smaller hideouts of Bahia and Rio de Janeiro depended to a large extent on Indian troops or auxiliaries"; and again, "Indians remained throughout the colonial period the best weapons against slave resistance."

7. According to Esteban Deive (1989, 41), Fernández de Oviedo, a contemporary chronicler, gives the impression that Enriquillo volunteered to apprehend runaways.

8. See chapter 7 on the use of the term *republic* in relation to Palmares.

9. Fouchard (1972, 365); Moitt (2001, 136); Borrego Plá (1973, 90); Pereira (1994, 102); Bowser (1974, 200); Gautier (1985, 230); Karasch (1987, 310).

10. Quarles (1969, 78) describes the Railroad as "a system of receiving, concealing, and forwarding fugitives".

11. See Hall (1992, 124–38); Esteban Deive (1989, 76, 80); Gautier (1985, 23–31); Romero Jaramillo (1997, 171).

CHAPTER 4

1. See also Aguirre (1993, 256).
2. La Rosa Corzo (2003, 21, 73) makes the astounding statement that Maroon settlements in Cuba carried out only infrequent depredations against the plantations. However, he later demonstrates that this was not the case, especially in the first half of the nineteenth century when such depredations were common (ibid., 98, 117–67).
3. Since 125 of them were either deserters from the French or born to French deserters, although led by Santiago, a Maroon from the Spanish side of the border, it was agreed that the whole group should settle on the French side (Moreau de Saint-Méry 1979, 140).
4. According to the *Shorter Oxford English Dictionary* (1978, 1190), a league varies in different countries but is usually estimated at about 3 miles. La Rosa Corzo (2003, 262) states that the Spanish league is 2.63 miles.
5. Borrego Plá (1973, 26); Mathieu (1982, 89); Arrázola (1967, 56, 57); Navarrete (2003, 64–69).
6. Information on the Suriname Maroons is taken largely from the following works: Beet (1984); De Groot (1975); and Hoogbergen (1985, 1990).
7. See Campbell (1990, 27) for the main clauses of these Articles. Campbell (ibid., 26) refers to them as "the first formal declaration of war against any Maroon group in Jamaica", and argues that the conflict that immediately preceded and succeeded the drafting of the articles should be viewed as the First Maroon War, rather than the wars of the 1730s that are usually assigned that title.
8. Dallas (1803, 1:27).
9. Patterson (1979, 266, 268, 285); Campbell (1990, 40, 41, 69, 84–85).
10. Reis (1993, 43–44) mentions the break-up of a *quilombo* along the Prata River in Brazil after being devastated by a military expedition. There, an originally substantial group of at least three hundred people lost many of its members through deaths and capture in the assault, and the rest decided to form small bands of four or five people to attack Whites and their property. The Maroon group led by Balla in Dominica suffered a similar fate after a lethal attack on it (Atwood 1971, 249–50).
11. Porter (1932, 323 passim); Blassingame (1979, 211); Krogman (1934, 421–23); Mulroy (1993, 2, 7–14).
12. Porter (1951, 260–64); Aptheker (1979, 156); Blassingame (1979, 211–12); Mulroy (1993, 14–15).

13. See also Porter (1943, 390–421).
14. See also Aptheker (1979, 162).
15. See also Porter (1932, 341, 342, 347).
16. The Mexicans referred to the Seminole Maroons as Mascogos (Mulroy 1993, 58). Many of the Seminole Indians eventually returned to the United States (ibid., 87–89).
17. Esteban Deive (1989, 47), a modern writer, estimates the population at that time at around 12,000.
18. A later, far more conservative figure put it at no more than two hundred (Debien 1979, 109).
19. However, in 1734 the leader of a military expedition that entered Nanny Town declared that it contained 127 huts, which he thought could house no more than three hundred souls, one hundred of whom were warriors. The expedition captured only a small number of the inhabitants, though it was a more successful enterprise than previous ones (Campbell 1990, 89–90).
20. See also Conrad (1983, 381).
21. Carneiro (1946, 23) states that between 1644 and 1694 there were sixteen expeditions that are indisputable, two by the Dutch and the others by the Portuguese. However, Anderson (1996, 552) declares that between 1654 and 1678 there were at least twenty expeditions.
22. See also Corro (1951, 17).
23. See also Brito Figueroa (1985, 215–18).
24. Carneiro (1946, 53) suggests that the name Zumbi might have been a sobriquet or an abbreviation of a longer name that signified "god of war", a term that a contemporary writer had attributed to him. Anderson (1996, 545) says that many people in Brazil still revere him as an ancestor and believe that his spirit is "inherently divine and immortal". He also states that "This belief is such that the tercentenary celebrated three hundred years of Zumbi's *immortality.*"
25. See Santos Gomes (2002, 486).
26. See also Brito Figueroa (1985, 216).
27. Maroons elsewhere also occupied abandoned plantations – for instance, in Haiti (Manigat 1977, 495).

CHAPTER 5

1. Bowser (1974, 187–221); Ortiz (1975, 362, 366); La Rosa Corzo (2003, 46–47, 62–72 passim).
2. Debien (1979, 115) suggests that these mounted police probably comprised free Coloureds and, later, enslaved persons who expected to be free.
3. See Thompson (1987, 160–61); Stedman (1988, 82); Campbell (1990, 69).

4. Buckley (1998, 214–47); Esteban Deive (1989, 48); Bowser (1974, 188); Campbell (1990, 40).

5. Patterson (1979, 263–67); Campbell (1990, 37, 40, 62–66, 86); Buckley (1998, 203–47).

6. Escalante (1979, 80); Stedman (1988, 81); Palmer (1976, 123); Esteban Deive (1989, 52–53); Bowser (1974, 212); Fouchard (1972, 367–68); Reis (1993, 41); La Rosa Corzo (2003, 4).

7. Black Shots were enslaved persons whom the Jamaican government recruited to assist in tracking down Maroons. Campbell (1990, 68–69, see also 73, 76, 81, 83–84); Patterson (1979, 265–66).

8. For a more detailed description of the Black Rangers, see Stedman (1988, 82).

9. Barnet (1996, 39); Davidson (1979, 95–96); Aptheker (1979, 154); Stampp (1968, 61); Fuentes (1979, 14); Campbell (1990, 2, 37); La Rosa Corzo (2003, 108). See Ortiz (1975, 366–68, 377–80) for a more detailed discussion of the use of dogs to hunt down Maroons in the Caribbean.

10. Ortiz (1975, 366–68); Dallas (1803, 2:55–71); Philalethes (1979, 60–63); Campbell (1990, 216).

11. See Franco (1973, 35–36) for a short statement on the terrible bites that bloodhounds inflicted on runaways in the United States.

12. See Campbell (1990, 61–69).

13. Stedman (1988, 99); Thompson (2002b, 196–97); La Rosa Corzo (2003, 85–86); Pinto Vallejos (1998, 188).

14. Thompson (2002b, 195–96); La Rosa Corzo (2003, 85–86); Escalante (1979, 75). La Rosa Corzo (2003, 86) informs us that, according to the regulations in operation in Cuba in 1796, no bounties were paid on runaways who were in such bad condition that their owners refused to redeem them. This must have led to bounty hunters killing such people and bringing in their right ears to collect the state bounty. According to La Rosa Corzo (ibid.), bounties were paid for right ears brought in; however, he also states (p. 97) that the regulations did not allow for bounties on dead runaways. It is possible that the law was changed later.

15. See Pinto Vallejos (1998, 188).

16. Navarrete (2003); Conrad (1983); Ortiz (1975); Frijol (1982); Borrego Plá (1973); Schalkwijk (1994).

17. See also Villaverde (1982, 80).

18. See also Lara (1988, 295–322); Boxer (1963, 170).

19. A similar kind of abuse occurred in Peru (Bowser 1974, 215–16).

20. These laws were based on imperial laws published periodically on the subject, though they were often modified locally as colonial officials deemed appropriate. For imperial laws between 1571 and 1619 see Franco (1973, 10–15).

21. Carneiro (1946, 37); Jordan (1968, 154, 156); Navarette (2003, 49); Stampp (1968, 61); Genovese (1976, 34, 67); León (1924, 10); Zips (1999, 36); Mellafe (1975, 83).

22. Some United States territories, such as Virginia and Georgia, began to prohibit castration as a form of punishment around the mid-eighteenth century (Jordan 1968, 155n38).

23. C.R. Boxer (1962, 171) writes about the treatment of captured Maroons in Brazil that "those Negroes who resisted arrest . . . [were] decapitated and their heads exhibited by the *capitães do mato*".

24. In the late eighteenth century in the Danish West Indies, the law decreed that leaders of runaways were to be pinched thrice with red-hot pincers before being hanged (Lofton 1948, 399).

CHAPTER 6

1. Lewis (1983, 27) notes that Africans brought with them ideologies and aspects of civilization that reinforced their identities in the Americas. Dealing specifically with ethnicity, Campbell (1990, 3) writes, "Among the rich gleanings we have from a study of Maroon societies is the fact that despite ethnic plurality, the cultural commonalities would seem to have taken precedence over particularism. There appears to have existed a kind of 'Africanness' that transcended regionalism, ethnic or linguistic affinities, on which these Maroons based their existence."

2. Franco (1979, 36); Acosta Saignes (1979, 65); Campbell (1990, 49–51); Stedman (1988, 404); Esteban Deive (1989, 37, 74).

3. The fact that each male had a female partner is said to have given it its name, which means "We All Have".

4. Mattoso (1979, 140) gives different details about this *quilombo*. According to her, Atanasio, a *Cafuzo* (mixed Black and Indian), established it in 1821 with enslaved persons who fled with him and survivors from two other *quilombos* that had been destroyed. It evolved into one of the largest Maroon settlements in the country and carried on extensive trade with neighbouring peoples and Dutch Guiana. Its original site was invaded and destroyed in 1823, but its leader managed to escape from custody and establish another *quilombo* elsewhere that endured until 1835. Those who survived the second *quilombo* founded the hamlet of Cidade Maravilha (the "Marvellous City"), which pursued such a peaceful existence that its merchants were allowed to ply their goods downriver without interference by the state authorities.

5. See also Zips (1999, 81).

6. This is how Fincham (1997, 438) describes a Cockpit: "An enclosed hollow in areas of topography showing an 'egg-box' like terrain. Generally, the depressions are polygonal or star-shaped and are contiguous. In Jamaica, cockpits are 50–100 m deep, heavily vegetated and often at least partially fringed with cliffs. [This is] typical of many limestone areas of Jamaica, including The Cockpit Country from which the term is derived."

7. Fouchard (1972, 424) points out that, in fact, the Bahoruco was part of "a Mountain chain going from Fond du Diable, to Sud de Mirebalais, to the eastern extremities of Jacmel towards Morne la Selle reaching into Spanish territory . . . and extends up to the Bahoruco Mountains".

8. See also La Rosa Corzo (2003, 14–15); Marcano Jiménez (2001, 21).

9. See also Hemming (1978, 355); Marcano Jiménez (2001, 51).

10. For a brief statement on washing and cleanliness in an African household, see Equiano (1789, 14–15). Long may well not have recognized the importance of bathing, since in Europe it was long regarded as a health hazard. It was not until around the mid-nineteenth century that the importance to overall health of regular bathing and frequently changing clothes was recognized in Europe and the Americas. For a short discussion on the use of soap in Europe, see Hunt (1999).

11. In spite of all the travails, what caused Domingos Jorge Velho not to attack Palmares at that time was a message recalling him from the campaign to fight a more urgent one against the Janduin group of Tapuia Indians who had risen up against the Portuguese. Following the peace struck with the Janduin in 1692, he resumed his expedition against Palmares and, according to Carneiro (1946, 15, 20–21), suffered defeat at the hands of the Maroons in the initial encounter. However, in 1694 he, along with Sebastián Dias and Bernardo Vieira de Melo, destroyed the state in a campaign that lasted into the following year (Hemming 1978, 356–69; Carneiro 1946, 15–16).

12. For a description of the demanding conditions that Francisco Estévez and his fellow *rancheadores* withstood to catch Maroons in Cuba, see Villaverde (1982, 31–35).

13. Dallas (1803, 1:42) observes of the soldiers in Jamaica that many of them "return to their posts, frequently without shoes to [*sic*] their feet, lame, and for some time unfit for service".

14. Stedman (1988, 84) also wrote: "Another settlement of the rebels was well known to exist in a corner of the colony known by the name of the *Lee shore* and situated between the Rivers Surinamc and Serameca [Saramaca] but here the situation by ma[r]shes, quagmires, mud, and water is such that it fortifies them, from any attempts of Europeans whatever, nay they are even indiscoverable by negroes, except by their own, so thick and impenetrable is the forest on that spot, and overchoaked [*sic*] with thorn–briers, and underwood of every species."

15. http://www.pinarte.cult.cu/palma/html/museo.htm#cimarron (last visited on 21 July 2004). For a discussion of archaeological work done on Palmares, see Funari (1995).

16. The original document containing Louis's testimony is deposited in the Archives Nationales in Paris. Sylvie Mirot published a copy of it as "Un document inédit sur le *marronage* à la Guyane Française au XVIIIe siècle", *Revue d'Histoire des Colonies* 41 (1954): 245–56. It was translated and included in Price (1979, 312–19).

17. See also Villaverde (1982, 82, 127).

18. Palmer (1976, 128–29); Davidson (1979, 94); Pereira (1994, 99). See chapter 9 for details of the treaty.

19. Villaverde (1982, 37, 43, 45, 46 passim); La Rosa Corzo (2003, 213, 235 passim).

20. The information about the relationship between the Creole and African settlements is somewhat contradictory, as can be seen in the pages that I have cited from Borrego Plá's work.

21. La Rosa Corzo (2003, 21), writing about Cuba, states that "[t]he runaways living in settlements were not traders; they were marginalized and hunted down". This is clearly much too sweeping a statement.

22. See also Palmer (1976, 128–29).

23. Campbell (1990, 95) states that the Jamaican Maroons sometimes sent "threatening" messages to the planters. This was perhaps a more subtle form of taunting in the Maroon context. See chapter 9 for further discussion on taunting.

24. See also Hoogbergen (1985, 84–85).

25. See Thornton (1991, 58–80) for a discussion of African military weapons and techniques that might have been employed during the Haitian Revolution and at other times.

26. The outstanding roles of the Seminole Maroons in the various European wars of the first half of the nineteenth century are well documented in Mulroy's (1993) excellent book.

27. Zips (1999, 86) is quite wrong when he asserts that "Machetes were so highly valued by the Maroons [of Jamaica] because of their superiority to the firearms. . . . The 'combolo' [machete] therefore assumed mythical proportions, feared exceedingly by the colonial troops." Similarly, his (1999, 86) citation of Montejo's acclamation of the virtues of the Cuban machete over the Spanish firearm in the Cuban War of Independence was more *ex post facto* glorification of this weapon than reality in contemporary times.

28. Iron was so important in traditional African societies that some communities revered local blacksmiths as mystical figures (Laude 1973, 42; Gillon 1991, 105). For a speculative discourse on secret African iron-working in the Caribbean, see Goucher (1990, 201–7). See Jean Libby (1992) for an interesting, though perhaps controversial, discussion of iron-working in Africa, on the American plantations and in Maroon communities.

29. See also Kent (1979, 177).

CHAPTER 7

1. Díez Castillo (1981, 49) says much the same thing about the Maroons in Panama.

2. The relationship between Grandy Nanny and Cuffee, who led the negotiations with

the Whites, is a matter of conjecture. One eyewitness account states that she was consulted on the treaty and had some misgivings about it. She was clearly the spiritual head of the community, but was she also the political head? (See Campbell 1990, 123; for further discussion, see chapter 10.) The treaty protocol is discussed in detail in Campbell (1990, 118–25, 135–63).

3. The information about Illescas comes largely from the writings of the Mercedarian friar Miguel Cabello de Balboa. He was dispatched by the colonial authorities in 1577 to offer Illescas a "pardon" from the king and name him governor of Esmeraldas, a title that he politely refused.

4. Landers (2000b, 3n9); Lane (2002, 29–44); Bryant (2004, 13–14); "Biografías de personajes Afro Ecuatorianos" http://www.edufuturo.com/educacion.php?c=427 (last visited on 20 December 2004).

5. See Price (1983a, 129–34) for a discussion on Maroon ambivalence towards mulattos.

6. A similar sentiment prevailed concerning the Indians. Several centuries earlier, Friar Tomas Ortiz, in a speech before the Spanish Council of the Indies, had asserted that they "thought nothing of killing themselves or others" (Williams 1963, 1:110).

7. Carneiro (1946, 11) explains that "the early documents used the term Republic in the wider meaning of State, *res publica*, . . . and, sometimes even referred to the Kingdom", a view with which Anderson (1996, 557) seems to concur. Marcano Jiménez (2001, 52) surmises that the term "republic" was intended to apply to the state's political organization.

8. Her views seem to have been based largely on those of contemporary White writers, one of whom declared that Cudjoe's captains "pay him the greatest defference [*sic*] imaginable, they are entirely under his subjection, and his word is law to them". However, in the same passage from which this extract was taken the writer had stated that Cudjoe was "a person of much humanity" (Campbell 1990, 114). The Dutch lieutenant Jürgens Reijmbach, who led a military expedition that entered the capital and several other settlements that comprised Palmares in 1645, also claimed that the king ruled with an iron hand (Marcano Jiménez 2001, 51).

9. See Thompson's (2002a, 141) very short statement on fictive kinship. For a more detailed study of kinship, see Higman (1984b).

10. Carneiro (1946, 11), Conrad (1983, 368) and Aguirre (1993, 260) emphasize the importance of such qualities as bravery and wisdom in the choice of Maroon leaders in Brazil.

11. Forde and Kaberry (1967); Akinjogbin (1967); Wilks (1975); Law (1977).

12. Zips (1999, 58) uses the term "fragmentation" (his quotation marks, implying some caution in his use of the term) to describe the Windwards' structure of government, but there is really no evidence to support this view.

13. A common but erroneous view among modern scholars is that women generally did all, or nearly all, the agricultural work in African societies. This is no doubt based

upon the observation of what has happened in Africa since the colonial period, but it
is largely incorrect, since men participated in cultivating a number of the cash crops.
In the pre-colonial era, the dominance of either sex in agriculture depended upon the
specific society and sometimes the specific crop. Women, for instance, were not
allowed to grow yams in most societies, since its planting and reaping involved
complex rituals in respect of the gods that men alone were allowed to perform.
According to Gloria Chuku (1995, 40), "[I]n the Oguta and Onitsha areas [of
Igboland], women contributed little or nothing to farm cultivation, only planting
vegetables around their compounds. It was the men who travelled to the distant
farms, living on the farms from the beginning of the planting season to the harvesting period." She points out, however, that in the colonial period the women tended
to do more farm work than the men (ibid., 39–40). In Senegal and Niger men and
women generally shared the agricultural work, whereas among the Yoruba and along
the coast men mainly did it. They also normally took charge of reaping and pulping
the boiled fruit of the oil palm, while women and children extracted the nuts from
the pulps and cracked them. Notably, however, until the late nineteenth century the
Wolof men of Senegambia considered agricultural work to be women's work, a view
that prevailed among some of them well into the colonial period (Chuku 1995, 39;
Udo 1978, 34, 37, 66; Haswell 1975, 84–85). Depending upon the particular crop, men
worked at digging up roots, ridging, burning, manuring, planting seeds, tree-top
cutting, weeding and harvesting, though women also undertook some of these tasks
(Berg 1965, 169).

14. See Porter (1943, 398).
15. See Forde and Kaberry (1967); Isichei (1976); Law (1977).
16. See Raboteau (1978).
17. See Barnet (1996) for numerous comments on the role of African religions in the
lives of enslaved Cubans. Zips (1999, 46) believes that nearly all revolts in Jamaica
involved religious rituals that were supposed to make the insurgents invulnerable to
their antagonists' weapons.
18. Great Britain (1825).
19. Stedman (1988, 521; see also 457) identified these rituals as including the *watra mama
(water mama)* or mermaid ritual, involving divination and exorcism. It was deemed in
many slave societies to be the most dangerous ritual. For one instance when it was
carried out, see *British Parliamentary Papers*, 1825, 25 (476): 29–30.
20. See also Geggus (1991, 41–57); Franco (1973, 27).
21. Long (1774, 2:451–52); Thoden van Velzen (1995, 126); Hall (1971, 58); Fouchard (1972,
359); see also Gargallo (2002, 63) and Lofton (1948, 414).
22. Brathwaite (1994, 120–21); Harris (1994, 46); Campbell (1990, 123, 177); Tuelon (1973,
21).
23. According to one interpretation, Vesey planned the revolt to liberate his children,

many of whom were still held in slavery (Lofton 1948, 402). This view seems far too simplistic, given the large-scale nature of the intended insurrection. It is more plausible to view his actions as emanating from his strong anti-slavery ideology that enslavement was incompatible with biblical precepts and human dignity (Lofton 1948, 403–5).

24. On Christianity as a revolutionary tool during the slavery period in the United States, see Harding (1969, 179–97) and Lofton (1948, 395–417). For an imaginative account of Turner's revolt, see Styron (1966). Douglass (1973, 118) – and possibly a number of other enslaved persons – rejected wholeheartedly the version of Christianity that the enslavers practised: "What I have said respecting and against religion, I mean strictly to apply to the *slaveholding religion* of this land [the United States], and with no possible reference to Christianity proper; for, between the Christianity of the land, and the Christianity of Christ, I recognize the widest possible difference. . . . I therefore hate the corrupt, slaveholding, women-whipping, cradle-plundering, partial and hypocritical Christianity of this land. Indeed, I can see no reason, but the most deceitful one, for calling the religion of this land Christianity. I look upon it as the climax of all misnomers, the boldest of all frauds, and the grossest of all libels." However, again in his own words (ibid., 118): "I love the pure, peaceable, and impartial Christianity of Christ". He was amazed at how slaveholders could pray fervently for their families and their servile charges and still treat them so brutally (ibid., 118–21).

25. For other references to the role of priests in influencing the decision of Maroons to return to their overlords see Marcano Jiménez (2001, 38), Kapsoli (1975, 70–73) and Marchand-Thébault (1986, 41).

26. See also Washington (1984, 18) on the subject of white devils.

Chapter 8

1. In Dominica, a group of Maroons, after burning the lieutenant-governor's plantation, named Rosalie, took away several valuable items, including some silver drinking utensils (Atwood 1971, 243).

2. See, for instance, Navarrete (2003, 35–36) and Schwartz (1979, 211, 218). For a refutation of this view, see Flory (1979, 118–21).

3. The diets of enslaved persons usually comprised one staple (for example, cassava, plantain or corn), provided year-round, and a small quantity of salted beef, fish or pork. Occasionally, such as during festival seasons, they might be given a slightly more diversified fare. Of course, they planted gardens and sometimes kept livestock, but most writers suggest that their diets were still very deficient in variety, quantity, and essential amino acids and vitamins (see, for instance, Sheridan 1985; Kiple 1984; Higman 1984a).

4. Maroons also adopted other aspects of the material culture of the Indians, such as hammocks and indigenous-type canoes, even though canoes had been used for a long time by the riverine and coastal peoples of Africa.

5. See also Debbasch (1979, 145) and chapter 10.

6. See Louis (1979, 315); Hemming (1978, 355); Kent (1979, 178, 179); Marcano Jiménez (2001, 39); Mulroy (1993, 19).

7. Mintz (1974, 141) writes that "The term *peasantry* is used here to refer in general to those small-scale cultivators who own or have access to land, who produce some commodities for sale, and who produce much of their own subsistence." Clearly, many Maroon societies fitted into this definition of peasantry.

8. See Pérez de Ribas (1896, 1:286–90); Franco (1973, 26); Escalante (1979, 80); Stedman (1988, 402, 404, 409–10, 449, 562); Campbell (1990, 47, 50); Thompson (2002b, 132); La Rosa Corzo (2003, 177, 180).

9. See also Marcano Jiménez (2001, 51).

10. Most portraits of Parkinson show him holding a gun. However, this image of him holding a spear or *junga* illustrates the kind of weapon with which most Maroons were equipped.

11. A Maroon settlement in Suriname is said to have had as many as five hundred chickens in 1765 (De Groot 1977, 524).

12. See Louis (1979, 316); Pérez de la Riva (1979, 53); Campbell (1990, 50); De Groot (1977, 524).

13. Price (1991, 112), however, states that times of near-famine were not rare, as too little or too much rain at the wrong time could spoil a crop.

14. See Thompson (2002b, 132); Pérez de Ribas (1896, 1:286–87); Esteban Deive (1989, 74).

15. See Carey (1997, 205); Patterson (1979, 262); Louis (1979, 317); Santos Gomes (2002, 488).

16. See also Mullin (1992, 59).

17. Long before the beginning of the transatlantic slave trade, West Africans had been mining minerals, including gold, tin, copper, silver, salt and iron. They practised surface and underground mining. The latter involved the erection of "steps" or shafts – sometimes, among the Akan, to a depth of 150 feet – by methods that were sophisticated for the period. Several of the early states and empires, such as ancient Ghana, Mali and Songhay (Songhai), depended upon the gold trade for most of the exotic commodities that they received. Gold was by far the best-known West African mineral, and in the later European Middle Ages the region gained an international reputation as the world's greatest producer of that commodity. The main areas from which gold was obtained were Bambouk and Lobi (in modern Mali), and Boure (in Guinea-Conakry), but the Akan of the Gold Coast were also well-known gold miners (Davidson 1959, 83–88; Davidson 1966, 81–89; Hopkins 1973, 46–47; Levtzion 1985, 156–57; Bovill 1968).

18. On the making of salt from ashes, see Campbell (1990, 47).
19. See also Carneiro (1946, 27–28).
20. See Stedman (1988, 410, 413); Price (1991, 117); King (1979, 298–99); Carneiro (1946, 28–29).
21. See also Long (1774, 3:747–48).
22. See Bastide (1978, 82, 86); Mattoso (1979, 140); Conrad (1983, 385); Esteban Deive (1989, 50); De Groot (1977, 524); Louis (1979, 315).
23. As Weik (1997, 83) points out, most of the archaeological work done so far has focused on locating Maroon settlements and marking out their physical dimensions. Orser (1992, 11), for instance, writes that colonial maps have not accurately depicted the location of Palmares. I am grateful to Professor Barry Higman of the Australian National University for locating Weik's article for me.
24. See also Gautier (1985, 231n50); Schweninger (2002, 5).
25. Larrazábal Blanco (1998, 147) makes a similar statement about the Dominican Republic.

CHAPTER 9

1. See Knight (1999, viii).
2. See Fouchard (1972, 336).
3. Each Black Ranger was given freedom, a house and garden plot, and payment as a soldier in exchange for satisfactory service (Price and Price 1988, xxii–xxiv). The Spanish imperial government decided that the Maroons in Gracia Real de Santa Teresa de Mose had to complete a period of military service before being accorded freedom (Landers 1998, 365).
4. It is interesting to note (in the passage cited) that the Rangers had adopted two of the White stereotypes concerning Blacks: that they were ugly and lazy. For another example of Black troops and Maroons verbally abusing each other, in 1755, see Price (1983b, 116).
5. Nevertheless, insurgents must initially have shown a great degree of bravery. As Zips (1999, 51) states, "Uprisings required an extraordinary willingness to accept risk on the part of all involved, given the severe punishments that might await them."
6. See Stedman (1988, 581–82); Sijpesteijn (1858, 92); Price and Price (1988, 666n581). Stedman (1988, 271) referred to the case of a Black man who wore a silver band on his hand with the words "true to the Europeans" engraved on it.
7. Belize gained some notoriety as a colony of exile for intransigents not only from St Vincent but also from other colonies. However, at least on two occasions the colonial officials of that settlement refused to allow the landing of such persons: in 1791, two hundred from Haiti (St Domingue), and in 1796, five from Jamaica (Bolland 2003, 70).

8. According to Marchand-Thébault (1986, 41), the Portuguese government agreed to restitution of the deserters on condition of a pardon for those who were deemed to have committed crimes worthy of death.

9. Paraguay honoured a similar treaty with Brazil only in a perfunctory way and gave lands, tools and sometimes wages to the runaways from Brazil (Borrego Plá 1973, 156–57). A mutual extradition treaty was also signed in 1777 in respect of runaways from Uruguay and Brazil (Isola 1975, 218).

10. See Hall (1992, 127, 129); Dookhan (1995, 146, 165); Thompson (1987, 138–40); Gautier (1985, 230–31); Moreau de Saint-Méry (1979, 140, 141).

11. On the subject of day-to-day resistance, see Bauer and Bauer (1971, 37–60); Schuler (1973, 57–75).

12. One example was the publication in 1720 of amnesty to Maroons who would turn themselves in to their overlords within two months of the publication of the ordinance granting them immunity from prosecution (Marchand-Thébault 1986, 39–40).

13. See also Derby (2003, 12–20).

14. For a detailed study of the Aristotelian concept as applied to the Indians, see Hanke (1959); for a shorter discourse, see Hanke (1965).

15. For other references to Maroons turning themselves in to the slaveholding authorities, see Villaverde (1982, 105, 112).

16. There is some debate as to whether these runaways should properly be called Maroons and their *pueblo* a *palenque* (see Díaz 2000, 4, 6, 405n2, 406n3).

17. For other cases of runaways negotiating for improvement in their conditions of work and life, see McFarlane (1986, 146–47).

18. See Davidson (1979, 96); Campbell (1990, 71–72, 105); Mulroy (1993, 15); Atwood (1971, 236–37, 242).

19. Cuba promulgated similar legislation in that year (Ortiz 1975, 364–66).

20. On the torture of runaways, see chapter 5. See also Porter (1932, 329); Franco (1973, 15); Fuentes (1979, 11); Conrad (1983, 390); Brito Figueroa (1985, 212–13, 217, 240); Zips (1999, 66).

21. For a detailed discussion of the treaties, see Campbell (1990, 126–63).

22. The reason that they gave for their action was that the San Andrés *palenque* had heard about the expedition sent against them and most of the warriors had temporarily vacated the settlement, probably to distract the expedition from attacking it, leaving twenty women and six men on guard. The two defectors, apparently among those left in the settlement, decided to turn themselves in at the plantation from which they had originally fled (La Rosa Corzo 2003, 99–100).

23. Contrary to official correspondence on the subject in 1763, which claimed that the Maroons were very aggressive, Mattoso (1979, 141) states that "To avoid possible reprisals, white planters preferred to collaborate with the fugitives of Buraco do Tatú,

who, because they were not inclined to make total war on the whites to liberate their captive brethren, were not felt to be particularly dangerous."

24. This last clause contained seeds of contention. It was left up to the colonial state ultimately to determine when mistreatment occurred, and to enforce the right of the enslaved person to secure his or her freedom at the correct price, assuming that he or she was in a financial position to do so. It is therefore doubtful that this clause was enforced with any regularity, though the abuses certainly occurred.

25. Treaties between the Indians and the Americans (British and then US) often contained clauses about the return of African runaways, though the Indians usually did not comply with this aspect of the treaties (Porter 1932, 308, 328).

26. Writers disagree on the date of the treaty. Some hold that 1609 was the definitive date, whereas others view that as the year when the first overtures began but resulted in a breakdown of talks and the continuation of Maroon activities by Yanga and his men. Others regard 1630 as the date when the viceroy of Mexico, acting on behalf of the imperial government, finally ratified the treaty, by which time Yanga was dead. The ratification in 1630 also conceded the Maroons' right to own land, something that the Mexican government had not accorded up to that time to free Blacks (see Pereira 1994, 99–101; Naveda Chávez-Hita 2001, 126; Palmer 1976, 127–30).

27. See Pérez de Ribas (1896, 1:290–93); Pereira (1994, 99–101); Naveda Chávez-Hita (2001, 126); Palmer (1976, 126–30).

28. In 1580 the Colombian government spoke about "the pacification of the black Maroons" of Santiago del Principe (De la Guardia 1977, 94). The Suriname government often referred to the Ndjukas, Saramakas and Matawais as "pacified Bush Negroes" or "pacified Maroons" (Campbell 1990, 112–14, 124; Thoden van Velzen 1995, 113, 124). The agreement of some Maroon communities to move from their hideouts to more accessible places, or their involuntary movement by the state authorities some years after they had demobilized, adds to the view that they had become pacified. This, for instance, was the case with the Cofre de Perote, Enriquillo and Windward Maroons.

29. Bev Carey (1997, 343–50) claims that it was only at the fourth attempt that the British managed to get the Windward Maroons to sign a treaty with them.

30. Pérez de la Riva (1979, 55) attributes the successful ambush of Sánchez and his chief men to one of his followers, who betrayed him to the Whites.

CHAPTER 10

1. See also Campbell (1990, 165).
2. See, for instance, Campbell (1990, 102–4).
3. See Carroll (1977, 498–99); Pereira (1994, 102–3); Corro (1951, 23); Naveda Chávez-Hita (2001, 167).

4. See Fouchard (1972, 162) concerning the clergy in Haiti in showing some consideration for the enslaved people.

5. See also Karasch (1987, 310).

6. Goveia (1965); Dayfoot (1999); Thomas (1971); Chauleau (1966); Bennett (1958); Banbuck (1935).

7. Note, however, that Count von Zinzendorf, founder of the Moravian (evangelical) missions, preached to a group of enslaved persons in the Danish Caribbean that they should be obedient to their masters and bombas (drivers), and that "The Lord has made all ranks – kings, masters, servants and slaves. God punished the first negroes by making them slaves and your conversion will make you free, not from the control of your master, but simply from your wicked habits and thoughts and all that makes you dissatisfied with your lot" (cited in Hutton 1922, 44–45).

8. See Stedman (1988, 80, 510); Borrego Plá (1973, 25–26, 28).

9. Pinckard (1806, 2:243n) records an instance in which an enslaved person who had saved a European officer from certain death in an encounter with Maroons refused to accept his freedom as a reward, but "only begged to have a silver medal to wear on days of festival".

10. Other groups suffered at the hands of the Ndjukas for the same reasons noted for the Boni people (Thoden van Velzen 1995, 127–28).

11. See Zips (1999, 75, 110–12) for further discussion of his views concerning Maroon treaties.

12. See Aptheker (1979, 156); Blassingame (1979, 211–12); Mulroy (1993, 14–15); also chapter 4.

13. A common fallacy, articulated by Zips (1999, 75), among others, is that most Maroon communities signed treaties with the slaveholding states.

14. See, for instance, Sharp (1976, 158); Debien (1979, 110); Hall (1992, 11); Dookhan (1995, 169).

15. See Aguirre (1993, 268–69).

16. For a recent discourse on the involvement of enslaved persons in the revolutionary struggles of the late eighteenth and nineteenth centuries, see Blanchard (2002).

CONCLUSION

1. For a discussion of social banditry in Cuba, see Pérez (1989).

2. See also Singelmann (1975, 59–83); Aguirre (1993, 265, 270–71); Flory (1979, 128).

3. See Schwartz's (1989) work on outlaws and liberators.

4. In a more lyrical moment, he (1999, 712) wrote, "Behind I left the whips and chains / Before me were sweet Freedom's plains!"

Bibliography

Acosta Saignes, Miguel. 1979. Life in a Venezuelan Cumbe. In *Maroon Societies: Rebel Slave Communities in the Americas*, 2nd ed., ed. Richard Price, 64–73. Baltimore: Johns Hopkins University Press.

Adams, A.R.D., and B.G. Maegraith. 1960. *Clinical Tropical Diseases*, 2nd ed. Oxford: Blackwell Scientific Publications.

Agorsah, Kofi E. 1994. Archaeology of Maroon Settlements in Jamaica. In *Maroon Heritage: Archaeological Ethnographic and Historical Perspectives*, ed. Kofi E. Agorsah, 163–87. Kingston: Canoe Press.

Aguirre Beltrán, Gonzalo. 1958. *Cuijla: Esbozo etnográfico de un pueblo negro*. México: Fondo de Cultura Económica.

Aguirre, Carlos. 1993. *Agentes du su propia libertad: los esclavos de Lima y la desintegración de la esclavitud 1821–1854*. Lima: Pontifica Universidad Católica del Perú, Fondo Editorial.

Akinjogbin, I.A. 1967. *Dahomey and Its Neighbours 1708–1818*. Cambridge: Cambridge University Press.

Akintoye, S.A. 1971. *Revolution and Power Politics in Yorubaland 1840–1893*. London: Longman.

Akroyd, W.R. 1967. *Sweet Malefactor: Sugar, Slavery, and Human Society*. London: Heinemann.

Albert Batista, Celsa. 1990. *Mujer y esclavitud en Santo Domingo*. Santo Domingo: Centro Dominicano de Estudios de la Educación.

Alvarez Nazario, Manuel. 1961. *El elemento afronegroide en el español de Puerto Rico*. San Juan: Instituto de Cultura Puertorriqueña.

Anderson, Robert Nelson. 1996. The Quilombo of Palmares: A New Overview of a Maroon State in Seventeenth-Century Brazil. *Journal of Latin American Studies* 28:545–66.

Andrews, Kenneth R. 1978. *The Spanish Caribbean: Trade and Plunder, 1530–1630*. New Haven: Yale University Press.

Aptheker, Herbert. 1979. Maroons Within the Present Limits of the United States. In

Maroon Societies: Rebel Slave Communities in the Americas, 2nd ed., ed. Richard Price, 151–68. Baltimore: Johns Hopkins University Press.

Arcaya, Pedro Manuel. 1949. *Insurrection de los negros en la Serranía de Coro.* Caracas: Instituto Panamericano de Geografía y Historia, Comisión de Historia.

Arrázola, Roberto. 1967. *Palenque, primer pueblo libre de América.* Cartagena: Ediciones Hernández.

———. 1975. *Más sobre Santa Marta.* Cartagena: Editora Bolívar.

Arrom, José Juan, and Manuel A. García Arévalo. 1986. *Cimarrón.* Santo Domingo: Ediciones Fundación García-Arévalo.

Asiegbu, Johnson. 1969. *Slavery and the Politics of Liberation, 1787–1861: A Study of Liberated African Emigration and British Anti-Slavery Policy.* London: Longman.

Atwood, Thomas. 1971. *The History of the Island of Dominica.* London: Frank Cass. (Orig. pub. 1791.)

Baker, Patrick. L. 1994. *Centring the Periphery: Chaos, Order and Ethnohistory of Dominica.* Kingston: The Press, University of the West Indies.

Banbuck, C.A. 1935. *Histoire politique, économique et sociales de la Martinique sous l'Ancien Régime (1635–1789).* Paris: Marcel Rivière.

Baralt, Guillermo A. 1982. *Esclavos rebeldes: conspiraciones y sublevaciones de esclavos en Puerto Rico (1795–1873).* Río Piedras: Ediciones Huracán.

Barnet, Miguel. 1996. *Biografía de un Cimarrón.* La Habana: Editorial Academia. (Orig. pub. 1968.)

Bastide, Roger. 1972. *African Civilizations in the New World.* New York: Harper and Row.

———. 1978. *The African Religions of Brazil: Toward a Sociology of the Interpenetration of Civilizations.* Trans. Helen Sebba. Baltimore: Johns Hopkins University Press.

———. 1979. The Other Quilombos. In *Maroon Societies: Rebel Slave Communities in the Americas*, 2nd ed., ed. Richard Price, 191–201. Baltimore: Johns Hopkins University Press.

Bauer, Raymond, and Alice Bauer. 1971. Day-to-Day Resistance to Slavery. In *American Slavery: The Question of Resistance*, ed. John H. Bracey, 37–60. Belmont, CA: Wadsworth.

Beckles, Hilary McD. 1986. From Land to Sea: Runaway Barbados Slaves and Servants, 1630–1700. In *Out of the House of Bondage: Runaways, Resistance and Marronage in Africa and the New World*, ed. Gad Heuman, 79–94. London: Frank Cass.

———. 1989a. *White Servitude and Black Slavery in Barbados 1627–1715.* Knoxville: University of Tennessee Press.

———. 1989b. *Natural Rebels: A Social History of Enslaved Black Women in Barbados.* London: Zed Books.

———. 1999. *Centering Woman: Gender Discourses in Caribbean Slave Society.* Kingston: Ian Randle.

Beet, Chris de. 1984. *De Eerste Boni-Oorlog, 1765–1778.* Bronnen voor de studie van

Bosnegersamenlevingen. Part 9. Utrecht: Centrum voor Caraibische Studies, Rijksuniversiteit Utrecht.

Bennett, J. Harry, Jr. 1958. *Bondsmen and Bishops: Slavery and Apprenticeship on the Codrington Plantations of Barbados, 1710–1838.* Berkeley and Los Angeles: University of California Press.

Benoit, P.J. 1839. *Voyage à Surinam; description des possessions néerlandaises dans la Guyane.* Bruxelles: Société des Beaux-Arts.

Berg, Elliot J. 1965. The Economics of the Migrant Labor System. In *Urbanization and Migration in West Africa,* ed. Hilda Kuper, 160–81. Berkeley and Los Angeles: University of California Press.

Bigman, Laura. 1993. *History of Hunger in West Africa: Food Production and Entitlement in Guinea-Bissau and Cape Verde.* Westport: Greenwood Press.

Bilby, Kenneth. 1984. Two Sister Pikni: A Historical Tradition of Dual Ethnogenesis in Eastern Jamaica. *Caribbean Quarterly* 30 (3–4): 10–25.

Biografías de personajes Afro Ecuatorianos. http: //www.edufuturo.com/educacion .php?c=427 (site last visited on 4 January 2005).

Birmingham, David. 1975. Central Africa from Cameroun to the Zambezi. In *The Cambridge History of Africa. Vol. 4. From c.1600 to c.1790,* edited by Richard Gray, 325–83. Cambridge: Cambridge University Press.

Blake, William O. 1857. *The History of Slavery and the Slave Trade, Ancient and Modern.* Columbus, OH: J. and H. Miller.

Blanchard, 2002. The Language of Liberation: Slave Voices in the Wars of Independence. *Hispanic American Historical Review* 82 (3): 499–523.

Blassingame, John W. 1979. *The Slave Community: Plantation Life in the Antebellum South.* Rev. and enlarged ed. New York: Oxford University Press.

Bolland, O. Nigel. 2002. Timber Extraction and the Shaping of Enslaved People's Culture in Belize. In *Slavery without Sugar: Diversity in Caribbean Economy and Society Since the 17th Century,* ed. Verene A. Shepherd, 36–62. Gainesville: University Press of Florida.

———. 2003. *Colonialism and Resistance in Belize: Essays in Historical Sociology.* Second edition. Kingston: University of the West Indies Press.

Boromé, Joseph. 1969. Dominica during French Occupation. *English Historical Review* 84 (330): 36–58.

———. 1972. Origin and Growth of the Public Libraries of Dominica. *Journal of Library History* 5 (3): 200–236.

Borrego Plá, María del Carmen. 1973. *Palenques de negroes en Cartagena de Indias a fines del siglo XVII.* Sevilla: Escuela de Estudios Hispano-Americanos. Consejo Superior de Investigaciones Científicas.

Bovill, Edward W. 1968. *The Golden Trade of the Moors,* 2nd ed. London: Oxford University Press.

Bowser, Frederick P. 1974. *The African Slave in Colonial Peru 1524–1650.* Stanford: Stanford University Press.

Boxer C.R. 1962. *The Golden Age of Brazil 1695–1750.* Berkeley and Los Angeles: University of California Press.

———. 1965. *The Dutch Seaborne Empire 1600–1800.* London: Hutchinson.

Brathwaite, Kamau. 1994. Nanny, Palmares and the Caribbean Maroon Connexion. In *Maroon Heritage: Archaeological Ethnographic and Historical Perspectives,* ed. Kofi E. Agorsah, 119–38. Kingston: Canoe Press.

Brito Figueroa, Federico. 1961. *Las insurrectiones de los esclavos negros en la sociedad colonial.* Caracas: Editorial Cantaclaro.

———. 1985. *El problema tierra y esclavos en la historia de Venezuela.* 2nd ed. Caracas: Ediciones de la Biblioteca de la Universidad Central de Venezuela.

Brown, William Wells. 1999. Narrative of William Wells Brown, a Fugitive Slave. In *I Was Born a Slave: An Anthology of Classic Slave Narratives,* vol. 1., ed. Tuval Taylor, 673–717. Edinburgh: Payback Press.

Bryant, Sherwin K. 2004. Enslaved Rebels, Fugitives, and Litigants: The Resistance Continuum in Colonial Quito. *Colonial Latin American Review* 13 (1): 7–46.

Buckley, Roger Norman. 1998. *The British Army in the West Indies: Society and the Military in the Revolutionary Age.* Gainesville: University of Florida Press.

Buckridge, Steeve O. 2004. *The Language of Dress: Resistance and Accommodation in Jamaica, 1760–1890.* Kingston: University of the West Indies Press.

Burnard, Trevor. 2004. *Master, Tyranny, and Desire. Thomas Thistlewood and his Slaves in the Anglo-Jamaican World.* Chapel Hill: University of North Carolina Press.

Burns, Alan. 1954. *History of the British West Indies.* London: George Allen and Unwin.

Bush, Barbara. 1990. *Slave Women in Caribbean Society 1650–1838.* Kingston: Heinemann (Caribbean).

Calcagno, Francisco. 1881. *Romualdo: uno de tantos.* Habana: Imprenta del Avisador Commercial.

Campbell, Mavis. 1990. *The Maroons of Jamaica 1655–1796. A History of Resistance, Collaboration and Betrayal.* Trenton, NJ: Africa World Press.

Carey, Bev. 1997. *The Maroon Story.* Gordon Town, Jamaica: Agouti Press.

Carneiro, Edison. 1946. *Guerras de los Palmares.* México: Fondo de Cultura Económica.

Carroll, Patrick J. 1977. Mandinga: The Evolution of a Mexican Runaway Slave Community, 1735–1827. *Comparative Studies in Society and History* 19:488–505.

———. 1991. *Blacks in Colonial Veracruz: Race, Ethnicity, and Regional Development.* Austin: University of Texas Press.

Chauleau, Liliane. 1966. *La société à la Martinique au XVIIe siècle (1635–1713).* Caen: Ozannie.

Chuku, Gloria Ifeoma. 1995. Women in the Economy of Igboland, 1900 to 1970: A Survey. *African Economic History* 23:37–50.

Cohen, David and Jack Greene, eds. 1972. *Neither Slave nor Free: The Freedmen of African Descent in the Slave Societies of the New World.* Baltimore: Johns Hopkins University Press.

Conneau, Theophilus. 1976. *A Slaver's Log Book or 20 Years' Residence in Africa.* London: Prentice Hall International. (Orig. pub. 1854.)

Conrad, Robert Edgar. 1983. *Children of God's Fire: A Documentary History of Black Slavery in Brazil.* New Jersey: Princeton University Press.

Corro, Octaviano. 1951. *Los cimarrones en Veracruz y la fundación de Amapa.* Xalapa: Veracruz Comercial.

Cracknell. Basil E. 1973. *Dominica.* Newton Abbot: David and Charles (Holdings).

Craft, William. 1860. *Running a Thousand Miles for Freedom; or, The Escape of William and Ellen Craft from Slavery.* London: W. Tweede.

Craton, Michael. 1982. *Testing the Chains: Resistance to Slavery in the British West Indies.* Ithaca: Cornell University Press.

Crowder, Michael. 1968. *West Africa Under Colonial Rule.* London: Hutchinson.

Dallas, R.C. 1803. *The History of the Maroons.* 2 vols. London: T.N. Longman and O. Rees.

Davenport, T.R.H. 1997. *South Africa. A Modern History.* 4th ed. London: Macmillan.

Davidson, Basil. 1959. *Old Africa Rediscovered.* London: Victor Gollancz.

———. 1966. *The African Past.* Middlesex: Penguin Books.

Davidson, David M. 1979. Negro Slave Control and Resistance in Colonial México, 1519–1650. In *Maroon Societies: Rebel Slave Communities in the Americas,* 2nd ed., ed. Richard Price, 82–103. Baltimore: Johns Hopkins University Press.

Davis, David Brion. 1966. *The Problem of Slavery in Western Culture.* Ithaca: Cornell University Press.

———. 1975. *The Problem of Slavery in the Age of Revolution, 1770–1823.* Ithaca: Cornell University Press.

Davis, John P. 1966. The Negro in the Armed Forces in America. In *The American Negro Reference Book,* ed. John P. Davis, 590–661. Englewood Cliffs, NJ: Prentice-Hall.

Dayfoot, Arthur C. 1999. *The Shaping of the West Indian Church 1492–1962.* Kingston: University of the West Indies Press.

Debbasch, Yvan. 1961, 1961. Le marronage: essai sur la désertion de l'esclave antillais. *L'Année Sociologique,* 3rd ser., 1:1–112.

———. 1979. Le Maniel: Further Notes. In *Maroon Societies: Rebel Slave Communities in the Americas,* 2nd ed., ed. Richard Price, 143–48. Baltimore: Johns Hopkins University Press.

Debien, Gabriel. 1966a. Les esclaves marrons à Saint-Domingue en 1764. *Jamaica Historical Review* 61:9–20.

———. 1966b. Le marronage aux antilles françaises au XVIIIᵉ siècle. *Caribbean Studies* 6 (3): 3–44.

———. 1974. *Les esclaves aux antilles françaises (XVIIe–XVIIIe siècles)*. Basse-Terre: Société d'histoire de la Guadeloupe.

———. 1979. Marronage in the French Caribbean. In *Maroon Societies: Rebel Slave Communities in the Americas*, 2nd ed., ed. Richard Price, 107–34. Baltimore: Johns Hopkins University Press.

Debret, Jean-Baptiste. 1834–39. *Voyage pittoresque et historique au Brésil, ou séjour d'un artiste français au Brésil, depuis 1816 jusqu'en 1831 inclusivement*. 3 vols. Paris: Firmin Didot Frères.

De Friedemann, Nina S. 1998. San Basilio en el Universo Kilombo-Africa y Palenque-America. *Geografía Humana de Colombia: los afrocolombianos* 6:79–102.

De Groot, Sylvia W. 1969. *Djuka Society and Social Change: History of an Attempt to Develop a Bush Negro Community in Surinam 1917–1926*. Assen: Van Gorcum.

———. 1970. Rebellie der Zwarte Jagers: de nasleep van de Bonni-Oorlogen, 1788–1809. *De Gids* 133:291–304.

———. 1975. The Boni Maroon War 1765–1793. Surinam and French Guiana. *Boletín de Estudios Latinoamericanos y del Caribe* 18:30–48.

———. 1977. Maroons of Surinam: Dependence and Independence. In *Comparative Perspectives on Slavery in New World Plantation Societies*, ed. Vera Rubin and Arthur Tuden, 520–29. New York: Annals of the Academy of Sciences.

———. 1986. A Comparison Between the History of Maroon Communities in Surinam and Jamaica. In *Out of the House of Bondage: Runaways, Resistance and Marronage in Africa and the New World*, ed. Gad Heuman, 173–84. London: Frank Cass.

De Kom, Anton. 1971. *Wij slaven van Suriname*. Amsterdam: Contact. (Orig. pub. 1934.)

Derby, Lauren. 2003. National Identity and the Idea of Value in the Dominican Republic. In *Blacks, Coloureds and National Identity in Nineteenth-Century Latin America*, ed. Nancy Priscilla Naro, 5–37. London: Institute of Latin American Studies.

Deschamps Chapeaux, Pedro. 1983. *Los cimarrones urbanos*. Habana: Editorial de Ciencias Sociales.

Díaz, María Elena. 2000. *The Virgin, the King and the Royal Slaves of El Cobre: Negotiating Freedom in Colonial Cuba, 1670–1780*. Stanford: Stanford University Press.

Díez Castillo, Luis A. 1981. *Los cimarrones y los negros antillanos en Panamá*. 2nd ed. Panamá: Impr. J. Mercado Rudas.

Dike, Kenneth O. 1956. *Trade and Politics in the Niger Delta*. London: Oxford University Press.

Donnan, Elizabeth, ed. 1930–35. *Documents Illustrative of the History of the Slave Trade to America*. 4 vols. Washington, DC: Carnegie Institute.

Donoghue, Eddie. 2002. *Black Women White Men: The Sexual Exploitation of Female Slaves in the Danish West Indies*. Trenton, NJ: Africa World Press.

Dookhan, Isaac. 1995. *A History of the Virgin Islands of the United States.* Kingston: Canoe Press. (Orig. pub. 1974.)

Douglass, Frederick. 1973. *Narrative of the Life of Frederick Douglass, An American Slave. Written by Himself.* New York: Anchor Books. (Orig. pub. 1845.)

———. 1855. *My Bondage and My Freedom.* New York: Miller, Orton and Mulligan.

Dubois, Laurent. 2004. *A Colony of Citizens: Revolution and Slave Emancipation in the French Caribbean, 1787–1804.* Chapel Hill: Published for the Omohundro Institute of Early American History and Culture, Williamsburg, Virginia, by the University of North Carolina Press.

Dusenberry, William H. 1948. Discriminatory Aspects of Legislation in Colonial Mexico. *Journal of Negro History* 33:284–302.

Dutertre, Jean-Baptiste. 1667–71. *Histoire générale des Antilles habitées par les François.* 4 vols. Paris: Thomas Iolli.

Edwards, Albert. 1994. Maroon Warfare: The Jamaican Model. In *Maroon Heritage: Archaeological Ethnographic and Historical Perspectives,* ed. Kofi E. Agorsah, 149–62. Kingston: Canoe Press.

Edwards, Bryan. 1966. *The History, Civil and Commercial, of the British Colonies in the West Indies.* 5th ed. 5 vols. New York: AMS Press. (Orig. pub. 1819.)

———. 1979. Observations on . . . the Maroon Negroes of the Island of Jamaica. In *Maroon Societies: Rebel Slave Communities in the Americas,* 2nd ed., ed. Richard Price, 230–45. Baltimore: Johns Hopkins University Press.

Equiano, Olaudah. 1789. *The Interesting Narrative of the Life of Olaudah Equiano, or Gustavus Vassa, the African. Written by Himself.* Vol. 1. London.

Escalante, Aquilas. 1979. Palenques in Colombia. In *Maroon Societies: Rebel Slave Communities in the Americas,* 2nd ed., ed. Richard Price, 74–81. Baltimore: Johns Hopkins University Press.

Essed, Hugo A.M. 1984. *De binnelandse oorlog in Suriname, 1613–1793.* Paramaribo: Anton de Kom Universiteit van Suriname.

Esteban Deive, Carlos. 1985. *Los Cimarrones del Maniel de Neiba.* Santo Domingo: Banco Central de la República Dominicana.

———. 1989. *Los Guerrilleros Negros: Esclavos fugitivos y cimarrones en Santo Domingo.* Santo Domingo: Fundación Cultural Dominicana.

Fanon, Frantz. 1967. *The Wretched of the Earth.* Trans. C. Farrington. Harmondsworth, Middlesex: Penguin Books. (Orig. pub. 1961.)

Fincham, Alan G. 1997. *Jamaica Underground: The Caves, Sinkholes and Underground Rivers of the Island.* Kingston: The Press, University of the West Indies.

Fleischmann, Ulrich. 1993. Maroons, Writers and History. In *Slavery in the Americas,* ed. Wolfgang Binder, 565–79. Würzburg: Königshausen and Neumann.

Fleming, James G. 1966. The Negro in American Politics: The Past. In *The American Negro Reference Book,* ed. John P. Davis, 414–30. Englewood Cliffs, NJ: Prentice-Hall.

Flores Galindo, Alberto. 1984. *Aristocracia y plebe: Lima 1760–1830: (estructura de clases y sociedad colonial)*. San Isidro, Perú: Mosca Azul Editores.

Flory, Thomas. 1979. Fugitive Slaves and Free Society: The Case of Brazil. *Journal of Negro History* 64 (2): 116–30.

Fogel, Robert. 1989. *Without Consent or Contract. The Rise and Fall of American Slavery.* New York: W.W. Norton.

Forde, Daryll and P.M. Kaberry, eds. 1967. *West African Kingdoms in the Nineteenth Century.* London: Oxford University Press.

Fouchard, Jean. 1972. *Les marrons de la liberté.* Paris: Editions de l'École.

Franco, José Luciano. 1973. *Los Palenques de los Negros Cimarrones.* Habana: Departmento de Orientación Revolucionaria del Comité Central del Partido Comunista de Cuba.

———. 1979. Maroons and Slave Rebellions in the Spanish Territories. In *Maroon Societies: Rebel Slave Communities in the Americas,* 2nd ed., ed. Richard Price, 35–48. Baltimore: Johns Hopkins University Press.

Franklin, John Hope. 1980. *From Slavery to Freedom: A History of Negro Americans.* 5th ed. New York: Alfred A. Knopf.

Freehling, William W. 2002. Why the US Fugitive Slave Phenomenon Was Crucial. Paper presented at the Fifth Annual International Conference, Gilder Lehrman Center for the Study of Slavery, Resistance and Abolition, Yale University, 6–7 December 2002.

Freire, Paulo. 1972. *Pedagogy of the Oppressed.* Trans. Myra Bergman Ramos. Harmondsworth, Middlesex: Penguin Books.

Freitas-Oliveira, Waldir. 2001. Economia de Palmares. In *Os Quilombos na dinamica social do Brasil,* org. Clóvis Moura, 61–71. Maceió-AL: EdUFAL.

Freyre, Gilberto. 1956. *The Masters and the Slaves: A Study in the Development of Brazilian Civilization.* New York: Alfred A. Knopf.

———. 1963. The *Mansions and the Shanties: The Making of Modern Brazil.* Trans. and ed. Harriet de Onís. New York: Alfred A. Knopf.

Frijol, Roberto. 1982. Introduction to *Diario del ranchador,* by Cirilo Villaverde. Habana: Editorial Letras Cubanas.

Fuentes, J. 1979. *El Cimarrón, 1845.* San Juan de Puerto Rico: Instituto de Cultura Puertoriqueña.

Funari, P.P.A. 1995. The Archaeology of Palmares and Its Contribution to the Understanding of the History of African-American Culture. *Historical Archaeology in Latin America* 7:1–41.

García, Jesús (Chucho). 1989. *Contra el cepo: Barlovento tiempo de cimarrones.* San José de Barlovento: Editorial Lucas y Trina.

———. 1996. *Africanas, esclavas y cimarronas.* Caracas: Fundación Afroamérica.

Gargallo, Francesca. 2002. *Garífuna Garínagu, Caribe.* México, DF: Siglo XXI Editores.

Gautier, Arlette. 1985. *Les Soeurs de Solitude: La condition féminine dans l'esclave aux*

Antilles du XVIIᵉ au XIXᵉ siècle. Paris: Editions Caribéennes.

Geggus, David. 1986. On the Eve of the Haitian Revolution: Slave Runaways in Saint-Domingue in the year 1790. In *Out of the House of Bondage: Runaways, Resistance and Marronage in Africa and the New World,* ed. Gad Heuman, 112–28. London: Frank Cass.

———. 1991. The Bois Caiman Ceremony. *Journal of Caribbean History* 25:41–57.

Genovese, Eugene D. 1976. *Roll Jordan, Roll: The World the Slaves Made.* New York: Random House.

———. 1981. *From Rebellion to Revolution: Afro-American Slave Revolts in the Making of the New World.* New York: Vintage Books.

Gillon, Werner. 1991. *A Short History of African Art.* London: Penguin Books.

Gordon, Edmund T. 1998. *Disparate Diasporas: Identity and Politics in an African Nicaraguan Community.* Austin: University of Texas Press.

Goslinga, Cornelis. 1985. *The Dutch in the Caribbean and the Guianas 1680–1791.* Assen: Van Gorcum.

Goucher, Candice. 1990. African Hammer, European Anvil: West African Iron-making in the Atlantic Trade Era. *West African Journal of Archaeology* 20:200–208.

Goveia, Elsa. 1965. *Slave Society in the British Leeward Islands at the End of the Eighteenth Century.* New Haven: Yale University Press.

Grant, John N. 2002. *The Maroons in Nova Scotia.* Halifax, NS: Formac Publications.

Greene, Lorenzo J. 1944. The New England Negro as Seen in Advertisements for Runaway Slaves. *Journal of Negro History* 30:125–46.

Guerra Cedeño, F. 1984. *Esclavos negros, cimarrones y cumbes de Barlovento.* Caracas: Cuadernos Lagoven.

Guillot, Carlos Federico. 1961. *Negros rebeldes y negros cimarrones: Perfil afroamericano en la historia del Neuvo Mundo durante el siglo XVI.* Buenos Aires: Librería y Editorial "El Ateneo".

Hall, Gwendolyn Midlo. 1971. *Social Control in Slave Plantation Societies: A Comparison of St Domingue and Cuba.* Baltimore: Johns Hopkins Press.

Hall, Neville A.T. 1992. *Slavery in the Danish West Indies: St Thomas, St John and St Croix.* Kingston: University of the West Indies Press.

Handler, Jerome S. 1974. *The Unappropriated People: Freedmen in the Slave Society of Barbados.* Baltimore: Johns Hopkins University Press.

———. 2002. Escaping Slavery in Barbados. Paper presented at the Fifth Annual International Conference, Gilder Lehrman Center for the Study of Slavery, Resistance and Abolition, Yale University, 6–7 December 2002.

Hanke, Lewis. 1965. *The Spanish Struggle for Justice in the Conquest of America.* Boston: Little, Brown. (Orig. pub. 1949.)

———. 1959. *Aristotle and the American Indians: A Study in Race Prejudice in the Modern World.* Chicago: Henry Regnery.

―――. 1974. *All Mankind is One: A Study of the Disputation Between Bartolomé de las Casas and Juan Guinés de Sepúlveda in 1550*. Illinois: Northern Illinois University Press.

Harding, Vincent. 1969. Religion and Resistance Among Antebellum Negroes, 1800–1860. In *The Making of Black America*, ed. August Meier and Elliott Rudwick, 179–97. New York: Atheneum.

Harris, Col. C.L.G. 1994. The True Traditions of my Ancestors. In *Maroon Heritage: Archaeological Ethnographic and Historical Perspectives*, ed. Kofi E. Agorsah, 36–63. Kingston: Canoe Press.

Hartsinck, Jan J. 1770. *Beschrijving van Guiana of de Wildekust in Zuid-Amerika*. Amsterdam: Gerrit Tielenburg.

Haswell, Margaret. 1975. *The Nature of Poverty: A Case Study of the First Quarter-Century after World War II*. London: Macmillan Press.

Hemming, John. 1978. *Red Gold: The Conquest of the Brazilian Indians*. London: Macmillan.

Heuman, Gad. 1986. Runaway Slaves in Nineteenth-Century Barbados. In *Out of the House of Bondage: Runaways, Resistance and Marronage in Africa and the New World*, ed. Gad Heuman, 95–112. London: Frank Cass.

Higman, B.W. 1984a. *Slave Populations of the British Caribbean, 1807–1834*. Baltimore: Johns Hopkins University Press.

―――. 1984b. Terms for Kin in the British West Indian Slave Community: Differing Perceptions of Masters and Slaves. In *Kinship Ideology and Practice in Latin America*, ed. Raymond T. Smith, 59–81. Chapel Hill: University of North Carolina Press.

Honychurch, Lennox. 1975. *The Dominica Story: A History of the Island*. Roseau: The Dominica Institute.

Hoogbergen, Wim. 1984. *De Boni's in Frans-Guyana en de Tweede Boni-Oorlog, 1776–1793*. Bronnen voor de studie van Bosnegersamenlevingen. Part 10. Utrecht: Centrum voor Caraibische Studies, Rijksuniversiteit Utrecht.

―――. 1985. *De Boni-Oorlogen, 1757–1860: Marronage en guerrilla in Oost Suriname*. Bronnen voor de studie van Bosnegersamenlevingen. Part 2. Utrecht: Centrum voor Caraibische Studies, Rijksuniversiteit Utrecht.

―――, ed. 1990. *The Boni Maroon Wars in Suriname*. Leiden: E.J. Brill.

―――. 1993. Marronage and Slave Rebellion in Surinam. In *Slavery in the Americas*, ed. Wolfgang Binder, 165–95. Würzburg: Königshausen and Neumann.

Hopkins, A.G. 1973. *An Economic History of West Africa*. London: Longman.

Hoyos, F.A. 1978. *Barbados: A History from the Amerindians to Independence*. London: Macmillan Education.

Hunt, J.A. 1999. A Short History of Soap. *Pharmaceutical Journal* 263:985–89.

Hutton, J.E. 1922. *A History of Moravian Missions*. London: Moravian Publication Office.

Ikime, Obaro. 1966. The Anti-Tax Riots in Warri Province, 1927–1928. *Journal of the Historical Society of Nigeria* 3 (3): 559–73.

Isichei, Elizabeth. 1976. *A History of the Igbo People.* London: Macmillan.

————. 1977. *History of West Africa since 1800.* London: Macmillan.

Isola, Ema. 1975. *La esclavitud en el Uruguay desde sus comienzos hasta su extinción (1743–1852).* Montevideo: Comisión Nacional de Homenaje del Sesquicentenario de los Hechos Históricos de 1825.

Jacobs, Harriet (Linda Brent). 1999. Incidents in the Life of a Slave Girl. In *I Was Born a Slave: An Anthology of Classic Slave Narratives,* vol. 2, ed. Tuval Taylor, 533–681. Edinburgh: Payback Press.

James, C.L.R. 1963. *The Black Jacobins: Toussaint L'Ouverture and the San Domingo Revolution,* 2nd ed. New York: Vintage Books. (Orig. pub. 1938.)

Jean-Pierre, Jean Reynold. 2000. *Sur la Route de l'Esclave: Saint-Domingue, une terre d'enfer, 1503–1791.* [Haiti]: Editions presses nationales d'Haïti.

Johnson, F. Roy. 1966. *The Nat Turner Slave Insurrection.* Murfreesboro, NC: Johnson Publishing.

Jones, G.I. 1963. *The Trading States of the Oil Rivers: A Study of Political Development in Eastern Nigeria.* London: Oxford University Press.

Jones, L. Oakah, Jr. 1994. *Guatemala in the Spanish Colonial Period.* Norman: University of Oklahoma Press.

Jordan, Winthrop D. 1968. *White over Black: American Attitudes toward the Negro, 1550–1812.* New York: W.W. Norton.

Jordan, Winthrop D., and Leon F. Litwack. 1991. *The United States. Combined Edition.* 7th ed. Englewood Cliffs, NJ: Prentice Hall.

Kapsoli, E. Wilfredo. 1975. *Sublevaciones de esclavos en el Perú, s. XVIII.* Lima: Universidad Ricardo Palma, Dirección Universitaria de Investigación.

Karasch, Mary. 1987. *Slave Life in Rio de Janeiro, 1808–1850.* Princeton: Princeton University Press.

Kelly, Alfred H., and Winifred A. Harbison. 1970. *The American Constitution: Its Origins and Development.* 4th ed. New York: W.W. Norton.

Kent, Raymond K. 1970. African Revolt in Bahia. *Journal of Social History* 3:334–56.

————. 1979. Palmares: An African State in Brazil. In *Maroon Societies: Rebel Slave Communities in the Americas,* 2nd ed., ed. Richard Price, 170–90. Baltimore: Johns Hopkins University Press.

King, Johannes. 1979. Guerrilla Warfare: A Bush Negro View. In *Maroon Societies: Rebel Slave Communities in the Americas,* 2nd ed., ed. Richard Price, 298–304. Baltimore: Johns Hopkins University Press.

Kiple, Kenneth. 1984. *The Caribbean Slave: A Biological History.* Cambridge: Cambridge University Press.

Knight, Franklin. 1970. *Slave Society in Cuba during the Nineteenth Century.* Madison: University of Wisconsin Press.

————. 1990. *The Caribbean: The Genesis of a Fragmented Nationalism.* 2nd ed. New York: Oxford University Press.

————. 1999. Foreword to *Black Rebels: African Caribbean Freedom Fighters in Jamaica,* by Werner Zips. Trans. Shelly L. Frisch. Kingston: Ian Randle.

Köbben, A.J.F. 1979. Unity and Disunity: Cottica Djuka Society as a Kinship System. In *Maroon Societies: Rebel Slave Communities in the Americas,* 2nd ed., ed. Richard Price, 320–69. Baltimore: Johns Hopkins University Press.

Kopytoff, Barbara K. 1976a. Jamaican Maroon Political Organization: The Effects of the Treaties. *Social and Economic Studies* 25 (2): 87–105.

————. 1976b. The Development of Jamaican Maroon Ethnicity. *Caribbean Quarterly* 22 (2–3): 33–50.

Krogman, Wilson M. 1934. The Racial Composition of the Seminole Indians of Florida and Oklahoma. *Journal of Negro History* 19:412–30.

Kubler, George. 1942. Population Movements in Mexico, 1520–1600. *Hispanic American Historical Review* 22:606–43.

La Guardia, Roberto de. 1977. *Los negros del Istmo de* Panamá. Panamá: Ediciones INAC.

Landers, Jane G.1998. Gracia Real de Santa Teresa de Mose: A Free Black Town in Spanish Colonial Florida. In *The Worlds of Unfree Labour: From Indentured Servitude to Slavery,* ed. Colin A. Palmer, 357–78. Brookfield, VT: Variorum.

————. 1999. *Black Society in Spanish Florida.* Urbana: University of Illinois Press.

————. 2000a. *Cimarrón* Ethnicity and Cultural Adaptation in the Spanish Domains of the Circum-Caribbean, 1503–1763. In *Identity in the Shadow of Slavery,* ed. Paul E. Lovejoy, 30–54. London: Continuum.

————. 2000b. Maroon Ethnicity and Identity in Ecuador, Colombia and Hispaniola. Paper presented at the meeting of the Latin American Studies Association, Hyatt Regency, Miami, 16–18 March 2000. http://136.142.158.105/Lasa2000/Landers.pdf (site last visited on 3 January 2005).

————. 2002. The Central African Presence in Spanish Maroon Communities. In *Central Africans and Cultural Transformations in the American Diaspora,* ed. Linda Heywood, 227–41. Cambridge: Cambridge University Press.

Lane, Kris E. 1998. *Pillaging the Empire: Piracy in the Americas, 1500–1750.* Armonk, NY: M.E. Sharpe.

————. 2002. *Quito 1599: City and Colony in Transition.* Albuquerque: University of New Mexico Press.

Lara, Silvia Hunold. 1988. *Campos da Violência: Escravos e Senhores na Capitania do Rio de Janeiro 1750–1808.* Rio de Janeiro: Editoria Paze e Terra.

Larrazábal Blanco, Carlos. 1998. *Los negros y la esclavitud en Santo Domingo.* Segunda Edición. Santo Domingo: Ediciones La Trintaria.

La Rosa Corzo, Gabino. 2003. *Runaway Slave Settlements in Cuba. Resistance and Repression.* Trans. Mary Todd. Chapel Hill: University of North Carolina Press.

Laude, Jean. 1973. *African Art of the Dogon: The Myths of the Cliff Dwellers.* New York: Viking Press.

Law, Robin. 1977. *The Oyo Empire, c.1600–c.1836: A West African Imperialism in the Era of the Atlantic Slave Trade.* Oxford: Clarendon Press.

Lemoine, Maurice. 1985. *Bitter Sugar.* London: Zed Books.

León, Nicolás. 1924. *Las castas de México colonial o Neuva España.* México: Museo Nacional.

Levtzion, Nehemia. 1973. *Ancient Ghana and Mali.* London: Methuen.

———. 1985. The Early States of the Western Sudan. In *History of West Africa,* 3rd ed., vol. 1, ed. J.F.A. Ajayi and Michael Crowder, 129–66. London: Longman.

Lewicki, Tadeusz. 1974. *West African Food in the Middle Ages According to Arabic Sources.* London: Cambridge University Press.

Lewis, Gordon. 1983. *Main Currents of Caribbean Thought: The Historical Evolution of Caribbean Society in Its Ideological Aspects, 1492–1900.* Baltimore: Johns Hopkins University Press.

Leyburn, James C. 1941. *The Haitian People.* New Haven: Yale University Press.

Leyten, Harrie M. 1979. *Goldweights from Ghana and the Ivory Coast: Tales in Bronze.* Amsterdam: Khepri van Rijn.

Libby, Jean. 1992. Technological and Cultural Transfer of African Ironmaking into the Americas and the Relationship to Slave Resistance. Paper presented at Seminar on Rediscovering America 1492–1992, Department of Foreign Language and Literatures, Baton Rouge, Louisiana State University.

Lichtveld, Ursy M., and Jan Voorhoeve. 1958. *Suriname: Spiegel der vaderlandse kooplieden: Een historisch leesboek.* Zwolle: W.E.J. Tjeenk Willink.

Ligon, Richard. 1976. *A True and Exact History of the Island of Barbadoes.* 2nd ed. London: Frank Cass. (Orig. pub. 1657.)

Llano Isaza, Rodrigo. 2002. Hechos y gentes de la primera república Colombiana (1810–1816). http://www.lablaa.org/blaavirtual/letra-p/primera/causas.htm (site last visited on 12 January 2005).

Lockhart, James. 1968. *Spanish Peru, 1532–1560: A Colonial Society.* Madison: University of Wisconsin Press.

Lockhart, James, and Stuart B. Schwartz. 1983. *Early Latin America. A History of Colonial Spanish America and Brazil.* Cambridge: Cambridge University Press.

Lofton, John M. 1948. Denmark Vesey's Call to Arms. *Journal of Negro History* 33:395–417.

Lokken, Paul. 2004a. Useful Enemies: Seventeenth-Century Piracy and the Rise of Pardo Militias in Spanish Central America. *Journal of Colonialism and Colonial History* 5 (2). http://muse.jhu.edu/demo/journal_of_colonialism_and_colonial_history/v005/5.2lokken.html (site last visited on 15 December 2004).

———. 2004b. A Maroon Moment: Rebel Slaves in Early Seventeenth-Century Guatemala. *Slavery and Abolition* 25 (3): 44–58.

Long, Edward. 1774. *History of Jamaica.* 3 vols. London: T. Lowndes.

Manigat, Leslie F. 1977. The Relationship between Marronage and Slave Revolts and Revolution in St. Domingue-Haiti. In *Comparative Perspectives on Slavery in New World Plantation Societies,* ed. Vera Rubin and Arthur Tuden, 481–501. New York: Annals of the Academy of Sciences.

Marcano Jiménez, Edmundo. 2001. *Los cumbes: visión panorámica de esta modalidad de rebeldía negra en las colonias americanas de España y Portugal.* Caracas: Academia Nacional de la Historia.

Marchand-Thébault, Marie-Louise. 1986. L'esclavage en Guyane sous l'ancien régime. In *Deux Siècles d'Esclavage en Guyane Française 1652–1848,* ed. Anne-Marie Bruleaux, Régine Calmont, and Serge Mam-Lam-Fouck, 11–62. Paris: L'Harmattan.

Marshall, Bernard A. 1976. Marronage in Slave Plantation Societies: A Case Study of Dominica, 1785–1865. *Caribbean Quarterly* 22:26–32.

———. 1982. Slave Resistance and White Reaction in the British Windward Islands. *Caribbean Quarterly* 28:33–46.

Martin, Norman F. 1957. *Los vagabundos en la Neuva España: Siglo XVI.* México: Edit Jus.

Mason, Philip. 1970. *Patterns of Dominance.* London: Oxford University Press. Published for the Institute of Race Relations.

Mathieu, Nicolás del Castillo. 1982. *Esclavos negros en Cartagena y sus aportes léxicos.* Tomo LXII. Bogotá: Publicaciones del Instituto Caro y Cuervo.

Mathurin, Lucille. 1975. *The Rebel Woman in the British West Indies during Slavery.* Kingston: Institute of Jamaica for the African-Caribbean Institute of Jamaica.

Mattoso, Katia M. de Queirós. 1979. *To Be a Slave in Brazil, 1550–1888.* Trans. Arthur Goldhammer. New Brunswick, NJ: Rutgers University Press.

May, Rollo. 1972. *Power and Innocence: A Search for the Sources of Violence.* New York: W.W. Norton.

McFarlane, Anthony. 1986. Cimarrones and Palenques: Runaways and Resistance in Colonial Colombia. In *Out of the House of Bondage: Runaways, Resistance and Marronage in Africa and the New World,* ed. Gad Heuman, 131–51. London: Frank Cass.

McFarlane, Milton. 1977. *Cudjoe of Jamaica: Pioneer for Black Freedom in the New World.* Short Hills, NJ: Ridley Enslow.

McManus, Edgar J. 1968. The Negro Slave in New York. In *American Negro Slavery: A Modern Reader,* ed. Allen Weinstein and Frank Otto Gatell, 64–73. New York: Oxford University Press.

Meier, C., and William L. Sherman. 1979. *The Course of Mexican History.* New York: Oxford University Press.

Mellafe, Rolando. 1975. *Negro Slavery in Latin America.* Berkeley and Los Angeles: University of California Press.

———. 1984. *La introducción de la esclavitud negra en chile: Tráfico y rutas.* Santiago de Chile: Editorial Universitaria.

Memmi, Albert. 1965. *The Colonizer and the Colonized.* Trans. Howard Greenfield. New York: Orion Press. (Orig. pub. 1957.)

Miller, Ruth, and Paul Dolan, eds. 1971. *Race Awareness: The Nightmare and the Vision.* New York: Cambridge University Press.

Mintz, Sidney W. 1974. *Caribbean Transformations.* Baltimore: Johns Hopkins University Press.

Moitt, Bernard. 2001. *Women and Slavery in the French Antilles, 1635–1848.* Bloomington: Indiana University Press.

Montesquieu, Charles de Secondat, Baron de. 1748. *De l'Esprit des lois.* N.p.

Moreau de Saint-Méry, M.L.E. 1784–90. *Lois et constitutions des colonies françoises de l'Amériques sous le vent.* 6 vols. Paris.

———. 1979. The Border Maroons of Saint-Domingue: Le Maniel. In *Maroon Societies: Rebel Slave Communities in the Americas,* 2nd ed., ed. Richard Price, 135–44. Baltimore: Johns Hopkins University Press.

Morgan, Philip. 1986. Colonial South Carolina Runaways: Their Significance for Slave Culture. In *Out of the House of Bondage: Runaways, Resistance and Marronage in Africa and the New World,* ed. Gad Heuman, 57–78. London: Frank Cass.

Morgan, W.B., and J.C. Pugh. 1969. *West Africa.* London: Methuen.

Moura, Clóvis, organizador. 2001. *Os Quilombos na dinamica social do Brasil.* Maceió-AL: EdUFAL.

Mullen, J. Edward, ed. 1981. *The Life and Poems of a Cuban Slave: Juan Francisco Manzano 1797–1854.* Hamden, CT: Anchor Books.

Mullin, Michael. 1992. *Africa in America: Slave Acculturation and Resistance in the Ameri-can South and the British Caribbean, 1736–1831.* Urbana: University of Illinois Press.

Mulroy, Kevin.1993. *Freedom on the Border: The Seminole Maroons in Florida, the Indian Territory, Coahuila, and Texas.* Lubbock: Texas Tech University Press.

Naipaul, Vidiadhar. 1974. *The Middle Passage: Impressions of Five Societies – British, French and Dutch – in the West Indies and South America.* London: André Deutsch.

Nassy, David de Isaac Cohen, ed. 1788. *Essai historique sur la colonie de Surinam.* Paramaribo.

Navarrete, María Cristina. 2003. *Cimarrones y palenques en el siglo XVII.* Cali, Colombia: Universidad del Valle.

Naveda Chávez-Hita, Adriana. 1987. *Los esclavos negros en las haciendas azucareras de Córdoba, Veracruz, 1690–1830.* Xalapa, Ver.: Universidad Veracruzana, Centro de Investigaciones Históricas.

———. 2001. De San Lorenzo de los Negros a los morenos de Amapa: Cimarrones ver-acruzanos, 1609–1735. In *Rutas de la esclavitud en Africa y América Latina,* ed. Rina Cáceres, 157–74. San José: Editorial de la Universidad de Costa Rica.

Northup, Solomon. 1853. *Twelve Years a Slave. Narrative of Solomon Northup, a Citizen of*

New-York, Kidnapped in Washington City in 1841, and Rescued in 1853, from a Cotton Plantation near the Red River, in Louisiana. Auburn: Derby and Miller.

Oldendorp, C.G.A. 1987. *History of the Mission of the Evangelical Brethren on the Caribbean Islands of St Thomas, St Croix and St John.* Trans. Arnold R. Highfield and Vladimir Barac. Ann Arbor: Karoma. (Orig. pub. 1777.)

Oluwasanmi, H.A. 1966. *Agriculture and Nigerian Economic Development.* Ibadan: Oxford University Press.

Orser, Charles E. Jr. 1992. *In Search of Zumbi: Preliminary Archaeological Research at the Serra da Barriga, State of Alagoas, Brazil.* Normal: Illinois State University.

Ortiz, Fernando. 1975. *Los negros esclavos.* Habana: Editorial de Ciencias Sociales. (Orig. pub. 1916.)

————. 1984. *Ensayos etnográficos.* Selección de Miguel Barnet y Ángel L. Fernández. Habana: Editorial de Ciencias Sociales.

————.1992. *Los cabildos y la fiesta afrocubanos del Dia de Reyes.* Habana: Editorial de Ciencias Sociales. (Orig. pub. 1921.)

Packwood, Cyril Outerbridge. 1975. *Chained on the Rock: Slavery in Bermuda.* New York: Eliseo Torres and Sons.

Palmer, Colin A. 1976. *Slaves of the White God: Blacks in Mexico, 1570–1650.* Cambridge: Harvard University Press.

Patterson, Orlando. 1967. *The Sociology of Slavery: An Analysis of the Origins, Development, and Structure of Negro Slave Society in Jamaica.* London: MacGibbon and Kee.

————. 1979. Slavery and Slave Revolts: A Sociohistorical Analysis of the First Maroon War, 1665–1740. In *Maroon Societies: Rebel Slave Communities in the Americas,* 2nd ed., ed. Richard Price, 246–92. Baltimore: Johns Hopkins University Press.

————. 1982. *Slavery and Social Death: A Comparative Study.* Cambridge: Harvard University Press.

————. 1991. *Freedom.* Vol. 1, *Freedom in the Making of Western Culture.* New York: Basic Books.

————. 2000. The Constituent Elements of Slavery. In *Caribbean Slavery in the Atlantic World,* ed. Verene A. Shepherd and Hilary McD. Beckles, 32–41. Kingston: Ian Randle.

Pereira, Joe. 1994. Maroon Heritage in México. In *Maroon Heritage: Archaeological Ethnographic and Historical Perspectives,* ed. Kofi E. Agorsah, 94–108. Kingston: Canoe Press.

Pérez, Louis A., Jr. 1989. *Lords of the Mountain: Social Banditry and Peasant Protest in Cuba, 1878–1918.* Pittsburgh: University of Pittsburgh Press.

————. 2005. *To Die in Cuba: Suicide and Society.* Chapel Hill: University of North Carolina Press.

Pérez de la Riva, Francisco. 1979. Cuban Palenques. In *Maroon Societies: Rebel Slave Communities in the Americas,* 2nd ed., ed. Richard Price, 49–59. Baltimore: Johns Hopkins University Press.

Pérez de Ribas, Andrés. 1896. *Crónica y historia religiosa de la provincia de la Compañia de Jesús de México en Nueva España.* Vol. 1. México: Imprenta del Sagrado Corazón de Jesús.

Perinbam, Barbara Marie. 1982. *Holy Violence: The Revolutionary Thought of Frantz Fanon, an Intellectual Biography.* Washington, DC: Three Continents.

Peytraud, Lucien. 1897. *L'esclavage aux antilles françaises avant 1789.* Paris: Hachette.

Philalethes, Demoticus. 1979. Hunting the Maroons with Dogs in Cuba. In *Maroon Societies: Rebel Slave Communities in the Americas,* 2nd ed., ed. Richard Price, 60–63. Baltimore: Johns Hopkins University Press.

Pinckard, George. 1806. *Notes on the West Indies: Written during the Expedition under the Command of the late General Sir Ralph Abercromby: including Observations on the Island of Barbadoes, and the Settlements Captured by the British Troops, upon the Coast of Guiana.* 3 vols. London: Longman, Hurst, Rees and Orme.

Pinto Vallejos, Julio. 1998. Slave Control and Slave Resistance in Colonial Minas Gerais, 1700–1750. In *The Worlds of Unfree Labour: From Indentured Servitude to Slavery,* ed. Colin A. Palmer, 171–204. Brookfield, VT: Variorum.

Pi-Sunyer, Oriol. 1957. The Historical Background to the Negro in Mexico. *Journal of Negro History* 42:237–46.

Plá, Josefina. 1972. *Hermano negro: la esclavitud en el Paraguay.* Madrid: Paraninfo.

Pollak-Eltz, Angelina. 1977. Slave Revolts in Venezuela. In *Comparative Perspectives on Slavery in New World Plantation Societies,* ed. Vera Rubin and Arthur Tuden, 439–54. New York: Annals of the Academy of Sciences.

Pope-Hennessy, James. 1967. *Sins of the Fathers: A Study of the Atlantic Slave Traders 1441–1807.* London: Weidenfeld and Nicolson.

Porter, Kenneth W. 1932. Relations between Negroes and Indians within the Present Limits of the United States. *Journal of Negro History* 17:287–367.

———. 1943. Florida Slaves and Free Negroes in the Seminole War, 1835–1842. *Journal of Negro History* 28:390–421.

———. 1951. Negroes and the Seminole War 1817–1818. *Journal of Negro History* 36:249–80.

Price, Richard. 1975. *Saramaka Social Structure: Analysis of a Maroon Society in Surinam.* Rio Piedras: Institute of Caribbean Studies of the University of Puerto Rico.

———. 1976. *The Guiana Maroons: A Historical and Bibliographical Introduction.* Baltimore: Johns Hopkins University Press.

———, ed. 1979. *Maroon Societies: Rebel Slave Communities in the Americas.* 2nd ed. Baltimore: Johns Hopkins University Press.

———. 1983a. *First-Time: The Historical Vision of an Afro-American People.* Baltimore: Johns Hopkins University Press.

———. 1983b. *To Slay the Hydra. Dutch Colonial Perspectives on the Saramaka Wars.* Ann Arbor, MI: Karoma.

———. 1991. Subsistence on the Plantation Periphery: Crops, Cooking, and Labour among Eighteenth-Century Suriname Maroons. *Slavery and Abolition* 12 (1): 107–27.

Price, Richard, and Sally Price. 1988. Introduction to *Narrative of a Five Years' Expedition Against the Revolted Negroes of Surinam*, by John Gabriel Stedman. Baltimore: Johns Hopkins University Press.

Price, Sally, and Richard Price. 1980. *Afro-American Arts of the Suriname Rain Forest*. Berkeley and Los Angeles: University of California Press.

Purchas, Samuel. 1950. *Purchas His Pilgrims*. Glasgow: J. Maclehose and Sons. (Orig. pub. 1613.)

Quarles, Benjamin. 1969. *The Negro in the Making of America*. Rev. ed. New York: Collier Books.

Raboteau, Albert. 1978. *Slave Religion: The "Invisible Institution" in the Antebellum South*. New York: Oxford University Press.

Ragatz, Lowell. 1977. *The Fall of the Planter Class in the British Caribbean, 1763–1833*. New York: Octagon Books. (Orig. pub. 1928.)

Rainsford, Marcus. 1805. *An Historical Account of the Black Empire of Hayti: Comprehending a View of the Principal Transactions in the Revolution of Saint Domingo; with its Ancient and Modern State*. London: J. Cundee.

Rattray, R.S. 1923. *Ashanti*. London: Oxford University Press. Reprinted 1969.

Raynal, Abbé [Guillaume Thomas François]. 1780. *Histoire philosophique et politique des établissements et du commerce des Européens dans les deux Indes*. Geneva. (Orig. pub. 1774.)

Reis, João José. 1993. *Slave Rebellion in Brazil: The Muslim Uprising of 1835 in Bahia*. Trans. Arthur Brakel. Baltimore: Johns Hopkins University Press.

Reitz, Elizabeth. 1994. Zooarchaeological Analysis of a Free African Community: Gracia Real de Santa Teresa de Mosé. *Historical Archaeology* 28 (1): 23–40.

Robinson, Carey. 1994. Maroons and Rebels (a Dilemma). In *Maroon Heritage: Archaeological Ethnographic and Historical Perspectives*, ed. Kofi E. Agorsah, 86–93. Kingston: Canoe Press.

Rodney, Walter. 1970. *A History of the Upper Guinea Coast, 1545 to 1800*. Oxford: Clarendon Press.

———. 1975. The Guinea Coast. In *The Cambridge History of Africa*, Vol. 4, *From c.1600 to c.1790*, ed. Richard Gray, 223–324. Cambridge: Cambridge University Press.

Romero Jaramillo, Dolcey. 1997. *Esclavitud en la provincia de Santa Marta 1791–1851*. Santa Marta, Colombia: Fondo de Publicaciones de Autores Magdalenenses, Instituto de Cultura y Turismo del Magdalena.

———. 2000. Pueblos de negros en el Caribe colombiano (3). *El Heraldo* (digital edition 808) http://www.elheraldo.com.co/revistas/dominical/00-06-04/index.htm (site last visited on 12 January 2005).

Rousseau, Jean-Jacques. 1762. *Du Contrat Social ou Principes du Droit Politique*. Amsterdam: Marc Michel Rey.

Rueda Mendez, David. 1995. *Esclavitud y sociedad en la provincia de Tunja siglo XVIII.* Tunja, Boyacá, Colombia: Editorial de la Universidad Pedagógica y Tecnológica de Colombia.

Rugendas, Johann Moritz. 1835. *Voyage pittoresque dans le Brésil.* Trans. M. de Golbéry. Paris: Engelmann.

Ryder, A.F.C. 1969. *Benin and the Europeans 1485–1897.* Harlow: Longmans.

Santos Gomes, Flávio dos. 2002. A "Safe Haven": Runaway Slaves, Mocambos, and Borders in Colonial Amazonia, Brazil. *Hispanic American Historical Review* 82 (3): 469–98.

Schalkwijk, J. Marten W. 1994. *Colonial State-Formation in Caribbean Plantation Societies: Structural Analysis and Changing Elite Networks in Suriname, 1650–1920.* 2nd ed. Paramaribo: By Author.

Schomburgk, Richard. 1922–23. *Travels in British Guiana 1840–1844.* 2 vols. Trans. and ed. W.E. Roth. Georgetown: Daily Chronicle. (Orig. pub. 1847–48.)

Schuler, Monica. 1970. Ethnic Slave Rebellions in the Caribbean and the Guianas. *Journal of Social History* 3:374–85.

———. 1973. Day-to-Day Resistance to Slavery in the Caribbean during the Eighteenth Century. *African Studies Association of the West Indies* 6:57–75.

Schwartz, Rosalie. 1989. *Lawless Liberators: Political Banditry and Cuban Independence.* Durham: Duke University Press, 1989.

Schwartz, Stuart B. 1977. Resistance and Accommodation in Eighteenth-Century Brazil: The Slaves' View of Slavery. *Hispanic American Historical Review* 57:69–81.

———. 1979. The Mocambo: Slave Resistance in Colonial Bahia. In *Maroon Societies: Rebel Slave Communities in the Americas,* 2nd ed., ed. Richard Price, 202–26. Baltimore: Johns Hopkins University Press.

———. 2002. Blacks and Indians: Common Cause and Confrontation in Colonial Brazil. Paper presented at the Fifth Annual International Conference, Gilder Lehrman Center for the Study of Slavery, Resistance and Abolition, Yale University, 6–7 December 2002.

Schweninger, Loren. 2002. Maroonage and Flight: An Overview. Paper presented at the Fifth Annual International Conference, Gilder Lehrman Center for the Study of Slavery, Resistance and Abolition, Yale University, 6–7 December 2002.

Senior, Bernard. 1969. *Jamaica, As It Was, As It Is, and As It May Be.* New York: Negro Universities Press. (Orig. pub. 1835.)

Shahabuddeen, M. 1983. *From Plantocracy to Nationalism: A Profile of Sugar in Guyana.* Georgetown: University of Guyana.

Sharp, William Frederick. 1976. *Slavery on the Spanish Frontier: The Colombian Chocó 1681–1810.* Norman: University of Oklahoma Press.

Sheridan, Richard. 1985. *Doctors and Slaves. A Medical and Demographic History of Slavery in the British West Indies 1680–1834.* Cambridge: Cambridge University Press.

————. 1986. The Maroons of Jamaica, 1730–1830. In *Out of the House of Bondage: Runaways, Resistance and Marronage in Africa and the New World,* ed. Gad Heuman, 152–72. London: Frank Cass.

Sigmund, Paul. 1988. *Thomas Aquinas on Politics and Ethics.* New York: W.W. Norton.

Sijpesteijn, C.A. 1858. *Mr. Jan Jacob Mauricius, Gouverneur-General van Suriname van 1742–1751.* 's Gravenhage: De Gebroeders van Cleef.

Singelmann, Peter. 1975. Political Structure and Social Banditry in Northeast Brazil. *Journal of Latin American Studies* 7 (1): 59–83.

Soler, Luis M. Diaz. 1970. *Historia de la esclavitud negra en Puerto Rico.* 3rd ed. Barcelona: Editorial Universitaria, Universidad de Puerto Rico.

Stampp, Kenneth M. 1968. Southern Negro Slavery: "To Make Them Stand in Fear". In *American Negro Slavery: A Modern Reader,* ed. Allen Weinstein and Frank Otto Gatell, 51–63. New York: Oxford University Press.

Stedman, John Gabriel. 1796; 1971. *Narrative of a Five Years' Expedition against the Revolted Negroes of Surinam.* Amherst: University of Massachusetts Press. Reprinted 1988, ed. Richard and Sally Price. Baltimore: Johns Hopkins University Press.

Stein, Robert Louis. 1979. *The French Slave Trade in the Eighteenth Century: An Old Regime Business.* Madison: University of Wisconsin Press.

————. 1988. *The French Sugar Business in the Eighteenth Century.* Baton Rouge: Louisiana State University Press.

Stowe, Harriet Beecher. 1852. *Uncle Tom's Cabin; or, Life Among the Lowly.* Boston: J.P. Jewett.

Styron, William. 1966. *The Confessions of Nat Turner.* New York: Random House.

Suret-Canale, Jean. 1971. *French Colonialism in Tropical Africa 1900–1945.* New York: Pica Press.

Suttles, William. 1971. African Religious Survivals as a Factor in American Slave Revolts. *Journal of Negro History* 56:97–104.

Tannenbaum, Frank. 1992. *Slave and Citizen.* Boston: Beacon Press. (Orig. pub. 1946.)

Taylor, S.A.G. 1965. *The Western Design: An Account of Cromwell's Expedition to the Caribbean.* Kingston: Institute of Jamaica.

Thoden van Velzen, H.U.E. 1995. Dangerous Ancestors: Ambivalent Visions of Nineteenth-Century Leaders of the Eastern Maroons of Suriname. In *Slave Cultures and the Cultures of Slavery,* ed. Stephan Palmié, 112–44. Knoxville: University of Tennessee Press.

Thomas, Hugh. 1971. *Cuba or the Pursuit of Freedom.* London: Eyre Spottiswood.

Thompson, Alvin O. 1987. *Colonialism and Underdevelopment in Guyana 1580–1803.* Bridgetown, Barbados: Carib Research and Publications.

————. 1990. African "Recaptives" under Apprenticeship in the British West Indies, 1807–1828. *Immigrants and Minorities* 9 (2): 123–44.

————. 1995. "Happy – Happy slaves!": Slavery as a Superior State to Freedom. *Journal of Caribbean History* 29 (2): 93–119.

————. 2002a. *Unprofitable Servants: Crown Slaves in Berbice, Guyana 1803–1831.* Kingston: University of the West Indies Press.

————. 2002b. *A Documentary History of Slavery in Berbice 1796–1834.* Georgetown: Free Press.

Thornton, John. 1991. African Soldiers in the Haitian Revolution. *Journal of Caribbean History* 25:58–80.

————. 1998a. *Africa and Africans in the Making of the Atlantic World, 1400–1800.* 2nd ed. Cambridge: Cambridge University Press.

————. 1998b. The Coromantees: An African Cultural Group in Colonial North America and the Caribbean. *Journal of Caribbean History* 32:161–78.

Toletino, Hugo. 1974. *Raza e historia en Santo Domingo: Los orígenes del prejuicio racial en América.* Santo Domingo: Editora de la Universidad Autónoma de Santo Domingo.

Tuelon, Alan. 1973. Nanny: Maroon Chieftainess. *Caribbean Quarterly* 19 (4): 20–27.

Udo, Reuben K. 1978. *A Comprehensive Geography of West Africa.* New York: Africana Publishing Company.

Van Lier, R.A.J. 1971a. *Frontier Society: A Social Analysis of the History of Surinam.* 2nd ed. The Hague: Martinus Nijhoff.

————. 1971b. Introduction to *Narrative of a Five Years' Expedition against the Revolted Negroes of Surinam,* by John Gabriel Stedman. Amherst: University of Massachusetts Press.

Vanony-Frisch, Nicole. 1985. Les Esclaves de la Guadeloupe à la fin de l'Ancien Régime d'après les sources notariales, 1770–1789. *Bulletin de la Société d'Histoire de la Guadeloupe* 63–64:131–38.

Vansina, Jan. 1966. *Kingdoms of the Savanna: A History of Central African States until European Occupation.* Madison: University of Wisconsin Press.

Van Wetering, W. 1979. Witchcraft among the Tapanahoni Djuka. In *Maroon Societies: Rebel Slave Communities in the Americas,* 2nd ed., ed. Richard Price, 370–88. Baltimore: Johns Hopkins University Press.

Veracoechea, Ermila Troconis de. 1987. *Documentos para el estudio de los esclavos negros en Venezuela.* 2nd ed. Caracas: Fuentes para la Historia Colonial de Venezuela.

Villa-Flores, Javier. 2002. "To Lose One's Soul": Blasphemy and Slavery in New Spain, 1596–1669. *Hispanic American Historical Review* 82 (3): 435–68.

Villaverde, Cirilo. 1982. *Diario del rancheador.* Habana: Editorial Letras Cubanas.

Wade, Richard C. 1968. Slavery in the Southern Cities. In *American Negro Slavery: A Modern Reader,* ed. Weinstein and Frank Otto Gatell, 98–111. New York: Oxford University Press.

Warner-Lewis, Maureen. 2003. *Central Africa in the Caribbean: Transcending Time, Transforming Cultures.* Kingston: University of the West Indies Press.

Washington, Joseph R. 1984. *Anti-Blackness in English Religion 1500–1800.* New York: Mellen Press.

Weatherford, Willis D., and Charles S. Johnson. 1969. *Race Relations: Adjustment of Whites and Negroes in the United States.* New York: Negro Universities Press. (Orig. pub. 1934.)

Webster, J. B., and A. A. Boahen, with H. O. Idowu. 1980. *The Growth of African Civilization. The Revolutionary Years. West Africa since 1800.* London: Longman.

Weik, Terry. 1997. The Archaeology of Maroon Societies in the Americas: Resistance, Cultural Continuity, and Transformation in the African Diaspora. *Historical Archaeology* 31 (2): 81–92.

White, Dorothy G. 1996. *Let My People Go: African Americans 1804–1860.* New York: Oxford University Press.

Wilks, Ivor. 1975. *Asante in the Nineteenth Century: The Structure and Evolution of a Political Order.* London: Cambridge University Press.

———. 1985. The Mossi and Akan States. In *History of West Africa,* 3rd ed., vol. 1, ed. J.F.A. Ajayi and Michael Crowder, 465–502. London: Longman.

Williams, Eric. 1963. *Documents on West Indian History.* Vol. 1, *1492–1655. From the Spanish Discovery to the British Conquest of Jamaica.* Port of Spain: PNM Publishing.

———. 1964. *Capitalism and Slavery.* London: André Deutsch. (Orig. pub. 1944.)

Williams, Joseph J. 1938. *The Maroons of Jamaica.* Chestnut Hill, MA: Boston College Press.

Williamson, Jane. 2002. Telling It Like It Was: The Evolution of an Underground Railroad Historic Site. Paper presented at the Fifth Annual International Conference, Gilder Lehrman Center for the Study of Slavery, Resistance and Abolition, Yale University, 6–7 December 2002.

Wish, Harvey. 1937. American Slave Insurrections before 1861. *Journal of Negro History* 22:299–320.

Wood, Peter H. 1975. *Black Majority: Negroes in Colonial South Carolina from 1670 Through the Stono Rebellion.* New York: Alfred A. Knopf.

Wright, Philip. 1970. War and Peace with the Maroons, 1730–39. *Caribbean Quarterly* 16 (1): 5–27.

Zips, Werner. 1999. *Black Rebels: African Caribbean Freedom Fighters in Jamaica.* Trans. Shelly L. Frisch. Kingston: Ian Randle.

Index